A

PRESBYTERIAN CLERGYMAN

LOOKING FOR THE CHURCH.

By One of Three Hundred.

SIXTH AND SEVENTH THOUSAND.

New York:
GEN. PROTESTANT EPISCOPAL SUNDAY SCHOOL UNION.
DEPOSITORY 20 *JOHN STREET.*
1853.

PUDNEY & RUSSELL, Printers.

TABLE OF CONTENTS.

CHAPTER I.

THE CONFLICT.

CHAPTER II.

TRADITION.

CHAPTER III.

APOLOGY.

CHAPTER IV.

PRINCETON.

CHAPTER V.

ABUSES AND DISUSE OF BAPTISM.

CHAPTER VI.

SACRAMENTS.

CHAPTER VII.

CONFIRMATION—THE LORD'S SUPPER—EXCOMMUNICATION.

CHAPTER VIII.

LITURGIES.

CHAPTER IX.

DOWNWARD TENDENCIES.

CHAPTER X.

A DREAM.

CHAPTER XI.

SCHISM.

CHAPTER XIV.

A UNITY POSSIBLE.

CHAPTER XV.

CATHOLICITY.

CHAPTER XVI.

ELDERS AND DEATH-BEDS.

CHAPTER XVII.

POPULAR LIBERTY.

CHAPTER XVIII.

LIBERTY OF WORSHIP.

CHAPTER XXI.

A FALSE ISSUE; OR, THE PHANTOM GIANT.

CHAPTER XXII.

THE TRUE ISSUE.

CHAPTER XXIII.

NUMBER FOUR; OR, PRESBYTERIANISM AMONG THE FATHERS.

CHAPTER XXIV.

PRACTICAL TEACHINGS.

CHAPTER XXV.

RAGS OF POPERY.

CHAPTER XXVIII

RETROSPECT.

CHAPTER XXIX.

THE CHURCH FOUND.

THE REV. FLAVEL S. MINES.

Born and nurtured in the bosom of Presbyterianism, graduated at her most honoured seat of learning in America, himself a Presbyterian clergyman of no mean reputation; the writer of the following pages came in due time, by the blessing of God, to see the errors of that system, and to look earnestly for the Church most clearly identified by doctrine and usage with that built upon the foundation of the Apostles and Prophets, Jesus Christ himself being the chief corner-stone.

Called to forsake error, he reasoned not with flesh and blood. How he reasoned, submitting himself to the light shining down from above on his faithfully continued efforts; how he searched the records which our Lord Jesus Christ, fulfilling His promise to be with His Church in all ages, hath caused to be preserved for its most certain guidance, let these pages testify.

But, was it nothing, to break asunder all the ties of youth and manhood, even though called as were Patriarchs, Prophets and Apostles, by no uncertain voice, and for the kingdom of God's sake? In a worldly sense it was the loss of all things; but he of whom we now speak was enabled to take up the cross; and to the earnest Christian man seeking for truth through many countries, over whom the billows of the world have rolled, he has left encouragement, in the certain traces of one who has but lately gone before. He has left—

"Footprints that perhaps another,
Sailing o'er Life's solemn main—
A forlorn and shipwrecked brother,
Seeing, may take heart again."

Being established in the faith and order of the Church, he was ready at a moment's warning, to go just where the way seemed appointed for him. After a short term of service in New York, as assistant of the venerable Dr. Milnor, he removed to the island of St. Croix, where he laboured, until his failing health compelling him to seek again a northern climate, he became, for a short time, Rector of St. Luke's Church, Rossville, Staten Island. From this position he was called to take the lead in the great enterprise of establishing the Church on our Pacific borders. He founded Trinity Church in San Francisco, and there he faithfully fulfilled the remaining days of his ministry, counting not his life dear unto himself. The success of his ministry was great, though attained through much tribulation. Tasks, dangers and difficulties that appalled other men were assumed and encountered by him with a firm reliance on Divine aid, and a perseverance that nothing could resist; self-denial was his daily habit; a power of self-sacrifice had been given to him when he first submitted his own to the Divine will. To other and bitter trials, disease, which had early fastened upon him, added its lingering pains and mortal sorrows; but, through all, his soul remained firm, and his heart and his hands faithfully maintained their devotion to Christ and His Church. He knew whom he had believed, and was persuaded that He was able to keep that which he had committed unto Him against that day.

He is now at rest. His grave is where the setting sun bids his latest adieu to this land; over it have been said the holy words,—Blessed are the dead who die in the Lord; even so saith the Spirit; for they rest from their labours.

A PRESBYTERIAN CLERGYMAN

LOOKING FOR THE CHURCH.

CHAPTER I.

THE CONFLICT.

The writer of this narrative was once a Presbyterian; I may add, that my numerous relatives, near and remote, with a single exception, are Presbyterians still. And that which I had been by birth and education, and without my consent or fault, I afterward became from conviction, and unhappily that species of conviction which is always absolute—satisfied with the potent reasoning, which even to a Nathanael, may sometimes seem conclusive—" Can there any good thing come out of Nazareth?" The question was unfortunately one, which modest worth has always found it difficult to answer; and I had never met with a Philip of Bethsaida to say, " Come and see."

Of the Episcopalians, whose friendship I had enjoyed from childhood up, not one, so far as my recollections serve me, ever made the slightest attempt to proselyte me to his faith; and even after it came to be suspected that my mind was disturbed upon the claims of Episcopacy—when an expression of sympathy, or an exchange of views, or a friendly consultation upon personal and local difficulties, that never find their solution in books and authors, would have been unspeakably refreshing to my mind, then grappling in its own solitude with its new perceptions of truth and duty—still, if the fact be creditable to Episcopalians, I may record it to their praise, that I never met with either layman or priest among them, who seemed so much as to care, whether a wanderer should come into his fold or not; but I felt many a time perplexed by the indifference with which they appeared to entertain a subject, on which my own mind was expending its most restless and intense anxieties. Whether those on the higher rounds of the ladder, reaching by God's ordinance from earth to heaven, were so far above me, as not to understand the pressure of an atmosphere that they had never breathed, or had not the skill to reach the helping hand so low; and that those lower down upon the same perceived so little difference between my elevation and their own, as to wonder that I should have suffered inconvenience or should have desired a change; or whether both high and low had forgotten that that ladder, with its facilities for climbing to the skies, was for me as much as for them; it would be irrelevant, and perhaps unbecoming, at present to inquire. It is enough to say, that I was excluded from the sympathies of Churchmen, both high and low; and, in looking at the past, I often feel like one who has made his way across some desert, where the foot-prints of the wanderers, in a thousand different directions, seemed rather to bewilder than to guide, and who therefore must ascribe his preservation and his better fortune to the grace that kept his eye upon the guiding star.

I may not be able to tell the precise moment, up to which I

remained a Presbyterian, nor the moment at which I became from conviction an Episcopalian; but one thing I know, that "whereas I was blind, now I see." To speak more accurately, while "seeing men as trees walking," I had been at no pains to form a definite or fixed conception of the ministry, the sacraments, the keys, the Church; but had rather passed these matters over, as things that we were not required to define, and which perhaps it were better not to define too nicely, lest, peradventure, by running lines and fences, we should be found "cursing whom God had not cursed, or defying whom the Lord had not defied." But now that, through the mercy of Him who hath touched my eyes and told me to "look up," I see all things clearly," I am more "ready to give a reason to them that ask me," and to say what that Church with its ministry and sacraments must be; and, standing on the great fact, that truth is positive and therefore exclusive, I am ready, too, to incur the imputation of an uncharitableness which I can only say my principles do not inspire, and of a bigotry which, I can only add, my private feelings are infinitely far from cherishing. As soon might we hesitate to allow the doctrine of the Holy and Ever-Blessed Trinity, for fear of branding with heresy the amiable Unitarian, the martyred Nestorian, or the ancient Sabellian: or, as soon should we hesitate to define carefully and guardedly the awful requisites of repentance, and faith, and prayer, and self-mortification, and holiness, lest we should cast a shade, perhaps a deep and disheartening shade, upon the safety, as regards the future life of many excellent persons—as to withhold accurate definitions of things pertaining to the Church, lest we should rouse the suspicion in others, or be accused of harboring the thought ourselves, that, however well our neighbors excluded by these definitions may be faring, we are persuaded that they might fare better still, and that however safe those beyond these lines may be, we feel some solicitude that they should be safer still.

The truth is, that in a world like this, and with such hearts as ours, and amidst the endless influences that within us and around us threaten to disappoint the very best of us of His salvation, where no fact is so certain or so terrific, as that even "the righteous shall scarcely be saved;" it is our duty to dig deep, if we would lay foundations for eternity—to make the definitions as accurate as possible—to place and wake the watch at every post—to spare nothing from the means of grace that a merciful God has placed within our reach; if by any means we "may apprehend that for which we are apprehended of Christ Jesus."

Although unable perhaps, as already stated, to determine the exact moment of the change which I have undergone, I may yet be able, before progressing a great deal farther with this narrative, to convince even the staunchest believer among my former brethren in instantaneous conversions, that mine to Episcopacy, however gradual and cautious, has been earnest and honest—the result of a conflict deep enough and enough prolonged, to furnish one plausible phenomenon more for the theory of irresistible grace. Indeed, one who has not been fated to pass the same ordeal, can never understand "the fightings without and the fears within," of a soul escaping, as it has been my happy lot to do, from the mazes of sectarianism, in its endless genealogies, into the genial bosom of the Church.

To abjure a well-compacted system of opinions, to which I have been publicly committed, and which I must now allow that I have held on insufficient grounds—to determine that I will "not consult with flesh and blood," where all who are dear to me in life would earnestly resist me; to resolve that I may not even "go and bid them farewell that are at home at my house," well knowing that I cannot answer their inquiries to their satisfaction; to disturb and break asunder the ties of brotherhood, which time and a friendly intercourse and many an occasion of "sweet counselling together," have long and endearingly connected; to withhold the homage that nature seems to claim for the ashes of the cherished dead, by appearing to insinuate a defect in their religion, and, with motives easy of misapprehension, to leave "the dead to bury their dead"—to overcome the countless expedients and sophistries to which the heart resorts, in order to persuade itself that whatever be the secret conviction, it is at least unnecessary to avow it openly; to encounter the obloquy that one must look for, in breaking old associations for reasons that, by implication, offend human pride; to admit that I have "run without being sent," and have performed the holiest offices of the altar without the Lord's anointing; to "go out not knowing whither," and incur the necessity of a long probation, before I may earn the confidence of my brethren in my new relations; to be day and night agitated and unhappy on a question, on which it would be imprudent to seek sympathy, either in the ties about to be sundered, or in those about to be formed; to "go up to this Jerusalem, not knowing the things that shall befall me there;" to feel *goaded on* by inexorable truth, to the fatal moment of proclaiming the change my mind has undergone; and, at last, under a pressure of conviction, which it would be unsafe longer to resist, and impossible ultimately to overcome, to take my new position, and yet to have not a doubt that I am right in taking it; this is a task that lays under exhausting tribute every resource and element of our frail nature. The patient investigations, and the sifting of reasons, the earnest longings for Divine guidance, and the searchings of heart; the wakeful nights and anxious days, wearing the spirits and corroding the health; now a determination to dismiss the subject, as one of externals and not of essentials, or of order and not of faith; now an effort to believe that it would be a lesser evil to continue, even at some hazard, in the old communion, than to suffer and to produce in others the necessary mischiefs of a change; now a recurrence to old prejudices, a carping at the theory in some of its details, or in its practical and local workings, or a magnifying of some incidental circumstance, to divert the mind, or to embitter it against the new relation, or to satisfy it that on the whole, the change would not be materially for the better; now the suggestion, that many learned and devout men, "of whom the world was not worthy," have believed that Presbyterianism was a scriptural religion; now the old feeling stealing over me, that my mother, who first brought me to Christ, and first taught me to pray, and who now "sleeps in Jesus," lived without blemish, and passed "the swellings of Jordan" without fear, in the faith which, *only as to its securities,* I am proposing to abandon; and again, the recollection that my venerable father, now leaning with Jacob on his staff, is in the same religion waiting with the bright anticipations of a holy hope "until his change come;" these are but some of the tumultuous tossings in the mind of the anxious inquirer. The happier child of the Church, who was "free-born," can scarcely conceive the tribute to be paid to old prejudices, old habits, old associations, old modes of thinking, and chiefly to the old pride of human nature, by one who would become "partaker of his liberty." In the words of one who purchased at great expense the freedom of Rome, when Rome was free—words which were appropriated by another, who long ago preceded me in this uneven path—"With a great sum obtained I this freedom."

A struggle like this may perhaps somewhat excuse the enthusiasm, which those, who "from without" have found their way into the church, have now and then betrayed. My own enthusiasm, if any I have felt, I have endeavored not to make offensive to my brethren, either old or new. I have chosen rather, under many provocations, to "keep silence even from good words," and to enjoy my liberty in quiet thankfulness to Him whose word hath made me free. Sometimes I have been questioned, and, it would almost appear, in the same spirit in which the man, twice unfortunate, if I may so say, unfortunate in having been born blind, and unfortunate in having received his sight, was persecuted with the questions, "What sayest thou? What did he unto thee? How opened he thine eyes?" And sometimes, "out of a good and honest heart," I have been asked to give "a reason of the hope that is in me." But from considerations that will readily occur to a discreet mind, I have felt it proper not to break the covenant with my lips. Time may however be now supposed to have sobered down the gushing impulses of the "new convert," and also to have in some measure healed the wound which only "the necessity laid upon me" could have induced me to inflict on those "with whom I once walked in company;" and therefore, from motives which I know will be approved by Him, who alone has the power to discern, or the right to judge, I now venture to give a degree of form and permanence to a brief chapter from my own "experience."

I am but one among more than three hundred ministers, who, in this country alone, have, within a few years, been 'grafted again into the good olive tree,' from which, on the responsibility of our forefathers, we had in evil and violent times been "broken off." In reaching this result, there has doubtless been no little variety in the trials that we have each encountered; but it is reasonable to suppose that "as the billows went over our soul, and deep answered to deep," in the general features of our "experience" we have resembled each other, as "face answereth to face in a glass." And forasmuch as few have taken in hand to give account of those things which are most surely believed among us, and especially of "that dark and terrible wilderness" through which the Lord hath brought us to the fold that was once "one," and is as certainly to be one again, it has been suggested by others and has seemed good to me also, "having perfect understanding of that way," that it might be a means of usefulness, and perhaps a source of consolation, or even an humble guide to those who may come after us in the same rough path, or who may be at this moment, grappling with the same rude difficulties to see that "the fiery trial has happened" to others before them, and that a goodly "cloud of witnesses," still panting at the goal, are looking on them with affectionate sympathy, as they run the same race from which we are now resting, and have their eye on the same invaluable prize which we have grasped.

CHAPTER II.

TRADITION.

It was enough to attach my young heart to the Presbyterian religion, that my mother, besides possessing in a high degree the most amiable and striking virtues of her sex, was formed in that religion to an elevated piety; that from her my mind had received those early religious inclinations which it can never lose; and that her flesh was resting in unclouded hope of a blessed resurrection. True, I was a child too young to know the nature of my loss, when I lost my mother; but never shall that mother's prayer pass away from my memory; never shall her tear dry away from my sight; never shall her hand be lifted from my brow, as she laid it there to bless me; never shall I forget the pleasing task she assigned me, as the little bearer of her basket and its burdens at her side in her alms-giving visits to the poor; never shall I lose from memory the little sanctuary, whither she often resorted with her child; and whence her soul soared upward and taught mine to follow; and, until death shall restore me to her, I shall feel her influence, and, for aught I know, enjoy the defence and succor of her spirit, hovering about me still. My venerable father, too, for half a century, had been a prudent and efficient minister of Presbyterianism; had, in the phraseology of that school, "dedicated me in baptism," and admitted me when yet a child to "the ordinance of the Lord's Supper;" had by much exertion expensively educated me; and had laid on me his hands, imparting the commission to bless the people and to preach the gospel and administer the sacraments as Presbyterians hold them. A few will find it in their hearts to censure me, if I shall here confess, that, when other and graver obstacles had given way before the force of truth, yet there remained this, which flesh and blood could not willingly profane, and found it no light matter to surmount; that the guide of my youth, now "old and well-stricken in years," might "go down with sorrow to the grave," if he should hear that his son had abjured the religion of his ancestors.

With that homage which parents such as mine seldom fail to command from their children, I could not for a moment doubt, so long as I yet "thought as a child, and understood as a child," that it was my duty to believe exactly as they had believed before me. And far be it from me to condemn this feeling, now that I have "become a man." If the commandment to "honor thy father and thy mother" be imperative, He who scarcely takes things temporal into the account, can hardly be supposed to have forbidden us to honor them, by embracing and defending their religion. It is unquestionably the original design of Providence, that this instinctive, and therefore divinely implanted, veneration for our parents' faith; a wise and holy instinct, which Cain first violated and Esau next; should have its application, not only to the Church in her perfection, where the case suggests no difficulty; but also to those forms of religion, which, although we call them defective, we rejoice to hope may be radically Christian. Nor do we feel free to limit even here the application of the principle; but we believe it to be as truly, although less obviously, wise and salutary, even when employed in the transmission of the faith of the Mohammedan, or the Socinian, or the Pagan, or the Jew. For, if the children of such were not trained in the religion of their parents, they would grow up to manhood without those ideas of accountability and retribution, which lie at the foundation of moral improvement and restraint. As we say of "the powers that be," that any government whatever is better than none, because its very existence affords a basis for progress and improvement; so we say that any religion whatever, Turk, Jew, or Heathen, is unspeakably better than none, because it makes man a creature of hope, and preserves the idea of accountability and law. Few, indeed, would be willing to see the experiment, if it could possibly be made, of severing the Mohammedan or Pagan from the teaching and religion of his parents, and of letting loose on earth, whole nations of Africans, or Turks, or Hindoos, without the conception of a God or of a future life. I need not extend this reasoning to the Atheist, until the question be settled, whether there has ever been this monster among men destitute of the first fundamental instinct of humanity; and until the Atheist should be willing, which the pretended Atheist is never, to initiate his children into the arcana and the consequences of his faith.

As it is then the duty of the parent to hold his own religion infallible, until he shall have seen convincing proof of its fallaciousness, so is it equally the obligation of the child to hold as inviolable the religion of his parent; his best friend under heaven; one who would not "for bread give him a stone, nor for an egg a scorpion"—until he shall, at the maturity of reason, have encountered *overwhelming* demonstration, or at least satisfactory proof, of some fatal flaw or falsehood in the system. And when Christians shall be again "of one mind and of one heart;" shall "eat the same spiritual meat, and drink the same spiritual drink;" shall acknowledge one baptism into one body, and with "one mouth" confess "one faith;" that faith shall be perpetuated, as once it was, from sire to son, through the happy and unbroken ages of millennial blessedness, to which we are taught to look exultingly forward. And although this instinctive and inviolable rule of entailing a particular faith, may work inconveniently, and often disastrously, in these days, when there be creeds many, and baptisms many, yet it is not to be set aside, except for the most serious and weighty reasons, to be cautiously considered in each particular case; for "from the beginning it was not so;" and, in happier days to come, the working of this very rule shall bring it to pass, that "all thy children shall be taught of God," and an unsullied faith and worship shall be entailed from generation to generation. Thus it is, that the laws of nature, grace, and instinct, have all been intended to cover vast circles of time, and to accomplish a vast preponderance of good, and are not to be suspended on account of any local and short-lived inconveniences that may result. As the wind must breathe, and the sun go on, the lightning play, and the volcano continue to blaze, the rains descend, and the rivers flow, and the ocean roll, and all nature keep in motion, to accomplish vast beneficent results, regardless of the partial evils that here and there may incidentally occur; so, without the necessity of tracing out the parallel, must the laws ordained for our religious nature, whether they come from revelation or from instinct, be implicitly obeyed.

Nay, we go farther and assert, that while the religion of tradition is the only religion of which childhood is capable, it is, almost to an equal extent, the only religion that we receive in manhood. Not more incapable is the pious child of demonstrating that the adorable Jesus, at whose name he bows and in whose name he prays, is both God and man, and must be God and man if He would lay his hand on both and reconcile the two, than older Christians for the most part are incapable of settling the canon of Scripture, or of establishing the fact, that the Scriptures have been faithfully preserved in their original tongues, or have been duly rendered in the received translations; although upon these facts, and others equally beyond their reach, they build the blessed hope of everlasting life.

Nay, this principle is one of still wider range. Our knowledge, on nearly all subjects, is the simple knowledge of tradition. The results in the whole circle of the sciences, and the facts in the whole field of literature, and the occurrences of every-day life, are received on tradition, or the word of others. Thus the child at school is the passive recipient of traditions. He believes, not only in innumerable facts, and histories beyond his sphere of observation; but he believes in facts, that his own observation would go far to contradict—that the earth is a sphere, although he sees it as a plane—and that the sun does not rise and set, although his eyes assure him that it does. He believes that an eclipse will occur to-morrow, although he cannot understand the stupendous calculations that furnish the result; he believes that there are a thousand countries, rivers, seas, and cities that he has never seen; and every event anterior to his birth, and every fact of which he has not been personally witness, he must and does receive on the testimony of tradition. He who would receive nothing on tradition must be without ideas, except as he acquires them in common with the brutes: carry the principle into religion, and he is an infidel and Atheist. Unless we could have lived from the times of Christ, and through all the succeeding ages from the Apostles down, we could not so much as know, that we have the Scriptures as they were then given to the Church.

When, therefore, I have said that mine was the faith of tradition; a tradition that I justly venerated, because it came from my parents to me, as it had done from theirs to them—but a tradition that I have since discovered to be not very venerable for its years—I do not repudiate, but mean most distinctly to sanction the principle; a principle, which, if from the first days of Christianity it had been, sacredly and without interruption, followed, would have found universal Christendom at this moment " of one heart and of one mind."

But as we have often remarked, that persons who pretend to have discovered the defectiveness of all creeds, and have made the high and flattering resolve to take *the Bible* as the expression of *their* faith, and with a sort of unwritten, unsettled, eclective and ever-varying creed, made up of shreds and patches from the creeds around them; or, as we have sometimes seen the teachers of religion, dissatisfied with all the existing churches, as though " the gates of hell" had equally prevailed against them all, broaching some new organization, or some inorganic spiritual brotherhood, which was presently, like Aaron's rod, to swallow up all others, but which after gathering some " itching ears" around it, shortly became but another of the innumerable " churches," that, like the dust of Egypt, are " found in all our borders;" so it is worthy of notice that greater practical sticklers for tradition, a tradition too of the most dangerous sort, the tradition of a mere yesterday, are nowhere to be found, than are every day met with, in the very churches and sects that declaim with lugubrious piety against it. And, as those teachers, who are constantly getting dissatisfied with all extant churches, or rather with those in which their own lot has fallen, and find something to complain of in them all, and profess to have left all " sects;" sometimes with the preposterous dream that all will presently fall in with *them;* cannot for their lives perceive, that they are only setting up themselves another " sect," which will by and by be right glad to get into a corner, dignified with the recently repudiated name of " church;" or, as those pious souls, women not less than men, " seven women," it may be, " at the skirts of one man," who " have thrown away all human creeds," cannot for the life of them understand, that the result of their " comparing spiritual things with spiritual," has been to invent with overbearing positiveness a new human creed, perhaps unwritten, and all the more dangerous for that; so the Presbyterian, the Methodist, the Quaker, the Sectarian in general, cannot at all perceive, that while professing to reject tradition, he is in fact the most rigid traditionist to be found on earth. The young Quakeress is compelled to swallow, as amicably as her years will allow her, the traditions of "mother Eunice and grandmother Lois," even to the gloss upon her hair, the shape of her bonnet, and the pinning of her shawl; and the Quaker boy comes up to manhood, with the traditions as he received them from his father, and the father from broad-brim ancestors before him, even to the curves and angles of his coat, and the wearing of his hat in meeting; while all the little ones preserve the traditions of the parents, even to the crucifying of the English tongue, in the everlasting jargon of thee-and-thou. In vain the boy remonstrates, "Why, Father, *thee* is a pronoun of the second person, and in the objective case; and *commands* is a verb in the third person, requiring the nominative; yet *thee commands me* to violate the first rule of grammar." The father finds it quite satisfactory to answer, "What has grammar to do with religion? O, son, we live in degenerate times! Thee had a great deal better violate a hundred rules of grammar, than one tradition of the Church." How fortunate it is for some religions, and especially for such as originated, and could have originated, only in a wild fanaticism, that there is such a thing as tradition! How long would Quakerism live without it?

The same is true, *mutatis mutandis,* of the Presbyterian, the Methodist, the Baptist, and all the host of them. Who, in times past, has more rigidly enforced traditions, creeds and catechisms on their children, than Presbyterians? For my own part, before I knew the difference between the nominative and the objective cases, I was a sincere believer that "the decrees of God are his eternal purpose, whereby, according to the counsel of his own will, he hath, for his own glory, foreordained whatsoever comes to pass." I never in my life met with but one consistent anti-traditionist; a good-natured Baptist preacher, who undertook to bring his children up unbiassed as well as unbaptized; that on coming to the years of discretion, they might investigate the conflicting claims of the Shaster and the Bible, and choose between Confucius and Christ, and settle the triple crown, yet in dispute, between Pius the Fourth and Calvin the First. But the worthy man soon grew tired of his consistency, and the unbaptized urchins had hardly got into their teens, before he discovered that "bodily exercise profitteth a little," (see marginal reading,) and by such exercise as the saints of the middle ages called *Flagellantes* or whippers, practised for godly discipline, the good minister found it quite necessary and highly edifying to inoculate his boys with somewhat of the *virus* of tradition.

The truth is, that the religion of tradition is universal. We see it everywhere. The principle is never violated. The Mohammedan, of every sect; the Pagan, of every caste; the Papist, of every order; the Jew, of every shape and form; all, equally with the true Catholic, transmit their religions in genealogical descent from sire to son, by a hereditary *sequitur*. And we repeat, that we find no fault with the principle on which this fact depends. We have seen good results from it already. And when "the glorious things that are spoken of Zion" shall "begin to come to pass," we look for it, by that prerogative whereby it now perpetuates both good and evil, to bequeath from age to age, in a millennium whose years no man can number, still "better things than these."

If then the abstract principle be so important, of what serious concern to every thoughtful parent must it be, to establish himself for his children's sake, in the current of a pure and safe and, if possible, unchangeable tradition! Before I became a Churchman, I had become a parent; and as I looked, first on the unruffled faces of my children, and then on the sea of clashing sects and creeds all claiming to be Christian; to-day noisily and fiercely jostling each other, and to-morrow sinking into oblivion again; now startling entire communities by the phenomena of a violent galvanic life, and lapsing once more as suddenly into silence and inertness; oh, many is the sigh I have ejaculated for a heritage to leave them, that should give some promise that it would not pass away with "every wind of doctrine;" and often have I felt a saddening, sickening of the heart, at the destiny that seemed inevitably to await them; *in* a church, whose actual condition in this country, and whose history in every other, gave me little reason to hope, that, however pure in my day, it would continue to be so in theirs; and *out of* the only church that seemed to possess the elements of perpetuity; the only church that history had proven to be conservative of our holy faith! Sad and still sadder grew my thoughts. I knew that if I should live and die a Presbyterian, so in all human probability would they; whatever *Presbyterian* might come to mean hereafter; for I saw that it continually changed its meaning, and I had more than once in England been mistaken for a Unitarian, because I had announced myself a Presbyterian. In short, could I feel satisfied or justified, in that hour when the things of Christ and of his church, and of eternity and our immortal part, assume their just magnitude in the eyes of men, to leave these children to the mercies of a sect, four-fifths of which, as a future page of this narrative will show, have become already, and with amazing facility and concert, Arian, Socinian, Neologian, or Pantheistical; and the only pure remnant of which has, under my own eyes, abjured the exalted view once taken in her own Confessions, of the ministry and sacraments as essential to the preservation of the more essential faith, and is rapidly declining into cheerless, intellectual theories, and has been rent within my own brief memory into a hundred schisms? Should I not be better satisfied, when looking on my little ones for the last time in life, to commend them to the nursing of a Holy Mother, that would enforce only the simple and sufficient creeds, which preserved the church's unity, so long as unity existed; and that would protect and perpetuate those creeds by liturgies, possessing some mysterious charm, whereby she binds her children from age to age in mutual and indissoluble union?

It may seem singular that this view of the subject should have occurred to me so forcibly. But, entertaining it, I could not hesitate; and with the instincts of parental love—though resolutely resisting, and scarcely conscious of, the slightest tendency toward that church myself—and at a moment when I fully expected to spend my own remaining days in a filial adherence to the communion in which I was born; seven years before I entered the church, I submitted my children, although "secretly for fear of the" synagogue and elders, to Episcopal baptism; that *they* might hereafter the more readily glide into a church, which at this time I regarded as having no other advantages above "the fair daughters of the Reformation," than in her manifest and tried conservatism, by virtue chiefly of her noble and unalterable liturgy.

One design of relating this circumstance, has been, to give the reader some just idea of the anxieties through which an inquirer must pass; and to teach the unreflecting that a conversion to Episcopacy, in certain circumstances, is not likely to be the result of caprice, or of blind or sudden impulse. For myself, so long as stern conscience allowed me to remain a Presbyterian; so long as my leanings toward Episcopacy involved, or appeared to involve, no fundamental principle, but were at most the suggestings of taste, policy, expediency, I was content to abide in the communion wherein I had been born. But knowing the difficulty and the danger of breaking asunder the tie that binds one to the religion of his childhood, I determined to make it easier for my children to glide out of the accidental religion of their father, into the church that he even then distinctly regarded, in the present state of the world and of human nature, to be sufficiently, and more than any other, and after ample trial, the conservator, amidst the world's changes and chances, of "*the faith once delivered to the saints.*" For the same reason, it was my determination, regardless of the inconveniences to myself from such a course, to recommend to them, in due time afterward, the religion in which by true-hearted clergymen of the Church of England I had caused them to be baptized.

And now the reader, having seen my children "received into the congregation of Christ's flock," will not be surprised to find the parent envying his children's lot, and, by more painful stages making progress, as he did for the seven following years—toward the same result.

CHAPTER III.

APOLOGY.

In my seventeenth year, I became a member of the theological seminary at Princeton; a village widely and justly renowned for its academical and theological learning. The Episcopal liturgy had probably, up to that time, never grated on the atmosphere, that lay in homogeneous repose, within a circumference of thirty miles. A priest, all dressed in white, as one uprisen from the grave of Popery, had never appeared to frighten the quiet villagers out of their propriety. The faces around us—the traditions around us—the very sepulchres around us—the strangers who came among us—the pious and venerated men, whose shoes we felt unworthy to bear, and under whose observant eye was passing, as we felt, our every thought—all were Presbyterian "after the most straitest sect." And what was I, at sixteen years of age, that I should entertain a doubt, that the men, whom there it was our privilege to know and to revere, had sifted their facts, and considered well their premises, and reached by the most cautious reasoning their conclusions? To me it would have seemed little less than parricide to have resisted the direction they were giving to my mind.

Being of an inquisitive turn myself, I would have pursued a doubt on any important alleged fact, to any extremity. But being also in my mental bias, both happily and unhappily, confiding and disposed to faith, and having been educated strictly a traditionist, I must confess, whether to my discredit or not, that, during a residence of more than three years at the seminary, I swallowed every fact and dogma as most wholesome truth, "asking no questions for conscience sake;" and, with a credulity that would have gained me laurels in a school of Loyola, I never for a moment doubted the essential truth of the prevailing system.

One exception I must briefly mark—as it is the key to much that is to follow in this narrative. I did, at one time, deeply doubt the lawfulness of infant baptism. The doubt did not last long; its consequences will last forever. A thorough investigation dispelled every shadow of misgivings that nature, revelation, and antiquity sustained the practice. But how to reconcile this fact with the popular idea of regeneration; or how it should be lawful to baptize an infant before it had given signs of a spiritual birth, when I was taught to believe that the very design of baptism was to proclaim that birth before men and angels; was a problem that haunted me, as the reader will see, both then and afterwards.

While my companions in study, either older in years, or more inquisitive, or less confiding than myself, were rash enough now and then to hint their dissent upon some point of merely metaphysical importance, there was certainly one subject on which no one ventured to suggest a doubt. During my long residence at that "school of the prophets," I am not able to say with a clear conscience, that I ever laid my eyes on a volume—a line—a syllable, in defence of Episcopacy. This may appear strange, but it is not inexcusable. Episcopacy came up of course among the conflicting forms of Christianity, but was summarily disposed of, to make room for some more plausible or more important theme. Everything else "came into our assemblies," as "a man, with a gold ring, in goodly apparel," while Episcopacy stood there as "a poor man in vile raiment," or as a woman not distant of kin to "the mother of abomination," and as an Episcopalian seemed in our limited horizon to be a *rara avis in terris*, and his sect unpopular and unimportant, and inevitably destined before the rising lights of Jerome and Augustine to melt like snow beneath concentric suns, or doomed more certainly, should it prove more obstinate, to be ridden over rough-shod by a more popular religion; and as we felt also sure that it could never thrive in a republic, we agreed that it was sufficiently honored in receiving at our hands the little notice that it got. "The sect is a small part of the Christian world. In this land it is and will continue to be, among the smallest of the tribes of Israel; its numbers are few in comparison with those of other denominations; its ministers are also comparatively few, and in point of talent, learning, piety and moral worth, not eminent above all others. . . . .—It is at variance with the spirit of this age and of this land. This is an age of freedom, and men *will* be free. The religion of forms is not adapted to the free movement, the enlarged views, the varying plans of this age. It makes a jar on American feelings. *It will not be tolerated by this community.*" So says Mr. Barnes, the serenity of whose dreams has been disturbed, if we are rightly informed, by the tumbling of this barley-cake into the hosts that lie round about as grasshoppers, smiting in its progress his own particular tent on Washington Square, and eliciting more than once, in that unanswered *ad hominem* of his to "the evangelical party in the Episcopal church," the lamentation, that "Episcopalians are everywhere endeavoring to win [we should have said, *are everywhere winning*,] the young from the churches of their fathers."

Although I was, and may say it without boasting, to an intense degree, a student, and my lamp at night often the last to be extinguished; and though, in the various departments of study, I was "not a whit behind the chiefest" of my companions, in giving satisfaction to my teachers, as their own obliging testimonials may show; yet one who has any knowledge of seminary life, or of the endless range of theological investigation; or one who has ever seen how impetuously the student must be hurried forward from one topic to another, without the possibility of pausing; will readily understand how it may have happened, that one young as myself; the youngest of a hundred and twenty brethren; should not have employed his time in poring over the defences of a religion, which seemed then to have scarcely an existence in the land, and which it appeared impossible that the republican should tolerate, or the formalist himself be able long to endure, and which "the spiritually-minded," even among Episcopalians, would by and by instinctively and loathingly repudiate. By referring to copious notes of lectures, which I had a facility of taking with great accuracy, I observe that we were employed from December the twenty-seventh to the seventeenth of January on the topics in question; that is, deducting the portion of this interval allotted to other duties, we were employed upon Episcopacy altogether, about *three days of continuous time.* How had we the opportunity to dwell on this silly question of "the washing of cups and pots and brazen vessels," in the space of three weeks, when all the other, and to us higher departments of study, were at the same time hungrily pressing upon our attention with the expectation that we should be equally proficient in them all?

Neither did I lay down Episcopacy, as I did most other subjects, with the intention of a deliberate investigation at some future time; but grudging it the little notice it had got, among what seemed to be "the weightier matters of the law," and fastening tenaciously upon several facts or points, which, if their verity might be depended on, were certainly enough to silence all the Episcopal batteries in creation—and I was not one to question the accuracy of traditions from those, who, to me, "sat in Moses' seat"—I laid the subject down, supposing, that in parting with it here, I had done with it for ever.

Besides this routine of study, which allowed us scarcely respite for our daily meals, the "revivals of religion," that broke out at the time in every section of the Presbyterian Church; exhibiting a wonderful mixture of good and evil, and accompanied by unusual and strange developments; were enough, with a temperament less ardent than mine, to absorb one class of energies and sympathies; while the theological disputes, that like a desolating flood were swelling in every direction to a most formidable height, and which resulted a little later in violent disruptions and in the addition of another large batch of sects to the already portentous list, were sufficient to engross the leisure moments of a young divine, in whose eyes, unread in history and unused to such phenomena, "the ends of the world had come upon us," and heaven and earth were mingling in the strife.

I permit myself to give prominence to these facts, as an apology (I am compelled to use the word,) for these, who have come out of the Babel—let me not call it Babylon—of sects and schisms, into the quiet home provided by the Church. Recantation is never a pleasing task. Even on the side of truth and goodness, it has its bleeding sacrifices. And we think that we lighten the harsh terms of penance to which we are condemned, by thus accounting for our having once conscientiously held opinions that we now conscientiously repudiate. If we had held our opinions on the Episcopal claim, believing it to be a subject of grave importance; or, if we had adopted them in circumstances that had allowed a fair opportunity for investigation; we should not have deserved the indulgence that we now presume to ask. But, so long as we regarded it as a question of the very least importance, the other engrossing topics of inquiry did not, either *de merito or de facto* allow us to pause.

It is but fair that this should be borne in mind, that we may be spared the objurgations which we sometimes hear, as though, in a moment of caprice, we had changed well-formed opinions, and might possibly hereafter change again; as though the vibration that brought us into Episcopacy, might, some day swing with us into Popery, or back again on the other side, to a position farther from the central truth than we were before. And yet among the Three Hundred Ministers to whom I have alluded, and among the thousand and thousand late lay converts to Episcopacy, I have never known of any such relapse, except of a Baptist in a recent instance in Ohio. I have known Episcopalians, baptised and educated in the Church, although I must suspect not educated on Church principles, to make the said transitions to Romanism and Dissent; but, personally, I do not know an individual, denied a birth and training in the church, and who has come to "this Mount Zion" at his peril, that has afterward lapsed into either of these errors. That such cases exist, we believe on the testimony of an excellent Bishop who has "taken pains to inquire," and has proclaimed the fact; and that such cases would exist, we should have thought not at all unlikely, especially if, of every two hundred and eighty-five persons ordained in the church, as was the case under Bishop Griswold, of Massachusetts, two hundred and seven are from other denominations; and if, as some have computed, two-thirds at least of the Episcopal clergy throughout the land, were once dissenters by their baptism or their education.* For, without undertaking

* "It is a curious fact," says Bishop De Lancey, in a Conventional Address, which has appeared in a number of our Church papers, "that as far

to extenuate their error, or wishing to become the apologist for these mistaken brethren, let us not use this sword against them, lest even in a bishop's hands, we find it a two-edged blade, that may wound in a different quarter from the one intended.

For, to tell the plain truth, the convert from sectarianism, whose conversion has been one of either his head or his heart, may well feel disappointed at finding the practical condition of the Church so vitally at variance with its theories. His conversion has been the result of long inquiry and anxious struggles. He has been converted to Christianity as ex-

as I can learn, almost all the clerical seceders in this country, from the Church to Romanism, have been originally educated and trained in bodies not Protestant Episcopal. The following is the result of my inquiries on the subject:—"

CLERGYMEN.

Names.	Dioceses.	Date of Defection.	Brought up as,
Rev. Virgil H. Barber, Jr. - - -	New York -	1815,	Congregationalist.
" Virgil H. Barber, Sen. - -	Connecticut	1815,	Congregationalist.
" John Kewley, - - - - - - -	New York -	1816,	Methodist.
" Pierce Connelly, - - - - -	Mississippi -	1836,	Presbyterian.
" J. Roosevelt Bayley, - - -	New York -	1842,	Episcopalian.
" Henry Major, - - - - - - -	Pennsylvania	1846,	Methodist.
" Nathaniel A. Hewitt, - - -	Maryland -	1846,	Congregationalist
" Edgar P. Wadhams, - - -	New York -	1846,	Presbyterian.
" Wm. H. Hoyt, - - - - - -	Vermont - -	1846,	Congregationalist.

...... *Candidates for Orders.*

Mr. Clarence Walworth. - - -	W. New York	1845,	Presbyterian.
" Benjamin B. J. McMasters,	New York -	1845,	Ref. Scotch Pres.
" ——— Putnam, - - - - - -	North Carolina	1845,	Congregationalist.

To this statement of the Bishop I beg most respectfully to add, that " as far as I can learn," but one of the twelve apostates here named, was ever a dissenting minister; and that one was the Rev. Mr. Kewley, who having been baptised in the Church, was in boyhood seduced by the Jesuits from his parents in England, and was educated at St. Omer's, in France, (his parents not knowing where he was, but only receiving anonymous as-

pounded by the Prayer-Book—a theory symmetrical, sublime, satisfactory. He has had little opportunity to discover the practical Puritanism that has reduced the church at so many points to a level, and into feeble and fruitless competition, with the sects around her; and can we wonder that when he finds himself in the church, still hampered and harassed by the same teachings, practices, and spirit, that he had imagined had been left forever behind him, he should in a moment of unlooked-for disappointment, throw himself with a desperation analogous to that of the weak-minded suicide, disappointed in the ideal object of his admiration and his love, into the arms of a more conservative system; conservative, although it be of error and wrong, as well as of truth and right? If the Church were actually the Church held up to the world in her Prayer-Book and in the writings of her great divines, the men who have thus been driven to a desperate deed, would more probably have been ready to lay down their lives in her and for her. We may be allowed to say, therefore, that we have felt it to be somewhat unkind, when one of these converts has happened to do something not quite churchmanlike, to attribute the error to a *residuum* of the old leaven; while the eyes of the veriest neophyte could see that the same errors, or errors still greater, and departures still more serious

surances that he was doing well the while,) and after a stealthy escape to England, became a Protestant, and a Methodist Minister. On coming to America, he entered the Church, and became Rector of St. George's Parish in New York city, which he afterwards resigned, shortly following this step by his return to Europe and to the Romish communion. Moreover, without being at much "pains to inquire," we ascertain that the churchborn apostates to Rome in this country, bear quite their proportion to the above lists among the clergy, and that in England the proportion is beyond comparison greater. Our only object is, to check these unnecessary and invidious distinctions, and that for no other reason than that they seem to us likely to check the progress, as they contradict the spirit, of a Catholic-hearted Church.

from the canons, liturgy, principles, and spirit of the church, were more numerously and more strikingly perpetrated by those whose better fortune should have taught them better manners toward their lawful mother.

It has been the occasion of satire to the Sectarian, and of pleasantry even to the Churchman, that the professed convert to the church of God should betray any earnestness in the cause, which he has at such peril espoused. For myself, although the feeling has never been officiously or offensively obtruded, because it has never been obtruded at all, upon the notice of others, and has been sometimes even studiously repressed, yet I am not ashamed to plead guilty to that sense of holy satisfaction, which only a great sacrifice to conscience can impart; and of gratitude, which only a great benefit conferred, can enkindle; and of comfort, which only a blessing long desired, and inestimable in itself, can bring; and, for one, I am content to put my hand, while living, to the sentiment which a noble son and father of our Church inscribed on all his actions, and again, for the thousandth and the last time, subscribed, with his dying hand, *Pro Ecclesia Dei! Pro Ecclesia Dei!* My answer to the dissenter is, Who but a Churchman, that has tasted the quiet delights of the sanctuary, can appreciate the church's excellence? My vindication to the Churchman is, Who but the soul that has been "tossed up and down like a locust," upon "the winds of doctrine" and the sea of sects, can understand the mazes, the dangers, the undercurrents, and the disasters, of Sectarianism? Sectarians, you know nothing of the church's blessings! Churchmen, you know nothing of Sectarianism's mischiefs!

The young churchman, as a theological student, has this advantage over the sectarian; that, besides his being tutored to a system better adapted to bind its sons in loyal attachment to itself, the subject of church order, in his course of study, is so prominently kept before his mind, and so assiduously followed out in its bearings, that he acts earlier in life under a clearer apprehension of the subject; and, if he have been but moderately attentive to the question in dispute, is not very likely to retract the results at which he has arrived. But it is right to recollect, that the case of the Sectarian is otherwise. His course of study is assigned, and every hour of his time so filled, as nearly to exclude, and certainly to force into a corner, the whole question of Episcopacy, and the still more vital questions, liturgical, catholic, and sacramental, that with the Episcopacy, as all experience teaches, are to stand or fall. Hence the phenomenon, arguing indirectly, but conclusively, for Episcopacy, that, in face of the outcry and the odious nicknames of the day, invented to arrest the wholesome reaction, hundreds of dissenting teachers, in England as well as in America, and thousands of their followers, are flocking back to the ark, from which, in an evil hour, they went out, seeking rest upon a turbulent and dangerous sea; and that in this country alone, within the memory of man, Three Hundred Ministers, with a corresponding number of adherents, have returned to the ancient fold!

If I may repeat what seems to be the only explanation of this fact, it is, that the church student is in little danger of meeting with new suggestions upon church polity; whereas, the dissenting minister is in continual peril of encountering new facts, or the refutation of the facts on which he has been accustomed to rely. And this defection from sectarianism must continue to annoy our "separated brethren," so long as the high prerogative of the Church, as the visible Body of Christ, witnessing His Word, perpetuating His Presence, and imparting His Forgiveness and His Grace, shall continue to be "privily thrust out." Let it also be remembered, that in subsequent life, the pressure of domestic avocations, the limited access to books, the *res angusta domi*, and the absorbing nature of parochial engagements, as effectually exclude it from the attention of the student, when promoted to the pastoral life; so that nothing but a seeming accident, or the ill-working of an intolerable system, is likely, in the first instance, to rouse his inquiries, or send him to the tomes of the Fathers and the fountain-heads of information.

Because these facts have not been allowed a hearing, the "new convert" has been regarded sometimes with a certain feeling of distrust; and attempts, that look like playing back into the hands of Dissenters, have been made, to make the period of probation, for those who have been dissenting ministers, so burdensome, as effectually to exclude them from the priesthood of the Church. We might be led into some curious speculations, were we to pry into the motives for these attempts. Is it, that the Church, so lax in her discipline at other points, wishes to be understood as taking the high ground, that we have committed some sin almost unpardonable in having been dissenting teachers? Or may it be, that in the judgment of some, we have perpetrated a most damning sin in abjuring communions, which are in their opinion, on all vital points, as much churches of Christ as the one we seek? Have you ever known one in a hundred of these converts from sectarianism, to return to his "first love?" Have you ever known one of them to apostatize to Rome, except in sadness and bitterness, at finding the living Church so flattered by its portrait in the Prayer-Book, and by the pencils of her masters? Are they not in general, as firm, and filial, and obedient sons, though "coming from far," as those that have been "nursed at her side," and as "able to give a reason of the hope that is in them?" But I mean not to argue. Take away those ministers at her altars who have been baptized or educated in dissent, and the Church in America will be left a widow indeed, with but little if anything more than her thirds for her portion.

Right sorry am I to tell it in this place, that there are quarters, in which the unchurchmanlike, unscriptural, unchristian, uncatholic, and behind-the-age sentiment is familiarly uttered, that you would rather these dissenters should remain where they are! Remain where they are! I confess I do not understand you. Remain where they are! Is your Church the living representative of Christ on earth, and you would rather they should not be baptized into that body, and derive through it, "by that which every joint supplieth," their nourishment and growth unto everlasting life? You pray incessantly, "Thy kingdom come," and yet you are startled at the first thaking of the dry bones, around you! You say that your Church is destined to absorb all others, and yet, the moment the bright result begins to dawn, and wake you from your slumbers, you deprecate the spreading light, and cry, "Yet a little sleep, a little slumber, a little folding of the hands to sleep!"

I speak not for myself. For myself I have nothing to ask. I have not found the Church the step-mother that my former friends predicted, and my own fears foreboded. I have found fathers among her elders; and among her sons I have found brothers; and from her breasts I have drawn consolations, for the sacrifices I have made. Yet I remember the words of a judicious writer, that "men are but men, what room soever among men they hold." Nor do I forget the words of a friend, dropped by the way-side, a few hours before I received the grace of holy orders, that "you will find human nature in the Church, as well as out of it; you must expect to meet everywhere with narrow minds and pent-up hearts." To which I have only to add, that the mere fact of our abandoning systems, that some within the Church regard with so much tenderness, may in some instances subject us to the mistrusting glance, as it is an awkward thing to be explained by those who at the Church's altars act as the apologists of dissent and schism, and over the Church's walls reach down the *left* hand of fellowship to "the brethren without."

My remarks look to the future, and, at the risk of incurring the rebuke, that "this one fellow came in to sojourn, and will needs be a judge," I cannot but confess, that it would be painful to see the Church—free as it is, and free as it ought to be preserved—legislating herself out of her own liberties, and inventing new and unnecessary hindrances to the enlargement of her borders. "Much land remains to you to be possessed." "The field is the world." If the dissenting teacher, applying for her orders, is not qualified for the responsibilities that they impose, then, though he be as old as Methuselah, use the Church's prerogative, and bid him away. But if he be ready with "the answer of a good conscience," then take all that come to you—for alas! you have room for all—and ordain them, though they be young as Timothy, and though, like his, their fathers have been "Greek." "What God hath cleansed, that call not thou common." Take the word of one, whose word in the present case may not go for nought, that you need inflict no greater penance, than that which these men have suffered, in crossing "the great gulf fixed" between them and you. What is the policy of Rome? What the policy of the Dissenter? *Fas est ab hoste doceri*—freely translated—*learn a lesson from your neighbors.* In days like these, when those who come to you must forsake the popular for the unpopular—must stem a breast-deep tide to reach you—must leave an unburied father, or an offended house, to follow you—must wear in no mean sense a crown of suffering and one of which for Christ's sake they are not ashamed—receive, as did Paul and Peter, all that come to you. Although, like Timothy, without our fault, we may not have been "of Israel, according to the flesh," yet "from a child we have known the Holy Scriptures," and have loved, "though half in the speech of

Ashdod," the faith that dwelt aforetime in our mothers and our grandmothers.

Only let the Bishops see, that ministers from other communions, seeking orders in the Church, leave no room for the suspicions that *cœlum non animum mutant;* and the Church may safely throw open her door. Her walls, the world over, and the world knows, are strong enough, and high enough: and if her gates be needlessly obstructed, those who would have entered, will go away wondering at the "grievous burdens" that your own scribes and lawyers "would not touch with one of their fingers." It was a fearful accusation, "Them that were entering in, ye hindered." Let the Church, that we believe to be "after the pattern of heavenly things," assert her prerogative, as "the mother of all living," and "travail," like her apostles, "the second time" for her disaffected children, and do nothing to deserve the reproachful name that sectarians have given her, and with which, if my own experience may testify, they seek to deter their adherents from her bosom, as a *noverca injusta.*

I am not ignorant of the discipline of the primitive Church toward those who returned to her from heresy and schism. Perhaps it is unfortunate that that discipline has been interrupted. But were it even in force, we might still without presumption remind you, that we were sectarians by tradition, and not by election; that few of us ever rejected any article of the Catholic Faith, as it is expressed in the ancient creeds; and that, in encountering all the inconveniences and hardships of a conversion, we have done a penance that should satisfy the Church, and at which a Hindoo breaking *caste* would justly marvel.

Perhaps few would be more ready than myself to bode danger from a sudden influx into the Church. I have seen disastrous consequences from the letting loose of Congregationalists into the Presbyterian communion—taking it by surprise, and cutting it adrift from its ancient moorings. It is notorious that her doctors have recently descended not only to Congregational mitigations of her faith, but to Congregational grounds in her defence—resorting, if I may give an example of recent and memorable date, to the silly hypothesis, urged formerly by Congregationalists against themselves, of a crew of Christians cast without the ministry and sacraments upon a desert island. And I know, that, when it was remarked in a circle of New School Divines, a few years ago, that a number of New England ministers were going into the Episcopal Church, a Congregational Doctor of Divinity, fresh from Ohio, replied, "I am glad of it; they will revolutionize the Episcopal Church, as we have done the Presbyterian." And it may be, that now and then an adventurer may make his way into the Church, from carnal or mercenary motives, (although, where Dissent is "fat and well-liking" in the land, this can hardly be conceived,) and such to their new spouse may be forever commending and canonizing their first love. It may even be, that the Cincinnati Divine has not been entirely disappointed, in seeing here and there the revolutionary hand at work. But let it be remembered, that the gliding from one sect into another, is a very different thing from a submission to the Church. In one you cross the street; in the other, a great gulf. One is a *caprice;* the other a *conversion.* Besides, I need not remind the Episcopalian, that Episcopacy has *guards,* which Presbytery has not—that Episcopacy has *claims,* which Presbytery has not—that Episcopacy has *promises,* which Presbytery has not—that Episcopacy has a *destiny,* which Presbytery has not—a destiny as catholic as the family of man—a destiny which she must inevitably fulfil, and can fulfil only by conversions as thick strown as "the drops of the morning dew." Either you must give up your high-sounding claim to be the Church of God, or every conversion must fill your heart with joy. Either you must not look for her future universality, and consequently must at once surrender her pretensions, and leave the undisputed field to Rome; or, like Rome, you must keep vigils for her straitness, and jubilees for her extension. Leave not these waters teeming with living myriads, to the Roman fisherman, who will let down his net at the Master's bidding, not fearing, like you, that "for the multitude of the fishes" *his* net will "break." Be ye not so like the brother in the field, who "was angry, and would not go in." "It was meet that we should make merry, and be glad; for this thy brother was dead, and is alive again; and was lost and is found."

CHAPTER IV.

PRINCETON.

Between the years 1830 and 1840, on the deck of a steamboat between the cities of Washington and Alexandria, I remember to have met, for the first and only time in my life, with the Reverend Mr. ———, an Episcopal clergyman, and one of three brothers "according to the flesh," who had themselves, as I was afterward informed, come "from without" into the Church. It so happened, in the course of conversation, that this gentleman made some allusion to the hurried notice taken of the subject of Episcopacy in certain theological schools, and hinted broadly that this was very much the case at Princeton. I do not recollect the reply that his remarks elicited, or whether I did not let them fall unnoticed into the Potomac; but I have not forgotten the indignation that burned in my young heart, at what I regarded as an unmanly and unfounded imputation upon my church, my alma mater, and myself.

Fortunately for me too, a few weeks before, on making my ministerial debut in the first Presbyterian Church in Washington, in the presence of President, Senators, and Rulers of the nation, the minister who "made" what is oddly but aptly termed "the long prayer," that is, the prayer before the sermon, thought proper to introduce me to his *audience* as "thy servant not yet nineteen years of age." For, although it was an extemporaneous error of more than a year, and intended to flatter the vanity of a *debutant*, still, by not allowing me to forget that I was yet a boy, it may have done me service in restraining me, on this occasion, from giving utterance to a feeling like this: "Sir! art thou a teacher in Israel, and knowest not yet the difference between the Gospel and the Church; between externals and essentials; between the casket and the jewels; between the net and the fishes; between the shell and the kernel; between the spirit and the body; between the chaff and the wheat; between the mere scaffolding and the glorious building?" And certainly, on this occasion, "discretion was the better part of valor;" for had the young bachelor in divinity given way to his pugilistic impulses, he might have been sadly puzzled; nay, I may fear, muzzled; if the excellent clergyman had, in his mild way replied: "My dear young friend—you will excuse me for reminding you again that you are young—would you deposit a jewel in a frail casket without a fastening? Would you expect to see the kernel come to maturity, if you should rend to tatters the protecting shell? Would you think to detain on earth the spirit of one you loved, if you should neglect or divide the body it inhabited? Would you, with a weak and broken net, expect, in all weathers and in all waters, to drag your fishes to the shore? Would you tear off the "useless chaff" that God has thrown around the grain, and hope, when the sickle should be thrust in, to fill your garner with the wheat? Would you throw down the scaffolding, and expect to see the temple rear its bright pinnacles toward the sky? The jewel would perish without the casket, and the kernel without the shell; the life would depart but for the body, and the fishes be lost but for the integrity of the net; the wheat would die but for the chaff, the temple never rise but for the scaffolding, and the gospel pass away from the hearts of men but for the Church, its channel and its witness. You must, then, my young friend, find other similitudes from the objects around us to support your theory. Ask nature. Does she furnish the analogies you want?" But fortunately for the reputation of Princeton, as represented in her youthful graduate, I did not lay myself open to the annihilation to which this would have been but the playful prologue.

Although the clergyman thus encountered was justified in the allegation, that the time allotted to the subject of Episcopacy, in certain schools, is unreasonably short; for, if I mistake not, he had been himself a pupil at Princeton, and now only "testified what he had seen;" yet the young graduate flatters himself into the consciousness that he is amply mailed and equipped to confront a universe of mitres, and all the ingenuity and learning of the heads that wear them. As we made our rapid transit over the ground, my own mind fastened distinctly upon what appeared to be its more plausible pretensions, and at the same time upon what promised to be the annihilating sources of attack. Contenting myself with these leading and, as I thought, strong positions, which I shall presently enumerate, I was the subject of a mental process, resting strictly on tradition, and fairly reducible to the following syllogism:

If what our Lecturer has drawn from the records of antiquity be true, Episcopacy is a fraud.

What our Lecturer has drawn from the records of antiquity is true by every guarantee of honesty, learning and piety:

Ergo, Episcopacy is a fraud.

Or thus:

Facts must settle this question:

Our Professor has given us the facts:

The question is therefore settled.

The nature of the facts on which my young mind had seized, and on which it had as undaunted influence, as had the

Hebrew stripling in "the smooth stones from the brook," may be inferred from the following examples, which I shall repeat in the form in which, for the most part, they were at that time presented to my imagination.

I. Episcopacy is, in its structure, anti-republican, and in its spirit, hostile to human liberty; in the pleasant places where our lot is fallen, we need not therefore fear its progress, nor concern ourselves about it.

II. It is now conceded, that the official names of Bishop and Presbyter in the New Testament are of the same exact meaning; therefore all Presbyters, or, which is the same thing, all Pastors are Bishops, and the setting of Bishops above Presbyters or Pastors is a usurpation and an anti-Christ.

III. The apostles were but twelve, and their number was no more intended to be increased than that of the twelve tribes or the twelve constellations. The apostles saw the Lord, whom their pretended successors have not seen; the apostles wrought miracles, which their pretended successors cannot show; the apostles possessed individually the gift of inspiration, which their pretended successors, unless indirectly or collectively, do not even claim; therefore their pretended successors are *Apostati,* non *Apostoli; Seductores,* non *Doctores; Pilati,* non *Prelati*—not Apostles, but apostates; not Doctors, but seducers; not prelates, but Pilates!

IV. Hilary declares that "In Egypt, even at this day [say, the end of the fourth century,] the Presbyters ordain in the Bishop's absence;" and Jerome a writer of unbounded learning, declares that Episcopacy was introduced "by degrees" into the Church; that at Alexandria even in his day, "not only the election, but the ordination of the Bishops was by the Presbyters themselves," and demands exultingly of the proud Bishop of Rome, "What *does* a Bishop, ordination excepted, that a Presbyter may not do?" in other words, "what prerogative has a Bishop, ordination excepted, that a Presbyter has not?"

These will answer for specimens of the positions, on which, as a graduate in this department, I relied for all future emergencies; and these, together with a few other quotations from the Fathers to save appearances, and especially a modest remark of the great Bishop of Hippo respecting his order, extracted, by a more searching process than is known in alchymy, from the fifteen huge folios of Saint Augustine; and also, the marvellous tradition we were taught, that "there is not one word in favor of Episcopacy to be found in the writings of the Fathers for the first three centuries;" and that, if there were, "the Fathers are not to be trusted," and their records are no better than "old wives' fables;" constituted the stripling's armor, as he came forth to meet "this uncircumcised Philistine." The Episcopal reader will readily understand the process, by which my mind was enabled afterward to perceive the irrelevancy or the inconclusiveness of these and the like assumptions; and the reader, to whom it may appear strange that they should ever have lost with me their force, may have his curiosity gratified by accompanying me a little farther in the story.

But those, who are curious to remark such things will see, that I was all this while a Presbyterian *by tradition*, believing with a loyalist's—I might almost write it, *Loyolist's* implicitness in the historical infallibility of my manuals and doctors. As yet, I had neither the motive nor the time to call in question these traditions, on a subject, as it seemed then to be, of infinitely secondary moment—the veriest "tithing of mint and anise and cummin;" and the sea of Presbyterian faces, lecturers, doctors, books, and temples, spreading to the horizon which my eye commanded, was hardly likely to disturb my confidence.

While in England, Episcopacy appeared to retain its footing by the argument of the sword and of a grinding aristocracy, in America it appeared to us to be breathing out a sickly existence, with scarcely a place of promise for its sepulchre, or any to "sing or say" its own burial service over it, when it should die. In some way or other, I got over the ground at Princeton, without knowing the causes that had held back the Episcopal Church from its destiny upon this continent, or the sorrowful fact, that from Massachusetts Bay to the Gulf of Florida, it was by friend and foe bound hand and foot, and systematically and perseveringly degraded to that miserable state, from which the wonder is, that it ever revived, or outlived the crisis of national independence. Although I knew that the solemn legislation of Connecticut made it *death* for a priest to be seen, after the first warning, within the settlements, yet I was not aware of the untiring and successful resistance, in the other colonies, to the introduction of the Episcopate into this land, whenever the attempt was made, and even when a Queen's bounty at one time, and private munificence at others, had furnished ample securities for its support. Soon after the Restoration, Dr. Murray was actually appointed the Bishop for Virginia, but the measure was defeated by the joint agency of Erastian indifference and Puritanical remonstrance. Again, forty years after, in 1704, the clergy in this country unanimously urged the like step on the attention of the English government, and, to avoid the odium of taxation, offered a tenth of their own substance to meet the expense. Again, about eight years after, in the reign of Queen Anne, and without oppression to any of her subjects, a fund was actually provided, by the sale of wild lands in the West Indies, for the maintenance of the Episcopate at four different points in the American colonies, where it would have been most cordially received; but the death of the Queen and a change of government gave fresh opportunity for the opponents of the Church to keep her under foot. Again, in 1713, the venerable

Society for the Propagation of the Gospel in Foreign Parts—a society still prosecuting its ancient work with the wisdom and dignity of age, and the ardor and energy of youth—purchased at Burlington (the very spot now redeemed by the exertions of a noble Prelate to the church) a house and glebe for a Bishop's residence. Within the twenty years following, not only the living, but the dying "wept when they remembered Zion" in America, and frequent donations and legacies from hands in England that would have reached that Zion if they could, and hearts that "it pitied to see her in the dust," from persons known and unknown, from male and female, from the humble layman to the highest dignitary of the church, continued to swell the fund, and invite the extension of the Episcopate to the American colonies. But government was deaf. And it was jealous. And it had its troubles at home. And the age was an age of indifference, such as experience has now taught us to look for, after a long prevalence of noise and cant, attended, as they usually are, and as they were with the English Puritans, by animosity and violence. In short, the Puritans and Presbyterians would not allow it; and they then held the balance of power.

A hundred and thirty years it was, after Dr. Murray was nominated Bishop for Virginia, that Samuel Seabury—a name impossible to speak, without associating it with the purest and brightest that have been "written in heaven"—was sent forth the first apostle to America. For nearly two centuries had the Church in this land travail and sorrow, before her first Bishop was born. In vain did she pray to be delivered. The marvel is, that she did not, as it was intended, perish in the crisis. And now the children of those very Puritans have the courage, or it may be in their case, as it was in mine, the ignorance to challenge this recurrence to the past, by turning the late, or if you please the present condition of our Church to our reproach. "Among the least," says

Mr. Barnes, "of the tribes of Israel." Be it so. "As for this sect, we know that everywhere it is spoken against." Not in the British Parliament alone, are Romanist and Protestant combined against her, and "Herod and Pilate made friends together." "Among the least of the tribes of Israel!" So was Bethlehem-Ephratah, "little among the thousands of Judah," yet wise men, and even the shepherds of flocks, got to hear how the Lord had made it beautiful with his presence, and found their way to it, and knelt in humble adoration in its dust. "Among the least of the tribes of Israel," says a Presbyterian; "Christianity was born in a manger," said a parishioner of mine, the son of a Presbyterian, "and ought to be kept there." Go a little further, I replied, and say, "she was once nailed to the cross, and ought to be kept *there*." Nearly two centuries was the Church down-trodden in this land; none to administer her discipline; her sacramental character obscured, and one-third of her pious sons, who were forced away to England for ordination, deterred from returning, or dying from the hardships of the voyage. Nor was the Church emancipated, or a Bishop allowed at her altars, until the drums of the revolution roused in her unwilling heart, at last, a sense of this injustice, and some of her very priests went girded to the field, and, with her own Washington at the head of the continental army, and her own White as chaplain to the continental Congress, she became forever free.

But, to return from this apology for the depressed condition of our Church, as the present generation has seen it in the United States: in England, as I have said, quite ignorant of the almost universal hold that the Church has there on the affections of the people, we were led to think that it retained its footing rather by the argument of the sword, and of an overawing aristocracy. Nor did it then occur to me, that it might be perhaps the conservative character of her religion, that had put into her hand that "glittering spear," and had given such power to her aristocracy, imposing upon Europe the hated policy—Pacem cum Anglo, bellum cum reliquis. Of the Greek and Oriental Churches I had scarcely heard. Rome was not to be taken into the account, and the whole world of orthodoxy, piety and common sense, seemed, in my youthful and honest eyes, to be Protestant and Presbyterian. The little island of Great Britain was accidentally Episcopal and liturgical—the universe beside, both earth and heaven was anti-liturgical and Presbyterian. "Why are you forever preaching against Bishops?" said a dissatisfied hearer to a Presbyterian divine. "Because," was the prompt reply, "I always find it in the text." "Well, I will give you a text where you will not find it; Genesis, first chapter, first verse." Accordingly the next Sunday the preacher began—"The Book of Genesis, the first chapter, at the first verse—'In the beginning God created the heaven and the earth,'—but not one word, my brethren, of his creating Bishops."

To speak plainly and honestly, Episcopacy was, in our estimation, a religion for masters and their slaves; but Presbytery for the free; Episcopacy for such as would be startled at the question, "Canst thou speak Greek?" and are therefore without the means of knowing that "Bishop and Presbyter are titles of the same import in the New Testament;" and Presbytery for those who can establish the synonymes in Greek, and *translate* Jerome, Chrysostom, Augustine, and even Clemens and Ignatius, by the hair of the head, over to the side of Presbyterianism: Episcopacy for men who must have books to tell them what to pray for; Presbytery for such as can get this information from their hearts: Episcopacy for "sentimental formalists and priestly drones," as a late writer in Connecticut has called them, who cannot be spurred by the warmth of an emotion, or by the abundance of the theme, to swell their sermons beyond twenty minutes; and Presby terianism for men, whose feelings can warm with their themes, and whose discourses bid defiance to the hour: Episcopacy for such as loiter in the cool shade, and beneath the ripe clusters of the vineyards; but Presbytery for laborers, who "bear the heat and burden of the day:" Episcopacy for those who would cling to the stereotypes of the past; Presbytery for those who can adapt, and modify, and change, as often as the times and the tide require: Episcopacy for intolerably plain and prosy preachers, dwelling continually on the tame maxims of morals and religion; Presbytery for ministers who can rise, and carry their flocks up with them, above such trifling matters as the obligations of daily life, and can entertain their audience by showing that they have at their fingers' end the intellectual universe. We regarded Episcopalians, at the time I speak of, and that time with many is not by any means past, as far behind us in piety and scholarship, owing in some measure, as I suppose, to the fact that individualism is happily lost in the Church, and that the Episcopal clergy are, for the most part, content with the fixed "yea, yea, and nay, nay" of the primitive creed, and are satisfied if they can imbue their preaching, like their prayers, with the simple learning and the simple piety of other days, gathering as they do from the short and melancholy history of Presbyterianism, that "whatsoever is more than these cometh of evil." Said an eminent divine, who was asked why he had exchanged the declamatory manner of his earlier ministry, for a style more dispassionate and mild, "When I was young, I thought it was the *thunder* that killed, but when I grew wiser, I discovered that it was the lightning; so I determined that in future I would thunder less and lighten more."

With these views, which might have been rectified by better acquaintance with the Episcopal Church, and particularly with her clergy, who for the most part deny themselves the luxury of exhibiting their learning or their piety, as incompatible in general with the intentions of their office, and their own proper fitness for its duties, I entered the Presbyterian ministry. I had been personally acquainted, in my whole life, with but two or three of the Episcopal clergy; and of these, the only one that I ever intimately knew, I had seen, in the day of "revivals" spying out, and to all appearance coveting the liberty of his dissenting brethren, and mingling, to great disadvantage, with all sorts of sects, who amused themselves much at his awkward balancings among them, and assigning as his best reason for not admitting these brethren into his pulpit, that "one of the canons of his church forbade it." By the way, it was an apology that elicited from an illiterate old lady, that had been for many years the housekeeper in my father's family, a remark having a range and force of meaning, of which she in her dotage, and myself then fourteen years of age, but little dreamed, that "if that were the case, she thought *they had better fire that canon off.*" Right! Thought I to myself—and so I acknowledge that it strikes me still—that if Episcopacy be of the small importance that some attach to it, "they had better fire that canon off."

Leaving Princeton with such impressions, it is not surprising that, with no temptation to call them in question; with "Bishop and Presbyter for convertible terms in the New Testament;" with "the testimony of the famous Jerome," called by Prosper in his own age the *magister mundi,* and by Erasmus long afterward "the prince of divines," ringing forever in my ear; with a faint echo from Augustine, "the most brilliant and orthodox link of the *catena* between Paul and Calvin;" I found neither time nor inclination, amidst the convulsive throes of revivalism, and the monstrous brood of theological shibboleths, to which those throes gave birth, to review opinions which had in their favor, as I had been taught, and as I still believed, the entire evidence of scripture, and "the unanimous consent of the first three centuries of the Church."

CHAPTER V.

ABUSES AND DISUSE OF BAPTISM.

I AM aware that it is quite easy to discover inconveniences and evils in the working of particular theories or systems, however wisely conceived, so long as those systems must depend for their preservation or efficiency upon the sagacity and purity of human counsels. But where the evils are found to be co-extensive with the system; and where the system is unshackled and free to work out its legitimate results, and yet makes no effort to throw these evils off; but they circulate invariably with its life, and pursue it as closely as the shadow does its substance, and eat as a canker to its very core; it is perfectly fair to suspect some radical defect, and to look into the system itself for an explanation of the fact.

One of the worst and earliest inconveniences, that I found adhering to the system from which I have been emancipated, was its unwarrantable restriction of the sacrament of baptism. I had received, so far as those around me could impart it, a power to baptize, and to "suffer little children to come"—and expressly, it had been, as I supposed, enjoined me by the Master, to "forbid them not." But I presently discovered that my church forbade them. So well is this prohibition understood among Presbyterians, that a minister is seldom, and many a minister among them never, called on to baptize a child, unless at least one of its parents be a communicant in the church. If it be said, that their written discipline does not necessarily impose this restriction, and that formerly a better custom obtained, I have only to reply, that this is then another of the instances, to be often adverted to hereafter, in which the written and fixed traditions of the system have been supplanted by the unwritten or the variable and the popular.

But before proceeding further, let us know what are the facts which we intend to employ as premises in this discussion. And let us first adduce those of a more general nature and from authentic documents, that, when we come to state those of our own private experience, they may not be suspected of exaggeration or distortion.

In the month of May, 1848, there were in connection with the General Assembly of the Presbyterian church, 192,022 communicants; and the number of infants baptized, within the ecclesiastical year, was 9,837; or, one infant to between nineteen and twenty communicants. It would therefore require nineteen and a half years to make the number of baptized children, if every one of them should live, equal to the present number of communicants.

Now take the Presbyteries of the great cities from Canada to Florida, and from the Atlantic to the Mississippi.

Presbyteries.	Communicants.	Infants baptized.	Proportion of inft's baptized to no. of com.
Albany,	4,173	125	1 to 33
New York,	4,729	226	1 to 21
New Brunswick,	4,534	165	1 to 27
Baltimore,	2,395	109	1 to 22
Cincinnati,	1,672	62	1 to 27
St. Louis,	1,159	57	1 to 20
Charleston,	843	35	1 to 24
	19,505	779	1 to 25

Now, in contrast with this, as far as I have access to annual Reports and Journals, the proportion of infants baptized to the number of communicants, in the Episcopal church, is a little more than one to five.* During a ministry of six years in the Church, I have with my own hand baptized as many children as the whole Presbytery of New York with its thirty-five ministers, according to the above table, would do in three.

But, to go still more into detail. The mother of Presbyterian churches in New York numbers 373 communicants; the Rev. Dr. Phillips reports *fifteen infants* baptized the past year. The Brick church has 668 communicants; Dr. Spring reports *twenty-six infants* baptized. The Rev. Dr. Potts, who has written against Episcopacy as "illiberal and anti-republican," has 282 communicants, and reports *twelve infants* baptized. The Rev. Dr. Smith, of Charleston, who was my classmate at Princeton, and has written a book in defence of Presbytery, has 408 communicants, and reports *six infants* baptized. The Rev. Dr. Boardman, of Philadelphia, also my cotemporary at Princeton, reports 482 communicants, and *one infant* baptized. He too, I believe, has written a book against the Episcopal church. Thus, while the books multiply, the flocks diminish.

Early in my ministry, a circumstance occurred, that forced this subject very affectingly upon my notice. I had in those days, a sister, in whose heart had long dwelt a measure of the grace of God, that is, if some of the most pleasing fruits of piety may make it lawful so to pronounce; although the spark often trembled for existence, unreplenished as it was from the fires of the altar. She was one of those many persons, who, under the influences of insufficient teaching, look

* In some few Calvinistic congregations, the proportion sinks to one half this estimate. Thus, in St. George's, New York, according to the last Report, the number of communicants was 463, and of infants baptized, 45; or one to ten. But the same year, the number of communicants in the Diocese was 13,486, and of infants baptized 2,658, or one to five.

unfortunately on the sacrament of the altar, not with too *much* awe—that were impossible—but with that *kind* of dread, which man's chief enemy employs to keep back the hungering and fainting heart from the strengthening nourishment of "the children's bread." And my sister's soul was of that sensitive and gentle texture, that it stood amazed, and at times half wild, at the exactions of a stern and frigid Calvinism; and the bruised reed had been often well nigh broken, and the smoking flax well nigh been quenched.

Having myself embraced with much satisfaction that view of the sacraments, which is yet to be found in the Confession of Faith, where it stands as a witness against an unbelieving age, I fell into conversation with my sister, respecting the education of the lovely children which the Lord had given her, and pressed her with the fact, that the only "good beginning" she could make with them, must date from the grace of baptism. She told me, that it had been the most painful desire of her heart, to have them baptized; but knowing as she was not a communicant herself, that the customs of her church did not allow it, she had never dared to ask it. She then inquired of me, if I would baptize them for her. "Can any man forbid water," said I to myself, "that these should not be baptized as well as we," we, who are far more filled than they, with all manner of unbelief and sin? What am I, that I should usurp the throne of judgment, and "visit the sins of the fathers upon the children?" What right have I, even were the parents visibly withering in the blight of a secret and eternal decree, to include in it those little ones, that, like the "six score thousand" in Nineveh, that turned God's judgment into mercy, "cannot discern their right hand from their left?" The practice of my church forbids them; but my heart, and One greater than my heart says, "Forbid them not." I could not hesitate. I felt it proper however to advise her, first to make trial of her own pastor, who was weary himself, as I knew, of some of the asperities of his theology; and who accordingly gave the sweet infants, *privately,* for fear of establishing an injurious precedent, the sacrament, which his church in the like circumstances, universally withholds. It must be added however, that this excellent man thought it necessary afterward to apologize for this act of mercy, on the ground that, in the right and might of his own "private judgment," he had himself for a long time regarded their mother as a believing Christian. Only in two other instances, during a ministry of seven years, can I recollect having been requested to baptize the children of a non-communicant. It is a pleasing reminiscence now, that, in all these instances, the practice of a purer age invited me to rise above the trammels of a new-invented theory, and to refuse to do it homage where it did violence to every feeling of the heart. And sad and chill would be my visits now to the silent field, where the three flowers, snatched from a sister's bosom, lie each in its bed, waiting to rise and bloom side by side again, when the Sun of righteousness shall return and shine upon the sod, were I to recollect, that, before they were planted in that dust, I had raised a finger to prevent their being watered, by *any* human hand, with the dews of baptism. But little did I suspect that that mother would have so soon been called to bathe with her tears the brows that had been so lately bathed at the fountain of grace. Not many have drunk, at a single draught, so deeply of the Master's cup as she.

"The shaft flew thrice, and thrice her peace was slain,
And thrice, ere thrice yon moon had filled her horn."

"For God, to draw her spirit heavenward,
Severed the golden chains that bound her here,
And placed her idols nearer to himself,
To lure her onward to the better land."

For, as they have been planted in the likeness of His death, they shall be also in the likeness of his resurrection. And it is sweet to think,

> "Babes, thither caught from womb and breast,
> Have right to sing above the rest,
> For they have gained the happy shore
> They never saw nor sought before.
>
> "We are the babes no more
> That gave their feeble wailing to thine ear,
> Free from the cumbering clay, we mount, we soar,
> Onward and upward through a boundless sphere.
>
> "We dwell no more with pain—
> We shed no tears—we feel no panting breath—
> Sweet mother, do not grieve for us again,
> We are so blest, we bless the hand of death.
>
> "Turn with unwavering trust
> From the green earth-bed where the body lies,
> Thou didst but lay our covering in the dust,
> Thy children live, will live beyond the skies.
>
> "There we shall meet again,
> O yes! believe it, meet to part no more!
> We'll welcome thee with heaven's angelic train,
> And lead thee to the Saviour we adore."

But again to the cold regions of speculation, and to my chilling theme. To me the reasoning was direct and just, that the child, that is unfit to be baptized, is unfit to die; the child that may not be admitted into the church below, for fear of tainting it, may not be admitted into the pure bosom of the church above. There is no evading the startling inference, and humanity shudders and falls back from the terrible conclusion! Tell me not, when my child is dead, that it has gone safe; why then did you withhold the token of its safety, that *antitupon* of St. Peter, of which he declares that the ark upon the water, and the water bearing up the ark, and both conspiring to save the eight members of the church of God, were together the type? "The like figure whereunto," he declares, "even Baptism, doth also now save us." Tell us not, when our children are dead, that although the Bible is not a revelation to infants, yet the intimations that it drops give us reason to believe that they have gone safe! for these insinuations pierce the heart with a sting more acute than death, and your withholding Baptism leaves with us the awful feeling—mistify and disguise it as you may—that you are not quite certain that our dear departed ones were born again.

The Presbyterian church, not content with making so prominent the disheartening view of election, which it has chosen to incorporate into her faith, has undertaken to intimate, at least in a general way, which of our very babes are not of "that happy number," by allowing Baptism—the "sign and seal," as they believe of that election—to one infant, and by refusing it to another. Yet the laity, for the most part, submit tamely to the usurpation—a usurpation unmatched, so far as I know, both in its essence and its extent, by any tyranny of priest-ridden Rome. Yet I have known instances, in which the parent, urged on by the cry of nature, and the voice of God within him, has taken his child "by night" to the minister of a Church, that claims to be "the Lamb's wife" and the "mother of us all"—a Church that, since the beginning of the creation, has never withheld her Baptism from the lost children of Adam. Yes, we proclaim it with unmingled satisfaction, that this same Church so denounced as exclusive, bigoted, intolerant—pours from her open hand the waters of pardon and of promise on the universal family. How is it that Presbyterianism—with a confession that speaks of "elect men" and of "elect angels" and of "ELECT INFANTS" (see Conf. chapters iii and x.)—and notoriously and every hour withholding baptism from new-born babes, for no other reason than the lurking apprehension that these babes may not be "of the happy number"—has claimed so long to be considered "liberal" and democratic; while the church that clasps your infant to her heart as soon as it is born, and beckons the whole family of man within her pale, has been branded as illiberal, intolerant, and bigoted?

The day for this ad captandum declaration is passing away, and the eyes of the people are opening to the facts. "Suffer the little children to come unto me, and forbid them not," say the Lamb and the Lamb's bride:—"Suffer the children of communicants whom we have privately examined, and pronounced to have in our judgment the marks of distinguishing grace to come," says the Presbyterian religion. "He died for all," "a ransom for all," "that He by the grace of God should taste death for every man," declares the Holy Ghost, and redeclares it by the church that he inspires:—"Neither are any other redeemed by Christ, but the elect only," contends the Presbyterian confession, (chap. iii. sec. 7.) "The grace of God, that bringeth salvation, hath appeared unto all men," proclaim the Bible and the echoing Church:—"All those whom God hath predestinated unto life, and those only, he is pleased in his appointed and accepted time, effectually to call, by his word and spirit," reasserts the Presbyterian confession. "Who will have all men to be saved," is the teaching of the Gospel and the Church:—"By the decree of God, for the manifestation of his glory, some men and angels are predestinated unto everlasting life, and others are foreordained to everlasting death," and, "These men and angels, thus predestinated and foreordained, are particularly and unchangeably designed, and their number is so certain and definite, that it cannot be either increased or diminished," is the sad wail of the Presbyterian confession, (chap. iii, sec. 3–4.)

We appeal to the understandings of men. Which of the two is illiberal and bigoted? Let the Presbyterian, whose child, for which Christ died, and which Christ pronounced more fit for the kingdom of God than we, and to be the object of an angel's watch and guard, has yet been excluded from the church on earth and from the only Sacrament which an infant can receive, answer this question. A day will come, when the Presbyterian ministry will be compelled to a better practice, or their people into a better Church. That day may be delayed by prudently keeping the subject in the back ground, and the people in ignorance of the efficacy and the grace of Baptism. Their ministers dare not bring it forward, and hold it up, as it is exhibited in their own Confession of Faith. Listen to its solemn and delightful testimony! "Baptism is a sacrament of the New Testament, *not only* for the solemn admission of the party baptized into the *visible church*, but also to be unto him a sign and seal of the covenant of *grace*, of his *ingrafting into Christ*, of REGENERATION, of *remission of sins*."—"The *efficacy* of Baptism is not tied to that moment of time wherein it is administered; yet notwithstanding, by the right use of this ordinance, the grace promised is *not only* offered, but *really exhibited and conferred by the Holy Ghost*, to such, whether of age or INFANTS, as that grace belongeth unto, according to the counsel of God's own will, in his appointed time." (Conf. chap. xxviii, secs. 1 and 6.) "Let but the commons hear this testament!" With the recovery of the lost doctrine of "efficacy," and "grace" and "regeneration," and "ingrafting into Christ" and "remission of sins" "*not only offered, but really exhibited and conferred by the Holy Ghost*," in Baptism, their ministers would be compelled to make its living waters again free for all, or parents, driven by the instincts of their natures, would fly, with their children in their arms, like doves into the church windows. Ministers of the Presbyterian church! I call upon you by the deep solemnity of an awful sacrament—and many a pained heart among your people joins me in the call!—to justify this language that you hold respecting "elect infants," or to abandon the practice that results from it in drawing a dividing line among infants, and excluding the majority from the grace of Baptism. The rains of heaven fall alike on all. The sun in heaven shines equally on all. The wind from heaven is wafted alike to all. The rivers and the fountains spring and flow for all. Free for all, is the plain handwriting upon every work of God. What then is this distinction you have drawn between my neighbor's children and my own? Speak! Tell us plainly, are some of them elect, and others not? or are some of them born but once, and others born again? I venture to term it an oppression that the Church in no age and in no instance ever dared to impose—nay, a cruelty, that Rome, in the days of her worst tyranny, would have shuddered to inflict; this punishing the parent in the child, repelling a redeemed infant, because its parents have sinned, from the only Sacrament of which it is capable, the heaven-ordained point at which grace is sent forth to meet it. It "asks bread," and, because its parents have not eaten the bread that you break, with a heart as cold and hard as your gift, you "give it a stone:" "it asks an egg," and, to sting the erring parent, you put into its little hand "a scorpion:" it "asks a fish," and you "give it a serpent," and leave it to become the serpent's prey.

It is a discipline that is fast driving off reflecting Presbyterians among the Baptists, or back by God's blessing to the Episcopal Church. So few already are the infants baptized in the Presbyterian denomination in this country, that it differs but little from a Baptist community, and may in strict propriety of phrase be called a semi-Baptist church. The difference between them is, that the one excludes all infants indiscriminately from Baptism; the other, venturing to discriminate, excludes more than three-fourths. As might have been expected, the Baptists in their position are altogether the stronger of the two. Every Presbyterian minister well knows that even his communicants often acquiesce in infant Baptism on vague and insufficient grounds, or are constantly harassed by most painful and perplexing doubts. Let me be rather the consistent Baptist, in a good conscience, denying Baptism to all infants alike, than the semi-Baptist, daring to tread where Gabriel would quake to follow, and to draw among the infants of a span long the tremendous separation between sheep and goats. As a layman I might have tamely submitted to the iron rule, and without resistance have heard the clinking key opening the kingdom to one infant and locking it against another; but, as a theologian, I could not endure the thought, or long believe, that this was the representative or the lawful almoner of God's love upon earth. I became early and clearly satisfied, that, on this most interesting point at least, Episcopacy was in the right, gathering, as the rightful mother, the universe of infants to her arms; and that Presbytery was in the wrong, to a degree that the world can hardly ever forgive or any longer endure.

That sectarianism has ever borne a singular resemblance to Romanism, has been remarked ever since its birth, and is not surprising, if we reflect, that they are of a common parentage, born at the same time, one at Westminster, and one at Trent, and that the twins alike decline to have their legitimacy tested, by bringing into court the ancient mother—the Catholic or universal faith. My musings on the abuse and disuse of Baptism brought the coincidence of the two systems strikingly to mind. If the Romanist has erred and played the tyrant in subtracting from "the people" the more significant part of the Christian sacrifice; the part, of which the Lord emphatically, as if to forestal the usurpation, said, "Drink ye *all* of it;" the Presbyterian has erred and played the tyrant, in subtracting the whole of another most precious sacrament from millions of little ones, all pure in heart, of which the Saviour of the world, with the like emphasis, as if to anticipate this usurpation also, said, and said in a moment when he "was

6

much displeased," "Suffer the little children to come unto me, and forbid them not; for of such is the kingdom of heaven." If then I am bid to fly from Romanism, for withholding the more significant portion of one sacrament, from those who are entitled to receive it; with all the holy instincts of parental love, let me fly from Presbyterianism, for withholding another sacrament—the only one of which my child is capable—from infants, who, by a Redeemer's legacy, are entitled to its benefits, and who, after the Testator's resurrection, were still upon his heart, when he said to a shepherd of his flock, "Feed my lambs," *If* ye love *me*, "feed my lambs."

I know the Pelagianism that thrives wherever Presbytery has prepared the soil, and the secret thought with many, and the practical feeling with more, that infants do not need the grace of Baptism, nor indeed any grace whatever. I was once invited in this land of ours into a pious family in New-York, for the purpose of baptizing a dying infant, whose Baptism had been already very carelessly delayed. Even at that time I had so far a glimmering perception of the truth, as to understand that Baptism was at least a joyful expression of the parents' faith in the new salvation; that it was the visible bond of the Christian brotherhood on earth; that it conveyed the grace which to one "conceived in sin and shapen in iniquity" is indispensable; and that infant Baptism, to take the lowest view of it, was a compliance with the will of Christ, and was the dictate of natural humanity and of parental instinct. Such were my musings as I went on my unaccustomed errand to baptize a dying child. Aware that Pelagianism had deeply tainted the minds of both the parents, I rather wondered that this should have been the only instance of the kind in which I had ever been invited to officiate. But on my arrival at the house, where the healing waters were already sparkling in the bowl, and the sweet infant about to return to the arms that encircled infants when He was on earth, the mother of the child, seeming to understand that the Baptism of an infant must after all mean *something,* interposed a murmur, that "it needed no Baptism—and was as safe without it—why should it be disturbed?" Her infant died—died unbaptized—went into eternity without faith's mark upon its brow—and was saved, as the child of the infidel or Hottentot is saved, with nought to impart to it a difference of glory in the resurrection, nought by which angels might know that it had come from a christian land, in fact without the only sacrament by which the gospel can be preached, or its distinctive grace conveyed to an infant mind. I have not to this hour recovered the shock that this occurrence gave me; nor could I now tell whether the stronger emotion was disgust or grief. Even then I sympathized not only with Baxter, and Owen, and Edwards, and Miller in their view of the privileges to which Baptism exalted the recipient, not only with Presidents Finlay and Smith, who, in the belief that original sin is washed away in this sacrament and the recipient placed on a new footing and under happier auspices, were in the habit of baptizing as many infants as they could reach; but my sympathies were entirely with the Confession of Faith, which, in common with all others of the period of the Reformation, exalts this sacrament to be the vehicle of quickening and regenerating grace. Such views, although I have never seen a Presbyterian layman that either embraced or understood them, have not, it is fair to say, entirely disappeared among the Presbyterian clergy. The present Professor of Theology at Princeton—perhaps as profound a divine as Calvinism in either hemisphere can boast of, and whose qualities of heart are not inferior to those of his mind, on the subject of Baptism, for a moment partially eluded the trammels of his system, as that system has been recently developed, and, consistently enough with the written confession of his church, has dropped the following language: "And when about to dedicate their children to God, in Holy Baptism, how earnestly should they [the parents] pray, that they might be baptized with the Holy Ghost—that while their bodies are washed in the emblematical laver of regeneration, their souls may experience the renewing of the Holy Ghost, and the sprinkling of the blood of Jesus. If the sentiments, expressed above, be correct, then may there be such a thing as *baptismal regeneration*" [the italics are his own;] " . . . . . and, what time in infancy is *more likely* to be the period of spiritual quickening, than *the moment* when that sacred rite is performed, which is strikingly emblematical of this change. . . . . . If by *means*, be understood something which is accompanied by the divine efficiency, changing the moral nature of the infant, then in this sense, baptism may be called *the means of regeneration*." *

But the view of this Sacrament, that stares them in the face, on the pages of their written standards, Presbyterians have for the most part lost; and we fear that there is no conservative or counteracting principle in the system, to which we can look with any hope for its recovery. We rather fear, that, having gotten so far away from their standards, the gravitation toward them is continually lessening, and the whole body is fated to go farther still into still chillier regions. Some few perhaps may fall in love with the opinions put forth in a volume some years ago by a living eminent divine of New York, that infants have a law written on their hearts, against which they are capable of wilful sin, and may be the proper subjects of everlasting perdition before they have even seen the light of day;—from which the inference will be direct, that they must not therefore be baptized, until they have given actual signs of repentance. Others will adopt the more popular Pelagianism, that infants, being not yet sinners, do not yet stand

* Thoughts on Religious Experience by the Rev. Archibald Alexander, D. D., Professor, &c.; published by the Presbyterian Board of Publication, 400 pages, see page 26 of the Third Edition.

in need of Baptism;—from which, though an opposite quarter to the former, the same result must follow, that infants by and by will receive no Baptism. A more consistent and ingenuous portion will adhere to the old Calvinistic ground of their Confession, that there are "elect infants," as well as "elect angels and men,"—which, from the difficulty of ascertaining them, will greatly abridge, as it has fearfully abridged already, the extent of infant Baptism, and must cause it ultimately to fall into disuse. With others, again, the Quaker or mystic notion of a spiritual church, into which Presbyterians are fast degenerating, will continue rapidly to gain ground, and will greatly discourage, and eventually wipe out the last vestiges of infant Baptism. It is demonstrable from facts and figures, that, if infant Baptism grow as rapidly into disuse among Presbyterians for the time to come as it has done for fifty years past, one hundred years hence, the Presbyterian church as a pœdobaptist society will exist no more. It is already as we have called it, a semi-Baptist denomination. In the Presbytery of St. Louis, the number of adults baptized the last year wanted but eight, to be equal to that of baptized infants; that of Cincinnati wanted but twenty-two; that of New Brunswick, including Princeton, wanted but twelve; the adults being one hundred and fifty three, the infants one hundred and sixty five.

The Baptists see distinctly that infant Baptism cannot be maintained, and is not worth maintaining, on the popular grounds adduced by Presbyterians in its defence. In fact they see that, separated from regeneration, it ceased to be a Sacrament; and not knowing "a more excellent way," and laying themselves the stress which Holy Scripture lays upon the ordinance, they will stand firm, and must necessarily increase by continual accessions from the Presbyterians, who will find it more and more out of their power to resist the encroachment. Meanwhile *the Church,* planting one foot on the ground of the Baptists, as to the value and efficacy of the Sacrament, and the other on the ground of the Bible and of humanity, and of historical Christianity, as to its extent, will continue to flourish, with a stability and growth that shall provoke the losers in this game to jealousy. Already, among the Presbyterians, infant Baptism has fallen into the disuse that Anabaptists could desire. Already thousands of parents, who still, from a vague compliance with old customs or with the wishes of a jealous pastor, "*suffer*" their little ones to come to the sacrament, are free to admit, that they scarcely see a necessity for what they do. Already, the pious Presbyterian is not made a whit more unhappy for having failed to imprint the token of its safety on the pale forehead of a deceased or dying child, than the pious Pelagian!

Indeed, Presbyterians are now but little behind the Quakers in reform. The "spiritual"—the "spiritual"—the "spiritual"—this is the sense in which every thing is to be understood; and if you speak to them of order and ordination, the daily prayer, the weekly oblation, outward reverence and external rites, bodily fasting and alms-deeds and worship, external Sacraments, and a visible Church binding the past to the present, and the present to the future, you seem but a Papist to many, and the lament of "a mixed multitude" rings sorrowfully in your ear, "Take these things hence! Are ye so carnal? Having begun in the spirit, are ye now made perfect by the flesh?" In the determination to be "spiritual," they are hardly a whit behind Swedenborg himself in his flight from the regions of flesh and sense. To them, as to him, it would seem that the Jewish Church was but the creeping worm out of whose shell the Church Christian was to take wing, and the Church Christian, as it has heretofore existed, but the shell in its turn, which the "spiritual" brotherhood are to despise and leave behind. This crying down external order and sacramental privilege, and this assuming superior "spiritual" discernment, as if they were "out of the body," or as if Christ had never come in the flesh may lull for a while the sense of injury on the subject which we are here discussing. But let Baptism get to be restored among them to the place assigned to it by the Westminster divines in the Confession which their ministers still vow at their ordination to defend, and not more certainly will the ice relax under the returning sun of summer, than the people will demand, according to the charter of their rights and of unlimited redemption, that the sign of that redemption be set on the foreheads of their children; and that, when infants die, no cold *perhaps* shall follow them to the bosom of God; no chilly *reasoning* shall come to bind up the parent's heart; no such *language* as "elect infants" shall be tolerated another hour; but that every heartless distinction and doubt shall be wiped out, and the brotherhood of the human family be restored, as the second Adam intended it to be, in the "One Baptism." If still they should be denied the heavenly boon—if still they should be driven from the healing waters, then their alternative will be, as with many it has already been, to fly from the chill atmosphere of an exclusive and repulsive system—a system so stern that it can frown upon an infant in its cradle—to the more genial bosom of the church.

Do not tell us that Presbyterians, in some other countries, still baptize children indiscriminately.

We have something to say hereafter of the system as it exists in other countries. In other countries it is hampered by the State, and "cannot do the things that it would." We are dealing now with Presbyterianism "under its own vine and fig-tree," where it is free, and freely working out its legitimate results. We raise our voice for the rights of parents among a preacher-ridden people—rights which a strange oppression springing up in this republic is trampling under foot. We lift our voice for the rights of infants to the blessings of "the kingdom of heaven"—infants, that like the "six score thousand" speechless but successful pleaders for the "salvation of Nineveh," have not known "their right hand from their left." We demand, in presence of a people who, like the Jews, suppose that they have never been in "bondage to any man," that there shall in the eye of the gospel be, at least among infants, no privileged or elect class. We demand the broad confession, that all our children have been redeemed by the blood gushing warm from a Saviour's heart, and that the water flowing with it from his side was intended to bathe their brow. In the ears of earth and heaven, we invoke the ancient charter of the Church against this encroachment on the inalienable rights and liberties of man.

If I could give no other reason for my return to the Church, than has been here presented, I might, with a heart full of peace, here rest my appeal with God and men—that God, who with a Parent's heart has said, "Suffer little children to come unto me, and forbid them not"—and that humanity, which He has endowed with the same sympathies and the same parental instinct.

But my dissatisfaction did not stop here, for the reason that the frightful evil does not stop here. Presbytery, like Popery, has, in its way, multiplied the sacraments, by, inevitably, suggesting the idea of two Baptisms. Or, as the Romanist has divided a commandment, to make up the ten; so the Presbyterian has divided the sacrament of Baptism, to answer private views. I can recollect a time, when I imagined that the chief practical virtue of Baptism consisted in imposing vows and obligations on the parent, and that its efficacy depended entirely on the faith of the parent in making the dedication of his child. Poor child! regenerate or not, according to the parent's mind! Wherein does this differ from Popery, which quickens the water or the wafer to its purpose, according to the intention of the priest?

Yet this is perhaps the prevailing explanation of this delightful sacrament among my former brethren. But if this be so, why—as I learned afterward to reason—why are not the words of the ceremony addressed to the parents? And why is Baptism considered complete, even if the parent be not present? And why, though the parent should immediately die, is the impressive ceremony never to be repeated, so that there should be never but the one Baptism? And why are the words of Baptism addressed to the infant? For instead of something impressive to the parent, the minister speaks in an unknown tongue—for it might as well be in Greek as in English—to a passive infant, saying, "N., I baptize *thee* in the name of the Father, and of the Son, and of the Holy Ghost!" Very extraordinary all this, thought I—that infants may not only be baptized in the same water with adults, but may be addressed in the same mysterious words, "I baptize *thee*"—if Baptism mean one thing—*regeneration*—in the adult—and something else *no mortal can tell what*—in the infant!

Let Presbyterians answer the charge which we here make, that they hold two Baptisms; a Baptism declaring to men and angels, as a fact, the regeneration of the adult; and a Baptism declaring something else, certainly not regeneration, in an infant. If, when administered to an adult, it signifies that he is born again and restored to the favor of God, and, when ministered to an infant, it signifies that he is *not* born again; we certainly perceive two Baptisms. Nor is there a possible escape from this dilemma, except on ancient and Bible premises, that neither adult nor infant is "born again," but as it is accomplished by the joint agency of "the Spirit and the Bride," or, as our Lord expresses it, "except ye be born of water and of the Spirit." Tell us not, that Baptism administered by you to infants, signifies prospective regeneration. This is Pelagianism. Tell us not, that it signifies their need of that regeneration; for why then do you not baptize them all, or even, like the Jesuit, catch the wild Indian, and *bon gre mal gre* baptize him, as the most solemn method of declaring that he "must be born again?" But you tell us, Baptism represents regeneration as accomplished, *un fait accompli,* in the adult; then tell us, we ask again, what it does signify in the infant? We repeat that we think you cannot tell. You know that your views are vague.

No, sirs; you must give up the ground you occupy to the Baptists, or you must go back to your Confession of Faith—the offspring of a more vigorous and healthy Reformation. You must go back to the principles with which you set out three centuries ago, "one Lord, one Faith, one Baptism;" for "by one Spirit we are all baptized into one body." What Baptism means in one, it means in all. What it signifies in the sinner of a hundred years, it signifies in the infant of a span long. "I baptize THEE in the name of the Father, and of the Son, and of the Holy Ghost." You tell us what this is in an adult; pray tell us, if you have the courage or the power, what it is in an infant. Only beware, that, in attempting it, you do not fall into a grand error of the Papists, and multiply sacraments, as they have done, or divide them, as they have divided a commandment, and as they have divided the communion, and that you do not give a *whole* sacrament to adults, and a *half* sacrament to infants. For, besides dividing the communion, and withholding the cup from the laity, we hear that Romanists, in certain cases of discipline and penance, to prevent scandal and to save appearances, will allow a prince, or any other individual where the motive is sufficient, to approach the altar, and receive a wafer, but a wafer not consecrated, and therefore without virtue; which has been called a blank or *white communion.* Precisely so, the Presbyterian ministry, it would now appear, give the same water and words, and, as the world looking on would think, the same thing, to the infant as to the adult; but to the cheated infant, it is not the baptism that an adult receives—it is a blank, *white baptism.* And while the Papist and the Presbyterian must look about them for a vindication of these strange abuses, I may in the meantime be allowed to think, that I have something to be gratified for, in being extricated from the toils of an oppressive system, and led out of the *sic volo, sic jubeo,* of Popery and Presbytery, into "the glorious liberty" of a Church—Catholic—Reformed—and Free.

CHAPTER VI.

SACRAMENTS.

I HAVE never remarked whether Presbyterian church edifices have eastern ends. Popish as it is, I suppose they sometimes have. But I have heard that in an old Presbyterian burying ground on Long Island, the feet of the dead of a certain epoch lie all toward the West, and that many years ago, an Episcopal clergyman, who desired to repose within its precincts, required by his will, that he should be interred, according to the ancient custom of all Christian folk, with his feet and face toward the East; and that so it was allowed, and that the burial-place is still shown, whereby, "he being dead, yet speaketh." But, in a Presbyterian church, that stood a few years since in Wall-street, there was a *Northern* window—I believe, behind the *pulpit*—of some ecclesiological merit—perhaps of stained glass. An Episcopal clergyman, wishing at that time to see the specimen, applied to a gentleman of that congregation, who very obligingly offered to accompany him into the church. As they stood together in the aisle, this gentleman, feeling doubtless safe in his own castle, took the opportunity to say to the clergyman, "Those Oxford men are doing an immensity of mischief; only to think, sir, of their altering the Bible?" "What!" said my friend, with some astonishment, "I was not aware that they had gone so far as *that*." "Yes, sir; if you will step with me into the pulpit, I will show you. Here, sir, is an Oxford edition of the Bible, that we have lately got out from England; and a young minister, officiating for our Pastor on Sabbath last, was reading the Revelation of John, and read it over and over—'the four living creatures—the four living creatures,' instead of 'the four beasts;'—I believe those Oxford men rather disrelish John's Revelation, particularly what he says about *beasts*;—yes, sir, they are altering the Bible?" "I hardly think that can be so," said the Episcopalian; "let us look!" The layman, as much as to say, "Now I have you," dashed into the Apocalypse, looking through grave glasses that had never deceived him before, for his "living creatures;" when, lo, and behold, "the four beasts"—"the four beasts"—there they were, "the four *beasts*, lion, calf, man, and eagle," staring him in the face, "with eyes before and behind." "There's something wrong," said the layman, after a pause, "he certainly did read it so." "Very likely he did," replied the clergyman of the weather-beaten Church; "There was nothing Roman however about it; it was your young man wanting to show off his *Greek*; I think I have heard that your Presbyterian ministers of late, in reading the Bible, often stop to correct the translation, and thus weaken the confidence of the people in its truthfulness; *but ours never do*; I do not think, Mr. N., you need be uneasy about the Oxford Divines; at least about their altering the Bible."

I have related this anecdote, because it is one of a class, and in my own mind is connected with another, which lies more directly in the plane of our narrative. A friend of mine —once, like myself, a Presbyterian minister, and now a clergyman of the Church—who had got a little weary of the pious lamentations of a Presbyterian neighbor, in the city of New York, over the fearful stridings of the Episcopal Church towards Rome, was at the house of his friend on a certain occasion, when, not much to his surprise, the old subject was brought forward. "Poh!" said the grave Elder of an up-town congregation, "your Church is going over to Popery as fast as it can!" "A very grave charge," said his reverend guest, "I confess that I do not see how you would support it; but, if you have any good reason for thinking so, no man would thank you more than myself, and no Church would be more thankful than the old acknowledged 'bulwark of the Reformation,' if you would let us know it." "Why," said the Elder, with a look over his spectacles more searching than his ratiocination, "you are teaching regeneration in Baptism, and something wondrous-like transubstantiation in the Lord's Supper;—just see that 'Churchman' published in this city! Is not that Popery?" "Let me understand you, my dear sir," said my friend, "for now-a-days we scarcely know what Popery is;—would you call *this* Popery?" (*Reads from the last number of the Churchman*)—"Baptism is a sacrament of the New Testament, *not only* for the solemn admission of the party baptized into the *visible Church,* but also to be unto him a sign and a seal of the covenant of *grace* of his *ingrafting into Christ,* of REGENERATION, of *remission of sins.*" . . . . "Yes, that's it! that's it! Don't you call that Popery?" interrupted the Elder. "Just wait a moment," said the clergyman, "let us hear it out:—'The *efficacy* of Baptism is not tied to that moment of time wherein it is administered; yet notwithstanding, by the right use of this ordinance, the *grace* promised is *not only offered,* but really exhibited and *conferred by the Holy Ghost.*' . . . . ." "There, I told you so," again interrupted the impatient Elder; "ah! you are all going over to Popery; just what I told you!" "Well, you object to *that*—what have you to say to *this?* (Reads) 'There is in every sacrament a Sacramental union between the sign and the thing signified. . . . . . Worthy receivers, outwardly partaking of the visible elements in the Sacrament of the Lord's Supper, do then also, inwardly, by faith, really and indeed receive and feed upon Christ crucified; the body and blood of Christ being then, not corporally and carnally, yet *as really and truly*, but spiritually, present to the faith of believers in that ordinance, *as the elements themselves are* to their outward senses. . . . . . And they that worthily communicate, feed upon his body and blood, to their spiritual nourishment and growth in grace." "Yes! there! I told you so! I told you so! All Popery! Popery! That's what your Oxford men are about! Well, John foretold it all;" (my friend had been a Presbyterian, long enough to know that *John* was neither the coachman of that name, nor the waiter that had answered the bell); "what is to be, will be; and *John* says, that 'the deadly wound,' that the Beast got at the Reformation, is to be 'healed,' and all the world is again to go after the—I beg your pardon—*beast!*" "Now, Mr. D.," replied the clergyman, "I have only waited to hear your opinions of the passages that I have read; I brought this paper with me this morning, on purpose that you might see what *your own church* teaches, or *did* teach, when she came from the hands of Knox and Calvin and the Westminster Divines. Just look and see for yourself; all that I have been reading has been taken from *your own Confession of Faith*." (*The old gentleman takes the hebdomadal and reads —fidgets in his chair—looks into the fire—then looks up at his antagonist.*) "I don't believe that the Confession of Faith teaches any such thing; I shall not believe it, until I see it." (*My friend draws from his pocket a volume, with a leaf turned down at a certain page, and hands it to the Elder—who reads a moment—fidgets—looks at the outside of the book—fidgets still more—examines the title-page—reads the marked passage —fidgets tremendously—gives back the book.*) "Well, I can't say," said the Elder, "I never saw that in the Confession of Faith before; *if it is* there, I shall go and ask my minister to explain it." "The truth is," said the morning visitor, "you Presbyterians formerly held upon these points about the same doctrines that we do; witness the strong language of your own Calvin and of Luther—but you have departed from your standards, and now imagine, because we adhere to ours, that we are going back to Popery. As you glide from the wharf, or recede from the shore, you imagine that the land is moving from you; but it is not the land that moves; it is your ship; the land stands still. In like manner, the Church, the building on the Rock stands still. *The Church is where it was.* It is you and your ship that are moving away, and throwing back the puny ripple against the everlasting Rock." Suffice it to add, that my friend still keeps up his acquaintance at the Elder's house, but that the old gentleman is by no means so lachrymose on the subject of Popery as formerly. It is said that he is waiting with some impatience for that explanation by his pastor.

Certain it is, that the Presbyterian Confession of Faith (much more the Dutch Reformed and the Lutheran) is as clear as the teaching of the Church Catholic, concerning the value and efficacy, both of Baptism and of the Lord's Supper. But Presbyterians, almost to a man, have departed more widely from their standards, on the design and uses of the latter, than we have shown them to have done on the benefits and efficacy of the former.

We have seen, that out of the doctrine of election, and of regenerating grace and of effectual calling reaching only to the elect, has sprung up as a natural growth, the refusal of the grace of Baptism to half the purest subjects of the kingdom of heaven. But, as if this were not enough for this "king of fierce countenance and understanding dark sayings," and opening the forbidden leaves of fate, the work of decimation must go further still. The Presbyterian standards enjoin, that "children, born within the pale of the visible Church, and dedicated to God in Baptism, when they come to years of discretion, if they be free from scandal, appear sober and steady, and to have sufficient knowledge to discern the Lord's body, they ought to be informed, it is their duty and their privilege, to come to the Lord's supper." And, for more than a hundred years, this order was universally obeyed. But now their baptized children are denied "the children's bread," as much as if they had been crowned in their infancy with the turban or a crescent, or had been devoted in the Ganges to the pollutions of Brahma. Only their communicants are complacently addressed as "fellow-citizens with the saints, and of the household of faith;" but all others, without regard to Baptism, are treated as "aliens from the commonwealth of Israel, and strangers to the covenants of promise, having no hope, and without God in the world." Such is this mother's love, and method of appealing to her children.

How often are my ears delighted, and my eyes gladdened now, to see the kind pastor going back with the youth of his flock to the bright fountains, where he had bathed them in the morning of life's sultry day, and to hear him speaking, in soft and winning tones, of sins forgiven, and of promised grace, of the Angel that troubled the waters, and of the Holy Ghost that descended like a dove, and of the ministering Spirit that hovered near to receive its new charge, when the Lord "sware and entered into covenant with them, as he said: In the day that thou wast born, and wast cast out on the open field, lo, I passed by and pitied thee and threw my skirt over thee; then washed I thee with water, and I girded thee about with fine linen, and I covered thee with silk, in the day that thou wast born; I decked thee also with ornaments, and I put bracelets upon thine hands, and a chain of pure gold on thy neck, and I put a jewel on thy forehead, and earrings in thine ears, and a beautiful crown upon thine head."

How often do I now see even "the strong man that keepeth his house," successfully resisting every approach, until, behold a stronger than he cometh, and by the chain that bound him when an infant, leading him back to the still waters, where, as in a glass, he too may see himself reflected, and how changed the crown fallen from his head, and the fine gold become dim, and the white robe, intended for his resurrection-dress, all soiled and rent, and now a deep shade, upon his brow once bright with the sign of the cross, and his bosom, once peaceful, now swelling high with the fears of eternity! Oh, I have seen "the keepers of the house tremble, and the strong men bow themselves," at the recollections of Baptism.

But long as I was a Presbyterian, I never knew a baptized child to be admonished from the pulpit, of any privileges, or of any obligations, arising from the fact of Baptism. A baptized child is taught and trained, precisely as a Baptist would train one unbaptized; and a Presbyterian congregation is addressed, as if the preacher were declaiming from a Baptist pulpit. And why is this, said I, when one apostle has called Baptism the *Antitype* (αντιτυπον) of the ark; and another has called it, "the washing of regeneration;" and he who poured water on an apostle's brow, said, "Arise, and be baptized, and wash away thy sins;" and He, who sent the same Ananias to Saul, said, "Except a man be born of water and of the spirit he cannot see the kingdom of God!" Are there two Baptisms—one admitting regenerate adults to all the privileges of the church—and the other admitting unregenerate infants to *nothing!*—Whether they live or die, poor children, they fare no better for their Baptism! The Bible says, "One Baptism," as distinctly as it says "One God." The Bible declares "Baptized into One Body" as plainly as it proclaims "One Lord, One Faith, One Hope." In the Bible, Baptism is the door of admission to all other promises and privileges of the church. "If you baptize your children, or any part of them, why do you not admit them to the Lord's Supper?" is therefore the standing and effective objection of the Baptists. The Confession of Faith long ago yielded to its force. Even

Dr. Miller, in the nineteenth century, succumbs to it himself. After advising that every means should be employed to retain baptized children in the communion of the church, he recommends, that if, after due admonition, they should continue to slight their birthright and neglect the communion; "they should be proceeded with, and cut off, as if they had been communicants, and had afterwards apostatized from their profession." But this is all theory. *Animum pictura pascit inani.* The new wine would make those old bottles burst and perish. Revivalism and election would go down together. No, Bible-baptism can never exist again among Presbyterians; it can never again be the door of entrance upon all the promises and privileges of the faithful; they will do as they have done—shut out more than half their little ones from the ark—and refuse, except on certain hard conditions, the bread for the voyage to few that are admitted. A new departure, I discovered, from the principles of the Reformation; let me fly with my children to a Church, where these principles are yet respected.

But Presbyterians cannot see their church thus falling off as under this discipline it must always do, in numbers; and therefore, repudiating the healthy increase by the Scriptural method of "discipling and baptizing," they fall into human expedients, fraught with amazing opportunities for abuses and corruptions, by which the baptized and the unbaptized alike are urged on to a crisis, at which they are encouraged to believe, that they are born again, in a sense that shall forever make temptation essentially powerless, and apostacy utterly impossible. Ingenuity is tortured: new measures are invented; methods still newer and still newer are resorted to, to urge the imagination on to the ideal point, at which the exhausted fancy, in its moment of collapse, "lets go" the world, "gives up" its sins and its associates, loses its relish for its former ways, yields every point it once disputed; like the death-bed penitent, when nature is too weak and weary any longer to sustain the controversy; and this collapse, with the hysterical relief, and, it may be, ecstacy, that follows it, is understood to be the essence of conversion. The soul is now supposed to have received the afflatus of an imperishable life, so that the person never can fall entirely from grace; and an incorruptible seed of the word is implanted in his understanding, which shall make him personally, and beyond what the Pope has ever claimed to be, infallible and indefectible in the doctrines of grace; in a word, because his consciousness has undergone a strange disturbance, he thinks that he has experienced the needful change—"the *ictus* from beyond the fixed stars," as Mr. Bushnell of Hartford, struggling in this net himself, has dared recently and manfully to call it. I know that many, who have felt as they think, this lighting down of the omnipotent arm, are pure and "meet for the inheritance with the saints in light." But it was not this sudden "ictus from beyond the fixed stars," that made them so. They have been under other influences, both before and since, that have made them what they are. I have been subjected, when a boy, myself, to the startling and electrifying agency of this species of machinery, and know it, even in the most prudent hands to be full of delusion and danger. Instead of being the one new birth, it is a regeneration that may be repeated at every camp-meeting. I have known the southern negro, and I have known the illiterate white man, to be twice, and thrice, and perhaps twenty times, regenerated in this way; although a mind more enlightened or better balanced is seldom caught in the snare but once. As a Presbyterian, I saw much of such regenerations, and the more I saw of them, like Mr. Bushnell, the more I doubted them. "What careful minister, seeing how many are gathered around him in the church, who manifest no real love to God in the practical duties of life, and have never shown any

Christian character, save that they once were subjects of a religious rhapsody, has not often staggered under the suspicion of some dismal error, in the current views of religious experience? For myself, I feel obliged, in faithfulness to God, to declare, that I have more than a suspicion on this subject." If the victim ever awake to the delusion, his awakening will be like that of the death bed penitent, who in a stormy and troubled hour built his hopes upon the sand—too late. The revival convert recovers his composure,—the powers of nature are restored,—the passions in their vigor return,—the world hangs out its lure,—and lo, the apostacy a little while ago pronounced impossible, has taken place! Sad memory here crowds its facts upon me. I will not speak of individuals, where troops and scores are rushing on my thoughts. I have known a congregation in New-York, of four hundred communicants, to disappear, "as the early cloud," not even outliving the revival that had given it birth. I was myself, in the city of New-York, the pastor of a congregation, of, nominally, five hundred communicants—the fruits, as the phrase was, of "powerful revivals;" but, when, as a shepherd, I made it my first business to "know my sheep and to be known of mine," and I sought them diligently in the ways and byways, and employed a corps of twenty deacons and elders to aid me in the task, and more than once read the names of those we could not find to the whole body of communicants, and also in a published church-manual designated them as missing, and though these inquiries were extended through a period little less than a year, one hundred and forty communicants could never be found. But what roused still more my suspicions respecting this theory of regeneration, was the fact, which I personally encountered early in my Presbyterian ministry, that the "Campbellites" or "Christians," or, to speak properly, Socinian Baptists, denying the Lord that bought them and the very existence of the

Holy Ghost, found it no difficult task to equal, and often to exceed, the Presbyterian and the Methodist, in the power of these "revivals," with singular readiness startling whole communities with the same phenomena, filling men's solitude with impressions, visions, dreams, and voices, and now numbering, after a career of less than thirty years, between three and four hundred thousand converts and communicants! If any thing could more than this shake my confidence in such a theory of the new birth, it would be a personal knowledge of the fact which I only know to be alleged, that similar phenomena, and especially the transitions from agitation to peace, from wild terror to ecstatic rapture, from agony of conscience to complete serenity, from actual prostration to actual shouting, are not at all unfamiliar to certain forms of heathenism and of demon-worship.

The reader will pardon this digression. My object has been, without entering on a new subject, merely to call attention to the fact, that human expedients have grown up, and have become necessary, for the continuance and enlargement of the denomination, in sheer consequence of having set aside the Scriptural view of the church as a "household of faith," with its "little ones," its "young men," and its "fathers," to be perpetuated and extended by the spontaneous increase of itself. The "anxious seat" or the "inquiry meeting" has been conceived to possess far more sacramental virtue to regenerate than any Baptism. And singular it is, that, amidst all the agitations and theories which have shaken the Presbyterian body, and among all the reformers, that have risen to purge and restore their temple, there hath not risen one to suggest the restoration of the Sacraments. My own awakening on this subject, I owe, by God's blessing, mainly to a careful revision of the Confession of Faith, which as a minister, I had with great tenderness of conscience subscribed. And in this state of mind, with many prayers for the Divine guidance, in a task so novel, and requiring a measure of wisdom greatly in advance of my years, I prepared for the press a treatise on the Sacraments; which, however, I withheld from publication, not only because it would have created one frightful element more of distraction, in a body already most sadly rent, but also, because I saw reason to fear, that the tendencies of Presbyterianism were, *et semper et ubique*, so uncontrollably downward, that it might as soon be expected to stop the stars in their courses. Still I wonder, that the men, who have undertaken to reclaim that body from the rationalistic influences of the new school of theology, have not first cast out the beam out of their own eyes. Only by the preservation of the Sacraments, will they preserve a vigorous theology. The Sacraments are the epitome of Christianity. As to the *Sacrament* of Baptism, we can scarcely say of it, *stat nominis umbra;* it has got to be regarded, and to be called, an unessential "rite." All idea of its efficacy has passed away, with the exploded dogmas of a less enlightened age; and with it, the doctrines of birth-sin, and of the new heart, and of regenerating grace descending on the soul, sit loosely on the popular mind, and are in danger of ultimate extinction. The Sacrament of the Body and Blood of Christ has been also degraded into a mere human commemoration; and, with it, the great Catholic doctrine of "a full, perfect and sufficient sacrifice, oblation, and satisfaction," as the Communion service of the Prayer Book defines it, "for the sins of the whole world," is openly excepted to, and, throughout New England absolutely lost. I have heard sermons upon free will, natural ability, "you can and you can't," the modus operandi in regeneration, and other metaphysical subtleties, until my soul was sick. I have heard sermons about some desolating fire; the stranding of some ship; the burning of some steamboat; the havoc of some storm; until fire, air, earth, and water, were exhausted. I have heard from the pulpit lectures upon great social enterprises, fourth-of-July orations, discourses on impending elections, eulogiums upon associations of men, and harangues upon the revolutions of empires and the abdications of princes. I have heard Unitarianism, Popery, Infidelity, dragged in from a distance, to supply themes for exciting declamation, and food for morbid appetites. I have heard sermons and lectures rambling into the future, pretending to "understand all prophecy," and helping, with startling events to come, to fill up that great moral and practical vacuum that Calvinism creates and leaves. But never in my whole life, have I heard, from Presbyterian lips, a sermon on the efficacy of the Sacraments: as, for example, on the graces, fruits, uses, promises, and helps, of Baptism. If Baptism has been ever named, it has been, perhaps amidst the heat of a revival, when converts must decide to which sect they would belong, or at the request of some unhappy questioner, to resist the encroachments of the Baptists, by endeavoring to make good the isolated, naked, cold, historical fact, that infants were baptized in the primitive church, or the still less edifying and more difficult assumption, that pouring or sprinkling was the common mode of its administration. Thus Presbyterians have retained the form, but have long ago denied the power of the Sacraments. They perform them mechanically. They keep the letter; they have lost the spirit. "The words that I speak unto you, they are *spirit* and they are *life*." *Qui manet in litera, hæret in cortice.* For myself, I went further in my own teaching, and well recollect, that one of my elders took me severely to task, in presence of his peers, for calling the Sacrament of infants, what Dr. Alexander has called it in the extract lately quoted, "holy Baptism." Still I preached the gospel of grace, and the grace of the gospel, in the Sacraments, and was able to do it in the language of their own confession, that "there is in every Sacrament a sacramental union between the sign and the thing signified." But like the Baptist in the desert, I was preaching to the rocks. When I asked them of the doctrine, "Is it from heaven, or of men?" they reasoned, I suppose, among themselves; "If we shall say, From heaven, he will say, why then do ye not bring *all* your little ones to Baptism? but if we shall say, of men, he will say, why then do ye bring *any?*" So that, although Presbyterians appear to have two Baptisms —one proclaiming that the adult is regenerate, and is now an heir of the promises of God—the other, implying only, that the infant either needs regeneration, or will need it at some future time, according as the *animus imponentis* is Pelagian or Calvinistic; and, although they seem to have a Sacrament in the Lord's Supper, yet, denying it the "efficacy" ascribed to it in their Confession, as a "*means of grace,*" it is perfectly clear, that they have after all, and strictly speaking no Sacrament at all. Not once in a thousand times do they grant Baptism to the dying penitent; not once in a thousand more, do they allow the Lord's Supper to the dying believer. The one is sent unwashed into the presence of his God; the other unfed into the solitudes and wastes of death. Both are compelled to violate, in the dying hour, the commands of Christ; while the living look on, and with easy aptness learn, that Sacraments may be neglected both by the living and the dying, as entirely unnecessary to salvation.

CHAPTER VII.

CONFIRMATION—LORD'S SUPPER—EXCOMMUNICATION.

Let us now suppose the child, baptized or unbaptized—it makes no difference with the Presbyterian, to have reached the next stage in life. We suppose him to be one of the elect, and to have received, at the "appointed time," that irresistible ictus of regeneration, for the want of which all the good things of his whole life before have been counted as evil, and by virtue of which, all the sins of his life afterward shall be so far counted to him for good, that they can no more "quench the spirit," than they can quench the stars, no more separate him from the favor of God, than they can separate him from his own existence.

He is now to "make a profession of religion, by the reception of the Sacrament." We stay not to find fault with the phraseology. We stop only to ask men who profess to be guided by the Bible alone, where in that book it is, that they find the "taking the Sacrament"—unless by that they mean the sacrament of Baptism—the authorized mode of "making a profession of religion?"

We suppose our candidate to have passed one ordeal in those agitating experiences, which so often rend and tear, and as if the evil one went out of them, are the accompaniments and signs of this species of regeneration. He has now to pass a more dread ordeal than the former, in relating these experiences to the company of the elders, or, if his lot have fallen among the Congregationalists, the Baptists, and the like, to the whole body of communicants. These elders, as my predecessor in a Presbyterian Parish is said to have remarked, have been sometimes "made when timber was scarce," and, like annuitants, of course they never die. Albeit, I knew an instance, in which one died, and with a dry smile and sigh the good man's pastor remarked to me, that it was one of those seeming afflictions by which the Lord works great deliverances for his people. Can we wonder, that men of education and fine feeling, shrink from a catechizing by a bench of elders? If they hesitate for months and years and even until the end of life—of which we have known many a striking instance—are we, therefore, to set it down as evidence of some irregularity in their conversion? Or, suppose these elders to be grave, dignified, well-read, capable of voting intelligently, when "deep answers to deep" in theological debate, and ministers may be on trial for abstruse opinions, that are supposed to involve and sap the foundations of religion—it is evident that in presence of such a company, the diffident and meritorious, the meek and humble babe in Christ will appear as a lamb before her shearers; while the rash and the vain will but reap assurance, from passing with the more eclat, the inquisitive—I might not err in calling it, inquisitorial conclave.

Thousands there are, to whom this "going before the Session," as the phrase is, to relate their experience, has haunted their lying down and their rising up, more than auricular confession has ever disturbed the papist, and, on the eve of the communion, when, above all other seasons, the mind should be quiet and self-possessed, has had a most painful influence in distracting and tormenting it. And scarcely a pastor but bewails the fact that, having passed this ordeal, his converts live thenceforth as light-hearted as if the day of judgment were appointed only to unseal and publish the verdict of the elders. And the monthly and quarterly repetitions of experience, and confessions in classes, under a complete system of espionage, adopted by the Methodists, is but a poor remedy for these pernicious results.

It has often been the case, that these elders in session have felt themselves moved to pry into private histories with unnecessary and annoying interrogatories. One of their own ministers has complained, that the conditions or tests of communion, have erected around the sacramental table in some of their churches, "a fence ten rails high." I have heard the modest maiden interrogated whether she belonged to a temperance society, and I have seen an indignant woman refuse to answer whether she drank intoxicating liquors. The purity of this page reminds me, that here I must arrest my pen. But I do so with the question, "*Quid domini facient, audent cum talia fures?*" If in a decent congregation, and against the minister's remonstrance, these impertinent questions have been asked, what may not be done, and what rights may not be trampled under foot, where the reins are thrown loose upon the neck? The legislation of these elders will admit a candidate to the Communion, at this moment, in one thousand congregations, only under the Nazarite and Popish vow of eternal abstinence from wine; and it is blazoned for the information and admiration of all mankind, that wine is now prohibited, even on their altars, in more than eight hundred churches. My spirit went heavily within me; it was more than I could bear. Compared with such arbitrary and irresponsible tyranny, to which there can be neither law nor limit, and which may forge new oppressions to-morrow, as it has invented these but yesterday, Rome, with its fixed and ascertainable exactions, is still gloriously free.

But now the experience is told, and the conclave adjourned. There frequently remains a third ordeal to be passed, by the baptized and the unbaptized alike, before partaking of the Lord's supper. The candidate, in face of the congregation, is to answer a series of questions, embodying, in some instances, nice metaphysical subtleties, that chance to feed the controversies of the hour; while the questions themselves are sometimes extemporaneously put, but are more commonly agreed upon, under the local and joint counsels of the pastor and the elders. To produce uniformity in this particular, a living divine, whose confidence I am not betraying in stating the fact, was a few years ago employed in preparing a confession—for creed-making is not yet at an end, and will live the lifetime of Popery and Sectarianism—to be adopted by the General Assembly, for the admission of communicants throughout the church. He proposed also—owing, I believe, the suggestion to myself—that the new formulary should clearly recognize the distinction between the unbaptized and the baptized. Such a measure was not likely to succeed; in fact, it failed.

With regard to this mode of admission to the Lord's supper, it is worthy of remark, that the whole thing is an innovation upon Presbyterianism, and although borrowed along with some other matters from the Congregationalists, within the short period of thirty years, has become almost everywhere prevalent. And the rapid spread of such a usage from parish to parish, demonstrated to my mind, many a year ago, *the conscious want, throughout the church, of a connecting link between Baptism and the Communion,* to ratify the vows and pledges of the former, and to conduct the maturing Christian to the grace and consolation of the latter. I certainly must have felt that want myself, when, thirteen years ago, in the printed formulary which I composed for the reception of new candidates to the communion, I used the following language: "*You acknowledge* the responsibilities whereunto you were appointed in Baptism, in which you forever renounced the world, the flesh, and the devil, and consecrated in a perpetual covenant your body, soul, and spirit, &c., ... (*Assent.*) . . . . This being the faith wherein you have witnessed a good confession before many witnesses, and as, from the beginning, you have been baptized into the privileges and promises of the Church Catholic, therefore I now pronounce and constitute you members of the body in which we worship the Father, and welcome you to share our grace and tribulation. And as we open before you to day the higher and wider mysteries of the kingdom in another ordinance, and *confirm you in the covenant* of the faithful, we beseech you, as strangers and pilgrims, &c."

When looking, in those days, at the baptized child, insensible to the responsibilities, and indifferent to the grace, accruing from his Baptism, or purposely taught, it may have been, to regard that Baptism as the lowest and merest rite of Christianity—forgetting that Christianity has in this respect no such rites, as had the Jewish faith before it, but has merged the shadow into the substance, and rites into realities—I have been often unable to check the thought, that, if Presbyterians had retained the use of Confirmation, it would not only have answered for an edifying link between Baptism and the Communion, but it would have brought many a baptized child, year after year, into personal contact with his pastor, and would have afforded a golden opportunity, in youth's fearful crisis, for admonition, for reproof, for instruction in the dangers and responsibilities of life. It seemed reasonable—so reasonable, that infant Baptism seemed incomplete without it, and unconnected with the after-life—by some solemn form to ask the child, now coming to the years of wisdom and discretion, "Do you abide by the terms on which you were baptized?" and, if the answer justified it, to renew the comforting assurance, that God would enlarge his grace, and most surely keep and perform the promises, which He for His part had vouchsafed to make.

About the same time, I ascertained, that Presbyterians, in portions of Germany and other countries, had not cast off the rite of Confirmation. Luther retained it, and his followers retain it still. "I sincerely wish," said Calvin, "that we retained this custom of imposition of hands, which was practised amongst the ancients." Beza and Owen and Adam Clarke speak in much the same strain. I had seen clergymen also in our own Communion, who would not have been unwilling to see the rite restored. Such facts induced me to look into the scriptural authority for this intervening ordinance between Baptism and the Holy Supper. For if any such rite be necessary for us, and if we betray our conscious want of it in the adoption of an awkward substitute, it could not have been less necessary in the times of the apostles, and we might therefore expect to find something in the word of God, beautifully intervening, as the connecting link, between the two Sacraments.

"To the law then and to the testimony"—what saith it? "Leaving the principles of the doctrine of Christ, let us go on unto perfection; not laying again the foundation of repentance from dead works, and of faith toward God, of the doctrine of baptisms, and of laying on of hands, and of the resurrection of the dead, and of eternal judgment." (Heb. vi. 1–2.) According to this, "*the foundation*"—"*the principles of the doctrine of Christ*"—what are they? "Repentance—Faith—Baptisms—*Laying on of hands*—the Resurrection—the eternal Judgment." For the first time in my life, I here saw that Christianity had filled the vacancy between the Sacraments, and had assigned a solemn rite to its place next after Baptism—the very place to which the human invention of a confession in broad aisle had been assigned by Congregationalists and Presbyterians. First, "Repentance;" secondly,

"Faith;" thirdly, "Baptisms," (whether that of John, or that of Jesus, or that of the Holy Trinity, or the double washing with water and the Spirit, or the trine immersion, which some allege to have been primitive,) fourthly, "Laying on of hands." Let me think, said I within myself;—is this the order of teaching among the Presbyterians? They teach, first, Repentance; very well; for St. Paul says, first, "*Repentance.*" They teach, secondly, Faith; very well again; for St. Paul says, secondly, "*Faith.*" They teach, thirdly, Baptism; very well once more; for St. Paul says, thirdly, "*Baptisms.*" But, at the fourth stage, St. Paul and the Presbyterians part; St. Paul says, fourthly, "*the Laying on of hands;*" Presbyterians break the chain, binding our youthful Isaacs to the altar, and our young Samuels to the temple, and cast the bright link away.

As a Presbyterian, I had nothing to gain, by supposing that ordination, was in the apostle's mind as a matter to be inculcated on a young convert next after Baptism, and in company with the tremendous doctrines, of repentance, faith, resurrection, and judgment. I came therefore to the conclusion, from which only an unnatural straining and dislocating of the passage could offer an escape, that St. Paul was speaking of the sacramental rite, or, if you please, the lesser sacrament, of Confirmation, coming next after Baptism, and filling up one of the confessed and conscious vacancies of Calvinism. Again, my attention was struck with the fact, that Baptism, and the Laying on of hands, were, in the apostle's estimation, of sufficient excellence and dignity, to lie at "*the foundation,*" and to be written down among the tremendous "*doctrines*" of "Repentance—Faith—the Resurrection—and the Judgment." What! Baptism mentioned in the same breath with Faith! the Laying on of hands raised to a correlative dignity with the Resurrection and the eternal Judgment! and both this and that lying at *the foundation*, where an apostle is deliberately reciting "*which be the first principles of the doctrine of Christ!*" Make of the passage what ye will, it falls upon our ears much more like the natural utterance of the Episcopal Church, than the teaching of Presbyterianism in the nineteenth century.

But did not "the Laying on of hands" impart the gift of tongues and miracles? Yes; and it was necessary that it should; *that the infant Church might understand, at once, the sacramental nature of the ordinance.* For the same reason, Baptism was at first, accompanied by the visible descending of a dove, that its sacramental character, the spirit brooding on the waters, might be a fixed and understood fact; so that apostles might preach, "Repent, and be baptized, every one of you, in the name of Jesus Christ, for the remission of sins, and ye shall receive the Holy Ghost." In like manner, Ordination was accompanied at first by the communication of the gift of miracles, even to the humblest deacon, that it might be an understood and settled principle of Christianity, that each vocation in the church should receive by the laying on of hands its proportion of grace. In the same way also, the first preaching of the gospel to the Gentiles was marked by visible and audible effusions of the Spirit, to establish the fundamental principles that the wall was broken down between the Jew and the Gentile. For the same reason, Confirmation at first had its "signs following," that the Christian, in confirming the pledges of his Baptism, might be assured of his own confirmation in grace, by a new afflatus of the Holy Ghost, for the higher responsibilities of the Christian life. Thus, in the city of Samaria, Philip, not the apostle, but the deacon, "one of the seven," we are told, preached to the people, and baptized a great multitude, "both men and women." More he was not empowered to do. But "when *the apostles,* which were at Jerusalem, heard that Samaria had received the word of God, they sent unto them Peter and

John, who, when they were come down—*laid their hands on them,* and they received the Holy Ghost." Philip, the deacon, converted and baptized them, "both men and women;" Peter and John came down, and "laid their hands on them"—certainly not to ordain them, for it says, "both men and *women.*" This was a rite that Simon Magus had never before seen; Philip had been there, preaching, baptizing, and working miracles, healing, we are told, the paralytic and the lame, and ejecting devils with wonderful success. But Simon, whom Philip baptized, and who "continued with Philip," never saw, until those that ordained the seven deacons came into Samaria, this rite of the imposition of hands. "And when Simon saw," says the narrative, "that, through laying on of *the apostles'* hands, the Holy Ghost was given, he offered," &c. (See Acts viii, 5–19.) We cannot see how the force of these simple facts can be evaded; and we set Confirmation down as one of the things which Presbyterianism has irrevocably lost.

Some of my ministerial brethren, I knew entertained upon this subject, a similar impression to my own. Presbyterian reviewers, I observed, and even gentlemen at Princeton, and in the Princeton Quarterly, touched tenderly upon the topic. The whole Lutheran church retained the practice. Those Protestants who had laid it aside, were already all feeling after something to supply the vacuum. I could not find, in antiquity, any beginning to this "Laying on of hands," but at the hands of the apostles. I would trace it beyond the apostles to the Jewish synagogue, where I could find it even to this day intervening between circumcision and the passover. I heard of it in the remotest East; in the heart of Abyssinia; in the fastnesses of Carmel and of Syria. I was glad that my children had been baptized and introduced before me into a fold, that would thus again throw its protecting shield of

Confirmation around them, when they should arrive at the years of discretion and of danger.

And if I was glad in the anticipation, what tongue, shall express my happiness in the result. One of those little ones; the first that was given me, and the first that I gave the Church; is now among them that sleep in Jesus. In the glow of childhood—in her fifteenth year—an age, when among Presbyterians, the minister is avoided, and the approach of a zealous elder dreaded and shunned; she expressed the usual desire to be confirmed, at the next visitation of the Bishop. As her father was beyond the sea, her friends advised her to await his return. But, with the grace already given her, she urged her request very importunately; and it brought her at once under the teachings and counsels of a judicious and affectionate clergyman. She was accordingly confirmed, under the most gratifying appearances of sincerity and earnestness. A new measure of the spirit evidently rested upon her from that hour; she spoke in a sweeter tongue; she led a more heavenly life: not noisy, but still; not ostentatious, but retiring; not even conscious was she of the impression made upon her heart and life, nor of that impression so sweetly reflected upon those around her. The solemn litanies of the Church were often observed to bring tears into her eyes; the church's fasts were her most pleasant feasts; morning, and evening, and at noonday, she was many a time observed to dwell long upon her knees; often was she known to retire from the midst of her young companions to the exercises of the closet; and such a life of gentleness and holiness, and self-denial, and prayer, and humble usefulness, and cheerfulness, it has never been my lot to know in one so young. And God has rewarded it. Within a year from the time that she knelt under the Bishop's hands, she entered joyfully into the rest, for which she had been unconsciously maturing; and was "*so* blessed, she blessed the hand of death."

And often have I been consoled in the reflection that Confirmation in a father's absence, espoused her by a new vow to Christ, *just at the moment* when the world first comes to claim the virgin-heart. What a happy opportunity it gives, in all times and climes, to bring the influences of religion to bear upon youth's generous affections! The father may be far away, and the mother sleeping in the dust; yet the Church is a mother that dies never; and the time comes round, the opportunity comes up, at the most critical period of life, for the hallowed associations, counsels, and instructions, incident to Confirmation. If I have introduced a case in illustration of this important point, it has been not without violence to my more tender recollections of a precious child; but as, in a former chapter, I had told of her Baptism, I have now, for a higher purpose, permitted myself to record her Confirmation and her end. And, to extend the illustration, I may add, that, during the six years of my Presbyterian ministry, not an individual, so far as I can recollect, seemed drawn toward me for counsel, or attracted onward by the arrangements and natural leadings of the system, to assume the responsibilities of Baptism. If an inquirer came to me, he came not from the gentler drawings of the common influences around him, (for Calvinism knows no gentleness,) but from some sudden ictus or impulse, that happened to him alone, and left hundreds undisturbed behind him. In contrast with this, during the first six years of my ministry in the Episcopal Church, more than six hundred baptized souls have come spontaneously within my personal reach and private counsels, for the ratification of the tremendous vows of Baptism. Some of them have been among my dearest friends on earth, towards whom I might otherwise have felt a reserve in offering religious advice; and *hundreds,* I have reason to believe, have thus been brought under my secret counsels, whom otherwise I should never have reached. Really, without Confirmation, or its positive equivalent, bringing back the infant to the altar, not only would infant Baptism appear cumbered with a real difficulty, but the provisions of Christianity would seem obviously incomplete.

Let us now go back to our candidate for the Communion. He has passed the ordeals of conversion, the confession to the elders, and the open profession in the congregation. Why he is not now baptized, to signify that he is born again, I cannot understand, except on the Pelagian hypothesis, that Baptism may be lawfully administered in anticipation of a possible future event. But why the person should not be now baptized, who is loud in reiterating, I had almost said, in glorying, that his Baptism in infancy "never did *him* any good" —a boast, and sometimes uttered in the form of challenge, which I have often heard—I leave for the elders and their minister to answer. And why the Anabaptist, who hesitates not to re-baptize an individual, though priest, prelate, or pope, may have baptized him in his infancy, on the assumption that he was baptized before he was born again or before he believed, does not *re-immerse* the grown up man, who, although he was immersed at twenty or at forty, now solemnly declares that the same mistake was perpetrated upon *him*, and that he too was immersed before he believed, and that his former immersion, so far from doing him any good, published to the world a lie, is entirely beyond my comprehension.

But, to follow our candidate to the Communion. If ever in his life he felt like lying low under the droppings of that most precious blood here flowing from the cross, it is now; but prostration is forbidden him, and his knees are not allowed to come in contact with the dust. If ever he desired to draw nigh and cling to the horns of the altar, it is to-day; but he is required to sit aloof from the table of the show-bread that showeth forth the Lord's death until He come. And, instead of receiving the emblems of his Saviour's own body and

9

blood, from that good man's hand, who perhaps received him when a little one in the person and the name of Christ, or who has led him in after years to Christ; and, instead of hearing a paternal voice speaking in words of comfort, and uttering a pastor's blessing, he is compelled to take the hallowed elements from hands that yesterday he saw employed in the counting-room, or in the market-place, or in occupations which the dignity of my subject will not suffer me to name. If out of the abundance of the heart the mouth speaketh; if a clean heart will naturally robe itself in a clean dress; so a true Christianity, properly alive to the purity and dignity and majesty of that worship in which Angels and Archangels join with men, must instinctively loathe this slovenly appearance, and these familiar manners, and, if she have more beautiful garments, although she can never mistake them for the beating heart and living soul within, will surely put them on, to appear before her King.

In early life, I had, at the south, been used to see the sacramental table spread, and the guests seated decorously around it. Princeton, which should have been the last place on earth, was the very first, in which I saw the communicants receive the elements while seated in their pews. I shall never forget the violence done to my feelings, and not to mine only, but to those of several others by this spectacle; a chill crept over me, a chill that returned as often as the festival came back; and I felt, because it was true, although I knew it not, that the sacramental character of the solemnity was vanishing away. Those very churches at the south, which, in my youth, or fifteen years ago, celebrated the Lord's supper with much decency and reverence around a table spread with the fair linen cloth, have been unable, even in the matter of "rue and mint and cummin," to resist the irruptions of the northmen, and have engrafted on their old, venerable forms, the rude and freezing usages of New England Congregationalism.

But so it is. Downward, and downward still, is the course of a system, that has once broken away from the unalterable past. Chilly, and more chilly still, becomes the atmosphere of a body, that has once left the warm orbit to which nature had assigned it.

I had noticed, when a boy, as the communicants in successive companies approached the table, that certain individuals waited their opportunity to secure the places immediately on the pastor's right and left, that they might receive the communion immediately at his hands; thus clearly betraying the natural working of a pious instinct. Later in life I reached the question: Why not indulge the generous desire, and kneel, and receive at the pastor's hand, and with the pastor's blessing, these seals of grace? Who would feel contented, that some tradesman should pour the water on his head, in Baptism, while the minister should say the sacramental words? And who should feel satisfied, to receive "that bread and that cup," from a merchant's or a tradesman's hands? Does it require a high degree of Christian reverence, to feel instinctively, through every fibre of the soul, a deep repugnance to such familiarity? "Is it not the communion of the body of Christ? Is it not the communion of the blood of Christ?" We feel that the minister is the only proper individual, to impart the water in Baptism; is he not the only proper and lawful person, to impart "that bread and that cup," wherein, it will be to our everlasting condemnation, if we "discern not the Lord's body." And why not also kneel, thought I, in the one Sacrament, as well as in the other? Adult candidates for Presbyterian baptism generally kneel. Candidates for Presbyterian ordination invariably kneel. Why not approach as near His sacred feet as I can, and kneel as lowly as I wish, in receiving "the true bread from heaven," while this sacrifice of Melchizedec, the bread and the wine, show the Lord's death upon the table, and plead for my soul with a fervour and a purity, which my own prayers are incapable of approximating? If it be objected, that kneeling may beget too much reverence for the symbols, we only answer, for the present, that sitting may beget the more dangerous too little. For more than a thousand years, there were but two upon earth, that sat at the communion; one of these was the Arian, "who, denying the divinity of the Saviour, thought it not robbery to be equal with Him at His table;" the other was, and yet is, the Pope of Rome, who, claiming the same equality in another and higher, although it is fair to remember, not in the highest sense, receives the Communion on certain occasions, in the posture of the Presbyterians. Treat the symbols with irreverence, and irreverence toward Him, whom they represent, will inevitably follow. Already, in this respect, are the Presbyterians where the Arians were once, and the Unitarians are now.

Again.. As the Episcopal arrangements bring every child of the congregation, just at the moment when the world breaks enticingly upon his eye, and whispers her meretricious flattery into his ear, and makes her resolute descent upon his heart, into personal intimacy with his pastor, in the preparatory steps to confirmation, so does the Episcopal mode of celebrating the Holy Eucharist, bring each communicant, many times a year, under the immediate eye of his pastor. who thus possesses the invaluable opportunity of noticing the absent, of kindling anew his interest in each communicant present, and of cherishing a personal acquaintance with them all. Under such a discipline, a fact like the one already stated would have been utterly impossible, that one hundred and forty communicants, or nearly one-third of the whole number in a parish, should have been lost sight of, from the recollections of the elders of the whole body of parishioners But so it ever is; under the workings of a true system, every thing falls naturally into its place, and harmony and beauty

and propriety are in all its parts; the machine regulates itself; the jar is not felt; anarchy is impossible. And, when the little things of a church, as we may perhaps consider them, like the joints and bands of the body, seem to be fitly framed together and to fill the very place that without them would be unseemly blanks, and to perform their minute offices in mutual and self-adjusting harmony, it would appear, that, as in Ezekiel's vision, "the spirit of a living creature was among the whole."

And when the painful necessity for discipline arises, although it be for sins that should not be named, Congregational Presbyterianism invests the whole body of communicants—male and female—young men and maidens—the wise and the unwise—the silent and the gossipping—with the equal right of investigating and pronouncing; while a numerous eldership, according to the theory of Presbyterians proper, neutralizes but a portion of this evil. How much more likely to be salutary are the private "admonitions" and "repellings" of Episcopacy. And under the Episcopal regimen, if an appeal be taken, it is conducted with the same delicacy and consideration, and with greater probabilities of rectifying mistakes, up to the Bishop; whereas, among Presbyterians, it must be dragged into open Presbyteries, and thence to Synods, and thence again to General Assemblies, where hundreds of ministers have lost hundreds of days, in adjusting some petty wrong, or in adjusting a neighborhood-quarrel in some remote and miserable village. And any attempt, such as an eminent divine among them has suggested, to arrest these appeals at the lower courts, is but an interference with the liberties of the people, and a departure from the Presbyterian theory. We shall not in this place notice that feature of Presbyterianism, which all jurists have established as the definition and essence of tyranny, and which places the sword, the sceptre, and the purse in the same hands; and combines the legislative, the judicial, and the executive functions, in the same body; so that the General Assembly, for example, is, at the same moment, legislature, jury, judge, executive and executioner.

The Confession of Faith declares, that "to the officers of the Church the keys of the kingdom of heaven are committed, by virtue whereof they have power respectively to retain and remit sins, to shut that kingdom against the impenitent sinners, by the ministry of the gospel, and by absolution from censures, as occasion shall require." Rome itself has scarcely a more terrific form of anathema than that which Knox, the reformer, devised, nor a more soothing absolution than the two, which the curious in such matters may see in the Liturgy which he prepared for the adoption of the Presbyterians in Scotland, but which ultimately fell of course, into disuse. But, now, the individual, thus assailed by a church censure, may laugh at the elders for their pains, and "join" some other of the sects which lie so numerously about his door. What is to prevent him? They are all "churches"—standing on the same basis of private judgment—equally pure; equally spiritual; equally free. Every day this evasion is actually practiced. I once knew a man, who, having lost a sum of money, was induced to consult one of those gifted individuals, that, not two centuries ago would have graced the stake or the gallows upon the shores of Massachusetts Bay. The good lady gave him information certainly very remarkable, and ventured some predictions, afterward most singularly verified. With this, however, my story has nothing to do. But out of the occurrence, an offence grew up, which made it necessary for the Presbyterian clergyman to excommunicate some two or three persons. The very day and hour of their excommunication, they were immersed by a Baptist preacher, and received triumphantly to the communion. A few years afterward, the same individuals were excommunicated by their new brethren, and became, and are now, members of the Campbellite sect, "in good and regular standing." Thus are the keys so held among the sects, that as one door of the kingdom is shut, another may be immediately opened.

This result of sectarian discipline is not varied, by enlarging the sphere of its operation. For, within a few years, we have seen whole synods, embracing sixty thousand communicants, "exscinded" from the Presbyterian church, and forthwith investing themselves anew with all the prerogatives of a Church of God. An ejected Presbytery, a Presbytery still; an exscinded Synod, a Synod still; an excommunicated Church, a Church still; standing on the conceded basis of private judgment—*tota teres atque rotunda*—equally pure; equally scriptural; equally competent to hold the keys; and with plenary right and plenary power, to originate a ministry, and celebrate sacraments, as valid as if the twelve apostles had risen from their graves, and had laid on them their consecrating hands.

CHAPTER VIII.

LITURGIES.

However well-proportioned I might have found the Episcopal Church in its structure; however safe-guarded against the outbreaks of fanaticism, and the incursions of heresy; however high her walls, or beautiful her gates, or strong her towers; however studded her whole frame-work with the inscriptions of the earliest ages; although on every portal I should have seen a martyr's name, and on every column the handwriting of an Ignatius or a Polycarp; yet I may confess, that all this symmetry and beauty, if it were possible that they should exist as a body without a spirit, ought to a devout mind, to present no irresistible attraction, if, upon closer inspection, the interior arrangements were found unfriendly to the great end to which every thing else in the temple must be secondary and subservient—the high and pure devotions of the heart. As in human friendships, we value not the lip's cold words without the heart's warm love, so, with an emphasis beyond comparison, as "God is a Spirit," "they that worship Him, must worship Him in spirit and in truth." But I have supposed a thing impossible. It cannot be, that

> "On the cold cheek of Death smiles and roses are blending."

Such symmetry and beauty as we have described, are the results of a life within; as the beautiful flower is the spontaneous evolution of a healthy seed, or as the proportions of a fair edifice are the developments of cultivated thought and feeling, or as the beauty and perfection of the material body are but the natural expression of an instinctive and vigorous life. As Nature, however, ever seeks a clothing verdant, bright, radiant with its Maker's image, so a true Christianity will lay aside the swaddling-clothes for the robe without seam, and in all that is external will exhibit strength, symmetry and beauty. I can, however, recal the time when Episcopacy was, to me, "the sepulchre, beautiful indeed, without, but full within," if not of Death's corruption, at least of Death's cold chill, and stiffened form; when lip-service and Episcopacy were as much convertible terms as Presbyter and Bishop were, in the New Testament. But this was at a time when I set a less relative value upon the worship of the sanctuary, than I have been led by God's blessing, since to do; at a time when I knew less of Episcopalians than I came, by God's Providence, afterward to know; at a time when I had not carefully observed the workings of the human mind with reference to liturgical worship, nor the influences of liturgical worship upon the human mind. If I found myself, or if I found others unprofited, or often pained and injured, by the crudities and defects of extemporaneous worship, to have sought relief in the Episcopal Liturgy, would, to me, have seemed like stepping from the regions of an occasional north wind, upon a zone of everlasting ice. Let me, then, conduct the reader along the line of reflection which brought me to the conclusion, that, agreeably to the analogies of the faith, as grace comes down to man, robed in the Sacraments and the Word in an external Ministry, and Christianity itself in the written Scriptures, so a permanent devotion will inevitably clothe itself in an abiding Liturgy.

I might here, at the outset, entrench myself behind a host of mighty names, that, having used a Liturgy through all their lives, had every opportunity to know its value, and have left a testimony which the Rev. Mr. Staunton has thus condensed: "Blame us not, then, if we value our Liturgy; it embodies the anthems of saints; it thrills the heart with the dying songs of the faithful; it is hallowed with the blood of the martyrs; it glows with sacred fire." I prefer to throw into the foreground of my argument the testimony of Presbyterians themselves.

Even Mr. Barnes, in a candid moment, and before his eulogium (of which we quote but a small part) had led any of his flock to seek our green pastures, and our still waters, permitted himself to say, "We have always thought that there are Christian minds and hearts, that would find more edification in the forms of worship in that Church than in any other. We have never doubted that many of the purest flames of devotion that rise from the earth, ascend from the altars of the Episcopal Church, and that many of the purest spirits that the earth contains, minister at those altars, or breathe forth their prayers and praises in language consecrated by the use of piety for centuries."

The New-York Christian Observer, the representative of the Dutch Reformed Church in this country, says of the Episcopal Church, "Her spirit-stirring Liturgy, and a scrupulous adherence to it, have, under God, preserved her integrity beyond any denomination of Christians since the Reformation."

Says a Scottish Presbyterian, the Rev. John Cummings, "I shall never forget how thrilling I felt one clause in the English Liturgy, on my first entering an Episcopal Church. It is perhaps the finest sentence and the sweetest prayer in the language:—'In all time of our tribulation; in all time of our prosperity; in the hour of death and in the Day of Judgment, Good Lord, deliver us.'"

Dr. Doddridge, an English Presbyterian and Expositor, says, "The language is so plain as to be level to the capacity of the meanest, and yet the sense is so noble, as to raise the capacity of the highest."

Dr. Clarke, the distinguished Commentator of the Methodists, declares it "superior to every thing of the kind produced either by ancient or modern times; several of the prayers and services of which were in use from the first ages of Christianity." "The Liturgy," he says again, "is almost universally esteemed by the devout and pious of every denomination, and, next to the translation of the Scriptures into the English language, is *the greatest effort of the Reformation.* As a form of devotion, it has no equal in any part of the Universal Church of God. *Next to the Bible, it is the Book of my understanding and my heart.*"

Robert Hall, the brightest light that ever shone among the Baptists, and one that would have been bright in any firmament, confesses, that "the *evangelical purity* of its sentiments, the *chastened fervor* of its devotions, and the *majestic simplicity* of its language, have combined to place it in *the very first rank* of uninspired compositions."

The heavenly-minded Baxter, another non-conformist, whose writings have prepared hundreds for that "saint's everlasting rest" which gave title to one of his choice productions, says, "The constant disuse of forms is apt to breed giddiness in religion, and to make men hypocrites, who shall delude themselves with conceits that they delight in God, when it is but in those novelties and varieties of expression that they are delighted; and therefore I advise forms, to fix Christians, and to make them sound." As Mr. Wesley for the Methodists, so Baxter prepared a Liturgy for the Nonconformists; and, like Wesley, he sought the consolations of the Church's Liturgy in the hour of death. And Watson, a Methodist divine, as great as either of these, said, just as his soul took wing for Paradise, "Read the *Te Deum;* it seems to unite one, in spirit, with the whole Catholic Church on earth and in heaven."

Let these suffice, after the addition of one testimony more. The Princeton Review, in a notice of Mr. Barnes's "Position of the Evangelical Party in the Episcopal Church,"—a work written, I am informed, *after* some members of his congregation had gone over to that Church, as the eulogium above quoted was written some months *before*, holds the following language:—"It is well for the Church of England that she has a Liturgy, which brings out so clearly the doctrines of depravity, atonement, justification, Divine influence, and a future Judgment. What would have become of these doctrines in the lips of worldly Ministers, &c.? Facts," it goes on to say, "are against this favorite position of Mr. Barnes, (viz., that the observance of forms is incompatible with the preservation of evangelical piety.") And, after reminding Mr. Barnes that God was himself the author of the forms in the Jewish Church, the Reviewer adds—"But to say, that a form of prayer, merely as a form, however evangelical, is destructive of piety, is to assert that the Gospel is not the Gospel, if it be read instead of being spoken." "Not that we object," said the Princeton Review of the year preceding, "to devotional composition, when happily exerted and wisely employed; on the contrary, we would wish that it were more common than it is."

With this amount of testimony, which could easily be multiplied into a volume, I am asked the question, Why is the Liturgy of the Episcopal Church so little esteemed, out of its own pale? I answer, simply because it is not known. The Wesleyans of England know it, and, to this day, they use it, at least once every Sunday of their lives. Other Dissenters there know it, and they use it in many of their chapels at this hour. It requires one, two, perhaps three generations to become insensible to the fascinations of a Liturgy. Calvin left for his disciples a Liturgy. Luther composed for his followers a Liturgy. Knox prepared a Liturgy for the people of Scotland. Baxter compiled a Liturgy for the Nonconformists. Wesley enjoined a Liturgy upon his followers. Twice, in the Scottish Kirk, did the Presbyterians adopt a Liturgy. Nothing but time and habit, or violent convulsion, can tear a Christian from his Liturgy. The separation once effected, a Prayer-Book becomes, to a Presbyterian, what the Bible is to the Papist—*an unknown book;* uncared for, unadmired, unread. Such was the Prayer-Book to me; and I probably regarded it with much the same aversion or indifference that the Romanist entertains towards the Bible, and for very nearly the same reason. Let the Bible be thrown into the way of the Romanist, as the Prayer-Book came into mine, and if he do not learn to admire, and venerate, and love and cherish it as I did the Prayer-Book, it will not be owing to any want in the sacred volume, either of intellectual sublimity or of moral loveliness. There must be, in ordinary circumstances, not only a taste, but an educated and cultivated taste, to appreciate beauty in a landscape, grace in a statue, refinement in manners, elegance in literature, force in eloquence, melody in music, purity in morals, and, to come to the point in hand, perfection in worship. Time, or opportunity at least, must be allowed, to correct and adapt the taste. It is impossible to rise, at a bound, from the impression that the sermon is the summum bonum for which we turn our feet towards the sanctuary, into the feeling—not new, I apprehend, to the heart of the veriest worldling among the Episcopalians—that, when we go within thy gates, O Zion, it is to worship God. It is not possible, from the heavy, dull common-places of an extemporaneous prayer, which it is enough to have heard once, to rise, by a single effort, to the dignity of a Liturgy, which, to be adequately admired, must be heard a thousand times. It is impossible to settle down, from the fitful, feverish and

10

momentary flights of the revival and the camp-ground, into the chastened and life-long fervor of the incomparable Liturgy. My own case may show.

Owing to the distance of any other place of worship, I was sent, in my boyhood, once a fortnight, to the Episcopal Church. But I went without the necessary guide to my devotions, and from a home, at which, among a thousand pious volumes, I do not recollect that I ever saw the Book of Common Prayer. I did not therefore learn, in childhood, so much as to "find the places," or to take part in the responses, or even to perceive that sacred amusement, if I may so call it, by which the varied service, as I have often since remarked, engages so easily the attention of the child of the Church. For, while an extemporaneous prayer from a pulpit, often as elevated as the ceiling will well permit, fails, and must fail to give employment to the mind of a child, there is something in Liturgical worship, when properly performed, strikingly adapted, as experience teaches, to occupy the mind and hands and lips, and, through all these, the heart of the little ones of Christ, and thus, to form, from the age of infancy, the great habit of devotion. We accept, therefore, most thankfully, the tribute sometimes paid to the Church, that her worship is well enough for the childish and illiterate. Like the Bible, it is a study for the learned, and yet giveth wisdom to the simple. Its language is, in part, literally the language of angels, and is yet within the comprehension of infants. It is a sun that will blind the gaze of the philosopher, but yet giveth light to the greatest and the least in the kingdom of heaven. It is as an atmosphere, full of wonders to the spiritual chemist, but feeding alike the life of the wise and of the unwise. Its alleluiahs are the alleluiahs of the Cherubim and Seraphim; its hosannas, the hosannas in which babes and sucklings perfect and echo back the praise. We think, with Robert Hall, that its simplicity is its majesty. All this we should not dare to say of a mere human composition. But the Prayer-Book is not a human composition; nineteen-twentieths of its language are taken, line by line, and word for word, from that volume which has the mysterious power to chain the understanding of a patriarch, and to charm the heart of a child. A Gabriel may desire to look into its pages; a Timothy may lisp them at his mother's knee.

For the want of teaching in childhood, I was in after-life, entirely at a loss when to stand, or when to sit, or when to kneel, or where to "find the places." The same is the general complaint of Presbyterians, and is the reason, in most cases, why they find the service not only unedifying, but embarrassing and painful, and why they leave the sanctuary with a growing prejudice against our Liturgy. Being myself seldom able to catch the responses of the people, as they were so often mouthed and mumbled, I had half the time unfinished sentences to dwell upon, more likely to distract attention, than to fix devotion. And as the Presbyterian goes to an Episcopal Church from the same motive with which he frequents his own, not so much to be heard in the outpourings of his own heart, as to hear the declamation of the preacher—of course, the whole service before the sermon is unedifying and irksome. I was myself nearly thirty years of age before I could find the Psalms for the day, or the Epistles and Gospel, or could lay my finger on the Te Deum, the Gloria in Excelsis, or the Litany.

Notwithstanding that I heard the Episcopal service under these disadvantages, I could not but notice, that the oftener I frequented it, the more it gained upon my heart. I could see nothing irreverent, to offend the eye. I could hear nothing, beneath the dignity of worship, to offend the ear. I heard large portions of Scripture, and the low concert of many voices, indicating that they were concerned in what was going on, and that they felt they had an individual part and right in the exalted service—that it was not sectarian eloquence which they had come as dumb Christians to *hear*, nor a mass-house pageant which they had come as speechless spectators to *see*.

As a Presbyterian, I felt certainly a little flattered by a tradition—I cannot now remember where I met with it—that, at the Reformation, the Presbyterians occupied so entirely every square inch with their serried hosts, that there was, in fact, not room to kneel, and that thence had arisen the custom of standing in prayer. But now that our ranks were not so crowded, I fell back into the instinctive feeling, that a sinner's place, before the Maker of the universe, is on his knees.

If kneeling be an aid to devotion in the closet, why may not its aid be permitted in the sanctuary? If kneeling be proper in our families, why is it not desirable where meet the visible and invisible of the one family in earth and heaven? If kneeling be thought indicative of life in the social meeting, why should it be abolished in the great congregation? The Saviour of the world lay low on the chill earth in prayer; why should I not bend the knee upon the cushioned floor? Such an one as Paul knelt on the bare ground at the water-side; why should not such an one as I kneel down within the warm and pleasant sanctuary? Even Solomon in his glory "arose from before the altar of the Lord, from kneeling on his knees;" why should not I with all my miseries fall down as low as he?

I have seen this instinct frequently betray itself in a Presbyterian congregation. In time of a revival, when there is indication certainly of deep impressions of the Divine presence; when the creature sinks into nothingness before Him; I have seen (and the same has been seen in a thousand places) the preacher kneeling in the pulpit; the suppliant kneeling in the pew; the "anxious seat" thronged with kneeling companies in presence of a kneeling minister; crowded prayer-meetings morning and night, where all could find "room to kneel;" and the most palpable proof, in vast assemblies prostrate on the floor, that *kneeling* or *prostration* is the posture indicated by the earnest mind in the presence of its God. Heathens, Mohamedans, Papists, Jews, all stand around Him while they praise, and fall down before Him while they pray. Presbyterians—and they alone in earth or heaven—sit down to praise, sit down to pray! Long will they search in the Scriptures for a license to this strange familiarity, and—let me say the word—this positive *indecency.* They will there find, perhaps, some standing, many they will find kneeling, others they will find prostrate in the dust, but none will they find sitting. And so indissolubly is the true idea of worship associated with prostration, that Presbyterian poetry swells above Presbyterian usage,—

> "Satan trembles when he sees,
> The weakest *saint upon his knees.*"

St. John has lifted the veil from the upper sanctuary and shows us four and twenty elders falling down before Him, and the universe of angels casting their wings into the dust and falling on their face around Him, as they present the vials with the prayer of the saints, or else fill the high vault above them with the song that is always new. How amazing the descent from such a scene into the midst of a company of mortals, separated at a distance measureless and well-nigh returnless from the favor and patience of God, against whom heaven's gates were once hopelessly shut; who are suspended by a hair over everlasting burnings, and who see the Son of God himself upon his knees in awful vigils for their safety, yet cooly sitting down when they praise, sitting or lolling on their seats when they pray! I have a thought—*an eloquar, an sileam?*—let me say, I mean by it no uncharitable judgment of my fellow-creatures, I infer it mainly from the sectarian principle on my own mind—it is this: that *the system is inca-*

pable of producing a degree of reverence which may properly be said to amount to WORSHIP. The whole theory of free-thinking reducing everlasting and boundless truths within the span of human reason, and in its extreme results refusing to acknowledge the Infinite *because* He *is* infinite, the unsearchable, *because* He *is* unsearchable, God *because* He is *God*—the whole theory, and the silent influences of the system are injurious, and in the end fatal to all reverence, and make the awful worship, which the Church Catholic has ever retained, a simple impossibility. That worship based on conceptions of the Divine nature, now almost lost among sectarians, is to be reached only from some different starting point. I feel certain that under the influences of that system, I never could have risen to that awe with which I am now taught to fall before Him, and from which, as from some "scale whose lowest round is planted on the skies," I behold an immeasurable expanse between the creature and Creator, which is but the opening of another and another, and yet another, which lie in interminable series between the frail child of dust and Him from whose hand he came. It may be doubted whether God, as conceived of under a sectarian, free-thinking system, and so irreverently regarded and approached, be not a creation rather than the Creator of the creature. God has been known many an age to the Church; yet late in the nineteenth century, as if the world still slept, we see a writer in the columns of the New-York Observer introducing *an argument* (*!*) advocating the propriety of *kneeling before Him*, with this extraordinary language: "The question as to the proper and appropriate posture to be assumed in the solemn duty of prayer, is one that *has begun* to awaken the attention of *the Christian public.*"

For many years, while yet a Presbyterian, I often attended Episcopal worship on the week day festivals, and often even on the Sunday have I gone "by night," when the labors of a weary day were over; and it was with me, as it has been with many, that the oftener I went, the oftener I was compelled to go, where "honor and majesty were before Him, and strength and beauty were in His sanctuary." As yet I had not the remotest expectation of ever being numbered among "the children of the elect lady." Only I envied the sparrow her house, and the swallow her nest, and although I might not stay there myself, I *did* lay my young at thine altars, O Lord, my King, and my God! But back to the miserable, empty, off-hand worship of my sect, like St. Paul to the body, I was obliged to go, less fitted to endure its husks and its inanity than I was before. Say, is it possible for the most gifted mind *extempore*, in the presence of a promiscuous assembly to hit upon thought and language adequate to all the high purposes of worship? If I ask the question, it is because all my recollections would compel me to doubt.

As I know that, in better days in the Presbyterian Church of Scotland, two books of public prayer were at different times set forth, so I have observed that in the heart of that Church, there is at this moment, a throbbing for their re-adoption. I know it from their own lips, that many of the Presbyterian clergy in this country admit, feel and, among themselves, deplore the vacuum which the loss of a Liturgy has left, and would gladly restore a written form, if the downward tendencies of the system and of the times allowed; a form not, indeed, to be invariably binding, this were incompatible with their ideas of liberty and gifts and inspiration; but to be of discretionary use, and of occasional obligation. But as experience has shown that the very reading of the Scriptures, when left to the discretion of the minister, has fallen into sad neglect, as has been proven by history, that Liturgies, when entrusted to the same discretion, fall into disuse, and even into oblivion. But having heard these unavailing regrets for the lost forms of worship, from some of the most distinguished of my former brethren, and having heard the like sentiments falling, even at Princeton, from "those that sit in Moses's seat," it is not strange that gradually the suspicion grew upon me, that, in this respect, also, namely, the great ends and uses of all religious worship, Episcopacy had a most enviable advantage. I was, too often for my peace, and comfort, disquieted and grieved by the so called devotions to which I was compelled to *listen;* their irreverent familiarity; their cold and wordy emptiness; their forced ejaculations; their sluggish drawl; the thousand blemishes, defects, redundancies, extravagancies of their off-hand homage with which we were taught to approach a Being in whose sight the heavens are dark, and the angels chargeable with folly.

But it is now so long since I was conversant with the evils which it is desirable to forget, that I shall refresh my memory by a method that will exempt me from all suspicion of drawing on my own imagination. The Boston Recorder has long been the organ of orthodoxy, in a community of great intellectual and moral elevation, and may be supposed to be quite competent, from its ample furniture of facts and from its own cultivated tastes, to express a judgment in the premises. The editor, whose language I shall not materially alter, but shall be obliged in some cases to abridge, puts forth the following as "*some* of the faults of *public prayers*." He does not notice, it will be observed, the blemishes of social worship, where the brethren indiscriminately try their "gifts." His remarks have exclusive reference to the classic ground and higher dignities of the pulpit and an educated ministry.

"Some of the faults of public prayers are the following:

1. *Doctrinal* prayers, or prayers designed to inculcate certain doctrines, which are regarded by the speaker as essential or important. Should a prayer be thus converted into a sermon?

2. *Historical* prayers, in which are comprised long narratives for the information of persons not acquainted with the detail of the facts referred to. But is narrative the business of prayer?

3. *Hortatory* prayers, intended to stir up the zeal of the congregation, in regard to some particular subject or enterprise, which at the moment may be thought interesting.

4. *Denunciatory* prayers, designed to warn the audience against certain errors or practices, to put down certain sentiments, or to awaken towards them indignant feelings, being appeals to men, not addresses to God." Fire from heaven is constantly invoked; temperance, abolition, revivals, missions, anything will furnish fuel for the passion; and the lash of a 'local public opinion,' manufactured, perhaps, in some miserable village, is mercilessly applied to some penitent individual or class of individuals in prayer. Innumerable instances tread one upon another in my memory; but it is needless to recite them. Now let the variances, emulations, and strifes, of Episcopalians, be what they may, we keep them out of our devotions; hence, when sectarians look on, expecting to see us the next moment separate in schism, 'we have an altar' where strife cannot come; we forget our differences at the throne of grace and prayer; 'with one mouth' still keeps us one.

"5. *Personal* prayer, which springs from a desire to administer a secret rebuke, or to bestow commendation, some individual being expressly in the mind of the person praying." How often have I heard the praises of a dead minister or deacon follow him, like the chanting of a requiem, from the pulpit, proclaiming to the Almighty the dead man's title to canonization. How often have I heard a visiting clergyman eloquent in eulogiums upon the blushing or unblushing pastor of a congregation, whose virtues and usefulness were represented to the Lord as reasons why his invaluable life or health should be prolonged! How often have I heard the pastor himself enumerate the merits of some elder or wealthy and generous individual now dangerously ill; and how often have I imagined that the enumeration of the good qualites of some dying woman fell upon her ears like the anointing of oil, and actually raised her up, or, if it failed in this result, had all the virtue of an "extreme unction" to soothe the pains of her departure. Contrasted with all this, how grave, and dignified, unexceptionable, and sufficient, are the varied prayers of the Episcopal Liturgy for the sick, and the impressive service by which the dead are committed to the dust; for so the greatest tragedian of this age, when asked what was the noblest composition in the English language, is said to have replied, "*the burial service of the Church of England.*" But let our Reviewer proceed.

"6. *Eloquent* prayers, in which there is a display of a brilliant fancy and of polished and elegant language, compelling the hearer to say, 'what a fine prayer that was.'"

"7. *Familiar* prayers, in which there is an evident absence of that sacred awe and reverence which should fill the mind in every approach to God." This is a miserable canker, but, strange to say, has been often interpreted as a note of high spirituality, entitling the individual as the phrase is, to "draw very near." "What liberty," said the man-worshipping elder, "our pastor had in praying this morning." "Why yes," replied the Churchman, "I must say I think he took very great liberties."

"8. *Sectarian* prayers, indicating very clearly an attachment to a particular sect among the multitude of Christian denominations." In contrast with this feature of public prayer, which is capable of being made singularly offensive, how chaste is the spirit of the Church's Liturgy, which although it "might have whereof to glory," yet vaunteth not itself, but remembereth only in her prayers "the holy Church throughout all the earth," and "all that profess and call themselves Christians," and requireth of her priests to bear all the tribes of Zion on their hearts before the Lord, as the Jewish high priest bore upon his breast the names, in precious stones, of the twelve tribes of Israel.

"9. *Long* prayers, which weary and exhaust the 'spirit of devotion.'" Whitefield is remembered to have said, "Brother, you prayed me into a good frame, and you prayed me out of it again." And we know how quaint has become the appellation, of "the long prayer," or the prayer before the sermon, in some portions of the country. The Episcopal Liturgy is not, to one engaged in its worship, liable to this objection, although to a dumb spectator it may be irksome. There is an animation and variety about it; and there are intervals and rests provided, which entirely preclude the fatigue incident to a long and continuous prayer.

Here endeth the editorial lesson. Ah me! if these are but "some of the faults," and such faults as these must be endured in bright New England, and in her classic capital, and from an educated and accomplished ministry, what must be the insufferable corruptions of public worship and of the very idea of Divine worship among the illiterate and extravagant sects that swarm over the land.

As the *catalogue raisonnée* of the Boston Recorder is professedly incomplete, we will take leave to continue it.

10. *Self-laudatory* prayers, heard chiefly from the agents of societies, which enter regularly into the work of reciting the merits of a particular society, or the self-denying labors of some devoted band of Sunday-school teachers, or Tract-visitors, or Scripture-readers, or the noble sacrifices about to be made by some embarking missionaries, or the wonderful successes of some particular branch of operations in which it is understood the speaker has borne a conspicuous part—*quorum magna pars fui*

"And all, in turn, essay to paint
The rival merits of their saint;
—For, be it known,
That their saint's honor is their own."

11. *Un-English* prayers, in which uncouthness of expression, and carelessness of composition, offend the ear, and unfit the mind for worship.

12. *Short* prayers, abridged and hurried, to make room for the sermon.

13. *Blundering* prayers, in which the recalling of words, and the remodelling of half-finished sentences and embarrassed pauses, constantly occur, so painful to the worshipper, and so fatal to devotion.

14. *Verbose* or wordy prayers, remarkable for the quantity of words, and the paucity and meagreness of devotional ideas.

15. *Eccentric* prayers, tainted with the sometimes intolerable eccentricities of the individual who happens to make them.

16. *Unforgiving* prayers; for I have heard the remark from persons who have been half their lifetime attendants on extemporaneous worship, that they never heard, in a Calvinistic congregation, a prayer for the forgiveness of their enemies.

17. *Defective* prayers, which not only exclude some particular petitions, but which omit some essential element of devotion, such as the confession of sin, the act of faith, the offering of thanks, the oblation of alms, the recognition of the Holy Trinity, even the mention of the name of Jesus. It is impossible, under the most urgent circumstances, that all the elements of proper worship, can be combined by an impromptu dash of the most gifted mind, hurrying on to the one great thing—the sermon.

18. *Common-place* prayers, repeating, till they lose all

meaning, the same trite and tiresome thoughts in certain worn-out phrases and matter-of-course quotations; that "we deserve to be made as miserable as we have made ourselves sinful;" that "others were as good by nature and better by practice than ourselves;" that "sinners may be convicted and converted;" that "multitudes may be heard inquiring the way to Zion, with their faces thitherward;" that "Zion may lengthen her cords and strengthen her stakes;" and that, finally, the Lord would "bless all for whom we are in duty bound to pray."

19. *Intellectual* prayers, by which the speaker seldom fails to intimate that he is versed in all the metaphysical logomachies and miserable subtleties of the hour. I recollect, that in presence of perhaps as large a Congregation as ever assembled in New York, a Presbyterian minister, in his prayer, first entered fully into the nature of the ability which he would *not* ask the Lord to grant the sinners then present, and which it was alleged they possessed sufficiently already; and that he then defined, with logical precision, the exact thing which he had it in his own mind that the Lord should grant.

20. *Theatrical* prayers, accompanied by painful gestures and grimaces, the latter resulting perhaps from the (unscriptural) custom of shutting the eyes, and of making at the same time a mental effort, under the unpleasant consciousness that the people are looking at the speaker.

21. *Bombastic* prayers, which approach the Majesty of Heaven with a solemn grandiloquence, familiar only to an oriental court.

22. *Declamatory* prayers, where the voice becomes excited to a fatiguing pitch, and often strung to a complete falsetto.

23. *Objurgatory* prayers, in which the pastor imputes, in an offensive manner, before the Lord, the low condition of his parish, and the departure and absence of the Spirit, and the

cessation of conversions, to the unbelief and other sins of the people.

24. *Inaccurate* prayers—inaccurate in facts, quotations, reasonings, and the like. A prayer was once made in my own congregation, giving the intelligence, that, "Thou hast taught us in thy holy word, man wants but little here below, nor wants that little long." I have shown, in another place, that the ablest divine may make a mistake of years in acquainting the Almighty with the age of a young clergy man.

25. *Presumptuous* prayers, petitioning for favors that it would be miraculous to grant, or thanking the Lord for the ascertained conversion of such and such, or for the undoubted translation of some deceased individual into His presence in Heaven, or for mercies that imply the prying into "those things that are not convenient."

26. *Political* prayers, that, even if they do not give offence to a party, yet are certain to put the politician on the *qui vive* to discover the political opinions of the minister.

A little reflection must make it obvious, that these evils are unavoidable, under the system by which they are generated. If a minister is to pray *ex tempore*—much more, if he is to pray *ab imo pectore*—unless he be endowed with rare discretion, to distinguish the promptings of passion and private feeling from the movings of a better spirit, his prayers must inevitably take color from the objects and influences around him. In times of agitation and violence, he cannot touch them without being drawn unduly, albeit, imperceptibly, after them: in times of spiritual declension and dearth, his prayers will move in the same sluggish current: in times of fanaticism and inflated zeal, his prayers must savor of the reigning extravagance: in times of heresy and of dangerous and doubtful disputations, his prayers will lie in the current of these subtleties and novelties, or else be painfully directed against them: in times of religious strife or of political convulsion, his prayers will be still infected by the prevailing leaven of uncharitableness and party discord; and party discord is never consummated, until it has become identified with "conscience," and, in another cant phrase, has "been made a subject of prayer." It is not in human nature to escape this snare. I care not how dignified the pulpit, or how good the man, the prayer will be graduated, as a rising or falling thermometer, to the religious *opinions* and the religious *fervor* of the times. The great regulator is wanting—a standing liturgy—to bind the clergyman, and to protect the devotions of the people, to day, from the strange fire that a heated imagination would bring to the altar, and to-morrow, from the cold nothings which would be offered up upon it. The Presbyterian, accustomed to the flaying process of such sluggish, jejune, drowsy prayers, as may be heard at any time, but especially in a country parish, or on a summer's afternoon, can hardly conceive with what amazing force the contrast strikes an Episcopalian ear, educated to the true harmonies of devotion. It was Wordsworth or Coleridge, I believe, who remarked, that he never so felt the sublimity and sweetness of the Church's liturgy, as, on returning to his parish Church, from a sojourn in a country place in Scotland, where he had been doomed to listen one or two Sundays to the extemporaneous effusions of a Scottish minister.

It is certainly worthy of remark, that not one of the more than twenty faults that have been enumerated, nor of as many more that might be named, can be alleged against the Episcopal Liturgy. Yet, within its compass, not a perfection of the Divine Being, but is becomingly adored; not a doctrine of the Divine Word, but is proclaimed upon the housetops; not a bounty of Divine Providence but is thankfully rehearsed; not a want of human nature but is affectingly spread out; not a relation in life, but has its turn to be con sidered; not a class or condition of society but is charitably remembered; not a traveller in the wilderness, not a voyager upon the wave, not a widow in her grief, not an orphan on her knee, not an infant at the breast, not a prisoner or captive in his cell is forgotten; all who are in any trouble, sorrow, need, sickness or other adversity, are cared for and prayed for; the absent and the distant, with all the Church visible, are remembered; the cherished dead and the Church invisible are not forgotten; and angels, and archangels, and all the company of Heaven are recognized and are admitted to the worship.

On entering the sanctuary, after doing silent reverence before the symbol of the Divine Presence, we hear, first of all, some sentences from God's holy Word, inviting us to prayer. The pastor then, not lifted high above us, but standing as a sinner in our midst, exhorts us earnestly to join in the devotions. Then follows the deep-toned confession of our sins, with the consoling absolution of the penitent, which joyful message of forgiveness is immediately followed by the voices of all present uttering that sweet prayer of children taken back to favor, "Our Father who art in Heaven." Then follow the Lauds and praises of the people, not in the words of human rhymsters, but in the words that inspired the harp of David, and even in the manner in which, on the banks of the Red Sea, in the temple at a later day, and in the synagogue until this hour, the people and the priests, or the people alone, answered and still answer one another, "by course." Then follow the Psalms, in such portions, that those delightful compositions are gone entirely through, once a month. We then listen to a well-selected chapter from Moses and the Prophets, which is followed by the noble *Te Deum*, which has earned the admiration, and swelled the devotions of the Church for more than a thousand years, or the rich *Benedicite.* When this is done, we hear a lesson from the New

Testament, corresponding in its drift, with the one chosen from the Old. We then repeat our simple faith, as the Apostle's Creed has transmitted it from the earliest ages. After which, we join in the prayers, thanksgivings, and litanies of the occasion. Then, after a psalm and special preparatory act of invocation, we listen next, upon our knees, to the Commandments, each of which we accompany with prayer for grace to "incline our hearts to keep this law." We then sit down and hear a part of some Epistle in which an inspired Apostle inculcates some of the precepts of the Christian life, and immediately afterward, in the attitude of servants standing to hear their Lord, we stand (for the same reason that we bow at the name of Jesus,) and listen to a portion of the holy Gospel, in which the Saviour himself speaks personally, and is always prominent. The Gospel and Epistle both are chosen in harmony with the lessons from the Scriptures, and all have bearing generally on some high doctrine or important precept of revelation, made prominent by the arrangements of the Church for the particular day. "In all which," we ask, with the great Hooker, "what is there which the wit of man can improve?"

After such devotions, it is not to be wondered at, that the preacher does not lapse into "endless genealogies," and "the oppositions of science, falsely so-called," or into Gnostic and Neologic vagaries, and the subtleties of intellectual learning, or into the contentions of conflicting schools, and the heretical and startling novelties of some last author he has read. Nor is it strange, that the laity, under such tuition, become familiar with the notes of the ancient faith, as they become inspired with the breathings of the ancient worship, and that, unlike the Athenian sects around them, "who spend their time in nothing else, but either to tell or to hear some new thing," they are little swayed by the dogmas and "private interpretations of the preacher," and, in all matters of religion, look upon any thing "new" with distrust, and deprecate the fond conceit of "development" in Christianity, whether it hatch its wretched brood in New England or in Rome. They may not become exact theologians under the teachings of the ancient creeds and Liturgies; but, with this milk from their mother's breasts, they imbibe a certain instinct to know food from poison, and *quod novum, hoc non verum,* which reduced to a simile of daily life, is simply this, that "no man, having drunk old wine, straightway desireth new; for he saith, The old is better."

With a growing feeling, which at that time I considered Catholic, although it was, in fact, the very opposite, I allowed myself, on several occasions, to receive, while yet a Presbyterian clergyman, the Lord's Supper in the Episcopal Church, both because I would not turn my back upon a table that the Lord had spread, and also because the form of its administration in that Church commended itself so entirely to my understanding and my heart. A Presbyterian Communion, borrowing yet another unsightly feature from Congregationalism, is now generally celebrated in the afternoon, when the flesh is full, the mind weary, the eye heavy, and the heart asleep. But, as it is now no longer a Sacrament, it can be thrust out of its place in the freshness of the morning, to make room for the preacher and his sermon! To this dull, drowsy service, dictated by a single mind, poorly qualified, at best, to raise me from the things of earth, and presenting to my longing lips a hard and chilling stone for warm, nutritious bread, I came, in the accidental way just mentioned, to prefer a celebration, more commensurate with the dignity, and more congenial with the sweetness of so august a Sacrament. The Episcopal Church forbids its depending upon one man, whether a whole congregation shall be edified or not, whether a glorious Sacrament shall be marred or not, whether the atonement shall ultimately be denied or not, and compels the minister to speak in "the words of sound doctrine,"—the words by which the martyrs passed away to their reward, and sainted millions in the ages gone by, grew so eminently ripe for Heaven.

The Communion office of the Episcopal Church is the resplendant gem in the girdle of devotions with which she belts the days of her holy year, and the hours of her holy days. In the immediate presence of her Master, showing His hands and His feet, she rises above herself, in the magnitude of her conceptions, and the fervor of her strains. No "thoughts" will suit her, but those that "breathe" in the bosoms of cherubim and seraphim; no "words" will answer her, but such as "burn" with the martyrs as they pass through the fires to God. Therefore, "with angels and archangels, and with all the company of Heaven," she pours forth the stirring strains of the TERSANCTUS, and the boundless chorus of GLORIA IN EXCELSIS DEO. Perhaps the Presbyterian who knows less of the Prayer-Book than does the Papist of the Bible, will be surprised to hear that these seraphic hymns, and other portions of our Eucharistic service, can be distinctly traced to the very days of the Apostles. Some hymns, some prayers the Apostles must have used; it is not likely that the early Church lost them all; the first Fathers of the Church tell us that these were some of them; at the same time they have a sublimity and sweetness that no human pen or voice can resemble. What then is the inference, but that ours is the Church, instinctively preserved, of the Holy Apostles, and of their glorious companions? But the rapt spirit of the Communion service, the Presbyterian can never know; because, to know it, he must enter into it, and taste and feel that it is his, as he falls down with an innumerable company, of every age, about the altar,—that great symbol of worship and of sacrifice.

When I had nearly resolved on entering the Church, I was

conscious of a fear that I might become some day impatient, under the restraints imposed upon my "liberty," forgetting that one very intention of a Liturgy is, to prevent men's taking liberties in the presence and the worship of their God. And, although my experience since, causes me to be astonished at such fears, finding, as I do, that I am not straitened in the Liturgy—an ocean, so to speak, without a shore—but am only straitened in my own heart, and in the earth-bound ties that prevent my launching on its free and untrammelled bosom; yet in those days I went so far as to inquire of Episcopalians, and particularly of a clergyman, in whose candor I knew I might confide, whether they did not sometimes in their hearts covet a larger liberty. But Low Church differed not from High, nor the oldest from the youngest, in the universal answer, that the oftener they used their delightful forms, the more all other services appeared defective and unedifying. Such, I remember, was the testimony particularly of a venerable and excellent clergyman, now fallen asleep, with whose friendship I was highly favored, and whom the "denominations" around delighted to honor.

Besides these assurances, I came to find, that I had had already an experience on this point, to which I had not been sufficiently attentive. I began to notice that prayers which I had learned in infancy, especially the prayer "*Our Father,*" came, morning and evening to my mind, so that it could never be forgotten, nor omitted. Also the little verse, which my mother taught me—

"And now I lay me down to sleep,"

was observed to be the instinctive good-night with which I closed my eyes upon the world, and must continue so to be, until I shall have closed them on the world forever; and even in what is called extemporaneous prayer, I noticed, that my private devotions had all fallen into set stereotype expressions, and that only an extemporaneous *effort*, in its very nature injurious to devotion, would secure any tolerable variety in the pulpit itself.

There was, too, another thing that struck my attention with considerable force. In those revivals, which, according to modern Presbyterian ideas, are the true thermometer of all that is kindling or spiritual in religion, when all remnants of forms are avowedly delivered to the winds, and a species of spiritual carnival or anarchy prevails, the effect of *repetition* is found to be what Episcopalians assert, and the very reverse of what Presbyterians at other times suppose. Not only is there, in time of a revival, a recognition of one of the great principles of Episcopal worship, in the increased proportion of praise and prayer, but the praises and the prayers, like the cries of Him in the garden, are constantly "in the same words." In those critical moments, when the interest is most intense, you do not find the minister announcing a psalm or a hymn never heard before, nor a judicious chorister selecting even a new tune, for the purpose of varying the effect, or of heightening the devotion; but the hymn and the tune that were sung with such effect at the last meeting, must be sung again at this, and, though they have been repeated for weeks and months, yet no voice nor heart is weary. A new tune or hymn daily resorted to for *variety*, would *kill a revival in one week!* And, for years, and throughout life, those same enlivening tunes and kindling hymns are echoed in the social meeting, and re-echoed at the fire-side, and in the darkest and coldest seasons are invoked, to warm and cheer by their lively associations, the Presbyterian, in his less happy "frames." How hallowed, then, thought I, by sacred associations with the past, and with all past ages, and how delightful, by a repetition that enables us to appreciate the force of words, and how sweet as the very language in which our dear departed ones, day after day, poured out their hearts to God, and how adapted to recover a lost or deteriorated spirit of devotion, not to say, too, a lost or overshadowed faith, must be *such* a Liturgy as is found among the treasures of the Episcopal Church.

As a "revival," therefore by throwing the Presbyterian off his guard, and betraying the religious instincts of a pious mind, is a species of agitation, in which truth comes accidentally to the service, we appeal to it as an authority which certain minds can comprehend. And as a revival restores simplicity to the style of *preaching*, and is fatal to that metaphysical haranguing which degrades the pulpit to a level with the schools; and as a revival rouses the worshippers from their cushioned seats, and brings them to their *knees;* and as a revival suggests also the public reception to the Communion, after a mode corresponding evidently to the rite of *Confirmation;* and as a revival elicits, moreover, the earnest *amen*, and the audible *response*, from worshippers who feel that they have a right to join in, as well as hear the prayer, and, in fact, makes the privilege of prayer the privilege of all, so that even the women, who are commanded to keep silence, have their conventicles, where the full heart, denied its utterance in a Liturgy, may assert its liberty, and speak out its pent up emotions—so a revival does to Episcopacy a still further homage, by discovering the fact, that our most earnest and delightful devotions and "frames" are invariably identified with *set psalms, and hymns, and forms*, of which the ear, the lips and the heart grow weary never. Even the Princeton Review, cool, dignified, dispassionate as it is, acknowledges this principle in *sound*, even if it do not adopt it entirely in *sense:* "The lovers of old tunes will not be disappointed in finding such as Old Hundred, Wells, Saint Martin's, Mear, &c.,—glorious old tunes, which our fathers sang, and handed down to us; time-honored, full of power, and deep religious influence, and which we are bound to use, and send down, unchanged and pure, to those that are to come after us." To me it is a perfect riddle, that the man who would thus gravely reason for mere *sounds—vox et preterea nihil*—should not feel the strength of his own argument, when dealing with such a Liturgy as the Episcopal. For we wish no better words than his, to express the same thought with reference to the Liturgy: "The lovers of old [*hymns*] will not be disappointed in finding such as [*the rich* BENEDICITE, *the noble* TE DEUM, *the heavenly* TERSANCTUS, *and the thrilling* GLORIA IN EXCELSIS DEO] glorious old [*hymns,*] which our fathers sang, and handed down to us; time-honored, full of power and deep religious influence, and which we are bound to use, and send down, unchanged and pure, to those that are to come after us." We cannot see how the Princeton Reviewer has escaped the *a fortiori* in this matter. We are quite sure he must think well of Liturgies. The principle, whether it apply to devotion or to tune, cannot be disputed. Could Napoleon reappear, to head his legions in the field, he would invoke the inspiration of the stirring *Marseillaise;* and could the martyrs and virgins and confessors return, nay, should the King Himself, in his beauty, come down, what strain more full of majesty and sweetness could we find for all earth's voices to go forth and greet Him, than the heavenly TE DEUM?

The revivalist finds all his machinery ineffectual, until he has drilled the congregation into set phrases and a fixed routine of hymns and spiritual songs; and nothing so electrifies a Missionary meeting, or achieves so successfully the difficult task of sustaining a high-wrought Missionary excitement on a great occasion, as the hymn of Bishop Heber—

"From Greenland's icy mountains."

Does the Presbyterian grow weary of the strain—

"Salvation, O, Salvation!
The joyful sound proclaim,

Till each remotest nation
  has learnt Messiah's Name."

Or does repetition lessen the thrill with which he sings

"Waft, waft, ye winds, his story,
  And you, ye waters, roll,
Till, like a sea of glory,
  It spreads from pole to pole;
Till, o'er our ransomed nature,
  The Lamb, for sinners slain,
Redeemer, King, Creator,
  In bliss returns to reign!"

It was, then, a mistake to have supposed that I had made no experiment in the principle of Liturgical repetitions. I found in myself, and observed in others, that the highest and happiest strains of devotion flowed always in the fixed channels of precomposed hymns—written and familiar words. And the Presbyterian may rest assured, that what he has already found in the Missionary hymn, or in the revival chorus, such will he find in the anthems and prayers of a Liturgy kept bright by the use of ages.

The worship of the ancient temple was Liturgical, and was made so at the express command of God. The worship of the synagogue was Liturgical, and Jesus took part in the same. The greatest prophet that was born of woman, prepared a form for his disciples. Jesus himself gave a brief form to his followers, as John the Baptist had done before him. We find the apostles and brethren, when at prayer, "lifting up their voice to God with one accord." St. Paul alludes to the familiar "amen" at Corinth, the "exhorting one another with the Psalms;" and tells us of irregularities and confusion created at first, by the popular participation in religious worship. To this, and much more in the New Testament, I could only oppose the instructions of Paul to Timothy, that prayer should be made "for kings, and for all that are in authority," "which does not look," says Dr. Miller, "as if the prayers of the Church at Ephesus, were cut and dried;" to which we *might* answer, that Timothy was now on his way to that Church to "cut and dry them," with instructions to include, among the subjects of prayer, "kings and all in authority," however vile or violent—a suggestion, we may add, carefully regarded in Liturgical worship, and too often unattended to in extemporaneous devotions. Even in heaven we hear the responsive worship—ten thousand times ten thousand voices, like the noise of many waters—the living creatures now upon their knees, and now standing before Him, the elders, the saints, and the angels, answering with voice and harp by turns, and proving, either that such, in St. John's day, was the Church's worship upon earth, which he transferred in a figure, to the heavenly choirs; or that such is the gorgeous ceremonial of the heavenly sanctuary, which it is right and meet to imitate on earth. If the Princeton Review has found an argument for the adoption of instruments in the music of the Church, "*from repeated intimations of their use in celestial worship,*" let the argument be pressed, until it shall unseal the lips of the worshippers, as they are unsealed in heaven. How strange to see in heaven the bright throngs all silently seated, and a single saint, standing and praying or praising for the rest! How strange to see a whole congregation upon earth all silently seated, and one man praying for the rest! We do not see why the preacher should not relieve the people of the singing, as he relieves them of their praying. As we demand, therefore, of the Papist, to restore the cup to the laity, so we once more demand of the Presbyterian to restore the privilege of lay worship, which the preachers have usurped, and to give back to the people, with their ancient Baptism, their ancient responsive service.

Is priestcraft a stealthy assumption, increase, and monopoly of rights and privileges? Right stealthily has Calvinism withdrawn Baptism from the infant; right stealthily (for Knox and Calvin allowed a Liturgy at first) has it usurped the prayers, and devotions of the laity. Here are two privileges, that Rome, in her haughtiest moods, never ventured to deny her laity. But, will say the Presbyterian, our laity do participate in the worship; they have a whole volume of psalms and hymns, and are permitted to sing. Very well; a printed form of psalms and hymns is, so far, a Liturgy, all full of prayers and praises, and is an argument for the use of forms. But let us hear once more the Princeton Review:—"It would seem as though the minister considered the interval of singing to be devised merely to give him an opportunity to attend to certain little matters of personal convenience. He starts the congregation upon a hymn, like an instrument wound up to go for a given time, and then proceeds to remove an extra wrapper from his neck, or to find the next hymn, or to arrange his notes and his collar, or, if it is the last tune, to undo his overshoes." Then follows the extraordinary intelligence,—"The singing is as much a part of the service of the house of God, as the prayer, *or the sermon.*"

It is quite true, as writers on this subject have said, that, strictly speaking, there is no such thing as Congregational extemporaneous prayers. A prayer may be extemporaneous to its composer, as it issues from a pastor's lips; but the instant his petitions and words are adopted by the people, it becomes to them a dictated prayer or form. The Rev. Mr. Barnes himself makes weekly prayers for a thousand people; the people have no choice, any more than have the Episcopalians whom he commiserates; they must use Mr. Barnes's prayers, or else use none. The only question, then, for his parishioners to settle, is whether they will adore and pray in the off-hand words that Mr. Barnes teacheth, or will worship in a Liturgy that has gathered to itself, in one glorious focus, the wisdom and the piety of all ages, or, as the dissenting divines, already quoted have expressed it, which is, "next to the translation of the Bible into the English language, the greatest effort of the Reformation, holds the very first rank of uninspired compositions, and has no equal in any part of the universal Church of God."

I have not dwelt upon the Scriptural argument, because it is of the same nature with that by which we maintain the Baptism of infants, and the observance of the Lord's day. It is the argument of allusion—rightly understood, the most unanswerable of all others. The temple and the synagogue services were those in which both the Master and the disciples worshipped, and we know that those services were rigidly Liturgical. But we do not need the argument from Scripture. The New Testament nowhere commands us to build Churches; but, throwing ourselves on the authority of the Old, which did, we find it to edification to build them still. So the New Testament may not command us to use Liturgies; but, falling back on the authority of the Old, which did, we find it unto edification to use them still. The New Testament could not prescribe a form for the Church, in all the varieties of place and condition under which the Church must exist; it could only settle a principle; and the example of both the master and the household established the great principle of Liturgical worship. Accordingly, we travel through the earth, and, wherever we find the Christian name, even among the Christians discovered by Buchanan, in the remotest East, and circled, since apostolic times, by the night of heathenism, we find the Liturgy; the Liturgy, be it remarked, always purer than the Church itself, and ever presenting the basis of a healthy reformation. We go back into antiquity, and find the fathers alluding continually to this feature of divine worship, and telling us of nearly fifty different Liturgies in use, in the different Churches throughout the world; in fact, they have left no record of a single Church in which public extemporaneous prayer was customary; they even tell us of Liturgies ascribed to the apostles; and fathers that lived within a hundred years of the apostles, speak familiarly of the Liturgy, for example, of St. James at Jerusalem, and others, of that of St. Mark, at Alexandria. And, throughout the world, there was, and there is, so striking a resemblance of phraseology, and especially of the leading points and their arrangement and relative position in these Liturgies, that they lead us necessarily to suppose some common origin of high and primitive authority. And it is to this authority, that we trace the loftiest strains of the present Episcopal Liturgy. Our "Therefore, with angels and archangels, and with all the company of heaven," we find in all the Churches of antiquity, however widely separated, both east and west; and it had become known even in Africa to Tertullian, within seventy years of the apostles. So the *Gloria in excelsis Deo,* we trace to the very infancy of Christianity, substantially as our Church hath used it in England, twelve hundred years. And, in like manner, the creeds in our Prayer-Book, we can find in the writings of an Irenæus, who was taught by Polycarp, the friend of St. John, and of a Tertullian, in more distant Africa, who, within seventy years of the apostles, informs us, that they had been "the rule of faith in the Church from the beginning of the Gospel." No marvel that the Liturgy commands the admiration of the world. Wesley for the Methodists, and Baxter for the Nonconformists, both adopted it in part. A hundred years ago, the Lutherans of Denmark adopted it, although in a mutilated form. In 1712, Prussia and Hanover came very near adopting it, together with the Episcopacy, in the lifetime of Archbishop Sharp. Perhaps, if Satan had not then hindered the labors of some learned and excellent men on the continent, that dreadful moral night which now blackens the face of Central Europe had not fallen upon Germany, whence its deadly shadows are reflected over the greater portion of the Protestant world.

Why should I say more? I went to the Jewish synagogue; the synagogue, on which the great, unreal argument for Presbytery is built; and there I found the Jews, amidst their loss of country, home, and temple, still perpetuating the Liturgical and responsive worship, as it rang of old through "the carved work of the sanctuary."

As to the objection, that it may become tiresome, the objection comes always from those who have not tried it. The users of Liturgies do not complain. It therefore falls to the ground. To hear the daily Liturgy, is to hear the voice of a friend that has supported us in sorrow, and has counselled us in danger, and has guided us in perplexity, and has raised us up from sickness, and has commended our dying into the hands of the Redeemer, and has, with pious hand, dealt tenderly with the dead, as it committed "earth to earth, ashes to ashes, dust to dust." To repeat it, is like repeating those endearing household words, of which the ear and the heart of true affection can never grow weary. We can no more grow weary of it, than we can grow weary of the air we breathe, or of the light we see, or of the bread we eat. The eye is diseased that grows weary of the light; the appetite is morbid that nauseates the sameness of its breath, its water, and its bread. And the heart is not right, and the spiritual taste is depraved, that would loathe this spiritual manna. Give back, thou man of Rome, the cup to a thirsting flock; give back, thou man of Geneva, the Liturgy to a congregation of dumb worshippers! Let not the cup of blessing be drunk by proxy; let not the great duty of worship by proxy be performed!

Again, What is the great business of the sanctuary? Worship. "My house shall be called the house of prayer for all people." How readeth the sectarian gloss? "My house shall be called the house of *preaching*." In former years I often went to my Church under feelings indescribable, of oppression and grief, that the pulpit—the pulpit—was the great central object around which my congregation were assembling, and that, could I have asked them, one by one, "Friend, why comest thou in hither," probably without exception, the answer would have been, "To hear the sermon." O, I have longed, a thousand times, to come down from the lofty pulpit, and lie low among my fellow-sinners at the throne of grace. But, the sermon—the sermon—the sermon; preach—preach—preach—was the everlasting cry. Even if our little ones could tell at night the text—the text—the text—it was enough. Is he a good preacher? Are his sermons eloquent—rousing—interesting—intellectual? Never was it asked on earth, in the selection of a pastor, are his prayers elevating? are they edifying? are they meet for the high purposes of worship? No! The preacher—the preacher—is the living-symbol, the *Grand Lama of Presbyterianism,* around which the people gather. In attempting, fruitlessly, in my humble sphere, to resist the overbearing tide, and to restore devotion and the Scriptures to their place in the worship of God, I encountered only the rebukes of my "most intelligent and pious" elders, not only for tempering my prayers with "the chaste fervor of the Episcopal Liturgy," but even for closing at least one prayer on Sunday, with the prayer which the Lord has commanded us to "say;" and this, although I conformed to the important order of Cromwell's High Parliament, in saying it at the end, rather than, as did the Church of England, at the beginning of my prayer. One of my elders happening to make this complaint to the late Doctor Milnor, the venerable divine replied, "Well, really, Mr. S., it seems to me, brother —— has very good authority for using that prayer." But Mr. S. had come from a land that is said, some years ago to have resembled heaven, chiefly in its color, and that in its palmier days, made it a statutable offence to eat mince pies at Christmas—to salute one's wife upon the Sabbath—to pray at a Christian man's funeral—or to say the Lord's prayer in meeting.

I entered, now and then, an Episcopal Church; nothing shocked at the Low-Churchman's mitre, which there I might have seen—the symbol of her apostolic order; nor at the High-Churchman's cross, which I sometimes saw—the symbol of her evangelical faith. If I entered with my hat on my head, or the world on my lips, the altar, the glorious altar, looked me reprovingly in the face, and said, "The place where thou standest is holy ground." The priest came in, in the white linen which the Lord commanded among a people whose salvation he had at heart, and, kneeling low among his flock, joined with them, and they with him, in the great business of the sanctuary. He then went into the pulpit—not, as I had elsewhere seen, to gaze around complacently upon an audience—but, remembering that he was dust himself, to fall again, upon the ground beneath him, into the dust before God. A sermon, not elaborate nor ostentatious, but generally Scriptural and simple, ended with prayer; and the whole was followed by a reverential silence, and a pause for secret recollection and petition among the worshippers; contrasting much with the hurried exit I had seen from a Presbyterian meeting, where overshoes, hats, canes, gloves, shawls, bonnets, overcoats, were adjusted, and the worshippers, or rather, the "hearers," were equipped for the street, before the benediction had been pronounced. What ideas Presbyterians may have of the benediction, it is needless to inquire; but the confusion in the congregation, while the minister is pronouncing it, savors somewhat of the *opus operantis* of a Popish priest, the benediction accomplishing its full mission, irrespectively of the faith or attention of the recipient.

It must be evident to my readers, that the whole atmosphere of sectarianism had now become to me uncongenial and unwholesome. To be losing my time and patience, and to be injuring my devotional taste and temper with the "gifts" of the brethren in a stupid prayer meeting, when I might be wafted toward heaven in the sublime strains of a holy Liturgy; to be frequenting a more public service, where prayer was curtailed, and holy Scripture almost excluded, and a few short verses of rhyme sung only as an interlude or rest, and all this done systematically, to make room for a labored sermon, often containing, unawares, in flowers of reasoning and rhetoric, the seeds of neology and infidelity; to be advocating a Baptism that had lost its inward and spiritual part, and was limited severely in its application to a certain number; to be upholding a more awful Sacrament degenerated into an external and unessential rite, and administered in a mode, and received after a manner comporting well with the new ideas of its virtue; in short to be fruitlessly contending with continual hindrances to my devotion and salvation, in the uncongenial and unseemly things remarked in the foregoing chapters, and, as a minister to be perpetuating a system thus tried and found wanting; when, by a single step, I might, (by paying a price, it is true,) enter the larger liberty of a Church which breathes, and believes, and prays, and praises as she did when Irenæus, Ignatius and Polycarp beheld her glory, and the noble army of her martyrs died for her, as the pure spouse of Christ—all this had now become a burden too great for me to bear.

Yet, if a Presbyterianism, such as my fancy had many a time imagined, could at this moment have been presented to my mind; that should have made the Scriptures conspicuous, and worship the great business of the sanctuary; that should have met the wants of a longing heart with a rich and noble, and wholesome Liturgy, all radiant with the gems of truth and holiness; that should have placed the Sacraments under guard of an inviolable form, as being Christianity itself in epitome; a Presbyterianism, in a word, with moderate attachment to old paths and landmarks; my inquiries might here have ended, and I have continued in the traditions of my childhood. Again and again did the question recur, Why can we not have a Presbyterian Church after the model that so many wish for? And again and again, did the disheartening answer fall like lead upon my ears—"These gifts are not for you." They are incompatible with the genius and destiny of the Presbyterian system. Its destiny is, *always to lose—never to recover.* Its genius is, *never to believe, always to reason!* Certain ideas of religious "liberty," enough to make one tremble as he reads the predictions of St. Peter and St. Jude; a new theory of religious "progress" and "development;" a certain vanity of "private judgment;" a preference of hebdomadal religion and spasmodic piety; a singular opinion of spiritual "gifts;" and a more singular fancy, that every man praying to be led by the Spirit, is actually so led, in his interpretations for himself—not only prevail coextensively with the system, but are so essential to its very texture, that they must be forever fatal, not merely to all endeavors to revive Liturgical and Scriptural worship, but, as we shall presently see, to all movements toward the recovery of the primitive faith.

CHAPTER XI.

DOWNWARD TENDENCIES.

HAVING discovered the tendency of Presbyterianism to throw off, more and more, the decent garments, ritual and sacramental, in which the Reformation had so disguised it at first, as to secure for it, for a time, the respect, even of the Church of England, I had to pursue the facts in the case but a little further, to perceive that the system was quite incapable of long preserving, or of perpetuating, unimpaired, the great principles of a Christian man's belief. There does appear to be a something ever preying on the vitals of the system, producing everywhere the same phenomena—the feverish irritation, succeeded by the long and languid ague—the high excitement, and its consequent collapse—the spasmodic life, and the succeeding torpor: or, to drop this figure, it ever and anon gives birth to revivals and revolutions, to fresh schemes and schisms, to strange fancies and fanaticism, to new experiments, new sects, new theories, new doctrines; until the old landmarks which the fathers set up are swept away, the reign of intellectual anarchy sets in, and the developments go on to infidelity—at first, in its more insidious phases—and, afterwards, in its stouter and more hideous forms.

Departures from unity, I shall consider hereafter. I am to notice, now, departures from the faith. I shall be content to stand, for the present, by those definitions of the faith, which the Wittemburg, Geneva, Westminster, Augsburg, Dort and Paris Presbyterians adopted at the Reformation. The proposition, then, is this:—That Presbyterianism is not conservative of things spiritual, more than it is careful for things ritual; and that, consequently, it could never have been intended to be the Lord's almoner of grace to men, or the steward of His mysteries to the household of faith.

In theory, Presbyterianism promises much for the Church's purity. The cords are drawn tight. The tests are severe. *The elect are numbered.* The tares are separated from the wheat, before the harvest. The good fishes are severed from the bad, while the net is yet in the deep. The door is shut against the foolish virgins, before the bridegroom has come: even infants, in vast numbers, are frowned away from the healing of its waters, and the porches of Christ's Bethesda are converted into the dungeons of man's Bethhoron, the house of mercy into the house of judgment. There is an unceasing *cutting off* of unsound members, and of unsound bodies, and a still more distressing *going off* of sect after sect, with the view of setting up a sounder faith and a purer worship.

With this rigor of discipline, was at first conjoined a severity of *creeds,* too well defined, one might have supposed, to be evaded; too solemnly subscribed, one might have thought, to be, by and by, denied; too evangelical, their abettors might have reasoned, to be ever undermined. Every avenue to error was foreseen and foreclosed. What then are we to think? We find no fault with the system, on the score of consistency; "elect angels," "*elect infants,*" "perseverance in grace," or the personal infallibility in doctrine, and indefectibility in grace, of each of the elect, and the "foreordination of all the non-elect to everlasting death,"—so repeatedly avowed in the Presbyterian Confession—are a bold but manly and consistent carrying out of the great first error, the πρωτον ψευδος, lying behind the whole theory, that "God, from all eternity, hath, for his own glory, by the mere good pleasure of his will, fore-ordained *whatsoever* comes to pass." But it proves too much—more than the common sense of mankind, and the common sympathies of humanity, and the common and obvious first truths of Christianity, allow us for one moment to believe. Hence we set the system down, as the effort of a daring and gigantic spirit, seeking new ground, instead of falling back upon the old, whereon to raise a barrier against Popery. The terrific features of Calvinism, as they stand out from the canvass, under the fearless pencils of Zuinglius, and Peter Martyr, and Hopkins, and Emmons, that "God is alike the Creator of evil and of good, and is, by the same right, the author equally of sin and of holiness," are but the legitimate offspring of the Genevan stock. The "Gethsemane plan of salvation," recently advocated by divines in Philadelphia, computing the number of the elect with such commercial accuracy, that, if another soul had been intended to be saved, our adorable Lord would have been condemned to bear another pang, and to shed another drop of his most precious blood, is but another child of the same fruitful mother. So the *reductio ad absurdum*, or, to speak our mind freely, the reduction to inevitable blasphemy, is fatal to the pretensions of the system. If it be true, that "God, from all eternity, hath, for his own glory, fore-ordained whatsoever comes to pass;" if it be true, that, for Adam's sin, all man kind are *born* "under God's wrath and curse, and are made liable to most grievous torments, in soul and body, without intermission, in hell fire, for ever," as the larger catechism teaches, (Ques. 27, 28, 29,) then is it reasonably true, as the same faith asserts, that certain *infants* are "elect," and it is truth to say,

"I, by my dire decree, did seal
His fixed, unalterable doom,
Consigned his unborn soul to hell,
And damn'd him from his mother's womb."

Presbyterians, if this be so, do right to ascertain, if they can, the dividing line, and to restrict their Baptism to such infants as they may suppose to be ceremonially elect and clean. But these results indicate that the whole theory is human, and, notwithstanding the recent evasive distinction of decrees, into decrees of *compulsion*, and decrees of *permission*, or of *preterition*—the decree of Εὐδοκησις, and that of Δυσαρέστησις—the decree sublapsarian, and the decree supralapsarian—how unlike all this, is the cheering voice of the Apostles and the Church, recognizing, as God's elect, in a sense high and full of comfort and of hope, the favored communities and individuals to whom His kingdom had come down, who had received the good word of God, and had been enriched with the illumination of his Baptism, raised, in a word, under the Gospel, to a new and bright probation, in which salvation is made, not only possible to all, but, to all who will, is made gloriously certain; an election comparative, not absolute; an election to means and not to their result; to intermediate privileges and facilities, and not to abstract, and ultimate, and everlasting destinies; an election always to good, never to evil!

These results, so repugnant to every feeling of humanity; so incompatible with the boundless grace of the redemption that is in Christ Jesus; so utterly at variance with the true sovereignty of an independent and infinitely happy Being; representing to a world, already disaffected, its Happy Father as producing, by His own inexorable and predetermined will, the blight and mourning that it suffers, and yet, insultingly protesting, in His name, that He has "no pleasure in the sinner's death;" these results, we say, so entirely unlike the weeping God who stood on Olivet, all bathed in grief over the destinies of wayward guilt; so amazingly unlike Him in the garden and Him on the cross, and Him on high with the golden censor, and so unlike His Image, as faintly reflected in the sympathies of Humanity itself, produce after a while, a reaction in the mind; demonstrate *to the heart* the rottenness of the imposture; and, at this point, too often leave the bewildered man upon a sea of doubt and weariness, of scepticism and adventure.

In this, the Presbyterian and the Papist agree: the one, defining Christ's gracious presence in the holy Eucharist, so as to violate our natural understanding; the other, defining the divine sovereignty so, as to shock our moral constitution: the one contradicting our senses; the other our sensibilities. And as, in throwing off Romanism, so in renouncing Presbyterianism, it is the natural tendency of the human mind to run, first, into religious anarchy, and, afterwards, by sure and measured strides, into downright infidelity. Hence the prevalence, at this moment, of infidelity and blasphemy in France and Italy and Spain; and the infidelity, at the same moment, of Germany, and Denmark, and Geneva. Popery has done, in the one case, what Presbytery has done in the other. Side by side, is England, on the West, and the Greek Communion, on the East, and the Swedish religion on the North, under the influences of whose purer Episcopacy, and more or less pure traditions, infidelity expires. As the spell-bound Papist, awaking from his strange hallucination, and abjuring the worship of the Virgin and her companions in glory, is tempted by the same effort to throw off the worship of her Son, Who was once a companion of their sufferings—so the Presbyterian, in casting to the winds the baseless fabric of a heartless system, rushes too often to the precipice, and takes the blind leap into a sea of irretrievable scepticism.

"Bless the Lord, O my soul, and all that is within me, bless his holy name," that He had planted on these shores a purer branch of His holy Church, with its sacramental signals waving high, inviting my sinking bark and failing heart into a quiet haven, at a moment when, in the liberty to which I knew not the proper check, I was tearing myself from a system uncongenial and unwholesome, and felt that the wide world was before me, and that all Churches, past, present, and to come, were equally at my election, and that none could say anathema, if, in the acknowledged right of private judgment, I should myself originate a "Church," and call it after my own name, as others have so often done, that the blasphemy has now ceased to shock or even to surprise: or, if, in the large latitude conceded me, I should glide more modestly into the existing confederacy of Socinians, Arians, Pantheists, Neologists, Eclectics, Deists, Infidels or Atheists!

For myself, however, I did not, at first throw off the Presbyterian creed, because I had discovered its defects or crudities. True, both its crudities and cruelties have caused me many a bitter hour. Perhaps I continued to believe it, *because* it was *unnatural*, and might therefore be *divine*. But the change I have undergone, in respect of creed, has been rather by the silent and supplanting influences of a more Scriptural and wholesome, a more rational and consistent theology, of which I must say that I caught its spirit before I understood its terms. As nearly as I can now trace the change, the first hint of a higher and purer faith, I owe to the Westminster Confession, which has erected a fabric, partly divine and partly human; an image, partly of gold, and partly of clay—*Desinit in piscem mulier formosa superne*—and, in attempting to blend the old doctrine of the Sacraments with the new dogmas of a speculative era—earthly philosophy with celestial faith—has left a flaw, which reveals the weakness of the whole structure, and thus has fortunately suggested a starting-point, from which individual minds may *begin* to recover, as I was enabled to do myself, the ancient consistencies and beauties of a purer faith.

But that which, more than all other considerations, loosened the hold of my former creed upon my confidence, was the historical fact, that it had been found, after long and fair experiment, in every possible variety of circumstance, *insufficient, in any one instance, to protect and preserve inviolate the faith.* And if the things I am about to allege, be true, I do solemnly appeal to my former brethren, to weigh well the matter, and to abjure a system, which all history has shown to lack that vital force with which every seed in Nature has been endowed by its Creator; to propogate its like and to perpetuate itself.

To cite the condition of the Scottish Kirk, might seem hardly in point; as the eye of the Church of England is upon her; and the legislation of an Episcopal Parliament would not allow infidelity or heresy to supplant the faith of the old realm. But, notwithstanding these safeguards, how fares it with the Presbyterian Church in Scotland? Her disruption into eight or ten Communions, all strictly Presbyterian, and all owing their origin to alleged unsoundness in each other's discipline and faith, shall be considered, when we come to speak of schism; and we allude to it here, only as indicating a general restlessness under the Westminster Confession, and a constant tendency to remodel its provisions. And what was the condition of the Kirk itself at the beginning of this century? Who will deny, that under the workings of an Arian, Arminian, and Pelagian leaven, in different proportions, what is now regarded as distinctively the Evangelical doctrine, was almost universally lost?

And what has been the fate of the Presbyterian Churches in England, where they have been sufficiently detached from the Scottish Kirk, to evade the legislation of an Episcopal Parliament? Of two hundred and sixty parishes established in their glory in the days of Cromwell, two hundred and forty are now Unitarian! I was personally informed, a few years since, in London, by men who bewailed the fact, that up to a recent date, every Presbyterian Church and Chapel in the metropolis had lapsed into Socinianism, and that, so instinctive seemed the tendency to this result, that the new and orthodox congregations had, for their safety, been compelled to adopt certain principles of allegiance to the Kirk of Scotland. On this account, I found myself advised and obliged, everywhere in England, to drop the name of Presbyterian, or if I still bore it, uniformly to explain it.

And what at the time we speak of, was the state of the denomination in Ireland, the last of the Three Kingdoms? Where it was not Unitarian, it was Arian, from centre to circumference; and that within a hundred years of the most wonderful "awakening" or "revival," that history has recorded. In that revival, "multitudes swooned, and numbers were carried out as dead, and whole days together were spent in fasting, and preaching, and prayer. I have known them," says an eye-witness, "to come several miles to Communions, and after the Saturday's sermon, to spend the whole Saturday night in company, in conference and prayer. They have then waited on the public ordinances the whole Sabbath, and spent the Sabbath night in the same way, and yet, at the Monday's sermon, were not troubled with sleepiness, and so they slept not, till they went home." Not long after this, as has been commonly the case, under the operation of like causes, opposition to creeds began to be made, and Pelagianism, Arianism, and Socinianism, and especially the views of Dr. Priestly, prevailed, and were current at the beginning of this century. I have stated these facts thus particularly, because the Presbyterian Church in the north of Ireland is the immediate mother of the denomination in America. It was from her, and not from the Kirk of Scotland, that several ministers came over, into Pennsylvania, Delaware and Maryland, and organized themselves into the first American Presbytery. The mother has since played the harlot, and denied her Lord; the daughter—but we shall speak of her afterward.

Let us first cross the channel that divides England from the Continent. The glorious Church of the Huguenots and the Vaudois—a Church planted in the learning and eloquence of Farel, and Viret, and Beza, and Du Moulin, and Calvin; dignified by the arms of its Condes and Colignys; fed by such pastors as Merlin, and Saurin, and Claude, and Daille, and Drelincourt; fostered by nursing mothers, in a Margaret and a Catharine of Navarre—a Church, that, for its influence, was dreaded by the Mazarins, and, for its virtues, was respected by the Fenelons of France—a Church that bared so often its intrepid bosom to the dragoons of the bloody Louis, and the musketry of the perfidious Charles, and that could spare, for a wedding banquet, in a single night, a hundred thousand victims from her fold, and the head of her noble Coligny, to grace, at Rome, the festivities of an execrable jubilee—where is this Church, after which, for its virtues, and its prowess, the whole world wondered? It is fallen! It is fallen! At Passy, and at Paris, at Rouen, and at Charenton, at Nismes, and at Lyons, it is fallen, like a millstone in the sea. It is a cage of unclean birds; It is the hold of every foul spirit; it is the worst of anti-Christs; it "*denieth the Father and the Son.*" The little flock of Moravians, no persecution has been able to diminish: the remnant on the mountains of Syria has survived the ravages of Islamism: but the Church of the Huguenots, only because it wanted the Apostolic descent, in which the Moravian and the Syrian are entrenched, has not only lost her numbers, but has lost her faith. Of her six hundred Presbyterian clergy, I was informed, a few years since, upon the spot, that "there was not found ten" who dared to affirm that Jesus Christ was "God manifested in the flesh." Who can wonder that infidelity has "hastened to the prey," and that Popery has "divided the spoil?" I am aware that, at this moment, there is a partial revival of orthodox opinions in that country; but I also know, that this revival, timid as it is, is not the spontaneous awakening of the Huguenot life, but is the effect of extraneous influences brought to bear upon that Church, not from Presbyterian Switzerland or Germany, but from Churchmen and Dissenters in Episcopal—Catholic England. Its character, too, is totally wanting in the manly features of the old Huguenot religion; it is pale, sickly, emaciated, and emasculated, presenting, at best, the melancholy spectacle of a distracted community, with here and there a solitary individual, sighing over its corruptions and its schisms.

Passing over to Switzerland, let us go through her twenty-two republics, beginning at the home, the Church, the pulpit, the grave of Calvin. I saw in the heart of Geneva, a proud sepulchral monument to Rousseau; but, to forgotten Calvin, "they raised not a stone, they carved not a line." The Confession of Faith continues, as it does in France, to be subscribed; but it is no longer believed. The ashes of Servetus, to whose fiery death Calvin gave his voice, have been scattered over lake and hill, and have broken forth in blains and boils, upon the whole Presbyterian body; while the opinions for which Servetus perished, are preached with trumpet-tongue, in the very cathedral from which Calvin hurled his anathemas against him. Of the whole venerable Synod of Geneva, but one solitary pastor, as I was informed when on the ground, was even *suspected* of believing in the divinity of Jesus. They began by denouncing it a superstition to bow at His name: they have ended by declaring it idolatry to bow to him at all. When, a few years ago, the venerable Malan dared to say, in his discourse, that Jesus "is the true God and eternal life," and that "there are Three that bear record in heaven," he was driven from his pulpit, and hooted on the streets, as profanely as if he had cast his pearls before a Mussulman mob in Mecca or Beyrout. The same was the state of things in the other republics. In short, the old Church of

Switzerland, the Church of Zuinglius and Bucer, of Farel and Beza, of Ecolampadius and Calvin, has become openly Socinian and infidel. Any child in Geneva could have guided me to the bright islet, where the statue of Rousseau looks proudly on the blue Rhone, as it gushes out at his feet from the lake; or to the house of Voltaire, which, from the French border, keeps sentinel over the city; but I could find no one in Geneva capable of pointing out to me the spot in the churchyard where the ashes of Calvin repose. Even the handful of "Evangelical" Christians in the place, I found, in 1838, divided, two against three, and three against two: the venerable Malan living in schism from his brethren, and Brownism and Anabaptism creeping into the fold. Such has been the fate of Presbyterianism in the place where it was born, and drew its first breath. Protected in its birth by a frowning and gigantic creed, as the place where it was born was hemmed in by scowling and terrific mountains, still it has obeyed the law of its existence, has run through the circle of its destiny, and has ended in the denial of its Lord.

In my younger days, I had been greatly prejudiced against Episcopacy, by the fact, that public functionaries under British law were formerly required to be Church Communicants. The Church of England, though so "little among the thousands of Israel," is so truly "a city on a hill," that all that happens in her is immediately noticed and known, it would appear, over the whole earth. Yet the same abuse existed wherever Presbytery was established, and existed within the memory of the living, in portions of New England itself. But I never heard of sacramental abuses so offensive as some that I have witnessed in Geneva. I happened, on one of the chief days of Communion, to be at the cathedral in which Calvin was the chief pastor in his lifetime. A large number of gentlemen and men stood in the streets about the Church, waiting until the sermon and preliminary services should end, that they might go in and receive the Sacrament. This, too, I was informed, was the common practice! With the views which I held, even then, that the unworthiness of the minister or of the congregation could not invalidate a Sacrament, and on the ground that the Creed yet remained as the Reformation had left it, and therefore that the Church was a Church of Christ, I remained in the cathedral, and, endeavoring to feel my own unworthiness, rather than that of the minister, I received the Communion without the smallest scruple. But here I may tell the world a secret. There was in our company that day, a Presbyterian clergyman, who thought, to use his own expression, that "the Church in Geneva had exceeded the limits within which a Church continues to be a Church of Christ," and with a conscience, I doubt not, as clear as my own, in the opposite direction, he would not and did not commune. It remains only to be said, that the clergyman, who thus turned his back on the altar at which Calvin ministered, and who dealt thus with the Church of Geneva as "an anti-Christ" in 1838, was the same who, in the controversy of 1845, made the following *ad captandum:*

"When Dr. Wainwright, a gentleman, a scholar, a Christian minister, (in each of which titles there seems to be implied the idea of refined *feelings*, as well as bland *manners*,) has taken so public, so extraordinary an occasion, for the purpose of *un-Churching* the whole of Protestant Christendom, the Churches of Germany, SWITZERLAND, France, &c., it is surely high time to demand that the public should be put in possession of the evidence by which so bold and unflinching an assertion is to be sustained; or, if that evidence is not forthcoming, it is equally high time that the enormity of the assumption should be exposed. There are hundreds who can perform the task better than myself, but still I believe it not a task which requires the strength of a giant."

Well said! Now then, Doctor, to your "task." If the

veriest Liliput is equal to it, I am sure that you are. You *did* not commune with the Church of Geneva, on the ground that it had "ceased to be a Church of Christ." I believe you *did* not, and *would* not, commune, and for the same reason, with the large Churches of Germany and France. It surely is high time to demand that *the public* should be put in possession of the evidence by which so bold and offensive an edict of excommunication is to be sustained; or, if that evidence is not forthcoming, it is equally *high time that the enormity of the assumption should be exposed.* Doctor Wainwright, in 1845, did only what you had done before him, in 1838. *He* did it, on the ground of Catholic and established law; but *you* have done it on the ground of private and independent judgment. *He* did it, with a thousand leagues of sea between; *you* crossed the sea, and did it at the chief altars of Geneva. *He* charged them only with erecting another *Church,* which is *not another; you* have charged them with preaching "another Gospel which is *not another.*" Whether of the two anathemas is most offensive? Pray, put "the public" in possession of "the evidence;" for, "if that evidence be not forthcoming, it is high time that the enormity of the offence should be exposed." But we will not wait.

Leaving Switzerland, let me ask the reader to go with me down the Rhine, and see how fare our "separated brethren," in Germany. It is well-known that the Protestants of Germany, like those of France, Holland, Switzerland, and, in fact, of the entire continent, with the single exception of Sweden, are Presbyterians. Many of them, from motives of expediency, or convenience—and it is a concession of great importance to Episcopacy—have created a class or order of Ministers, at first called Superintendents, but dignified, latterly, with the Babylonish name of Bishops; and, in this respect, resemble the Methodists of America, who have this spurious Episcopacy. But, in fact, the Protestants on the Continent,

Sweden only excepted, are Presbyterian. And what has been the fate of the faith in Germany—the land of Jerome, and Huss, and Grotius and Melancthon—THE LAND OF LUTHER? "I could not find," says a recent American and Presbyterian traveller, "a single individual in Germany who believed in the eternity of future punishments." Even the Evangelical and excellent Neander, given up to what is known in Germany as the *theologia pectoris*, or religion of the affections, thinks that "the doctrine of universal restitution does not stand in contradiction to the doctrine of eternal punishment *as it appears in the Gospels*; for a secret decree of the divine compassion is not necessarily excluded, by virtue of which, through the wisdom of God, in the discipline of free agents, they may be led to a free appropriation of redemption." The father of the new philosophy of Germany has been deified as "Messiah the Second;" and our awful Baptism, I was informed, had, by some of her clergy, been administered in the name of Liberty, Equality, Fraternity, or of Reason, Humanity, and Love of Country. It is taught by her pastors, that there is no other God than in the things we see, and that man himself is the highest impersonation of Divinity, and, in such a one as Christ, man may therefore be lawfully adored! As to the Bible, it has been justly said, that "if Luther could return from the dead, he would find the Bible as much banished from the communities professing his doctrine, as it was, in the worst times of the Papal policy." And if the Bible has begun to reappear in those lands at all, it has been in many an instance, if not in absolutely all, by the direct or indirect agency of *British* residents, or of a *British* and Foreign Society.

Nor would this be so terrific a result of Presbytery, if the "Evangelical" clergy of Germany, of whom one here and there is to be found, gave hope of a brighter day. But Luther himself bequeathed to them the dangerous precedent of setting Scripture itself aside, when it stood in the way of some favorite opinion. *Epistolam Stramineam*—an Epistle of Straw—he did not hesitate to style the Epistle of St. James, because it laid the axe effectively at the root of his *articulum ecclesiæ stantis vel cadentis.* Other books of the Bible fared with him but little better. The German Evangelical Clergy, still profiting by the courage of the master, are able, by a dash of the pen to settle, on the basis of "private judgment," the canon of Scripture which the whole Catholic Church was cautiously substantiating for three hundred years. "Scarcely a book of the New Testament," says a Presbyterian writer well acquainted with his subject, "has escaped the *obeliscus* of some Aristarchus; and we know not that the Doctor's hat could be duly conferred, in Germany, on one who had not singled out some book for elimination. . . . There are in Germany scores of scholars whose tact enables them to pick out a Pauline epistle as confidently as a bank-cashier can detect a counterfeit note. . . . Several attribute the Apocalypse to a disciple of John. Eichhorn pronounces it a drama on the fall of Judaism and Paganism. . . . Semler condemns it as a work of a fanatic. Ammon thinks the author and the editor of John's Gospel to be different persons. Vogel, Rettig, Ballenstedt, and Bretschneider, deny its authenticity. Schleirmacher rejects First Timothy; Eichhorn rejects all the Pastoral Epistles. Schmidt throws doubt over both the Epistles to the Thessalonians. Cludius treats those of Peter in the same way. Baur and Schneckenburger consider Luke, in the Acts, not as giving a faithful narrative of events, but an apolegetic statement, to vindicate favorite opinions. Kern maintains that the Epistle of James was forged by a Jewish Christian, in the name of this Apostle, to controvert the Pauline doctrinal views which prevailed in the Gentile Churches. Gfrorer finds undeniable marks of falsehood in the account given of Cornelius. And it is significant, that even *the sounder*

German writers, when called upon to combat such views, rehearse them without any approach to a shudder. . . . Neander himself regards the Epistle to the Hebrews as the work of a Christian, a learned and eloquent Alexandrian, who stood to Paul in the same relation as Melancthon to Luther. He denies the genuineness of the First Epistle to Timothy, and exceedingly doubts that of Jude, and entirely gives up the Second of Peter. As to the inspiration of the Scriptures generally, Neander holds it, both in degree and in kind, far below what is regarded as orthodox among ourselves." Such are the fancies of German divines and universities, to which the Stuarts, and Hodges, and Alexanders of Presbyterianism, and her seminaries in America, are sent to learn the Art of Exegesis. And these are the elaborated fancies of Neander, "A venerable theologian," according to the Princeton Review, from which I have just quoted, and am now quoting again,—"a venerable theologian and a noble scholar—perhaps the most celebrated Professor in Germany, and whose works we never open without instruction and delight." [!] And such is the sea of doubt and wild conjecture, in which even the "Evangelical" remnant in Germany are driven. And, unless the Church be invoked as the true Witness, to say, what *were* the books of Scripture confided to her, *from the beginning*, who shall settle, either for the German Presbyterian or American, the canon of Scripture, and give them again *the Bible*, of which Presbyterians in this country yet unthinkingly boast, as the rule of faith, but whose claims they are consistently enough beginning, like their more advanced brethren in Germany, to reinvestigate, in all the unbounded plenitude, and the *jure divino* of untrammelled "private judgment."

Thus has Socinianism, with her pestilential train, trodden, with giant step, the causeways of Irish Presbyterianism; planted her banners in the Presbyterian encampments along the Thames and the Seine; written her insulting creed on the tombs of the Vaudois and the Huguenots; reared her towering head above the Alps and the Appenines; dashed on, like the winter avalanche, into the fair vallies of Switzerland; and kept her insulting jubilee in the cathedral of Geneva, and over the dust of Calvin. Rolling with the turbid torrents of the Rhine, she has scattered its seeds of death into a congenial soil upon its right bank and its left; she has entered the seats of learning, and, by her resistless spell, has won over to herself the renowned universities of Germany. Leyden and Leipsic have fallen down before her. Wittemberg and Heidelberg have kissed her feet: and Göttingen and Berlin have anointed them with ointment. In a word, the lawful child of Presbytery has succeeded to the Empire, *wherever* Presbyterianism had reigned before her. She would fain have crossed the stormy Baltic, and have planted her icy tabernacle in the north, and, like the maelstrom on the coast of Norway, have swallowed, in her capacious throat, the Churches of those empires. It was not the stormy wave of the Baltic that arrested her progress; for she had stridden a continent and an ocean before. It was not the hills of Dofrefield that turned her back, for she had conquered the Jura and the Alps. But, with the music of those waves, there were borne to her ears the strains of a Catholic *Liturgy*, and beautiful upon those mountains she beheld the feet of Apostolic Bishops. "It would be interesting," says a writer, on whose accuracy, I must, for the present, rely, "to compare the two kingdoms of Saxony and Sweden. Both are almost exclusively Lutheran; the people of both are generally well educated; religion is one of the studies in every grade of the public schools of both. One is universally Rationalistic; the other universally Orthodox. One has not more than half a dozen Evangelical preachers, out of six hundred clergy; the other has not as many Rationalists, out of three times that number! One is Episcopal, and has retained the Apostolic succession; the other is Presbyterian, and without it."

I know of but one other spot in Europe, out of which this spirit has departed "naked, and wounded and bleeding." The Church of England has, by the daily incense of her wholesome Liturgy, enbalmed an atmosphere around her, which Socinianism has never with any comfort, been able to breathe, and, by her Apostolic descent, has inherited a blessing, which Socinianism, with her mess of red pottage, has never been able to supplant. Socinianism, like a local malaria, with her train of diseases, has been invited from Geneva, into the ruins of a few Presbyterian and Baptist Congregations in England, but to them has been rigidly confined; not a congregation of the Church of England, throughout an empire on which the sun never sets, has ever caught the infection. Mr. Lefevre, of New-York, on his return from a visit to England, complains that "the system of American Universalism has not a single defender in England." In a single word, the fact—enough to make one shudder at its contemplation—must now be obvious, that, if Presbyterianism had retained its footing in Great Britain, the whole Protestant world would at this moment have been Socinian or Infidel! During four years that it triumphed under Cromwell, one hundred and seventy-six sects, or forms of heresy and blasphemy, appeared; and, as stated before, of two hundred and sixty Presbyterian Congregations that survived the Restoration, two hundred and forty have lapsed into Socinianism. Well may the Church of England be called "THE BULWARK OF THE REFORMATION;" and we marvel not that all that touches *her*—since it touches the apple of the world's eye—is at once felt at the Earth's heart, and in all Earth's extremities; and the least speck upon her face, like a spot on the great luminary in heaven, instantly attracts the observation of the world. Still, there is the owl and the bat that would rejoice in her eclipse! These are the facts that drove me rapidly on toward the result contemplated in this narrative.

But give Presbyterianism the opportunity of one more experiment. Follow the "May-Flower" in her ocean-path, and wonder to yourself, whether the flood from the dragon's mouth shall pursue this woman and her child into the wilderness. Behold the Pilgrims disembark: a noble race, a virtuous people, a godly congregation, who fast, and give alms, and pray, and establish once more, not unaided by sons of the Church of England, a Christian empire, far from the contact and contamination of the old leaven, and fortified in fence-work deeper, higher, broader, than any that had been contrived before. And are we to see this new empire of faith uprooted? Is the same death-worm to gnaw at the root of the transplanted tree? Are we to behold the same mysterious plague-spot appear in a new clime, upon a healthy and vigorous frame, until from the crown of the head to the sole of the foot, it shall be "a leper white as snow?"

And tell us ye divines and ye diviners, when shall all this be? Shall it be soon? Shall not generation after generation, washed in the Lamb's blood, be placed first beyond the reach of sin and death? No! we tell you, *no!* Scarcely have the feet of the Pilgrims touched Plymouth Rock, before the empoisoned waters gush from its bosom. Scarcely have the children that gambolled on the decks of the May-Flower, grown up to manhood, ere Arminianism, at once the offspring and the antagonist of Calvinism—an Arminianism not grounded in Catholic truth, nor guarded by Catholic restraint, but guarded and grounded in the vain sanctions of human reasoning, and the simple reactions of human instinct,—has overspread the land, and an Egyptian darkness has stretched its curtain over the new empire.

Time rolls on. Reformers again rise, and again bare their

breasts to persecution. Whitefield, with his Episcopal orders, and a heart moulded in a Liturgical faith—a man of fasts and vigils, who, at Oxford, spent whole nights on the cold earth in prostration and prayer, but a man whom the Church of England preferred to drive from her communion, with the Wesleys and their companions, into schism, because she wanted the wisdom to employ them in her own bosom—Whitefield, and a few individuals like-minded, come, as another Moses and Aaron, to spread their hands over the land, and dispel the unnatural darkness, and once more we see New England, through Whitefield of the Church of England, recovering, to some extent, the faith and its practices, which, in the short space of a hundred years, it had unaccountably lost.

But again, men who sat entranced under the burning eloquence of Whitefield, what have they seen at the beginning of the present century? The Church of the Puritans, after as fair an experiment as it was possible to make—with the whole ground again to itself—eaten up, to its very heart, with Socinianism; and a Socinianism not imported, like the plague, by any intercourse with degenerate Geneva, or Halle, or Berlin, or Belfast, or Montauban, but springing up by the natural law of generation, in the moral world, from the latent germ, that, in a free-thinking theory, is at once the *primordium vitæ* and the *primordium mortis* to the system. The blighting angel drops again the cursed dew from his wing, over bright New England, and the pulpits of her capitals, and of her quiet villages; the pulpits of her Mathers, her Davenports, her Hookers, her Robinsons, her Rutherfords, are occupied by preachers who, confronted by no Liturgy of purer times, preach fearlessly and blasphemously that Jesus is *not* "the true God," and that the Son and the Father are *not* "One." "I am verily afraid," said Increase Mather, in the heyday of Puritanism, "that, in process of time, New England will be the wofullest place in all America." "Yea, we are fain to that madness and folly," said Edwards, "that I am persuaded, if the Devil came visibly among many, and held out independency and liberty of conscience, and should preach that there were no devils, *no hell*, no sin at all, but these were only men's imaginations, with several other doctrines, he would be cried up, followed, admired." And the result has made good these singular predictions.

The Universalists alone, teaching that "there is no hell," boast of having come into possession of a thousand pulpits, among the sons of the Puritans, in this ill-fated land! In 1840, they had but eighty-three preachers; now they have seven hundred preachers, and eleven hundred congregations; and claim, in point of numbers, to be the fourth denomination in the country. Nearly all New England was Socinian. Every old congregation in Boston, except the "Old South," was Unitarian. The Church that looked down so long in pride on Plymouth Rock itself, has yielded to the destroying heresy. I have even heard that Emmons and Hopkins, the Calvinistic leaders, of a later day, could they come back, would find their Churches and flocks engulfed in the one *gurgite vasto*. No wonder that we hear, in the middle of the nineteenth century, that, in America, the lineal descendant of Mather the Puritan has returned to the Episcopal Church; that in Germany the descendants of Luther the Reformer have taken refuge in the Romish Communion; and that, in Great Britain, a descendant of Cromwell, the Protector, ministers at the altars of the Church of England.

As to New England, we regard the last experiment of Calvinism as made. "Ten years," says a sagacious Presbyterian divine, "will place the [*orthodox*] Churches of Massachusetts beyond redemption." Says the Editor of "The Presbyterian," "The ground they assume in the contest with the Socinian is absurd and futile. The latter may lie on his arms, without striking a blow, and confidently await the issue." "It has been long prepared in itself," says a discerning Unitarian, "for a reform in its theology; but its allegiance to the public sentiment of more sluggish communities has retarded it. It is laboring along, like an active steam-tug with a half-dozen logy ships in tow. Andover, for example, could she have been freed from her deference to Princeton, would long ago have fallen into the arms of an essentially liberal Christianity." This is the tendency—downward and downward—still everywhere downward. There is no remedy—and so the people begin to understand—but in the time-worn Church, to which a goodly multitude are coming back, with the cry, as one has uttered it, "O my Ancient Mother, take back a weary and heavy-laden wanderer to thy bosom; give me thy yoke and thy burden, that I may find rest to my soul." "If the Episcopal Church had been known in New England," said one of her wisest and most celebrated statesmen, to a Churchman, "we should never have been Unitarians; we are Unitarians only in the ignorance and the absence of something better." And the late growth of the Church there appears to justify the remark. In Connecticut, where the chanting of the service when first introduced by Bishop Seabury, was laughed at and hooted by the people on the street as an "Indian pow-wow," there are now one hundred congregations that so worship God. And of Newburyport where the bones of Whitefield are entombed, it has been said of this man and that man in the list of the Episcopal clergy, that he was born there. That single town, as if Whitefield had repented in the dust, and had warned them from the dead to return to the bosom of their ancient mother, has given birth to at least twenty living pastors and divines of the Episcopal Church.* Yet so it must be; for thus it is written, "the sons

* Their names are as follows:—

The Rev. Wm. Bartlet, St. Luke's, Chelsea.

" " Josiah M. Bartlet, Pierpont Manor, W. N. Y

also of them that afflicted thee, shall come bending unto thee."

When I first became acquainted with the facts narrated in this chapter and in the one preceding, I was more startled than if seven thunders had uttered their voices, and as much convinced as if seven angels had poured their plagues before my eyes on the seat of Presbyterianism. I conjure the Presbyterian to account for these *frightful* phenomena, by any explanation that shall not make it his first duty to abjure the system he has espoused. There is a *semper*—there is a *ubique*—there is an *ab omnibus* about it, that fills me with amazement. Why is it, I inquired that, in different languages, and in distant lands; sundered from each other by oceans and untrodden hills; separated even by mutual jealousies and hates; antipodes to one another in education, and taste, and habits of life and modes of thought; and with mutual antipathies, in

The Rev. Moses B. Chase, Chaplain U. S. Navy.
" " Thomas M. Clark, Trinity Church, Boston.
" " George H. Clark, late of All Saints' Church, Worcester.
" " Samuel A. Clark, Church of the Advent, Philadelphia.
" " Samuel Cutler, St. Andrew's Hanover, and Trinity, Marshfield.
" " Benjamin Dorr, D. D., Christ Church, Philadelphia.
" " Samuel M. Emery, Trinity Church, Portland, Conn.
" " William Friend, St. Peter's and Grace Churches, Port Royal, Virginia.
" " Benjamin Hale, D. D., President Geneva College, N. Y.
" " William Horton, St. Thomas's, Dover, N. H.
" " Jacob B. Morss, St. Thomas Parish, Baltimore Co., Maryland.
" " Moses P. Stickney, St. Peter's Church, Cambridgeport.
" " Charles C. Taylor, St. Andrew's, Ann Arbor, Michigan.
" " Stephen H. Tyng, D. D., St. George's Church, N. Y.
" " James H. Tyng, Jr. St. George's Church, N. Y.
" " Frederick Wadleigh, St. James's Church, Arlington, Vt
" " George D. Wilde, Grace Church, New Bedford.
" " John Woart, Christ Church, Boston.
" " Charles C. Adams, St. Paul's Church, Key West, Florida.

some instances wrought up to the highest pitch by protracted and barbarous wars—why is it, that the religion, that has once divorced itself from its Bishops and its Liturgy, is downward and ever downward in its tendency, bequeathing her sceptre in all lands, without a single exception yet, first to the Socinian, and then to the Infidel? Particularly I asked myself, and now I ask the candid Presbyterian, to tell me, how it is, that the system established by these pious men; men of fasting and alms and prayer, of learning and untiring zeal, of intellectual power and virtues sufficient to have given them a control beyond their times; men "of whom the world was not worthy"—has suffered in so short a time this awful retrogression? Why is it, that a Church, which they would joyfully have defended with their lives, and which they guarded by an uncompromising creed and by a vigorous discipline—a Church, that, less than a hundred years ago, amidst a universal re-awakening, returned for a while to the manly faith of the earlier Puritans—should now, *again*, while hearts are yet beating that kindled and beat under the eloquence of Whitefield and Brainerd and Edwards and the Tennants, have lapsed into Socinianism—Universalism—Deism? One of their favorite divines we find, in a New-York pulpit, associating, in a breath, the names of "Socrates and Cato, of Howard and Lafayette, of Jefferson and Jesus!" "Such is the era," says one of their orators in the mesmeric trance—and not unendorsed by a number of their clergy—"such is the era foreseen by David, Isaiah, Zechariah and Daniel, and impressed upon Confucius, Zoroaster, Brahma, Jesus, Mohammed, Fourier—it was sung on the Orphic lyres of Egypt—preached and anticipated by Paul—and described by John in the Apocalypse!" We hear Boston divines beginning at last to deny the personal existence of their Maker; and the learning of old Harvard University is at this moment employed in the grave business of seeking to convince her sons, that, although they be right in denying the "*three* that bear record in heaven," yet there is sufficient reason to believe that there is One! Herself the plaything of a hundred schisms and sins, the old New England Church is now abandoning her children to "the delirious wanderings of the transcendental philosophy;" and some of her leading divines are echoing the huge atrocity of Germany, that Jesus was but one of a series of Messiahs, whom the world has a right to look for, until society shall be conducted by the paths of liberty and progress to its longed for perfection.

Once more. That small portion of the Presbyterian Church, to which it has been my happier lot to be attached—what, said I, cautiously, within myself, is its condition? Is it also on the downward road to doubt and dissolution? Let me think. Under my own eyes, and while enjoying, as some have said, "the most remarkable revival since the days of the Apostles," it has been rent into irreconcilable parties, which have ended in the adoption of opposing creeds, and separate communions; the same philosophizing spirit is stalking in its midst, which has, all around it, entirely supplanted the old faith. On the principle, "Nec Deus intersit, nici dignus vindice nodus," we are told that natural causes may have dried up the Red Sea; that natural causes may have rained fire on the plain; that natural causes may have hung a meteor in the heavens over Bethlehem; that natural causes may have produced all the phenomena ascribed by our Lord to demoniacal agencies, in accommodation to the prejudices of the Jews. Not very far, all this, thought I, from the German discoveries, that the Ascension of Jesus was his disappearing in a mountain-fog, and his stilling the tempest was his settling a dispute among the sailors.

And, in doctrinal theology, almost afraid that my very thoughts should be overheard, I yet thought within myself, Where do we stand? "Original sin is an original absurdity"

—"Imputed righteousness is imputed nonsense,"—"Natural inability makes sin a natural misfortune, but certainly not sin"—"We must be willing to be damned, that God may be glorified, or we cannot be saved"—"We are as much indebted to God for sin as for holiness"—"God is as much the Author of evil as of good"—"God was bound to introduce sin, as producing, through grace, the greatest possible amount of knowledge and of happiness"—"Regeneration is simply a resolution of the will, in view of motive, or is the result of moral suasion"—"Were I as eloquent as the Holy Ghost, I could by the presentation of motives, regenerate the world"—"When the laws of mind shall be better understood, regeneration will universally take place, as the natural result of the proper selection and adaptation of motives"—"As God cannot govern the sun by motives, nor the stars by the ten commandments, so neither can He regenerate mind, and give it a new direction, by the direct and immediate power of His grace"—"Spiritual Christianity is to be henceforth the standard; perish forms and creeds"—"The Church must be re-built upon broader *bases* of faith"—"Its discipline must be altered, and other tests of communion, adapted to the times and the societies around us be instituted"—"The eternal generation of the Son it is not absolutely necessary to believe"—"In fact, we subscribe the Confession of Faith, only as indicating the outline or substance of doctrine"—"And the old forbidding doctrine of the Atonement, an eye for an eye, and a tooth for a tooth, must be abandoned for that of an At-one-ment, by which man shall become morally at-one with God"—"for, (to use the language of one of our eminent divines, whose pen seems not to have understood the first lesson of reverence,) no debt was due from us to God, and consequently, *none was paid by Christ;* we had not deprived God of His property; we had not robbed the treasury of Heaven; God was possessed of as much riches after the fall, as before;

the universe and the fullness thereof still remained His; we neither owed money to the Deity, nor did Christ pay any on our behalf; *His atonement, therefore, is not a payment of our debt.*"

These, and numberless like propositions, continued I to myself, emenating from the Edwardses, the Beechers, the Barneses, the Skinners, the Emmonses, the Hopkinses of Presbytery, have, within my own brief recollection, become the absorbing themes of our pulpits, our schools of theology, and, in the absence of a Liturgy, of our very prayers. The Old School, or Orthodox Presbyterians, occupying themselves, for the most part, the doubtful and slippery ground of the New Lights of the last generation, are awhile in doubt whether they can rally in sufficient strength to "exscind" their unsound brethren, or whether they shall be driven to secession, as the only escape from evils under which the body is groaning. The crisis comes. The Church is rent. Heresies multiply. The Catechism, in a thousand parishes, gives place to "Union questions," and to "The Child's Book on the Atonement," "The Child's Book on the Soul and its Immortality," and perchance, "The Child's Book on the existence of its God!" The Catechism once neglected, there is no possible way of commending such a system to a ripened understanding, in after life; and the whole body, loosened in its joints and bands, is preparing for its dissolution. Even that portion of the Presbyterian body, which, by setting adrift sixty thousand communicants, aimed at becoming purer, is still entirely below the requirements of its Confession. The Sacraments, in the sense of that Confession, are almost lost; the eternal generation of the Son not held to be at all essential; the distinction between moral and natural inability, ultimately so fatal to the system, allowed; salvability of all, in a certain sense, assented to, at the necessary expense of election and a limited redemption; and Princeton itself, becoming daily more remarkable for the patience, respect, and "delight," with which the student and the reader are conducted through its Reviews and its Exegetical Chairs, to the laboratories of the German theologians. In fact, the Old School Presbyterians, while boding that "ten years will place the Churches in Massachusetts beyond redemption," are unconsciously far out on the ebbing tide, toward the gulf of Continental Neology.

There is certainly a chain of hands from Calvinism down to Atheism—Calvin reaching the hand to Luther, Luther to Arminius, Arminius to Pelagius, Pelagius to Arius, Arius to Socinus, Socinus to Messiah the Second, and even Messiah the Second to another, and another still, whom this theology teaches us to look for. At Calvin, the uppermost link of the theological chain, retaining yet much of its ancient Catholic consistency and polish, the series stops; and between Calvin and Cranmer, Presbyterianism and Episcopacy, human philosophy and celestial faith, private judgment and Catholic consent, there is an interval, wide as the earth, high as the stars, and lasting as the heavens. Why then should Episcopalians be blamed for not wishing to bridge the gulf, or to break down the dividing wall? Or why should they be derided for seeking to restore that wall, where it may have been weakened? Is there not a hid treasure in its corner-stone? Pray, gentlemen, desist from calling names. Pray, for a trifling, temporary advantage do not endeavor to stultify us to the world, and expose us to its sneer, by creating the impression, that it is for forms and shadows that Episcopalians contend! We will not tell you you know better; but we do tell you *it is high time that you knew better.* The advantage this mode of warfare gives you, will not last you long. We bide our time. When Presbyterianism, where it is new, shall have run the course and reached the decay that it has run and reached wherever it is old, the world will see—alas, too late for many!—that it has not been a war for forms. It is not an archangel contending with Satan for the body of Moses. It is the Bride, the Lamb's Wife, contending with anti-Christ for the divine perfections of her Lord. Has *she* ever—has she *ever*—since the moment of the Reformation, sympathized with the heresies on every side of her, which not only deny that the Lord hath "bought us with his blood," but deny that He who bought us is the Lord? Wherever Apostolical Episcopacy exists—and it now belts the earth—Jesus is worshipped as "very God of very God;" His blood, in all places, the price of our redemption; His cross, save where your own hands have torn it down, the symbol of our hope; and the Creeds of the earliest times, recited with a lowly bowing at the name of JESUS. How different, where Presbytery has fulfilled its course—in London or in Belfast, in Paris or Geneva, in Berlin or in Boston—it matters not where—*wherever* it has run its course, there Jesus is rejected, and his crown trodden in the dust. It is the "invariable antecedence and consequence" of the philosopher—the plain "cause and effect" of common sense—the *semper post hoc, ergo, propter hoc,* of all human experience.

After attentively considering the terrible experiment of three hundred years, I sought in vain, to fly from the conclusion, that Presbyterianism embodies in it, by an inherent and innate necessity, the elements of its own decay. Certainly its undying worm is nurtured in the heart of its unhealthy bud. The *punctum saliens*—the principle of the system, is fatal to the system: the very condition of its existence fatal to that existence: the freethinking on which it is based, its own death-warrant. Its leading, hinging, fundamental article, "the right of private judgment," is a cup of sorceries. But it is a golden cup, and "the wine therein giveth its color, and it moveth itself aright." When once "the right" to taste has been established, impossible it is to fling the intoxicating bowl away. Deeper and deeper must the victim drink, until, in a wild delirium, he will suck out its very dregs. The "right of private judgment" is the very key, by which the intellectual sophistries of Calvinism are reached and detected, and, unless the conservative principle of Catholic consent intervene in time to give my mind a new and safe direction, I am lost. Yes, I have been myself upon the slippery descent. What held me back? Calvinism as history has shown, and as the operations of my own mind would lead me to suspect, is the first step of a liberal intellect towards honest infidelity. Presbyterianism, with empires in her arms, has been commonly two hundred years, in running its course. But the individual mind, borrowing her impetus, can easily outrun her. A philosophical mind, like Doctor Priestly's, or a mind formed like Mr. Belsham's, in a physical and utilitarian mould, or an active, imaginative mind, like Milton's, may, in a single lifetime, run through this circle of opinions. Milton, to take but one of those examples, whose fingers swept with such inimitable grace and grandeur the strings of a seraphic lyre, alas! with a like facility, almost poetic, swept over all these notes in the descending scale of theology. Leaving the Church of Rome, and from political animosities, unwilling to stop at the Church of England, he became a Presbyterian—then, an Independent—next, Anabaptist—afterward, an Arian—and eventually a Socinian—although it is believed that later in life he returned to a better mind. So the freethinking mind of Watts, the great poet, whose words of praise form chiefly the present liturgy of Presbyterians, labored, it is understood, anxiously and painfully on the question of our Lord's divinity, while the chair that he occupied as a preceptor has in latter years, we are informed, been filled by a Socinian.

Yes, I have stood myself upon the topmost round of this slippery descent, and have seen the depth as it darkened below me. And from my soul I bless the hand of Providence for interposing the faith of the earliest and purest ages as an alternative to my distracted breast. I ascertained that there was a clearer and steadier light than the sparks of reason's kindling, in which Christianity might be considered—not the light of a volcano, bursting in Germany, and leaving the earth strewn with ashes and cinders—not the light of a meteor, flashing on Geneva, and leaving the heavens darker than in the nights of Popery—not the light of a planet, reflecting for a while the bright rays of the body from which it is broken, and then sinking into silence and eclipse—but the steady, unfluctuating light of a primitive age, all radiant with innumerable constellations, that, like the light of the natural firmament, has come down to us undimmed and unimpaired. O it is refreshing beyond all utterance, after following these human guides and wandering stars—the Luthers, and the Calvins, and the Wesleys, of yesterday—to see at last a Christianity shining with that same full-orbed light in which Polycarp and Ignatius and Irenæus beheld its glory, and to know as a historical fact, that it is as much the same, as the light of the celestial bodies above us is the light that shone upon their natural eyes.

I may therefore repeat, that to my mind the inference was irresistible and, may I not say, philosophical, that for the uniform defection of Presbyterian communities from the faith, or their continual tendency to that defection, there must be a uniform cause; and that this cause must be inherent in the system; for the frightful phenomena are everywhere the same; in empires and nations and in narrower localities, separated by sea and mountain, and diverse from each other in language, government, education, taste, and all the habits of mind and modes of thought. And I thought I could perceive that, next to the self-sufficiency of private judgment, and next to the principles on which they depend, of exegesis and of argument, by which everything must be clearly defined and proven, the chief secret of this terrible decay is in the want of a liturgy to protect the faith, and of the order of Apostles to whom the promise was given by our Lord, "Lo, I am with you alway, even unto the end of the world." Though we say it in sorrow, we must say it in candor, aye, in fidelity to the Master, that, as a matter of historical *fact*, "the gates of hell" *have*, to an extent that should inspire the most serious misgiving and dismay, "PREVAILED against" the Presbyterian communion. Only two out-posts—one in Scotland, and one in part of the United States,—and in both a sad breach has been made in the walls,—remain to be taken, and *the work is done!* In this country, Presbyterianism, save in New England, has not fulfilled its course; and yet it is rent into conflicting schisms, and agitated with wild "winds of doctrine," and is the unhappy plaything of what one of their own divines has called "the eternal Eurekas of some new divinity." But of Presbyterianism in New England, in France, in Switzerland, in Denmark, in Germany, in Holland, in Prussia, over nearly all which countries it has had an uninterrupted run and reign of three hundred years, we can speak now historically. Gather the Presbyterians of all these lands into one vast assembly, and you will find, that they have, almost to an individual, "denied the Lord that bought them with his blood." Ask them again, if the Bible that we acknowledge contains the inspired and infallible communications of God to men, and, with scarcely a dissenting voice they will tell you NO! More than three hundred years was Popery in laying her hand upon the laity, and repelling them from the cup; but in less than three hundred, in all the countries we have named, Presbyterianism has laid her hand upon the crown of JESUS, and torn it from his brow, and declared Him to be no God of hers. Again and again has she surrendered the Divinity of her Lord, taken off from His exalted Person the purple robe, and suffered Him to be crowned with shame and spitting. Rome, with all her abominations, never did it. Which then is *the Anti-christ* of the present day? I dare not answer—but one, whom the catholic faith has always held to be inspired, has said, "He is anti-christ, *that denieth the Father and the Son;*" and again he says, "Many deceivers are entered into the world, who confess not that Jesus Christ is come *in the flesh.* This is a deceiver and an *anti-christ.*" (I. John ii. 22, 23: II. John 7.)

"Have you heard the dreadful news?" said a very remarkable lady, and *active* parishioner of mine, not many years ago.—"another clergyman in England gone over to Rome!"

"Indeed!" I replied; "it is really very sad; but" (endeavoring to adapt my answer to one who had been nearly Swedenborgianized out of the doctrine of the resurrection, and liberalized and spiritualized, as I had heard, into the celebration of the communion with friend Gurney and his companions,) "I think he might have done worse—better believe too much than too little." But this did not damp, in the least, the ardor or the satisfaction with which, sometime afterward, she renewed the lamentation, "O, Mr. ———, have you heard the dreadful news—have you not heard it? another of our clergy gone over to the Papists!"

"But why do they leave the Church," said I; "do they believe the Church of England to be Erastianized and Puritanized beyond redemption? If so, I can only say that I do not agree with them." Still, after a certain interval, the old song came back, "O Mr. ———, have you heard the dreadful news—have you seen the papers—have you not heard—another clergyman apostatized?"

"Is it possible," I replied, "apostatized to what?"

"To *Popery!*"

"Ah, indeed!" I remarked; "I did not know but you meant, to the Independents or the Baptists, or possibly the Unitarians; however there is this consolation," said I to the lady, who carried the Church of England as some better employed ladies take their knitting, in her lap, "it is a consolation that not a speck nor mote can appear in the eye of the Church of England, but it seems instantly to give pain to the extremities of the body social; surely this is the Church of God!"

But as this continual dropping began, in the course of time, to wear a little on my powers of endurance, I said one day to the good lady, "Oh, Miss ———, have you heard the *dreadful news?*"

"No! pray dont tell me, if it is any thing bad—I want to hear something good—but I believe there is no more any good—but do not tell me—any more apostacies to Rome?

"Worse than that," I answered very solemnly.

"Why, what do you mean? What can be worse than that?"

"Indeed, Miss ———, I wonder you should not have heard it—very little is said about it however—a great many people do not even know it—but still, I think it ought to be known, and I hope you will do your part in letting our parishioners know it. How singular it is, that three or four men cannot leave the Church of England, for that of Rome, without rocking the earth to its centre and turning all faces black, when fifty thousand Presbyterians in Switzerland may deny the Lord and reject His word, and no one's equanimity be disturbed throughout all Christendom!"

"But tell me," said the lady, "that *news* you had to tell me."

"Well, Miss ———, I am endeavoring to break it to you by degrees, as you thought you could not bear it very well this evening; *that* is the news—not that fifty thousand, but that more than *thirty millions* of Presbyterians, in Switzerland, in Germany, in Ireland, in New England, in Old England, and wherever Presbyterianism has held sway, both pastors and parishes, in one terrific mass, have disowned the Trinity, and denied the divinity of JESUS. Now, Miss ——, let me beg you not to make yourself so unhappy about half a dozen men, who imagining that our Church bids fair to run the same course, are seeking refuge in Rome; but, if you must be unhappy, take up your lamentation over the thirty millions of Protestants going down this moment to the grave, and the fifty or one hundred millions, who have already gone, with the open denial on their lips of "Him who bought them with His blood." This was, however, a sad experiment with my parishioner. *She never forgave me.*

And if here and there amidst the general apostacy, the continental mind is seen returning to some dim perceptions of the truth, with what crudities of mysticism or fanaticism is the effort marred, how partial is the acknowledgement of ancient doctrine, how sceptical and mutilated the re-appropriation of the books of Scripture, how abandoned the mind to the *theologia pectoris*, as it has been termed, or the theology of sentiment, as the phrase imports. As the famished sailor, taken from a wreck, has lost the power of discerning wholesome and appropriate food, and impelled by blind hunger, seizes on the first nourishment that offers, so a German or Continental mind, thus waking out of infidelity, plunges at once, under his new impulses and new wants, into all the revelry of a wild and licentious divinity; or else, as Popery is the only other religion within his reach, flies to her bosom as a shelter from his own intolerable distractions; and we therefore hear without surprise, that the present family of Luther, for want of the purer Catholicity which Cromwell's descendant has found in England, and three hundred dissenting ministers have found to their heart's joy in America, have fled from the horrid and wild developments of Presbyterian metaphysics to the more genial bosom of the Papacy.

Having now seen that, as a Presbyterian, I was not in the Rock-founded Church, entitled, after the death of the Testator, to his gracious promise to be with her "until the end of the world," and that the gates of hell should not prevail against her, I felt a deep anxiety to quit the house thus fallen already, or else its last timbers shaking on the sand; but believing that the part of it in which I dwelt might "last my time," I had only resolution enough to introduce my children into a Church, already belting the earth, every where acknowledging her Lord, and now, as eighteen centuries ago, 'continuing steadfastly in the Apostles' doctrine and fellowship, and in breaking of bread, and in prayers." Yet I was unconsciously beginning to move in the middle path between Popery and Sectarianism—the too much and the too little in Christianity—toward what was now fast becoming the Church simultaneously of my affections and my understanding. An influence invisible attracted me on, a feeling unaccountable sustained me, that to go on would be safe. I inhaled already the fragrant air of a morning that my eyes had not yet seen: I beheld, though at a distance still, bright gleamings from the windows of a temple that my feet had not yet trodden.

ADVERTISEMENT.

PECULIAR causes, entirely beyond the control of the Author, have occasioned the irregularities and delays that have occurred in the publication of this work. A large portion of it has been written, also, during an absolute separation from books, aggravated by the loss of memoranda which the Author had with difficulty gathered, and found it impossible to replace. Errors in quotations or facts will gladly be corrected in subsequent editions.

F. S. M.

CHAPTER X.

A DREAM.

NOT more delusive is the worldling's hope that he may outwit the providence of God by hovering about the borders of the kingdom, so that when he shall see the approaching storm, and shall feel the earthly tabernacle giving way, he may make good his escape: than the confidence of pious individuals, that *their* portion of the Presbyterian Church shall not be overtaken by these consequences. As soon might the eye, by its vigilance, or the hand, by its vigor, expect to beat back the poison coursing through the veins of the corporeal system. There is a certain *vis a tergo*, as we have seen, invariably pressing, through every artery and channel of the Presbyterian body, on—on—on—to the terrible results that we have been considering. In vain do you resist—you who were formerly my brethren. Like the actor, poised upon a rope, or on a pillar's point, you will one day be weary of this continual effort to preserve your balance, and you will fall into the pit where your brethren are fallen. You know that misgivings constantly assail you, and that the hard things of your belief hang often painfully upon you, and that *you are conscious of this effort* to maintain your balance. Vain are your lamentations for the apostasies with which your Church has filled up the ranks of the Socinians; and as vain will be your exertions to prevent their recurrence in the future. *Naturam expellas furca, tamen usque recurrat.* As soon may you chain the death-dealing miasma, or hedge up the secret path of the pestilence, as check the progress of "private judgment," when, once upon the slope, you have let go the reins. Dash on the coursers must. Dash on the impetuous coursers will. There is no arrest till they have reached the bottom. When Calvin entered on his work, his heart said,

> "Jamque opus incepi, quod nec Jovis ira, nec ignes,
> Nec poterit ferrum, nec edax abolere vetustas."

It was a tower, whose steps were to lead earth's sons, in all future time, to heaven. But shibboleths and sibboleths have distracted the workmen; and what the fathers builded in their pride, the sons have in their folly destroyed. Is it not true that great numbers of your ministers, your Barneses and Skinners, your Stuarts and Taylors, and Bacons and Bushnells, ambitious only of a *nullius magistri* celebrity, are toiling to leave your theology better than they found it? Is it not true that, as an ill-taught child forgets to-day the story as he told it yesterday, and can never tell it the same way twice, so your doctrines, as expounded by your ministers, have never remained for fifty years the same? The last pastor in Dr. Mason's pulpit did not preach the preaching that did Dr. Mason, who forty years ago was the Cephas of Presbyterian Christianity. Nor does the present minister in Pearl-street teach or administer ordinances, as did the well-remembered McLeods and Romaines before him. The fatal leaven is leavening the lump, and the night-plant creeping stealthily beneath the walls. Already the destroying insect has deposited its egg upon your vines and olives, and the green things of to-day will be the withered things of to-morrow. Amidst it all, the Church, bright and yet brighter from the crucible of truth-telling time, "*sibi constans, semper eadem*," and judging with her ancient saints *verum non esse, quod variat*, tells now, and will tell for ever, the same simple, consistent story she told when she first went forth with the Eleven from the cross. What necessity there is laid upon you I know not. I only see results. Causes are hidden; effects are obvious. But do not suppose you can escape. Already you admire the exegesis of the Germans. Already their authors fill your libraries. Already your tone is lowered. Already you have learned not to hate; next you will begin to love. Go on with your experiments. At all hazards the majesty of "private judgment" is to be supported.

"What millions died, that Cæsar might be great!"

I fear your resistance to the Antichrist of the age will be short, and you will drop as a wounded bird into his hand. You may abjure the tyrant, but you cannot break his chain. You may have your moments when you would fling the specious cup of free-thinking to the earth, and bow before the faith of the ancients; but the thirst returns, and all is again at stake upon the supremacy of individual reason.

Here then is the sum of the matter. Every ecclesiastical system, not Episcopal, is, by virtue of the negation, Presbyterian. I look then over the whole Episcopal world—European, Asiatic, African, American—in the mountains of the East—beyond the deserts of Sahara—in the islands of the seas—in the snows of Siberia—in the farthest Indies—in the wilds of Australia, and of the Western Hemisphere—can I anywhere find a clergyman in this vast domain who would deny the supreme divinity or the redemption of Jesus Christ, or the direct and renovating influences of the Holy Ghost upon the hearts of men? No, not one.

Again, I look over the Presbyterian or Sectarian world—German, French, Dutch, Genevan, Scotch, Irish, English, Dane, Saxon, Prussian, American; everywhere Presbyterian, because everywhere disowning the order and authority of Bishops—how many pastors and how many flocks do I see, by whom the majesty of an everlasting Trinity, and the mystery of Redemption by the blood of Jesus, are now regarded as the exploded eccentricities of the half-emancipated Reformers? If I must answer my own question, I will say, from fifteen to twenty thousand such congregations, and from fifteen to twenty thousand such pastors!

There must, said I, be something in the two theories, and something in the providence of God, stamping the two systems with such opposite results.

If four-fifths of the Presbyterian world had been smitten with the plague or leprosy, paying no respect to the *cordon sanitaire*, or even to non-intercourse itself, we might have pronounced it the visitation of God. But for this blight upon the souls of men, we must look for some other cause; "for God tempteth no man, and no man when he is tempted may say, I am tempted of God." But either the tree has its seeds of death within itself, or else the afflatus of the serpent breathes death into its branches. Satan, finding that he could no longer prevent the Reformation, for which the heart of the whole Church was inwardly breaking, may have resolved to urge it on, on a principle that would make the last state worse than the first. That principle was every man's right to form a faith for himself. But human reason was an unlawful weapon for the purpose, and the blow aimed at "the beast" has recoiled fatally upon the men who dealt it. Not satisfied with driving the sellers of indulgences from the temple, they must needs pull down the temple also to the ground. Haman perishes by the instrument erected for Mordecai. Perillus burns in his own brazen bull. Popery lives to see Socinus exulting over Calvin. Wherever Presbyterianism *was*, Socinianism *is*. Lift up your eyes and see! *Ubi Troja fuit, jam seges!*

And as the kind reader has listened to my waking thoughts, I shall beg him now not to chide me for speaking a little in my sleep; for his own experience may have led him to observe that "the heart often wakes when the senses slumber."

Luther, when travailing with the birth of Protestantism, assures us repeatedly that he had dreams and visions, and personal encounters with the devil appearing to him in broad daylight, in a bodily shape. Melancthon saw, in a dream, a lone man, in the garb of a monk, thrusting his sickle into a boundless harvest, and was at last persuaded to join him, when, after the two had some time reaped together, a multitude of reapers came to help them in their labors; and to this dream is due, in part, the association of Melancthon with Luther at the beginning of the Reformation. Frederick, the renowned elector of Saxony, saw, in a dream, a monk, with a great pen that reached to Rome, and that wounded with its point the ears, and shook terribly the crest, of a *lion* that was there. Empires in vain tried to break the pen; it grew, and still grew, until out of it came a great number of pens. The elector then asked the monk to tell him where he got that pen. That pen, said the monk, is from the wing of a *goose* in Bohemia, a hundred years old. The reader should be reminded that the name of *Huss*, to whom the dream alludes, signifies *goose*, as *Leo*, the name of the Pope at the time, signifies *lion*. And this dream the elector, surnamed the Wise, who stood in the foreground of the German Reformation, has related as a reason for siding with Luther in his labors. And thus the three felt called from above to open the continental reformation. Let no admirers of the Reformers of Germany, therefore, despise my dream.

At a later day, the Puritans were singularly favored in this way, although the recent editions of such authors as Bunyan and Flavel, I have observed, suppress the remark-

16*

able relations contained in the older biographies. But it is no secret that Puritanism came in, as Popery had come in before, and as Mormonism has come in since, and as Swedenborgianism is endeavoring to come in now, under the cloak of inspiration, dreams, clairvoyance, and miracles. It was enough that a dweller in some cloister had seen the Mother of our Lord crowned and worshipped as the queen of heaven, to establish Mariolatry upon earth. Another had been favored with a letter from Saint "Peter and Mary, and the thrones and principalities of heaven," claiming universal jurisdiction and political supremacy for the Bishop of Rome; and thus was Pepin, the king of France, persuaded to crown the Pope with the titles of universal empire. Another had seen the Host bleeding in the Eucharist, to verify the dogma of transubstantiation. To another it was given to see souls, by virtue of the mass, escaping from the fires, to make good the claims and the profits of purgatory. Another had seen particular individuals admitted to the rights of saintship, while others had dreams, to indicate the place where their relics could be found for the adoration of the faithful. It was thus that many of the pretensions of Popery were privily brought in. In the same way the Puritans, Baptists, Quakers, Mormons, Swedenborgians, as every one familiar with the facts must know, relied upon dreams, and revelations, and impressions, to a most fearful extent, for their practices and innovations. Let no admirer of the Puritans, therefore, despise my dream.

There are among us whole communities, in which, even now, a conversion is regarded as certainly more edifying and complete, if enlivened by something bordering on the supernatural—dreams, voices, lights, smells, sounds, or sudden sensations and impressions. They have perhaps heard that Luther and his coadjutors, that Flavel and Bunyan and their brethren, that Tennant and Newton and their associates, and a host of others, have had wonderful dreams, or trances, or swoons, or ecstacies, as indubitable proofs of the divine approbation; and they leap to the conclusion that they must have them too. On this Procrustean bed of conversion, Mr. Belsham tells us that, when a youth, he stretched himself out to the extent prescribed in Doddridge's Rise and Progress, as thousands have been taught to do; and when exhaustion and reaction came on, in after years, he became a miserable prey to Socinianism and infidelity by turns. How often have we seen revival converts keeping journals of their frames and feelings and swoons and rhapsodies, laboring to work themselves into the exact experiences of some male or female model, until the effort wearies, and they fall away. It has been often observed, that if one attempt to imitate another, he will be more likely to copy the blemishes than the graces of his model. We have in such instances been often amusingly reminded of the piece of cracked china sent back to the celestial empire, that a whole service might be made according to the pattern, and which the celestials most scrupulously copied, even to *the crack*. And so with the journals, dreams, voices, impressions, and swoonings of model conversions; the very thing to be avoided runs through them all. They have become so interwoven with the new ideas of conversion, that the subject has been deemed worthy of grave consideration in Dr. Alexander's work on "Religious Experience," published under the sanction of the General Assembly. Without therefore disturbing the question, whether God "by dreams turneth man aside from his purpose," if I venture, in giving this history of my conversion, to tell my dream, or rather to open my dark saying, since I have such authorities and precedents, let no man despise me.

I and my father's house, and many of the people of our religion, were led away captive into the regions of Babylon.

And it was my custom to walk with a certain friend by the banks of the river Ulai, where we hanged a harp that we had, upon the willows that were there; and we spake often one to another of the place of our fathers' sepulchres, because it was desolate, and its hedges were broken down, and the landmarks of the ancient ones were carried away. And we saw that some of our brethren had set up in the plain of Dura, hard by the province of Babylon, an image of earth, washen over with gold, so that the simple folk took it to be gold; but the inner part was earth; only its feet were of brass, to trample and break in pieces. And the name of the image was EUREKA; and it had three faces. One face was of a man, with a high forehead, as one that understood dark sentences; and he held a cold, phosphoric torch in his hand, whereon was written, REASON; and three cries continually issued out of his mouth—No Superstition, No Mystery, No Creed. And the second face was of a strange woman, and her lips were smoother than oil; a head-dress was upon her head, and on it was written, LIBERTY; and a cup was in her hand; and three cries went day and night out of her mouth—No Kings, No Governments, No Dignities. And the third face was of a flying dragon, and he held a telescope to his eye, as if he saw something afar off; and on his wings was a scroll, whereon was written PROGRESS; and three cries, that shook the land continually, issued from his mouth—No Monopoly, No Property, No Inequality.

And a day was set when all the teachers of our religion should be assembled in Babylon; and I saw them entering through a hundred gates, multitudes, multitudes, from the morning until the going down of the sun. They came from Geneva and Wirtemberg, Montauban and Lyons, and the parts of Navarre and France; from Belfast and Ulster, and the parts of Ireland; from Cambridge and Boston, and the regions of New England; Prussians and Hollanders; Danes and Saxons; and the men of Heidelberg and Leipzig and Leyden and Berlin; they came as a great cloud over the land, and over the sea. And I saw among them men of lofty countenance, with their brow knit, as though some great thought occupied them; and they seemed as gods walking on the ground. Yet their words were the words of the humble and meek; for they said much concerning "parity," "despised governments," and "spake evil of dignities," and promised men "liberty." And between their eyes, upon their foreheads, where the fathers wore the sign of the cross, I saw that they had frontlets, and within the frontlets was written, "The Right of Private Judgment;" and they had every man a pair of balances in his hand, wherewith one might weigh a hair, and a bag of weights was in their girdles. And one whispered in my ear and said, "This is Gog and Magog."

Now I saw in my dream, that, when the assembly were set down, and there was silence, they brought in a Man, or one in the likeness of men; His head and His hairs were white like wool, and He was clothed with a garment down to the foot, and girded about the waist with a golden girdle, and a crown of gold was upon His head. And His coming was on this wise: if the sick saw Him, he was straightway healed of whatsoever sickness he had; if the leper heard His voice, immediately his flesh came on him like the flesh of a little child; if a tear from His eyes fell on any grave, the grave gave back its dead, and the widow's heart sang for joy; if His sandal touched the waters of the sea, its waves slept like an infant at His feet; if His shadow passed over the chains of a maniac, the chains immediately fell off, and the maniac came to himself; if but His spittle fell to the ground, the clay where it fell opened the eyes of the blind; if His fingers but touched the bread of the perishing, their loaves were immediately multiplied; and wherever the poor "saw the print of His shoe in the earth, there they coveted to set their foot too."

Then the Moderator of the Assembly rose up and said:—"Brothers, this is Jesus of Nazareth, gorgeously arrayed; but if you will handle Him and see, you will find, that He hath flesh and bones as one of us, that He hath slept and been hungry, that He hath thirsted and been weary, that He hath suffered and hath died the death of mortals. Yet Popery, that could make demi-gods of monks and hermits, hath made this man a God. For fifteen centuries, the world had been bowing at the bare mention of His name; and even our own forefathers, although they nobly refused to bow any longer at His name, nevertheless worshipped Him for a time in their hearts. Nay, it is not to be denied, that certain portions of our brethren worship Him still. Yet, there be many that would know of this learned and grave Assembly, whether He who on all hands is admitted to be a man, is at the same time God; and, in giving your response to many an aching heart, let not old prejudices influence you. Give traditions to the winds, that have time to attend to them. Forget the legends of the nursery. Let not the opinions of early Christians and Apostles terrify you. *Show to the world that you can think for yourselves.* Remember your name is *Protestant;* your motto, the Right of Private Judgment; your guide, the light of Reason; your atmosphere, Liberty; your watchword, Progress. But I will first examine Him, for it is not right that you should judge a man before you hear him." So he asked Him these questions:

Who art thou?

"No man knoweth who the Father is, but the Son; neither knoweth any man who the Son is, but the Father."

What is thy name?

"Emanuel; which being interpreted is, God with us."

Whose son art thou?

"The Son of God, the Only Begotten of the Father."

Art thou not the son of David?

"David in the Spirit doth call me Lord; how am I then his son? I am the Root and the Offspring of David."

How old makest thou thyself? thou art not yet fifty years old?

"Abraham rejoiced to see my day; he saw it, and was glad; before Abraham was, I am."

When wast thou born?

"I am Alpha and Omega, the beginning and the ending, the First Born of every creature; even as I said, O Father, glorify thou me with the glory which I had with thee before the world was."

What is thy rank?

"Ye call me Master and Lord, and ye say well, for so I am; on my vesture and my thigh my name is written, KING OF KINGS AND LORD OF LORDS."

Where is thy dwelling?

"Where I was before. I came forth from the Father, and am come into the world; again I leave the world, and go to the Father."

What sign showest thou that we may believe?

"If I do not the works of God, believe me not; for what things soever the Father doeth, these doeth the Son likewise."

Who made all things?

"All things were made by me, and without me was not any thing made that was made; I was in the world, and the world was made by me, and the world knew me not;" "for by me were all things created, that are in heaven, and that are in earth, visible and invisible, whether they be thrones, or dominions, or principalities, or powers; all things were created by me and for me, and I am before all things, and by me all things consist."

Wilt thou then show us the Father, and it sufficeth us?

"Have I been so long time with you, and yet have ye not known me? He that hath seen me, hath seen the Father."

Dost thou then make thyself equal with God?

"I and my Father are one."

How long dost thou make us to doubt? What wilt thou have us to do? Tell us plainly.

"That all men should honor the Son, even as they honor the Father."

Then an old man, a hundred years old, who sat not far from "Him in the likeness of men," and whose head was white so that the snow could not whiten it, rose up, and leaning on his staff, he said: Brethren, to me, who am a child of other days, it seemeth strange that there should be any question concerning this man, whence He is.

I grant you, that He hungered and ate; that He thirsted, and drank; that He was weary, and slept. Many of His first followers found it more difficult to believe Him man than God, and were led into an opinion that His body was an appearance, or phantom, and quoted for this opinion His being "*in form and fashion as a man.*" The writings of John combat this very opinion, in saying, that "every spirit that confesseth not that Jesus is come *in the flesh*, is not of God."

I grant you, then, that He was flesh and blood; nor can we spare a single proof of the delightful fact; but I ask you to tell me why this fact is so often and so strongly stated in the Scriptures. It is nowhere said, that Paul, or Peter, or John, "was made flesh and dwelt among us;" or that Esaias, or David, or Moses, "came in the flesh," or "was made in the likeness of men." But incessant pains are taken to impress us with the fact, that He of whom we speak was "born of a woman," and "took on Him the nature of men," and "was made flesh and dwelt among us," and was actually "*seen of angels.*" To me the proofs of His Humanity are the proofs of His Divinity.

I grant you, that He wept and suffered; that He groaned in spirit and was troubled; that He suffered a desertion which martyrs never knew; that He endured an agony which martyrs never felt; that He was baptized with sweat and blood that never flowed from the flesh of martyrs; that He died amidst a darkness that martyrs never saw. But I expect you to explain why apostles and a hundred millions of their followers may pour out their blood upon the earth as unnoticed as the rain, while, among all deaths before or after, the death of JESUS CHRIST stands out alone, with a virtue that a universe of martyrs and an ocean of their blood could not possess? Read the testament of the Testator, and mark how often, and in what amazing terms, the blood of Christ is named. Nay, in an hour of deep humility, when He washed His servants' feet, humble and meek though He was, He commanded that, as the streaming altar, four thousand years, and in a thousand lands, had pointed the nations forward to His death, so the red CUP on the altar still should point us for ever backward to His blood. And while this was the absorbing theme on earth, if you will believe His servant John, he saw in heaven a Lamb as it had been slain, the only Being in the universe that had carried into heaven the vestiges of suffering, while prostrate thrones and principalities did their unwearying homage to the Lamb.

Have you never observed in Scripture, how an immeasurable gulf is spread between the Creator and the creature, to prevent the possibility of creature or man-worship? But with respect to Jesus Christ, when the world had now been waiting, and the whole creation groaning, through forty centuries, for the Seed of the woman to bruise the serpent's head, a pomp and circumstance attend Him, eclipsing the visions of the prophets. A star is born at His birth; a sun expires at His death; and the choirs of the angels that sang and shouted together when man was "made in the likeness

17

of God," sang in a yet sweeter strain when God was made "in the likeness of men." The natural world, with its winds and its seas, obeys Him; the world celestial, with Moses and Elias and its angels, ministers around Him; the dark infernal world falls at His feet, and cries, "Art Thou come to torment us before the time?" For three hundred years, the very Jews disputed not these facts, but attributed them to Beelzebub, or to the Great Name stolen from the temple. Tell me, if you can, a name by which God is known, that the Scriptures do not challenge for Christ. Tell me, if you can, a work of God, even to the creation of the Universe, that the Scriptures do not ascribe to Christ. Tell me of a heaven, if you can, where the Scriptures do not represent the high and happy myriads as paying Him their highest worship. That this should be the case at all I call upon you to explain. That it should be done without one word of caution against mistaking Him for God, I ask you to account for. And that it should be done, where the Scriptures well know the tendencies of the world to man-worship, and the belief of the world that gods had appeared in human form, and that the greatest of these Avatars was yet to come, is a problem I *demand* of you to solve.

But yourselves have heard His answers. Tell me, are they the answers of one who wishes to be remembered as a man, or as a God? Yet they are the answers of one meek and lowly of heart, who gave His back to the smiters, and hid not His face from shame and spitting, who washed the feet of the fishermen, and dipped in the dish with Judas, who pressed the cross to His bosom, and for a universe of crowns would not have pretended without right to the glory of the Father. When they of Lystra fell at the feet of Paul and Barnabas, to worship them, they ran in among the people, and rent their clothes, and cried "Sirs, why do ye these things? we also are men of like passions with you;" but Jesus did not lift up from the earth the women that "held him by the feet and worshipped Him." When Cornelius fell down to worship at the feet of Peter, "Peter took him up, saying, I myself also am a man;" but when the same Peter fell down to worship at the feet of Jesus, crying, "Depart from me, for I am a sinful man, O Lord," Jesus did not raise him from his knees. When John fell down before the angel to worship him, the bright angel raised him up and said, "See thou do it not, for I am thy fellow-servant, and of thy brethren the prophets;" but when the same John, with the eleven, fell "wondering and worshipping at the feet of Jesus," Jesus neither reprimanded nor forbade. In all the Scriptures there is not one word, to put the world upon its guard. And the coming of Christ, instead of destroying idolatry, has restored and fortified it, according to yourselves, through the space of twenty centuries; while the only nation that has taken ground against the idolatry, is torn from its sanctuaries, and scattered to the winds. Six hundred years ago, a devout Rabbi exclaimed, "I would fain learn, out of the law and the prophets, why we are thus smitten with this long captivity, which I may call the perpetual anger of God. For it is now above a thousand years since we were carried away captive by Titus; and yet our fathers, who worshipped idols, and killed the prophets, and cast the law behind their backs, were punished only with seventy years' captivity, and were then brought home again; but, for us, there is no end of our calamities, nor do the prophets give signs of any."

And what have you to oppose to all this reasoning? Only that you have discarded mysteries, and will believe nothing that you cannot comprehend. You will not acknowledge the Infinite, because he is infinite—the Incomprehensible, because he is incomprehensible—God, *because he is GOD!* For my part, I adore Him, *because* I cannot comprehend Him. A being *I* could comprehend with my understanding would no more be God than the idol I could comprehend within my arms. Ye say it is the province of reason to account for facts; account to me, then, for the facts I have adduced concerning the meekest of the sons of men; and beware lest, in escaping from a single fact beyond your comprehension, you do not involve yourselves in labyrinths out of which reason cannot light you. It is the province of reason to discover truth, not to create it. Ye talk of Liberty, as if liberty consisted in denying and defying truth. If to believe that two and two are four is to surrender our liberties, or is to prevent our progress, then are we all yet slaves, and only the brutes are free. And are we no longer to believe that two and two make four, because it is an old opinion, or because the Papists have believed it? No! Let *Truth* be wedded to *Liberty;* then will the healthy progeny be *Progress.* Ask not with Pilate, "What is truth?" and, like Pilate, turn away and go out; but weigh the answers that ye have heard Him give. To use, with slight variation, the words of one whom you admire, and who confesses that he "had his moments of conviction,"*—"If the answers of Socrates were those of a philosopher, the answers of Jesus are those of a God." Even as one of your own poets† has said, "If ever God was man, or man God, Jesus Christ was both." I therefore give my sentence, that "THIS IS THE TRUE GOD AND ETERNAL LIFE."

Then a young man, of exceeding beauty, whose locks were like the raven's, and his forehead white like the lily, and his cheek the color of the summer rose, and none could perceive that it was the hectic pencilling of a deep disease, stood up and said:—Brethren, it is one of our principles, and is now getting to be better understood, that "man is not responsible for his belief;" and therefore, I have heard the venerable father patiently. But, I have weighed his reasonings, and

* Rousseau. † Byron.

although they appear to have consistency and fervor, I find them to be but exhalations and mists from the cells and cloisters of the dark ages. For me, I rejoice to say, with one styled "evangelical," that "I know nothing of those ages which knew nothing." We live in the happier days of Light, Liberty, and Progress. We have carried all the outworks of Popery; to-day, we take the citadel. That Jesus was in advance of His countrymen and times, or that He stands, if you please, "in the foremost list of those true heroes who have died in the glorious martyrdom of Liberty, braving torture, contempt, and poverty, in the cause of suffering humanity,"* many of you will admit. But do not tell us that He was God, because the Church through a long age of ignorance and tyranny believed it, for that, to an enlightened mind, is reason for discarding it. Do not tell us, that the Apostles worshipped Him and believed Him to be God, as the Hindoos believe in their Avatars; for if the dogma be absurd, we have better facilities for detecting that absurdity than had the fishermen of Galilee. Do not tell us, that Jesus himself, feeling himself far in advance of His age and nation, believed himself that a God dwelt in Him; for of this we have the means of more dispassionately judging than had the carpenter of Nazareth. We have long since agreed to break the spell of superstition, creed, and dogma, and to believe those truths alone that Reason alone can reach. "He that will not reason is a bigot; he that cannot reason is a fool; he that dare not reason is a slave." Our fathers took the name of Protestant, and did nobly in their days; let us add new lustre to their name, and do as nobly in ours. What they began, let us finish; they began by not bowing at the Name, let us finish by not submitting to the Thing. They began by banishing from men's eyes the symbol of atonement; let us finish by banishing from men's minds the dogma of the Cross.

* Shelley.

Our watchword is Progress; but Progress we shall never make, until we shall have burst the chains that have bound humanity these sixty centuries. We must throw off the whole encumbering and entangling load at once. Jesus was Messiah, if you please; and the inspiration and the developments of Nature dwelt largely in him; but there have been other Messiahs, and there are Messiahs still to come; for nature hath understanding, and knoweth when to throw off decay, as a tree throweth off its dead limbs and leaves; the whole creation travaileth in pain; and the womb of our mother earth, made fruitful by the Spirit of Nature, is pregnant with the apostles of her own regeneration. I give my sentence, then, that Jesus was God, only as the Soul of the Universe, which breathes in all things, made Him a partaker at once of her divinity and of her agony for the world's amelioration. But we do not need the individual Messiah any more. The people have their redemption in their hands. The Spirit of Nature has kindled in their hearts an inspiration that many waters cannot quench. There is an afflatus upon the nations, not to be mistaken, inspiring them with the same simultaneous thought, impelling them to the same enrapturing goal. The past is hopeless, and belongs to others; the future with "hope's flowing urn" is ours. Judaism made its experiment, and with its iron age is gone; Christianity has made also its experiment, and its age of brass is departing. The age of gold now glitters in our eyes. I am no prophet, and claim only to be a sharer of the inspiration with which the breast of the nations is swelling, when I utter the bursting conviction, that as Christianity emerged from Judaism, so out of the carcass of this gigantic worm, in its turn, a new and bright and glorious Trinity, of Reason, Liberty, and Progress, is about to rise and scatter upon earth, from its bright wings, the dew of a celestial morning, the light of an unclouded day, the magnificence of a true millennium.

So when the youth, who spake partly in the New-England tongue and partly in the German, had done speaking, many of the multitude cried out, "Messiah the second!" and threw garlands at his feet. But many did not approve the deed of them.

And after there had been no small dissension, one rose and said, Brethren, ye should have hearkened unto me. Catholics teach dogmas; Protestants, as the august title imports, should be contented with negations. We may never be agreed if we attempt to determine who Jesus was, or what was the extent and nature of His inspiration. But the question before us, as I conceive, requires us, not affirmatively but negatively, to say what Jesus Christ was *not*. If then you are principally agreed that He was not *God*, let us not lose time on a barren dogma, but settle the question, as Protestants, negatively, and proceed to those matters of practical importance that are yet before us.

And the saying pleased the whole multitude, and they held up their balances and weighed the matter, and gave their voices that Jesus should be worshipped as God no more.

Then the old man, that spake at the beginning, called for a basin, and washed his hands, and said—"Now have the evil days come, when I may say I have no pleasure in them; henceforth the grasshopper is a burden, and the sun, and the light, and the moon, and the stars are darkened. Alas, that I should see the day! The glory is departed! The ark is taken! Would that the silver cord were loosed, and the golden bowl were broken!" And with that he fell backward, and gave up the ghost.* And I saw certain come around him, and they carried him out, and said, Let us die with him; and they that went out were for the most part

* A few years ago, the King of Holland appointed to the highest theological chair in his kingdom an individual of the new German school; and when the fact was reported to a very aged Professor, who had survived a better day, the old man, like Eli, fell back in his chair, exclaiming, "Then Christianity is done for."

superannuated men, and were chiefly from the parts of Scotland, and, as I was comforted to see, from the land of my own nativity.

But when the multitude gave their voices that He should be worshipped as God no more, I beheld a sight that but to remember almost turns me into stone; His hands bled again in the palms, and blood issued out from His feet and from His side, and I saw blood running down from His temples to the ground, and the crown which I saw on His head turned of itself into a crown of thorns, and Jesus, without any touching Him, was extended on a cross, and one Ananias caught His blood in a napkin. Then I remembered it was written, "THEY HAVE CRUCIFIED THE SON OF GOD AFRESH." Then my spirit went from me, and I fell on my face and desired to die, but could not, and a horror of great darkness came over me, and it seemed that the mountains fell on me; and one came and touched me, and said, Brother, it is a dream, yet the dream is certain, and the thing is true, and I am sent to tell thee. Our brethren have almost everywhere "denied the Lord, that bought them with His blood." Remember how we spake together, when I was with you, and with our sisters in the flesh, seeing and wondering whereunto all this would grow. And with that he wiped my eyes with a handkerchief, and said, Weep not; only come out of her; for "it is an Antichrist, that denieth the Father and the Son." Then I saw an angel descend upon earth, covered with sackcloth, and crape was on his wings, and tears fell from his eyes like a great rain upon the earth, and he cried with a voice that shook the hills and caused the curtains of the land to tremble, Woe, woe, woe to the inhabiters of the earth, and of the sea; the times are well nigh ripe; that which hath let is taken out of the way, and the earth hath made herself ready; the Incarnation of Evil is at hand; now "shall that Wicked be revealed;" behold, it is at the doors! And while I lingered, my brother, who came to me at the first, laid hold upon my hand, and upon the hand of others of my father's house, and led me into a path that went over the great river Euphrates, for the river was dried up, and I could see, at a great distance, that the path I was in led toward the city of Jerusalem.

Then, many days after, as it seemed in my dream, I stood upon the Mount of Olives, and my feet were covered with the dust of my journey; and one whispered and said, Thou shalt see the Bride, the Lamb's wife, to-day, and the virgins that stand round about her; the King's daughter is all glorious within, her clothing is of wrought gold, and she shall be brought unto the King in raiment of needlework; thou shalt see it with thine eyes; only thou hast no right to enter through the gates, for thy feet are not washen, and thy garments are not changed. And I saw, upon Mount Zion, the holy city; and the length and the breadth of it were equal, and harmony was in its proportions. Its walls were of jasper, and were laid on twelve foundations, and in them were the names of the apostles, for on apostles only could the walls of the city of God be built. And the city had twelve gates; on the north three gates, on the east three gates, on the south three gates, and on the west three gates; and each several gate was of one pearl; and the three gates were the Trinity, through which, by baptism, we must enter the habitations of Zion. And as I beheld, a great multitude passed by, and upon their foreheads I saw the sign of the cross, by which I knew that they were Catholics; and they were clothed in fine linen, and by this I knew that they were priests. But, though their number was so great, yet order prevailed among them, and each appeared to know and to keep his place. And they were of three orders; for it is meet, said my interpreter, that the Three that bear record in heaven should have, as They have had from the days of

Moses, in the grace of the One Priesthood, three to bear witness on earth. Thus they were of three orders, and the dress of one order was not like the dress of another order; for so I knew them by their dress. And they were divided into companies, and the overseers of the companies had two staves, one they called Beauty, and the other they called Bands, to feed the flock; and they had mitres upon their heads; only, on the head of one, I saw a tiara, unlike the mitres on the heads of his brethren; and he that had the tiara claimed, when they came within the city, to sit above his brethren that had the mitres, which when his brethren that had the mitres saw, they said it had not been so from the beginning, and communed together and were sad.

And the priests that I saw were men of every tongue and color and nation of the earth. And when I would know the meaning of this multitude, my interpreter said, Six days, a day for a thousand years, have passed heavily away; the Sabbath, to give rest to a troubled world, is near; and these are the sons of Antipas, the faithful Witness, going up to the Sabbatical or Seventh Council of the universal Church, to bear testimony, for the last time, to that which was from the beginning, is now, and ever shall be, even to Him, which is, and which was, and which is to come.

And when the multitude came up to the Mount of Olives, and the city was now full in their view, and they could see its streets of gold and its ivory palaces, I heard them sing a Song of Degrees, which they sang by course, and their singing was like the chanting of the cherubim, and thus they sang as they went:—

Beautiful! Beautiful! Beautiful for situation, the joy of the whole earth, is Mount Zion; on the sides of the north, the city of the great King!

For there are set thrones of judgment: the thrones of the house of David.

O go your way into His gates with thanksgiving, and into His courts with praise: be thankful unto Him, and speak good of His name.

Our feet shall stand within thy gates: O Jerusalem.

As we have heard, so have we seen: Jerusalem is builded as a city that is at unity in itself.

Walk about Zion, and go round about her; tell ye the towers thereof.

Mark ye well her bulwarks, consider her palaces; that ye may tell it to the generation following.

Peace be within thy walls, and plenteousness within thy palaces; they shall prosper that love thee.

Glory be to the Father, and to the Son, and to the Holy Ghost:

As it was in the beginning, is now, and ever shall be, world without end. Amen.

Thus they went into the gates of the city, which opened of themselves to let them in. And when they were set down in a place appointed, each one according to his rank, I saw in my dream that one came in, in the form a servant, and sat before the council. And lo! upon His back the furrows wherewith He had been ploughed, and His face was marred with shame, and spitting, and the marks of blows that men had given Him; and there was a crown of thorns upon His head; His eyes were held with a napkin, and His robe was taken from Him; and there were prints of sharp iron in His hands, and in His feet, and in His side, and He seemed as one that treadeth in the wine-press; and one said, *Ecce Homo!* And one said, What are these wounds in thy hands? And He said, Those with which I was wounded in the house of my friends. And another said, Wherefore art Thou red in thine apparel, and thy garments like him that treadeth in the wine-press? And He said, I have trodden the wine-press alone, and of the people there was none with me.

Then understood I that it was the Lord. And when I saw the staves of the overseers, and the mitres, and the priests' vestments, I shut my eyes, and put my fingers in my ears, lest I should see or hear some fresh indignity done to Him; for I had heard always, from a child, that these were the marks of Antichrist. But when the council saw Him, they cried out, above the space of an hour, "Oh! it is the King in His beauty!" And they fell upon the earth, and became as dead men. Then they that had garments spread them in the way, and they that had mitres cast them down at His feet, and he that had the tiara threw it to the earth among the mitres before Him, and they cried one to another, above the space of an hour, "Lo! this is our God! we have waited for Him, and He will save us: This is the Lord; we have waited for Him, we will rejoice and be glad in His salvation!" Then all the bells of the city began to ring, and the "streets were filled with trumpeters and players upon instruments," and the light of the city was clear as crystal, and the children in the streets cried, "Hosanna! Hosanna! Hosanna!" and the stones in the streets joined in the cry, and all the trees of the field clapped their hands. Then He in the form of a servant, looking on them with a look I never beheld until then, said, "It is expedient for you that I go away, but I will come to you again." And with that, as He breathed on them, and said, "Lo, I am with you alway, even to the end of the world," He was caught up into heaven. And I saw ten thousand times ten thousand, and thousands of thousands, casting their crowns at His feet, and they rested not day nor night, falling down and crying,—"Worthy is the Lamb that was slain, to receive honor, and glory, and might, and dominion, and riches, and power, and blessing!"

After this I saw that the whole council ate bread and drank wine together, and they gave each other the kiss of peace, and they washed each other's feet. And again there was great joy in the city, and the streets were filled with trumpeters, and the bells rang so that the nations in the uttermost parts of the earth heard them, and came running to the gates of the city. And when the angels at the gates had washed them, and set "the sign of the Son of Man" in their foreheads, they let them in. And when they were entered into the city, I saw that some went forth to meet them and said, "Welcome, brothers!" And they said, "All hail!" and fell upon their necks and kissed them. And they said, "Brothers, whence come ye?" And some answered and said, "From the regions of Babylon, which is by interpretation, Confusion, are we come;" and with that they broke out into a song, with timbrels and dances,—"Our soul is escaped as a bird out of the snare of the fowlers; the snare is broken, and we are escaped."

So "I awoke, and wished myself among them."

CHAPTER XI.

SCHISM.

As in a circle a thousand radii meet at a single point, so truth—I mean moral truth—is central in its nature, and may be approached by a variety of avenues. A truth in mathematics can usually be reached but by *one* line of reasoning, and depends essentially on the link that immediately precedes it in the chain. But, in the moral world, an important truth is reached by many and different lines of reasoning—no one of them, in the present obscuration of our moral nature, demonstrative in itself alone, because God never intended that truths so high should hang by a single thread—but all of them, when pursued, leading by various routes to one result, and producing the same conviction in varieties of mind, by varieties of reasoning. How surpassingly grand, on this account, are the demonstrations of providence, of God, of immortality, of revelation, of judgment! We reach the truth upon these points by a line of reasoning, and we wonder and adore. Again we go back, and by another route, we find ourselves at the same goal, and our wonder increases. Once more we set out, and still the new route conducts us to the old result, and new wonder fills our hearts. Away, then, with the boast of your exact sciences, that coldly compel belief; and bind upon living limbs the icy links of their resistless chain! Away with the infidelity that demands for a generous, freeborn mind *such* links and *such* a chain, in proof of God, of Immortality, of Christianity! And away with the frigid sectarism, that asks of Episcopacy or Catholicity to produce such a line of reasoning! No, she has no such chain to bind you to her altars. She has different lines of reasoning for the mind, and different lines of feeling for the heart, by which those who have either mind or heart may see or may feel their way to the centre, which rests in tranquillity, one and the same, while all is motion and commotion around it. If Episcopacy be truth, like Immortality, like Christianity, like the Divinity of Jesus, it may not have its one, cold, convincing, and *resistless* ray, but it will emit its beams in all directions, and those beams, bright and warm, may be traced, by either heads or hearts, like so many radiations, to the common centre.

I have conducted the reader already along different paths that led me to a particular and central truth, and perchance he has expected me, ere this, to loose my girdle, unbind my sandals, throw away my staff, and rest from the toils and fatigues of the journey. But if the refuge we have found be one that the King has prepared, there are yet other roads and highroads that will lead his people up to it—let us then set out upon another:—

UNITY is a holy reality, consecrated by the more than human prayer, "that they all may be *one*, as Thou, Father, art in Me, and I in Thee, that they also may be *one* in Us, that the world may believe that Thou hast sent Me." It was cherished as a holy mystery in the hearts of the Apostles, who dwelt continually on the oneness of all things in Christ—one Lord, one faith, one God, one baptism, one hope, one body, one spirit, one Shepherd, one fold,—a vine, a tree, a temple, a household, a bride, a Church—the Church at Colosse—the Church at Corinth—the Church at Ephesus—the Church of Sardis, although "ready to die," still "*the Church* of Sardis"

—the Church of Pergamos, although corrupted with "the doctrine of Balaam and of the Nicolaitanes," still "*the Church* of Pergamos"—the Church of Thyatira, although "suffering that woman Jezebel to seduce her servants to commit fornication, and to eat things sacrificed to idols," still "*the Church* of Thyatira"—the Church at Philadelphia—the Church at Philippi—the Church at Rome—the Church of God—"that there should be *no schism* in the *body*." What if these Churches, instead of being hampered with the apostolic rod and staff of *unity*, had enjoyed the *liberty* of the "nineteenth century!" How soon the remedy could have been applied by separating from a Church thus paralysed and darkened by Balaam, Nicolas, and Jezebel!

Come with me now, kind reader, to a country-village—of some sixty families—on the borders of the Potomac, within the shadow of the National Capitol. The spot is sacred to me: on its green turf I gambolled in boyhood; from its atmosphere I imbibed my first ideas of Christianity; in its neighborhood still live the living whom I revere; and under its sod are sleeping the dead whom I love. As we enter this village, by a southern road, we see on an elevation at our right a Romanist chapel, that was never completed, and is already going to decay, and a fallen cross lying and rotting in an open church-yard. As we proceed, we see on our right a Methodist meeting-house upon an open common; and, at the same time, on our left, an Episcopal church, to whose green pastures not only the sheep of the fold have freedom of access, but the goat, and the ox, and all cattle are grazing at its doors. A little farther on, the Presbyterians have their place of worship, and on the western borders of the village is a tabernacle for the Baptists, and another for the Campbellites; besides the public court-house, in which visitors and "distinguished preachers" of other and yet other sects continually let down their nets; six churches, six ministers to be provided for, and not one of them "living by the gospel," as the Lord ordained; six schools to be supported, if each should carry out the parochial system, or otherwise the vital union of Christianity with education to be given up; a handful of people not "dwelling together in unity," but disunited, disaffected, and now and then devoured by jealousies, and worshipping by half-dozens in a place aching to the eyes, and freezing to the hearts of ministers and people, and a standing byeword to them that hang "around the corners of the streets."

Far from this home of my childhood, I now invite my reader to accompany me, where I have several times been, upon the deep. Here, in our noble ship, is a broad and well-swept floor, kept bright by the hands of men. Above us is the blue vaulted roof, made without hands. On every side the sea is pouring its music into its Maker's ear, and the "very fish leaps up and means His praise." The emblems of Eternity and God are all around us. It is the holy hour of sunset; even the skeptic is devout; and the child at home, taught by maternal love that God made the stars, and watching from its window to see the first evening gem launched from its Maker's hand upon the sky, cries, "Mother! Oh mother! God has made a star!" Was ever place, was ever time, more suitable for praise and prayer? The heathen are at their rites; the Mussulmen at their devotions; the Romanists at their vespers. Where is *our* censer, and where *our* altar? And what has thrust them into a corner? I answer, SCHISM.

Once more, I beg the reader to go with me to the new settlements in our Western wilderness. *We* cannot, like Columbus and his men, go forth and plant the Cross, and, before we have climbed up into our beds, find a habitation for the God of Jacob. Whole years pass on; and other years roll by; and still years roll, and yet there is not unity enough to give either Church or sect dignity enough to rise above the miserable worship of the log-cabin or the school-house. And what fills all the West with this portentous difficulty? And what keeps thousands of the Western clergy, of all denominations, pensioners upon the East themselves, and beggars for congregations that feel no longer the least remorse or shame? I answer, SCHISM.

But if neither the sea nor the wilderness be a refuge, let us seek it among people that "lie in the region of the shadow of death." But why seek we the living among the dead? The shrewd mandarin exultingly demands, "How can I agree with you, when you are not agreed among yourselves? One of your missionaries tells me that my children are not capable of the grace of baptism; but you assure me that they are even more capable of grace than an adult. One would convince me that your bishops are to be revered; another teaches us that they are impostors. Some of you tell us there is a place of everlasting burning; but others tell us there is no such thing. One says your Bible is inspired; another affirms that it is not. Your Bible does not settle the questions that divide you. Your best men are not agreed." And while he is yet speaking, the intellectual Brahmin takes up the argument; "Some of you tell us, that Jesus is the true God, and that we must worship Him; but I have seen others of your missionaries, who declare, that to worship Him is as much idolatry as to worship Juggernaut. Which are we to believe? Have you no authority, no tradition, no watchword, no priesthood, to perpetuate in unbroken line the fact on this tremendous question?" O Schism! what a murderer thou art!

Look over the land, and behold the multitude of sects—their intermitting fits of feverish zeal—their jealousies and strifes—their dwarfish and dilapidated temples—their separate and weakened action in charities, and schools, and missions—each professing a purer doctrine than his neighbor's—each differing from each in his modes of worship, from the sealed lips of the Quaker, to the open countenance of the Methodist—from him of Pennsylvania, who has no sacraments, to him of Rome, who has seven—Methodist Episcopal, Methodist Primitive, Methodist Protestant, Methodist Radical, Presbyterian Old School, Presbyterian New School, Presbyterian Associate, Presbyterian Reformed, Presbyterian Covenanter, Presbyterian Relief, Presbyterian United, Presbyterian Cumberland, Presbyterian Scotch, Presbyterian Independent, Presbyterian Seceder, Dutch Reformed, Baptist, Baptist Campbellite, Baptist Sandamanian, Baptist Christian, Seventh-Day Baptists, Church-of-God Baptists, Seven-Principle Baptists, Free-Communion Baptists, Free-Will Baptists, Hard-Shell Baptists, Soft-Shell Baptists, Ironsides Baptists, Little-Children Baptists, Glory-Alleluia Baptists, Unitarian, Irvingites, Congregationalist Orthodox, Congregationalist Independent, Lutheran, Lutheran Evangelical, German Evangelical, German Reformed, Quaker Orthodox, Quaker Hicksite, Restorationists, Universalists, Perfectionists, Swedenborgians, Latter-Day Saints, Come-Outers, Live-Forevers, &c., &c., &c.—*Eheu, jam satis!* cries the reader; *Eheu, jam satis!* cries the writer.

As I give the foregoing catalogue entirely from memory, there are probably as many more that I have omitted. A gentleman informs me, that, travelling in the West a few years since, he saw on one occasion about a thousand men and women in a grove, rolling hoops, flying kites, playing ball, shooting marbles, leaping, running, wrestling, boxing, rolling and tumbling in the grass, the women caressing dolls, and the men astride of sticks for horses, and the whole company intently engaged in all the sports of childhood. At last he ventured to ask what it meant. They told him that they were the little children to whom the Lord had promised

His kingdom, and affected some surprise, that he seemed not to have known that it was written, "Except ye be converted, and become as *little children*, ye shall in no case enter into the kingdom of God." He told them that that was true; that it was very well to imitate the virtues of childhood, but not its foibles; that the Apostle had said, "in malice be ye children, but in understanding be men;" and that this extraordinary conduct was the folly of childhood, without the immaturity of childhood to excuse it. "We are not surprised that you think so," they replied; "for we are a reproach unto our neighbors, and they of our acquaintance do hide themselves from us; but we are willing to suffer persecution for the kingdom of heaven's sake; for these things are hidden, as it is written, from the wise and prudent, and are revealed unto *babes*." My friend now found that they were persons not to be outdone in the quotation of Scripture, and as he related the facts, I could not but exclaim within myself, Oh, the luxury of private judgment, and the blessedness of exegesis! He afterwards learned that they were a numerous sect, calling themselves Little-Children Baptists; and the reader may see in the histories of the Reformation, and even in D'Aubigné himself, that this sect in the West are the genuine successors of the original Baptists in Germany, Switzerland, and England, who ran many of them naked and half-naked, in the pretended innocence of childhood, through the streets, rolling and tumbling, and affecting all the sports of children, on the ground that the truth is revealed by the Spirit to babes, throwing the word of God into the fire, exclaiming, says D'Aubigné, "The letter killeth, but the Spirit giveth life." It is well known that the origin of the Quakers, as well as of some other sects, now grown to be quite respectable, was equally extravagant. But wherever the Episcopacy was respected, the Reformation was conducted to its dignified and glorious consummation without any such exhibitions of extravagance. And so it has ever been, from the Baptists to the Mormons; they are carried about of the winds, and in approaching them with common sense, you but break your lance against a mill. You cannot reason, for they are mailed in Scripture; if you quote Scripture, they tell you, as *you* tell Episcopalians who adduce Scripture for the church, and for her order and her sacraments, that you have not the Spirit.

> "Alchymists may doubt
> The shining gold their crucible gives out;
> But faith, fanatic faith, once wedded fast
> To some fond falsehood, hugs it to the last."

Not very long ago, two clergymen of the Episcopal Church, travelling in Kentucky, called at a farmer's house, and not finding him at home, waited awhile for his return, as night was near, and they had occasion to claim his hospitality. By and bye the farmer came home, and as he rode into the yard, or rather after he had dismounted, *sang* out to his man, in a most extraordinary tone:

> "Go, give that horse some ears of corn,
> He has'nt had any since I've been gone,
> Glory Alleluia!"

Then leading the two gentlemen into the house, he said:

> "Come in, my friends, and take something to eat;
> Go, Katy, go, cook them a portion of meat;
> Glory Alleluia!"

In this manner the travellers were condemned to hear every thing done up in "the language of Canaan," and sung to the same everlasting tune or tone, with the perpetual Alleluia, until the next morning effected their release. They differed from their Little-Children brethren about the nature of regeneration, holding it to be an outpouring of the Spirit, whereby those who were born again were inspired, like the prophets, with the language of poetry. They were numerous in the country, and went by the name of the Glory-Alleluia Baptists. And yet we are to believe that all this is better than to have remained in the one fold of the Episcopal Church, which would in that case have been able to unfold her bright banner, with the *Agnus Dei*, in every vale and village of the West!

It is time to meet the questions—Who is the mother of all these sects? and—Who is the father that begat them? The father that begat them, is the unbridled lust of private judgment; the mother that bare them, is Presbytery, who has carried them in her womb, and nourished them from her breasts. If Presbytery had never lived, then these had never been. *Episcopacy has not brought one of them into the world.* They are all the living generations of Presbyterianism; and other children she has had, even as many more, but they are dead; and there is every indication, in the throes and perils of the body, that others are yet to come.

And if from wholesale sects, we pass to individual fancies and opinions, where "every one hath a Psalm," (a Glory Alleluia,) "hath a doctrine, hath a tongue, hath an interpretation," rendering him a sect, as it were, within himself, where shall we end? In the parlor and the street, in the stage-coach and the bar-room, in the city, the sea, and the wilderness, and in mixed companies everywhere, how constantly is religion dragged, like her Divine Master, from tribunal to tribunal, to be catechised, exposed, and judged? O, how often has my very heart sickened, to hear the crude fancies and conceits of men and women, uttered with a flippancy that nothing could intimidate, and yet with an obstinacy that nothing could disturb, on themes in the midst of which Gabriel adores, and into which the whole company of heaven "desire to look." It is said that there were times when "Shakspeare thought himself no poet, and Raphael believed himself no painter;" but can sectarianism produce a washerwoman or a cobbler in the land, that is not confident of being an infallible theologian? From every settled article of faith, one and another will clamor his dissent, and iterate it, and reiterate it, until you are disposed to withdraw the sacred thing from the unholy gaze of the lookers-on, and to leave the field to a combatant whose only ambition has been to establish a reputation for thinking for himself. Ever and anon you meet a new Protagŏras, who, according to the account in Plato, "had nothing but confused notions, such as he had collected by desultory reading, and, instead of knowledge, had a monstrous heap of opinions, which, when compared, contradicted and destroyed each other." One you find asking, Can I not be saved, even if I reject this—and this—and this, in Christianity? Another demands, Is it necessary to salvation that I should fast?—that I should receive the communion?—that I should be baptized?—that I should be a member of the church? And another wishes to know, Cannot the Mohammedan be saved?—the Jew?—the Unitarian?—the Hottentot?—the Infidel? Still another asks, Do you think a man is responsible for his belief? Is not a man safe, provided he be sincere? Questions like those which the Jews put to our Lord, apparently to seek information, really to ensnare him in his answers, and to which it would, in general, convey a wrong impression to answer either *yes* or *no*. The intention is, not to believe more than they can help—not to do what they can avoid—not to yield what they can withhold—*to pare down the terms of salvation to the minimum*, and secure the crown of eternal life on the most reduced terms. Hence (O, the depths of Satan!) the artful distinction between fundamentals or essentials, and non-essentials, in religion. "It is not necessary to salvation to belong to a church; it is not necessary to salvation to receive the sacraments; it is not necessary to salvation to believe the Trinity:"—go on, gentlemen; I cannot see where you will stop; revelation is itself unnecessary; for we all believe that a heathen may be saved without it. How plausible this old reasoning in our new Adams and Eves: "The prohibition of a visible and outward tree it is enslaving to the mind to regard, and we honor our Maker in not imputing to Him so unessential a condition of salvation." Shame on such heartless reasoning. There may be circumstances, in which, to refuse a cup of cold water may bring upon my soul, at the last, the awful words,—"Inasmuch as ye did it not to one of the least of these, ye did it not to me." O, may my soul escape the woe, and gain the promise of the Preacher on the mountain, who said, in words that hang, as the cloud between the Israelites and the Egyptians, dark to the latter, but bright to the former,—"Whosoever shall break one of these least commandments, and shall teach men so, he shall be called the least in the kingdom of heaven; but whosoever shall do and teach them, the same shall be called great in the kingdom of heaven." I praise my Maker for having opened my eyes to this one thing, that whatever God has thought it necessary to reveal or to command, it is, *for me*, necessary to believe and to obey.

Such is the nature of SCHISM. Even the sects are continually throwing off individuals and groups, who have found the atmosphere too relaxing or too bracing. One has but to pretend to greater sanctity and a purer discipline, and he finds himself at once the founder of a sect; or, he has but to lower the terms on which salvation may be had, and his followers will form around him. I heard a Presbyterian divine once say in a lecture to his class, that if in this country a man should require his disciples to walk upon their *heads* as the evidence of grace in their *hearts*, he would not be without followers. Presbyterianism throws off the discipline of her ancient mother; and her children, in the retributions of Providence, throw off hers. Who are the restless multitude, constantly discussing, in all companies, questions of religion? Who are the leaders of the new sects, that continually spring up, like mushrooms in our midst? Who are the beginners of new and startling opinions, that are continually crying "Lo, here is Christ, or lo, he is there," unsettling the communities through which they run? Has any man ever found an Episcopalian indulging such ambition? I trow not; in every instance that I have ever known, in the whole land, they have been the descendants, directly or indirectly, of Presbyterianism. And why should this be so?—a fact quite worthy to be called a phenomenon! I see the first reason in Scripture, that the gates of hell shall not prevail against the Church; and I see a second reason in philosophy, that there is nothing in the mild discipline, or the moderate teachings, or the dignified deportment of the Episcopal Church, to drive men to new inventions or to infidelity. I remember well the terror with which, when a boy, I related my stammering "experience" before the elders; and I remember, when a boy, under the chestnut and the oak, discussing with boys the mysteries of predestination and free-will; and I remember, when a boy, my misery at the possibility of having been left out in the purposes of God's electing love, and my *agony* on that terrible engine of torture and revivalism, "the unpardonable sin," and, when my life was well-nigh faultless, and my heart ten thousand times purer than it now is, my dreadful fears that I had done "despite unto the spirit of grace," and my doubtings whether my heavenly Father's mercy could extend to "such a wretch as I." Ask not what fills the land with sects, and darkens it with every shade of novelty and infidelity!

Go into England, and, while you find the fifteen millions of her Church in solid and inseparable column, you find her two millions of dissenters rent again into conflicting sects, and never united except in combination against the Church.

Go up into Scotland, and the locusts swarm about you still—Independents, Baptists, Wesleyans, Irvingites, Arians, Unitarians, Quakers, and besides these, not less than eight well-known Presbyterian denominations, holding alike the Westminster Confession, observing alike the extemporaneous form of worship, clinging alike to Rouse's Psalms; yet, without any available principle of cohesion, splitting upon matters generally indicated in their names—Burghers and Anti-burghers—Relief and Cameronian—Associate and Reformed—Covenanters and Seceders—New Light and Auld Light—Established and Free—and so forth and so forth. Even the gigantic soul of a Chalmers has, under our own eyes, fallen into the snare of the schismatical Reformers, and rather than bear up awhile against odds in defence of an obviously righteous principle, which would certainly have triumphed in the end, has been betrayed, with more than half the ministers of his communion, into a fresh and fatal schism.* And the

* It is remarkable that Dr. Chalmers, who directed some of his best energies and efforts against dissent and schism, should, so immediately after his celebrated Lectures in London on this very subject, in a moment of impatience, under a just sense of wrong, have become the head and leader of the great schism that has recently taken place in Scotland; nor can we reconcile it with the Erastianism with which he was imbued respecting establishments of religion. I believe it is known that this truly great man was very favorably affected toward the Church of England, and perhaps it was his Erastianism alone, or deference to the religion recognized in Scotland by the CIVIL MAGISTRATE, that at one time prevented his connection with the Episcopal Church. I was once in England when Dr. Chalmers was in London, and I heard from good authority that the Doctor, on laying down a certain book treating of the Scottish Reformers, and of Knox particularly, made the remark, that he thought they had been rather in a hurry in separating from the Church and setting up the Presbyterian Communion. By the by, Presbyterians generally imagine that the present kirk of Scotland is the rightful successor of the original Reformed Church in that country. But it is not so. The church as reformed and settled, was Episcopal. The Presbyterians, led on by men who had been in Geneva, and had gotten new ideas about a more *thorough* reformation than that in England, separated from the church of the country, and set up a new and *Presbyterian* communion, and ultimately, with great violence, uprooted and placed under severe penalties the old Church of Scotland. The present Episcopal Church, only recently disenthralled from those penalties, and growing fast in numbers, is the only historical successor of the ancient Church of Scotland.

same tendencies to disruption and secession are constantly manifested on the European continent; and it is not the genius of Presbyterianism, but the despotic temper of jealous and arbitrary governments, that has hitherto suppressed *instanter* the ebullitions of private judgment and the formation of new societies; thus strikingly verifying the sagacity of Melancthon, who warned the more impatient and impetuous Reformers, that the safe reformation of a whole church was a work of prudence and of time, and that, if they attempted to go on *without the bishops*, the whole thing would end either in division and anarchy, or in the despotism of the kings over the church.

There is, there must be, something wrong. From the beginning it was not so. It was in the middle of a dark and stormy night, when the great drops were falling from Him to the ground, that the Saviour of the world, with the redemption of the world upon his heart, and knowing the connection between the world's redemption and the church's unity, lifted His eyes in the tempest to heaven, and cried,— "that they all may be one, as Thou, Father, art in Me, and I in Thee, that they also may be one in Us; that the world may believe that Thou hast sent Me." And there was a time, when His apostles carried out the Master's will, that there should be "one body, even as there is one Spirit;" that "there should be no schism in the body;" and when the "I am of Paul, and I of Apollos, and I of Cephas, and I of Christ," instead of commending these discriminating individuals as more spiritual than their brethren, was the evidence to their apostle, that they were "yet carnal," and he gave solemn commandment that the schismatic, after due admonition, should be given back to Satan. And there was a time, after the apostles, when those who received from them the keys of the kingdom, regarded the schismatic with the abhorrence that they did the murderer, because the act of schism was a striking at "the body of Christ," and a wound to the heart of all believers at once; when they regarded him as partaker with the parricide, because he had plunged a sword into the Mother that bare him; nay, when they regarded him as vying in guilt with the soldiers at the cross, for, said the noble patriarch of Alexandria who excommunicated Arius, and who held a seat in the great council of Nice, "That seamless garment which the murderers of Christ would not divide, these men have dared to rip asunder." Make what we will of all this, the feeling on this subject was evidently in those days intense and deep, and can be as evidently traced to the teachings of the Master. Schism in the early church but gave her the opportunity to raise her voice for Unity, just as heresy gave her occasion to bear testimony to what had been the Faith from the beginning, or as spurious gospels and revelations gave occasion to settle the book of canonical Scripture. Even when sectarianism could count in some places more followers than she, still she lived to see them melt away in her presence like snow before the sun. Let any man read the case of Korah and his followers, in the sixteenth chapter of the book of Numbers, and then make up his mind, whether, for the causes commonly alleged to justify schism, God will hold it excusable in the last day, when all its remotest consequences shall have been brought to light. When God would establish a great fact or principle for the faith of after ages, He has uniformly done it both by revelation and by miracle. The credentials of the first ministers were miraculous; baptism, the laying on of hands, the preaching of the Word, the act of discipline on Ananias and Sapphira and others, were at first attended by miracle. Many were visited with disease and death at Corinth, for presumptuously undervaluing the dignity and benefits of the Lord's Supper. The great first schism of Korah and his company, soon after the Church had been organized, was punished by a signal miracle in a storm of earthquake and of fire. So the schism and the heresy of Simon Magus, and of Arius, and of many others, were punished as signally, perhaps, as the pride of Herod and the treachery of Judas. And is there no cloud from heaven resting over Geneva? And is there nothing dark and lowering in the horizon of Germany? And have we not seen the giant of Socinianism, with his sickle in his belt, reaping in our own New England, and *all* other fields where Presbytery had sown? It is not for me to doubt that precious gold and silver may be recovered from these ruins, as the brazen censers of the company of Korah were commanded to be rescued from the burning, "inasmuch as they had been an offering to the Lord." But these were the facts that led me to perceive, that the old Faith and the old Church must go together; separate them, and you separate old friends—the soul from the body; the body perishes, and the faith disappears. It is a transmigration into another body, that the faith will not bear. "There is one Body, and there is one Spirit."

The Episcopalian will at once see that this is reasoning which a Presbyterian may elude, but with which he cannot grapple in a manly contest. How is it then to be eluded? How is *the fact*, that the Presbyterian is now in a state of actual separation from the church to which all the faithful formerly belonged, to be excused? Are there no fig-leaves with which he may cover up the rent? Yes! here comes the dark spirit that prompted the schism, and that first carried division into heaven, and then suggested schism upon earth, saying, "In the day ye separate, ye shall be as gods, dwelling and exulting in a purer and holier atmosphere; and God, who looketh only at the heart, doth know, that a forbidden tree, or a visible church and ministry and sacraments, are externals and non-essentials, above which the spiritual man should learn to soar, honoring them rather in the breach than the observance." "And no marvel, for Satan himself is transformed into an angel of light." Excuses for sins once committed, are as easily gotten at as leaves upon the trees; and these were the fig-leaves with which I was to cover up the rent in the body of Christ:—

The church, it is maintained, is an "invisible" body. I know that there is an invisible church, a blessed company who have gone before, waiting our coming, "that they without us should not be made perfect." They have dropped the body, and can be no more seen.

One army of the living God,
We at His bidding bow;
Part of the host have crossed the flood,
And part are crossing now.

But if the church of the Bible be, what is now pretended, *an invisible* church, then every *visible* thing on earth, calling itself *church*, is unscriptural and wrong! But an "invisible church!" It were as rational to talk of an invisible sacrament, an invisible ministry, an invisible revelation, an invisible resurrection. In fact there are many sectarians now spiritual enough, with the Swedenborgians and Quakers, to deny the external and visible resurrection of the flesh. And there are others who have their invisible callings to the ministry, and their invisible baptisms and communions. I have often heard the spiritual Calvinist affect a perfect indifference whether the external body should be raised in the resurrection, and we all know that the questions are gravely entertained in the Calvinistic world, whether there is such a *place* as hell, and whether there is such a *place* as heaven, and whether the very mother shall recognize the fruit of her womb, or a pastor the stars in his crown, in the *invisible state!* If then there be no such place as heaven, but it be a bright spiritual impalpability, and if there be no such place as hell, and if it be a matter of no moment that the bodies of the just shall rise, then it is no wonder that the church itself has become invisible. Where will end this effort

"—— to darken and put out
Eternal truth by everlasting doubt?"

An "invisible" church! Did our Lord cast His teachings on the unseen wind, to float through ether to the end of time? Or did He not rather call men visibly around Him, and form them into a community, and give them sacramental signs, and officers, and guides, and promise to be "with them always, even unto the end of the world?"

An "invisible" church! The word "church" occurs more than a hundred times in the New Testament*—quite often enough to satisfy the churchman,—and I beg the candid Presbyterian to sit down and attentively compare the places, and mark how often it will *bear* the interpretation of a thing invisible. A pure, spiritual, invisible church at Pergamos, infested with the Nicolaitanes! An invisible church at Thyatira, with "that woman Jezebel" for a member! An invisible church at Sardis, "ready to die!" An invisible church at Laodicea, fit only to be "spued out of the mouth" of Christ!

How can the church be "invisible?" "Tell it to the church," says our Lord; how can we tell it to an invisible community? and how can a man be cast out from an invis-

* This very striking fact has its equally striking counterpart in the circumstance that the words *Baptism*, *Baptize*, *Baptizing*, &c., occur *ninety-four* times in the Gospels and Epistles of the New Testament, besides innumerable allusions to the sprinkling of the heart from an evil conscience, and the washing of the body with pure water. That dreadful word "Baptism" ninety-four times in the Gospels and Epistles! I venture to say that, in the preaching of Presbyterians, it does not occur *once* in ninety-four sermons. Only think of St. Peter saying, "Repent and be baptized every one of you in the name of Jesus Christ, *for the remission of sins; and ye shall receive the Holy Ghost.*" Only think of Ananias saying to so intellectual a man as Saul of Tarsus, "Arise, and be baptized, *and wash away thy sins*, calling on the name of the Lord!"

ible church? Though you cast him out, if he be a good man, he still belongs to your "invisible" church as much as before; and if he be a bad man, you cannot cast him out, because he does not belong to it at all.

How can the fold be invisible?—The Shepherd prays, "that they all may be one, as Thou, Father, art in Me, and I in Thee, that they also may be one in Us, that *the world* may believe that Thou hast sent Me." How can *the world* discover an "invisible" unity? But let all things return to the faith and unity of the first centuries, and *the world* will again see, and the world will *again believe.*

If the church of Christ on earth be an invisible brotherhood of spiritual believers, then is schism an impossible sin, and charity an impossible virtue. *Schism an impossible sin;* because, go where you will; set up what sect you please; cry, I am of Paul, and I of Apollos, and I of Luther, and I of Wesley, as you may; as a spiritual Christian, you cannot, by any act of visible and external separation, divide an invisible community of spiritual members; and as schism is an impossible sin, so *is charity an impossible virtue.* Charity is no longer to be extended to all who have been baptized into one body, nor to all who eat with us the children's bread; but we are to spy out those who are spiritual according to our ideas, and give them, and them only, our charitable fellowship, as members of our invisible communion. In the *visible* church, where doubt commences, charity begins; in the invisible church, where doubt commences, charity dies under the new prerogative we take upon us of discerning *spirits.* Peace in a family were always easy, if we were allowed to choose our brothers and our sisters; and charity ceases to be a virtue, where we have exercised the prior assumption of selecting who shall be our brethren.

The church an "invisible" body! How has such an idea found its way into the minds of men? The truth is that the histories of Presbyterianism have always been in advance of its theories. The "invisible" church they talk of, would never have been thought of, if they had not perpetrated schism after schism, until the identity and unity even of their own sect can be no longer traced. As the doctrine of predestination, (or, as its advocate Doctor Priestley calls it, of philosophical necessity,) which has been inherited from Calvin, to whom it descended from the Romish Schoolmen, who had derived it from the Greeks, who in their turn had received it from the Persians, among whom it still flourishes in all its vigor, must be first believed, before men can find it in the Bible: so must Universalism, and *isms* without number, be first believed, and the proofs sought afterward. According to the same rule, schism is first perpetrated, and palliation sought for it afterward. But who can find it in the Scriptures? "*Ye take too much* upon you," said Korah and his company to Aaron and his sons, "seeing *all the congregation are holy.*" "Ye take too much upon you, ye sons of Levi," answered Moses, and the earth opened and swallowed them up. Korah and his company were the second of the three orders of the priesthood, casting off the authority of the first; and, if such events of the old dispensation typify events in the new, then here is the order of Presbyters rising up against the order of bishops with the same plea, "Ye take too much upon you, ye sons of Aaron." Show me one instance in the Bible, where the pretence of superior purity or piety ever was alleged to justify a *schism*, and I will show you thousands where the possession of that purity and piety was demonstrated by a noiseless adherence to *unity*. Show me thy spirituality without thy unity, and I will show thee my spirituality by my unity. Noise is easy; silence is severe. Rebellion is the child of nature; obedience is the daughter of grace. Elijah, who for his purity was carried up alive to heaven, would not separate himself or the seven thousand that had not bowed the knee to Baal, from the seven millions that had fallen into the pollutions of idolatry. Daniel, the holy captive, who inspired the lions with awe, did not separate from the church of his fathers, but turned his face in Babylon toward Jerusalem. John the Baptist ate the passover with Herod, and the Holy Jesus sat down to supper with Judas. They did not withdraw from the temple, though it was now a den of thieves; nor from the synagogue, although Satan had his seat there. In Samaria our Saviour found the only schism in the Jewish church, and, passing by their mountain to go up to Jerusalem himself, he said to the woman at the well, "Ye worship ye know not what; we know what we worship; for salvation is of the Jews." "But into any village of the Samaritans enter ye not," He said to His first heralds. Where is schism or separation, in any one instance, tolerated in the Scriptures?

To this there can be no *reply*, but there will be certainly the *retort*—Why then did the Episcopal Church separate from the Church of Rome? I answer, the Episcopal Church separated from Rome in precisely the same way that she separated from Geneva; that is—*Rome separated from her*. She condemned the corruptions of Rome, threw them off herself, and warned her children against them; and for so doing, *Rome* anathematized *her*, and withdrew from her, and set up a schismatical communion in opposition to the Church of England. Both in the case of the Romanists and that of the Presbyterians, the *separation* was the work of the *Separatists*,—not of the Church. In both, the Separatists pretended to justify their separation, simply because the Church of England chose to exercise, in a way which did not please them, those powers which are the inalienable right of every National Church. And that Church still calls upon both to do, as she has herself done;—return from novelties to the ancient and universal faith, and from schism to the ancient and universal discipline.

Pray, do not tell us any more of your invisible church. For "unto what is the kingdom of God like, and whereunto shall I resemble it?" It is the vine and its branches; and "every branch in me (*in Christ*) that beareth not fruit, is cut down, and cast into the fire." It is the vine, then, with its *living* branches and its *dead.*

It is a vineyard; and the barren fig-tree, so long the keeper's care, is cut down and *cast into the fire:* how can it be then the spiritual vineyard now alleged?

It is the company of guests at the marriage of the King's Son, among whom was the man *without the wedding garment:* it is not then the company of the elect and good, but the assembly of sacramental guests, some in a sinless and seamless garment, and others in impurity and rags.

It is the retinue of virgins going forth to meet the Bridegroom; and while the lamps of five burned on, the lamps of five went out, and left their possessors *in darkness and despair.*

Such are the parables by which our Saviour has made plain this important subject. The kingdom of heaven is the family of servants, to whom their Lord distributed the talents. By some these talents were improved; others digged in the earth, and in earth centred and buried all. "Cast the unprofitable servant *into outer darkness:* there shall be weeping and gnashing of teeth."

Again, saith our Saviour, it is the field of wheat and tares so mixed and interwoven, that even an angel's eye cannot discern them now. Ye are not to be continually and continually separating from your brethren because the tares are among the wheat, and ye would, at the expense of unity, set up a purer church. What if men cast up to us that there are bad men in the Church? We know it; we see the wisdom of it; we can give them many reasons for it; it is intended to be so; the work of rooting out the tares would root out charity from the heart; root not up the tares, lest ye root up the wheat; let both grow together until the harvest. John bore the hypocrisy of Herod; Jesus received the kiss of Judas. Are we better than the Elijahs and Daniels in times of apostasy? Are we purer than he with the leathern girdle, or He that hanged upon the tree, that we must ever and for ever be separating from our brethren? Who, then, are "uncharitable?" Those who are satisfied with the Church as it is and as it was, and are content to live and die in her bosom? or those who, like the ungracious child of Noah, take delight in exposing a parent's nakedness, leaving it to other hands to walk backward with the mantle? Who are the "uncharitable?" They who left *us*, counting *us* as *tares?* or we, who were willing that both should grow together until the harvest?

These continual illustrations show how the heart of our Lord sighed for His Church's unity. He would that the wheat and the tares should grow together, rather than trust to the judgments of men, and sacrifice to continual experiments the great principle of unity. "He knew from the beginning who should betray him;" yet He never broke the secret to the disciples, that the bond of charity might not be broken. And when we think that parables have been exhausted, He returns yet again to the subject, and says that the Church is the net cast into the sea, which gathered into it both good fishes and bad. The world is the sea. Millions are in its bosom. It has its calms and its starry nights; but the storm is often on the deep. Bleak, barren, rocky, and full of danger, are its shores. Whirlpools and currents, and shoals and reefs, lie in ambush under its deceitful face. This is the sea in which the fishers are to let down the net. Stormy may be the day, starless may be the night, dark may be the bosom of the deep, wild may be the hurricane as it comes lashing its way from the mountains: still they must let down the net. They may have toiled the live-long night, and taken nothing: but still they must let down the net. That net, then, takes both good and bad. But let no opening be made, to let out the bad, for the good will leave it too. Depend upon it, you are mistaken. The Church is the Beth-esda of the world; and we are not to say, Get thee away, thou miserable man, who for thirty and eight years hast lain here, a libel on the virtue of these waters, and art nothing better; and give thy bed to one more likely to be healed—for thus we should turn the Beth-esda of God into the Beth-horon of man—the house of mercy into the house of judgment. The Church is earth's hospital, not for the hale, but the halt; not for the recovered, but the convalescent. With a living bread she feeds the poor; from her cup she pours wine and oil into the wounds of the bleeding, and enables the weak to go on their way rejoicing; at certain seasons, an angel, with healing in his wings, moves upon the waters and imparts a fresh virtue to the wave; and the heavenly Physician, with healing in his very looks, walks the porches of the hospital. Do not then tell us that the kingdom of heaven is an "invisible" Church. *Schism has lost you a reality; do not grasp at a shadow.*

You know yourselves that this shadow does not satisfy. You know yourselves that you are feeling after a visible and more tangible union. What was the meaning of a meeting held in New York a few years ago, (of which I was a silent spectator,) for the purpose of devising a comprehensive basis of faith, that should recover unity—a meeting remarkable for its oversight of the Apostles' Creed, but not singular in its result, the giving existence to a new sect? And what is the meaning of the more recent and abortive movement, known as "the evangelical alliance," from which, we are informed, the dogma of future punishments was, out of deference to the Germans, well nigh excluded? And the Bible Society, and the Tract Society, and the Sunday-School Unions, what are they all, but concessions to the great principle of visible Unity? What are they all, but a confession that you feel your columns broken and feeble before the solid phalanx in which Rome moves? You affect to undervalue Unity—then why do you tremble at the growl of the lion and the thunder from the Vatican? Has Rome truth on her side? Has she reason? Has she antiquity? Has she the Bible? No! but she has—what you have lost—Unity. And, as an eloquent clergyman of New York once said, (whose name I might give, if I could from memory recite the passage without marring its beauty,) speaking of the sects into which the land is rent, "While this is so, and they are divided into sects and parties, the Roman eagle is hovering near, as he did over Jerusalem of old, biding his time, until, weary of endless faction and division within, and of the interminable siege without, the people shall in despair throw open the gates, and let the conquerors in." *Divide et impera*—divide and conquer—was a maxim of Rome, even when Rome was pagan.

If "invisible" unity had been in the mind of St. Paul, why could he not as well have allowed one to be of Paul, and another of Apollos, and another of Cephas, as that one should now be of Calvin, and another of Wesley, and another of Swedenborg? No, it is a flimsy substitute for a vital and holy reality—a fig-leaf apron over a miserable nakedness—an oratorical flourish on an anniversary platform, appearing, as one of the three hundred and sixty-five islands of Bermuda is said to do, one day in the year, and again disappearing till its anniversary returns. It is a curious thing, living only on its birthdays; at all other times, it is a union from not uniting, a *lucus a non lucendo.* Instead of a church, we go into the

Broadway Tabernacle or Exeter Hall. Instead of an altar, we surround a platform. Instead of priests, we are occupied with orators. Instead of the Bishop, the emblem of unity is the chair of the Dairyman's Daughter. Instead of incense to our Maker, a cloud of applause and dust is sent up as a grateful offering to the speakers. And instead of sacraments,—the holy, the blessed, the love-constraining sacraments,—there is a shaking of hands, and the curtain drops. Is it right—*is it right*, thus to suppress the symbols of unity and of communion with which Christ bound his Church together? Can any end on earth justify the means? And what does such unity amount to? It is well known, that it is with great difficulty a half-dozen orators can be selected, skilful enough to step for a day over a platform, without treading on each other's toes. And not unfrequently, with all the tact and caution that are used, the toes are trodden, and the challenge follows, as promptly as a card the insult in the ball-room. We must confess, that the alleged union has in our judgment just the same existence with the alleged transubstantiation of the Romanists. In either case, our external senses are not to be allowed to testify. One of the Live-Forevers in the West was asked by a gentleman, "Suppose I should put the ball in this rifle through your heart, would you not die?" "No," said the Live-Forever, "I should not; I might seem, to unbelievers, to fall down and die; but it would not be so; for 'He that believeth in me shall never die.'" The same is the pretence to spiritual unity; "we may seem to dispute and wrangle and to be divided; but we love one another, and are all united, heart to heart, in the tie of spiritual and invisible unity. What is this, but the old argument for transubstantiation? And what is all this cry about a spiritual Church, but downright Quakerism? And what is all this anniversary and platform unity, but a got-up thing,

"Which at the best lasts not a day;
"Like frost-work in the morning ray,
"The fancied fabric melts away."

All this while, the Episcopal Church is one and the same—unaltered in her creed—undivided in her unity—free as the air—universal as the light—firm as the earth's centre—everywhere, always, indissolubly one—the old olive tree of the Bible:—

"Moored in the rifted rock,
"Proof to the tempest's shock,
"Firmer she roots her, the harder it blows."

She is known to the sects, that carry their mutual strifes into distant lands, as the universal, the indivisible, the unalterable. Wherever she is found, no one is left to conjecture what teachings the nations will hear at her lips, by what prayers she will teach them faith's ascent to heaven, what hymns she will send up from ships far off at sea, by what comforts she will soothe the last hours of the stranger in a foreign land, with what solemnities she will lay him on his pillow in the dust. All over the world, in answer to our Lord's last prayer with the disciples, she is one—"often, like the seamless garment in the soldier's hands, just on the point of being rent," when a better thought comes into the minds even of her soldiers and her fighting-men,—No, it is so beautiful, "let us not rend it!"

CHAPTER XII.

THE SUBJECT CONTINUED.

WHAT, then, it may be asked, were the Reformers to do, in Germany, and Switzerland, and France, and Holland, where the bishops were not willing to reform? Answers are easy. Do as Melancthon entreated them to do, and not attempt to go on without the bishops. Do as did Elijah and his seven thousand amidst the altars of Baal. Do as did Daniel and his companions amidst the idolatries of their countrymen in Babylon. Do as did John, who kept the passover with Herod. Do as did Jesus, who ate the supper with Judas. Do as did the Reformers of England, who waited in the days of Mary, until the time came, and God sent them His wonderful deliverance. These all waited, and many of them died in faith, not having yet received the promises, but being confident of this one thing, that He who had purchased the Church with His blood, would redeem it in due season by His providence. But do I blame these Reformers? I blame them the less, when I remember that they relied upon their children, when times should be more propitious, *to restore the Episcopacy*. But the language of the children has been, "We are wiser than the ancients; we have more understanding than all our teachers."

Now, supposing the Romanist to have been the first schismatic of modern times, by violating the ancient terms of unity, in adding to the ancient creeds, and in riding over the authority of bishops, and in imposing new conditions of communion, who was the next that fell into the sin of schism? We answer, the Presbyterians, and in identically the same manner, first, by unheard-of additions to the ancient creed, and secondly, by annulling actually, as Rome had done virtually, the powers of the bishops. And there is here a singular historical coincidence. Until about the eleventh year of Elizabeth, there was but one Church in England, the Episcopal Church that now is. No one doubted its validity. Even the Pope offered to acknowledge it, reformed as it was, if Elizabeth would concede the supremacy. A spectacle it was, to make glad the hearts of angels—a whole Church gloriously reformed, and bright from the fires of Smithfield and Oxford—and not a Romanist in England, nor yet a Presbyterian, to break the universal brotherhood! So things continued until the tenth or eleventh of Elizabeth's reign. About this time, some who had fled from the persecutions of Queen Mary to Frankfort and Geneva, returned to England, and brought with them the idea that the Church of England was not sufficiently reformed, and must be reformed further. They did not like the kneeling at communion—they did not like the surplice—they did not like the altar in the east—they did not like the rails around the chancel, the ring in marriage, the sign of the cross, and many other such things they now abhorred. The bishops were now "popelings," and the Episcopal order a "stirrup for Antichrist to get into the saddle," and the Prayer-Book, which is now the admiration of the world, was the "ill-mumbled mass-book." At this the lovers of ancient order grew alarmed, and some drew back from the Reformation in despair; and it is a remarkable fact, that in 1570, the very year that the Romanists first separated from the Church of England, on the ground that she was reforming too far, the Puritans organized their opposition on the ground that she would not reform far enough. Fiercer and fiercer grew the cry for more reforms, until at last the sympathizers with Geneva proposed a Prayer-Book with which they would be satisfied, with six hundred alterations from the one in common use. The Church saw at once that concession was hopeless, and took back her imprudent consent, at one time, to give up the surplice, the sign of the cross, and the kneeling at communion. And now the cry of Popery grew louder than ever. Jesuits came in disguise into the Church, and by violent harangues swelled the cry for further reformation. The tumult increased. Men's minds were unsettled. Endless confusion followed. The result is known. The clergy of the Church were deprived of their livings, immured in dungeons, sent into exile, or executed by the common hangman, and often not a brother allowed to attend them to the gallows, or read the Burial service over them when dead.* The cathedrals

* The following lines, by the Rev. Mr. Hollingsworth, (Eng.,) have reference to the case of the Rev. Mr. Lowes, who, having been for fifty years the laborious Vicar of Brandeston, in England, after being tried by water and the rack, was condemned by Calamy, a Puritan divine, to be hung at Bury, with certain other wizards and witches:—

"'Good judges, hear my sole desire,
And grant my latest prayer,
That when I stand at the gibbet foot,
A priest may meet me there!'

"But out then spoke Judge Calamy,
A wrathful man was he,
'We'll have no Popish mummery
Beneath the gallows tree!'

"''Tis hard to die on gibbet high,
Like vile unchristian hound,
To yield unblest my parting sigh,
To lie in unhallowed ground!

"'But I am a Priest of England's Church,
I'll read my own funeral prayer;
God will accept His servant's act,
For the sake of His Son so dear.'

were converted into stables for horses—the pleasant organs were broken into pieces, that their Babylonish tones might no more fall upon the people's ears—they broke down with axes and hammers the carved work of the sanctuary—the records of the Church were burnt—the commandments were torn from their place over the altar, and "the covenant" was set up in their stead—the Prayer-Books throughout the realm were collected and publicly burnt—the bones of bishops were dragged out of their tombs and scattered on the streets—and, (until the present work of restoration going on under the recent movement in the Church of England,) scarcely was there a church, as my own eyes to some extent can testify, that did not exhibit the remains and marks of the violence of those unhappy times—and it was forbidden in any part of England to kneel in the communion, to wear a surplice in prayer, to use any portion of the liturgy, to decorate a church at Christmas, *or to bow at the name of Jesus.** An aged archbishop laid

"In this free English land of ours,
No soul shall now be shriven,
Then seek alone, as best you may,
Your passport up to Heaven!"

"'Tis hard to die on gibbet high,
Like vile unchristian hound!—&c."

As a special favor, he was allowed, under the gallows, before being swung off, to read the Burial service over himself!

* A resolution had passed the House of Commons "that the Communion-Table should be removed from its place, the rails around it be pulled down, the chancel levelled, and that no man in the realm should bow at the name of Jesus." Sir Edward Dering opposed the decree with much feeling; and the reader will notice the presentiment of *the back stairs to Socinianism*, which was so fearfully verified, as we have seen, in the case of the 258 Presbyterian chapels that remained after Cromwell—all of them, save twenty-three, becoming afterward Socinian.

"Hear me," said he, "with patience, and refute me with reason. Your command is, that all corporal bowing at the Name of Jesus shall be henceforth forborne. I have often wished that we might decline these questions in divinity.—I say it again and again, that we are not *idonei et competentes judices*—proper and competent judges in doctrinal determinations. The theme we are now upon is a sad point. I pray you consider severely on it. You know there is no other Name under heaven given among men, whereby we must be saved. You know that this

gladly his hoary locks upon the scaffold, and Charles, like his Master, sold for pieces of money, and three days under sentence of death, as he was preparing to lay his head upon the block, exclaimed for the Church of his heart, in words well fit to be the last from a martyr and a King,—"I go to-day from a corruptible to an incorruptible crown!" Nor was it long before the people of England, grown weary of endless confusion and division, took refuge in the Church that had been so recently repudiated, and which to this day is the glory and the strength of England, for ever one, and for ever the same; while the churches of Frankfort and Geneva, after which the Church of England was to have been remodelled, are now openly Socinian, and of the two hundred and fifty-eight Presbyterian chapels in England, remaining after the times of Cromwell, two hundred and thirty-five, as I have before stated, are Unitarian! What is the inference? Where are

is a Name above every name. *Oleum effusum Nomen Ejus*—His Name is as ointment poured forth; it is the carol of His own spouse. This Name is by a Father styled, *Mel in ore, melos in aure, jubilum in corde*—honey in the mouth, music in the ear, jubilee in the heart. This—it is the sweetest and the fullest of all the names and attributes of God—God my Saviour. If Christ were not our Jesus, heaven were then our envy, which is now our blessed hope. And must I, sir, hereafter, do no exterior reverence—none at all—to God my Saviour, at the mention of His saving Name *Jesus?* Why, sir, *not* to do it—to *omit* it—to leave it *undone*—is questionable—is controvertible—is at least a moot point in divinity. But to *deny* it—to *forbid* it to be done! take heed, sir! God will never own you if you forbid His honor. Truly, sir, it horrors me to think of this. For my part, I do humbly ask pardon of this House, and therefore I take leave and liberty to give you my settled resolution—I *may*—I *must*—I *will* do bodily reverence to my Saviour, and that at the mention of His saving Name—*JESUS.* Mr. Speaker, I shall never be frightened from this, with that fond, shallow argument, 'Oh, you make an idol of a name.' I beseech you, sir, reduce this dainty species of new idolatry under its proper head, the second commandment, if you can; paint me a voice; make a sound visible, if you can. When you have taught mine ears to see, and mine eyes to hear, I may then perhaps understand this subtle argument. Was it ever heard before, that any man, of any religion, in any age, did ever cut short or abridge any worship, upon any occasion, *to their God?* Take heed, sir, and let us all take heed, whither we are going! If Christ be Jesus, if Jesus be God, all reverence, exterior as well as interior, is too little for Him. *I hope we are not going up the back stairs to Socinianism!* In one word—certainly, sir, I shall never obey your order—so long as I have a head or an eye to lift up to heaven."

men's eyes? For myself, I confess that I was *ignorant of the facts.*

And as Schism opens the gates to Infidelity, so is it the breach through which Popery comes in. For I wish the reader to bear in mind, that it was not until the eleventh year of Elizabeth, that Pius the Fifth undertook to excommunicate the queen, and authorize the separation of the Papists from the Church; and this was about the time that the ultra-reformers came back from Geneva, and, by throwing the Church of England into confusion, gave that Pope his opportunity and his apology. And it is equally remarkable that (excepting for a brief space of six years) there was not a Romish bishop in England for one hundred and forty years after the Reformation, nor until *the very year* (say 1685) that the Puritans ultimately *separated from* the Church. And when more than one hundred and seventy-six subdivisions and heresies had overspread the land. Puritanism made the breach in the wall; Popery then entered with the sound of a trumpet: and it is to my mind extremely problematical, whether the Popish schism would to this day have been attempted either in England or America, but for the confusion that thus invited her return. She could never, in open day, except under this pretext, have set up altar against altar. Remember, then, that the Reformation had been established one hundred and forty years before Rome sent her bishops into England, and that the opportunity was afforded her by the schism of the Puritans. And one hundred and ten years before, (say in 1570,) Pope Pius V. excommunicated Elizabeth, absolved her subjects from their allegiance to her crown, and gave her dominions to the king of Spain; and an inducement for *that* was given by the Presbyterian Protestants, who were then returning, with new ideas, from Geneva, and were likely to succeed in the outcry for a further reformation.

How very disingenuous and unfair, then, is the charge that

the Episcopal Church is intolerant and bigoted! Ask history. In order to prevent schism, and appease the Calvinists, she offered to give up the surplice, the kneeling at communion, and the sign of the cross, all which even Luther and his followers retained; and she receded from the projected compromise only when she saw that she had undertaken to satisfy "the cry of the daughters of the horse-leech," and that six hundred alterations more were demanded in her ritual. Intolerant and bigoted! *Gentlemen, you forget!* Episcopalians did not separate from Presbyterians; Episcopalians did not foment secession in Geneva, where Presbyterianism held the field. But Presbyterians from Geneva and Papists from Rome did foment and did accomplish schism in the reformed and quiet churches of England, Ireland, and Scotland. Presbyterians too, *let it be remembered*, separated from them for an offensive reason, openly and constantly avowed;

> "For then a bishop or a priest
> Were held for 'limbs of *Antichrist*.'"

and I am at a loss to say, whether it strikes me as more strange that they should represent the Episcopal Church as bigoted and intolerant, when she did not repudiate them, but *they* repudiated *her;* or that they should now desire her amalgamation with the "denominations," when she has not made one of the six hundred alterations they demanded, at the time they denounced her as "a vile old withered harlot."

But, supposing the Presbyterians had separated for a less offensive reason, is the Church of Christ to vary her terms, to reconstruct her liturgy, to remodel her orders, to alter her faith, and to chisel another door into her pulpits, as often as a new sect appears? Where could she draw her lines? The English Unitarian would say, "I am known in England as one of the original Presbyterians, established about the times of Cromwell; admit me to your pulpits." And while he is yet speaking, the German Transcendentalist would say, "I am a Presbyterian, older than the former, in direct succession from the days of Luther; admit me to your pulpits." And while he is yet speaking, the Geneva Socinian would say, "I am a Presbyterian, and have lifted my voice in the cathedral, as I have derived my succession from the hands, of Calvin himself; admit me to your pulpits." And, in the rear of these, I see Arians, Mormons, Baptists, Campbellites, Swedenborgians, Methodists, Independents, and a multitude more, darkening the road for leagues. Is it possible that the Church can go into details with all these, examining their claims, and listening to their tedious interpretations? It would occupy her whole existence! But she has general principles with which she meets them all:—"We did not separate from you; you separated from us. You have all alike departed from the ancient creed, and substituted your own confessions. You have all alike departed from the ancient discipline and ministerial succession, and substituted new ones of your own." No, the Church never banished them. They took a portion of her goods and went their way; and now that their good things are spent, as we have seen, still, like the loving parent, she will welcome their return, and will run and fall upon their necks, and kiss them, and put the ring of reconciliation on their hands, and lead them with songs and timbrels to the banquet.

The sorrow that I now felt, at the discovery that my own communion was the first, the very first, to open the grand modern drama of schism, was not to be described. I felt that I had taken part in the scenes, and that, remembering the Church as she looked forth in England, "as the morning, fair as the moon, clear as the sun, and terrible as an army with banners," I was now keeping the raiment of them that had accused and stoned her. As I said before, like the Wesleyans, they had no intention at the beginning, of perpetrating schism. But schism once accomplished, like the boy's first oath, like the youth's first game of chance, like the maiden's first false step, makes the sequel easy. The French tell us: *Ce n'est que le premier pas qui coute;* and the Latins, *Facilis descensus.* How was it with the Methodists? Wesley, their founder, said in 1739: "A clergyman desiring to know in what point we differed from the Church of England, I answered, To the best of my knowledge, in none." Twenty-seven years after, he said again: "We are not dissenters from the Church, and will do nothing willingly which tends to a separation from it. Our service is not such as supersedes the Church service, [for it was not held at the same hours,] and we never designed it should." In 1789, half a century after the first of these declarations, he said again: "I never had any design of separating from the Church. I have now no such design, and I declare once more, that I live and die a member of the Church of England, and that none who regard my judgment or advice will ever separate from it." And again, hear his dying charge, as I may call it; his sermon at Cork, *only ten months before he went to his account*, upon the text, "No man taketh this honor upon himself, but he that is called of God, as was Aaron:" "Did we ever appoint you," said the Presbyter, "to administer sacraments? to exercise the priestly office? Such a design never entered into our minds; it was the farthest from our thoughts. . . . In doing it, you renounce the first principle of Methodism, which was wholly and solely to preach the gospel. The first attempt of this kind was made, I apprehend, at Norwich. One of our *preachers* there yielded to the importunity of a few of the people, and *baptized their children;* but as soon as it was known, he was informed it must not be, unless he designed to leave our connection; and he promised to do it no more. As long as Methodists keep to this plan, *they cannot separate from the Church; and this is our peculiar glory.*

It is new upon the earth. . . . The Methodists are *not a sect* or party; they are still members of *the Church;* such they desire to live and to die. And this, I believe, is one reason why God is pleased to continue my life so long, to confirm them in their present purpose, *not to separate from the Church.* . . . It does by no means follow that ye are commissioned to baptize or to administer the Lord's Supper. Ye never dreamed of this for ten or twenty years after ye began to preach; ye did not then, like Korah, Dathan, and Abiram, seek the priesthood also; ye knew that 'no man taketh this honor upon himself, but he that is called of God, as was Aaron.' . . . . You were yourselves first called in the Church of England; and though ye have, and will have, a thousand temptations to leave it, and set up for yourselves, regard them not; *be Church of England men still.*" No! Mr. Wesley and his preachers had no more intention of perpetrating schism, than the preachers and exhorters upon temperance or anti-slavery had, at the first, of establishing separate communions; but both have accomplished what neither of them purposed.

And how was it with the Presbyterians? What were their views, once, of the sin of schism? When, in 1643, they gained the upper hand in Parliament, and appointed the Westminster Assembly of Divines to settle things upon the Presbyterian platform, and the Congregationalists petitioned for toleration: the Divines of that Assembly replied, that to grant their petition would be "licensing perpetual division in the Church;" that it would be "conceding the lawfulness of getting new Churches out of true Churches, in countenance of which there is not the least example in all the Holy Scriptures;" that "if the Church requires that which is evil of any member, he must forbear, but without separation;" and "the same ground of separation (scruple of conscience)," say they, "may be pleaded by any erroneous conscience whatever, and thus the Church be broken into as many divisions as there are scruples in the minds of men."* Right nobly argued, venerable fathers! But how have your sons been reasoning since? "These different denominations," says one, "are but regiments, under different colors, of the same great Captain." "The different sects," says another, "are but the children of one father, each with a different Christian name, but all belonging to the same household of faith." But from the days of the Conformists and Nonconformists let us come down to the days of the Platformists. The place is New York. The scene is the Tabernacle. The occasion is the anniversary of the New York and American Sunday School Union. The Rev. Dr. Ferris presides. The Tabernacle is "thronged with interested spectators." Time, the nineteenth century. "Pursuing the thought," said Mr. S., "respecting the power of our benevolent institutions, he saw in them some features of peculiar excellence that he discovered in no other organization. The Christian world is divided into a great many sects, and he was ready to say, let the division go on, and go on, and perhaps by and by, when the present ecclesiastical organizations are dissolved, there may be devised some new system more conformed than any now existing, to the model of the Apostles and the Prophets, Jesus Christ himself being the chief corner-stone. There is now no Church that may with propriety be called '*the* Church,' and it might be matter of question, whether it were not a greater distinction to belong to one of these benevolent institutions, than to any of the so-called churches of the day." O Presbytery! Thou wast the Eve in all this sin. Thou wast the first to taste the forbidden tree. In sorrow shalt thou bring

* This answer of the Presbyterians who had just separated from the Church, to the Congregationalists who were about to separate from *them*, reminds us of the Bengalee tiger-hunter: "Tiger hunting," said the man, "is a very fine amusement so long as *we* hunt the *tiger*; but it becomes rather awkward when the tiger takes it into his head to hunt *us*."

forth thy brood all the days of thy life! In vain dost thou deplore the continual splitting;

> "Like one who stems a stream with sand,
> Or fetters flame with a flaxen band."

Where is there a principle of cohesion—a centre of unity? Each man is a centre, if he can find seven women to hang upon his skirts. You have no excommunication that cannot be reciprocated on the very principles on which you would issue yours. You cannot cast up to these sects that they were born to-day, for they will cast it back to you that you were born but yesterday. There is in your system a facility for schism—a premium upon schism. In the Church, an Ignatius may be thrown to the wild beasts for his faith, a Polycarp may give his aged limbs to the fire: but they leave no followers to bear their name; the Church made them what they were; to the Church they leave what they have. A holy archbishop may lay his head upon the block, but there are no Laudists to tell the story; a Cranmer may go up in a chariot of fire into heaven, but there are no Cranmerites to trumpet his fame. In the Church, in all ages, individuality is surrendered, as the Christian sacrifice to Catholicity and unity. Calvin and Luther, and Wesley and Arminius, and a multitude of others, who died in their beds, enjoy the sweet flattery that thousands are called by their names; and so was it with Arius and Sabellius, and a multitude more, and with Nicolas, the founder of the Nicolaitanes under the very eyes of St. John: but in the Church of God "we call no man master;" our Polycarps and Cranmers may die in a blaze of glory, but it must all "be done away, by reason of the glory that excelleth." In the Church, not even a Paul may have a follower, nor any man in Corinth say, I am of Apollos, or, I am of Cephas. But saddest of all it is to see, that the body of Presbyterians has ceased to feel any longer *the pain* of schism! Majorities "exscind," minorities "secede;" "any three ministers," says Doctor Breckinridge, "may form a Presbytery;" schism is accomplished, especially after periods of agitation and revival, even with sensations of pleasure; just as a state of high inflammatory action in the body, is sometimes followed by a condition in which amputation is unaccompanied by pain. But in the vigorous and healthy condition of the Church,—"the true body of Christ," partaking the life and unity of her Head,—the very thought of *division*, the very idea of *the knife*, causes the cold chill to pass through every fibre of her frame. You may wonder often that she does not consent to be split and rent; you must not wonder; she is a Living Body.

And you must not wonder that Her children will not consent to see her, like Agag, hewn in pieces; for she is their Mother. She is "the Lamb's wife," saith St. John, "the Mother of us all," saith St. Paul; "and he hath not God for his Father, who hath not the Church for his Mother," was the maxim of the earliest antiquity. The schismatic can therefore be known by this, that he has little compunction in rending, or in seeing others rend, the Church which is Christ's body. As the pretended mother, in the presence of Solomon, was willing to see the child *divided* between the real Mother and herself; but the true Mother threw herself frantic between the child and the knife, and cried, "No, do not divide it, let the other take it, rather than divide it:" so says the Catholic heart, "O, it is our Mother, do not divide our Mother!" But the schismatic says, "Yes, divide, and distribute her amongst us all."

O God! I cried, why have I been left motherless upon the earth? Why have not our fathers risen from the dead to tell us that never, never would they have begun the schism, if they had seen the things that we see, or had heard the things that we hear? Why do not the graves of Geneva and Wirtemberg open, and Luther and Calvin, and Melancthon and Grotius break the silence of the dust? If I have reason to believe that my British forefathers would not have perpetrated schism, had they foreseen its consequences, and that they did not even intend to perpetrate it, as it was: how shall I answer in the Judgment if I perpetuate it now, with these frightful results before my eyes, and aid in its expansion, and help to plant this upas tree of Christendom on heathen shores? If to me is now given the opportunity which Melancthon at the beginning, and Grotius afterward, and even Calvin himself, and a multitude of the continental reformers, so much desired, of recovering the Episcopacy, and with it the Unity: am I not *free*—am I not *bound* to embrace it? The days were evil, and the times violent, in which my ancestral branch was broken off from the ancient olive-tree. I must not condemn them for motives of which I cannot perhaps judge at this distance of time. But from their sturdy answer to the Congregationalists, I know that they never, never, *never* dreamed of the endless schisms of which they were unconsciously sowing the seeds. Which of them, in the most incoherent dream of night, would ever have imagined that his son, bewildered in innumerable isms and schisms, should in a few years find cause "in a Sunday School *Union*" to say—"It may be a question, whether it be not a greater distinction to belong to one of these benevolent institutions, than to any of the so-called churches of the day!"

Am I influenced, said I, in remaining out of the Church, by the considerations that tempted my fathers to leave it? If with the Puritans her Episcopacy *was* to be "the stirrup for Antichrist to get into the saddle," has not Presbyterianism already *been* the ladder, by which Genevan, German, Englishman, New Englander, and whole communities, have glided down into Socinianism? Is not her Prayer-Book so unexceptionably beautiful and excellent, that, in the calmer times which have succeeded, a distinguished dissenting divine, without fear of forfeiting his reputation, either for correct taste, scholarship, or piety, may say: "Next to the Bible, it is the book of my understanding and my heart?" Is her language on the sacraments any higher-toned than that of the Westminster Confession? And have not many of the things for which my fathers separated from the Church, been gradually re-adopted by the Puritans themselves? Expensive churches —the mystic emblems of the Gothic style—the massive tower and pointed steeple—the "dim religious light" and dark-vaulted roof—the solemn chant, once hooted as the "Indian pow-wow"—flowing gowns and deep-toned organs, called by the Puritans "the devil's bagpipe"—praying at funerals, which was once abolished—the Lord's Prayer and the Doxology, which were pronounced by the Scots to be "a superstition"—kneeling in the time of prayer, once not customary even in family devotions—and written sermons, formerly the detestation of the faithful—have they not all been re-adopted by the Presbyterians? What have I to do then with these childish "scruples" that drove my fathers from the Church? What have I to do with the political influences that tempted them to schism? If they had to choose, *as I have to do*, between the old Church yet abiding in her strength, and the Presbyterianism now overtaken in all lands by a deep and mortal decay, would they ever have left the fair bosom of the Church of England? Would they have left a Church which had weathered storms that Frankfort and Geneva never knew, which had just beaten back the Spanish Armada that came against her by water, and the legions of Queen Mary that came against her by fire, and had walked unharmed over the black vaults of the Gunpowder Plot, and which, with Germany and Geneva submerged in infidelity, is left, the only lighthouse of the sea, confessedly "the bulwark of the

Reformation?" No! Luther, like his descendants, would have perferred Popery to Pantheism; Calvin, as many a Genevese has lately done, would have abhorred the religion of Servetus, and fallen back upon the Papacy; and I have charity enough to think that Cromwell himself would have remained in the Church for which Charles died, and at whose altars one of his descendants now ministers; that even Cotton Mather would have continued in the Church, to which his descendant and namesake has lately fled from New Englandism; and that Wesley would have so shaped his course, as to have made unnecessary his avowal that he lived and died a member of the Church of England. They all left the Church for reasons they would not now approve. They left it to entail evils they did not then foresee!

Now a theory is true, when it will account for and harmonize all the facts and phenomena of the case. If, then, the Church of which we speak be *the Church of Christ*, and if separation from it be *the sin* contemplated in the Scriptures under that name, and if the ancient faith be confided to the Church, so that, in her keeping, the gates of hell shall not prevail against it: then the present condition of the schismatical communions is identically that which we should have some day looked for, in the displeasure and blight of Providence. The great phenomenon can in no other way that I see be accounted for. We live in a world where God has blended and combined the visible with the invisible—the body with the soul—the letter with the spirit—the sacrament with the grace—THE CHURCH with THE FAITH. If this be so, sectarism and the Faith can never exist long together. You despise the pot, and carry off as you suppose the hidden manna; but for want of *the ark*, in which, like Aaron, to lay it up, your manna becomes corrupt, and your generations cannot "see that bread" on which your fathers were fed. When you first leave the Church, you take with you a portion of her jewels of silver and her jewels of gold, but in the German and Genevan workshop you soon convert them into a golden calf. Where there is schism, you cannot keep the faith. You have cut a limb from a tree, and its hidden life will depart. You despise and break the vessel, and profess to care only for the oil and the light; but you, by-and-by, return and cry, "Give us of your oil, for the winds are high, and our lamps are gone out." If you sever a limb from the human body, the limb for a while may exhibit signs of life, but the convulsive action will soon subside. Schism is like the buckets of the daughters of Danae; you may with great toil be continually pouring in; but it will be as constantly escaping. Only the unrent Church without effort can retain it.

There is then, said I, *a Church yet* on earth. As the sick may die amidst the nursings of a hospital, or may sometimes meet with mercy and health upon the street: so many may perish in the Church, and "children of the kingdom be cast out," and many not in it may be saved, for "they shall come from the east and from the west, and from the north and from the south, and shall sit down in the kingdom of God." Esau may sell his birthright; a daughter of Canaan may find crumbs under the table. But yet there is a Church. It is builded on a rock. It has possession of the keys. It is the elect Lady. It is the heir of the promise. It is rich with provisions and facilities for our salvation. It tells us what was the Bible of the early Christians; it tells us what was their faith and discipline. The intention of its Founder was to help men on in virtue and a holy life, by Baptism and the succeeding confirmations and teachings of a holy Mother; by filling it as His symbol or Shechinah, with His perpetual presence; and, chiefly, by the continual exhibition of the memorials of the great Sacrifice for sin: to hedge men's path along from the cradle to the skies, to render their salvation as certain as the nature of probation will permit. The Church is therefore one, and never can be two. Moses did not establish two churches; the temple did not allow of two priesthoods; Christ did not leave two bodies to perpetuate His presence upon earth. If there be two churches, one is the Church of Christ, the other a device of man; "on this rock I build *my* church;" "unto *thee* I give the keys of the kingdom." "One body as there is one spirit," saith St. Paul, "even as ye are called in one hope of your calling." There can be no more two Bodies than there can be two Heads. There can be no more two churches than there can be two Gods. Man can no more make a Church, than he can make a Bible.

This view of the subject made me still more unhappy. Here, said I, I find myself a member of the oldest and first sect among the moderns—a sect that had little cause to leave a Church fresh and resplendent from the fires of Smithfield and of Oxford—the experimenter on the untried sea of schism—the great forerunner and lineal parent of all the sects and schisms in the land. I feel that the current to which I am committed is downward, and is sweeping me on. What, then, is before me, but to make those frightful cataractic leaps into the deeper and darker speculations, into which the bolder Presbyterians of Europe and New England have plunged before me? Or, even if I should not myself be drawn over the abyss, what may be the fortune of my children?

"—— O when the grave
Has swallowed up thy memory and thyself,
Dost thou desire the bane that poisons earth
To twine its roots around thy coffin'd clay,
Spring from thy bones, and blossom on thy tomb,
That of its fruit thy babes may eat and die?"

As a Presbyterian layman, I should now have sought repose in the Episcopal Church. But as a minister, I had motives for adhering, while I could, to the validity of my orders. As I remarked in the early part of this narrative, it was a subject I could not be said to have examined. I dreaded, too, to be convinced. Sometimes I almost determined that I would shut my eyes. I saw the fiery trial into which it would precipitate me. In every other point of view, Episcopacy had now conquered my judgment, and won the more cautious admiration and affections of my heart. Before, however, I explain the manner in which I was compelled to yield this scruple, some may be curious to know the further operations of a bewildered mind, admiring unity as a thing beautiful, loving it as a thing most excellent, deploring its loss as the greatest calamity since the expulsion out of Eden, and longing for its restoration as the promised harbinger of the world's regeneration. And if the reader be somewhat weary of the detention, let him remember the significant re-iteration with which a mother in Israel sang—"For the divisions of Reuben there were great thoughts of heart . . . . For the divisions of Reuben there were great searchings of heart."

CHAPTER XIII.

A UNITY IMPOSSIBLE.

As I looked with dismay and sorrow on the *membra disjecta* of Presbyterianism, lying around me in wild disorder, like the broken columns of some tower, rent and scattered by the bolts of an angry sky; and particularly as I gazed on the torn and withering limbs of the venerable tree under which my fathers worshipped two centuries ago, now riven and strown over the land, as by the visitation of some mighty wind from heaven: if the question had been put to me, "Can these broken columns rise again into their tower, and can these shattered branches be gathered again into their ancient tree?" I must have answered, with the prophet over the bones of the valley, "O Lord God, thou knowest!" Still, I believed that a day was yet to come when there should be a noise, and a shaking, and a restoration of the branches to their tree. Not a pulse of my heart ever beat in sympathy with those now numerous Presbyterians, who regard it as a matter of gratulation, rather than of regret, that such differences exist in the Christian world. I could never have been brought to think that it was either the intention or the proper result of Christianity, so to alienate and sunder the members of the body. I held it to be a libel on the dignity of our religion that, without a centre—a mouth-piece—a church, to regulate such matters, it should be so vastly accommodating as ever and anon to change its hues with the different varieties of mind on which it might happen to alight, like the chameleon, assuming the various complexion of the objects over which it passes. These varying forms and creeds, which to the eyes of many of my brethren were like the variegated plumes and banners of the different regiments of an army moving together under One Great Captain: were to me like the hectic hues of autumn, the result, not of vigor, but of decay; the harbinger, not of a mellow sunshine ripening the fields into a golden harvest, but of a cheerless winter arresting the circulation of nature, and killing the life of all that is green upon earth. And there was a time, as we have seen, when the Presbyterians themselves made noble answer to the Congregationalists, when the latter offered the plea of conscience as a plea for schism. They never undervalued unity, nor spoke of it in so *sour* a tone, until unity, like the vine, binding its grapes joyfully together in its branches, grew up *beyond their reach:* just as Melancthon, and Calvin, and Grotius, and Le Clerc, and the Synod of Dort, entertained a veneration for the ancient Episcopacy; and their children never thought slight of it until they perceived that it was irrecoverably gone, and that they must cast about them for a new foundation.

I know the "philosophical" objections to the resurrection of the flesh: How can the elements that now compose this body, when drifted and driven in a thousand combinations through the world, be brought back, and restored to the unity and identity in which they now exist? And I know the objection to the restoration of Unity in the Body of Christ: How can the elements of thought, drifting and driving wildly in a thousand combinations through the world, be recovered and remoulded into the beauty and harmony of One Body, feeling the same life, thinking the same thought, moving with the same will, and happy in the same affection? But why should it be thought a thing incredible with *us* that God should restore us Unity? Like the resurrection, it may be the great miracle in reserve, the crowning beauty of the fullness of the times of grace. Whether the elements that go to form the body do or do not acquire a mysterious affinity for each other that shall one day re-unite them: it is certain that the members of the Body of Christ *have* an affinity and fondness, and will draw together, so soon as "that which letteth"—*the force* that keeps them so unnaturally apart, be it the pride of private judgment, or be it the dark influence of Evil hovering over for a time—"shall be taken out of the way." The power of God is equal to His goodness. His goodness has promised it; His power shall perform it. "And there shall be one fold, and one Shepherd."

But, as we believe in the resurrection of the body, chiefly because Christ is risen from the dead and become the first-fruits of them that slept: so, while yet a Presbyterian, I believed in the future unity of the Church, because the Church, in the time of her first-fruits, had long ago been visibly one upon earth. I had but to look through the dust of recent creeds, and beyond the ruins and fragments of sectarianism piled around me, back to a period of glorious memory, when the smallest beginning of "I am of Paul, and I of Apollos, and I of Cephas, and I of Christ," was arrested by the burning admonition, "*Is Christ divided?*" Yes, there was a time when Asiatic, European, African, and Islander, the white man, the red man, and the negro, Greek and Barbarian, Jew and Scythian, the bond and the free, were in one communion and brotherhood: and this, too, not in an age friendly, like the present, to coalescence and coalition, but presenting formidable barriers of language, country, clime, government, education, tastes, and manners, and a thousand influences, social and political, to keep the Christians in the different nations irreconcilably apart. I had but to look back to happier days, when the smallest schism was frowned out of the pale of Christianity, as unworthy to exist within it ;—the glorious days, when a question so unimportant as *the time* of keeping Easter, brought holy Bishops out of Asia, over many a league of sea and land, to consult their brethren in Europe, when, at every step of their way, the sword of persecution gleamed in the sun by day, and the fires of the martyrs burned on the hills by night ;—all from the heavenly motive of producing concert in the *time*, as well as consent (which was universal already) in the *fact*, of the observance of Easter :—glorious days, when such questions, only because they might possibly have a remote bearing upon Christian unity, were matter of painful and prolonged anxiety throughout the Christian Church. How sublime this spectacle ! How perfectly identified with the birth of Christianity, this doctrine of visible unity ! Nations just emerging from the isolation, and selfishness, and wars of heathenism, grasping the mighty conception of universality and unity ! And be it remembered that these men who made the journey out of Asia into Italy, were born in the days of the Apostles. And was not the same spectacle exhibited when dissensions about circumcision, and other such matters, arose among the Apostles themselves, and Apostles left their flocks in the wilderness, to "go up to Jerusalem" and settle, in holy synod, a uniformity of practice ? And was it not still the same, three hundred years after, when a like question, whether infants should be baptized chiefly or exclusively on the eighth day after birth, brought together a great council of bishops in Egypt ? Such was the sublime unity of the Church in the first few centuries—the faith settled—the Apostles' Creed the bond—the Episcopacy the symbol of Union—and the Church *One* ;—nothing in which to differ from each other, throughout the body universal, but the exact *time* for commemorating the Lord's resurrection, and the precise *day* for receiving infants to His Baptism : questions absurd to the modern sectarian, but important indeed. to men who felt that touching Unity was "touching the apple of the eye."

How could I, *as a Presbyterian*, undervalue unity? *As a Presbyterian*, let me go back to the fourth century. I here find Episcopacy universal on the three continents. Yet so wonderful a revolution as the entire overthrow of the apostolic institution of Presbytery, and the supervening of Episcopacy on its ruins, did not tempt a solitary country, or province, or city, that we hear of, to produce a "schism in the body!" What, therefore, said I, did the Presbyterian Church, think of Unity *then?* Why, evidently, they thought it of such paramount importance, that apostolic Presbytery must be universally and unresistingly surrendered, rather than retain it in any church on earth at the expense of Unity! They parted with Presbytery to purchase Unity: but our modern Presbyterians give Unity to the winds, to get back Presbytery! Which horn of the dilemma will you choose? Either it is not true that Presbyterianism existed, and was overthrown: or else the universal Church was pleased to see every Presbytery on earth sunk into the sea, rather than behold celestial charity broken in the violation of Unity. The Church of the first century, according to your own showing, would not purchase tinsel at the price of gold—Presbytery at the expense of Unity! No, none but heretics would perpetrate schism in those days; Ebion, Arius, Pelagius,—the daring heretic alone ventured out from the Ark upon the wave, and exhibited, in those days, the hideous phenomenon of *schism.* And it is to be observed again, that the "heresies," and "damnable heresies," spoken of in the New Testament as things then future, signify also, in the Greek, "*schisms*" and "*damnable schisms.*" And when, after six hundred years of Unity, Rome set up her peculiarities, and created breaches, by claiming a new authority, and proclaiming new terms of communion: all the rest of Christendom declared in an agony against the *novum et inauditum nefas*, and protested in thunders that echoed from the plains of Syria to the mountains of Wales. And, after Rome, there was no other schism to be noted, until the local individualism that contrived the Creed of Trent, contrived in the same century the creeds of Westminster, Augsburg, Geneva, Dort, and Heidelberg. If, then, the Church was one and undivided for so many centuries, so that the universal overthrow of Presbyterianism could not shake a single province or city from its adherence to unity: surely it is now more likely that the "Christian world," having suffered the endless mischiefs of sectarianism, may at some future day afford to return to the creed and the order of the centuries when all were One. This, then, I took for granted: that "the thing that hath been is that which shall be;" that the Church has been One, and the Church may be One once more. Nor is it half so likely that the unconverted world shall be converted, as that the converted world shall be united. There is a window in heaven, which, if opened in answer to our earnest prayers, will pour us out an influence that shall accomplish both results at once, and shall a second time "Baptize us all into One Body."

Now, in that glorious day when all shall be one again, shall the Church be Presbyterian? For it seemed to me, that whatever it was in the past, when the Church was One: it is likely to be in the future, when the Church shall be One again. And it was my duty to seek the Church that should give the fairest promise of harmonizing conflicting opinions, of satisfying the purposes of organization, of meeting with the concurrent approbation of all who profess and call themselves Christians. Shall the Church of the talked-of millennium be Anabaptist? Shall sacraments, and rites, and priesthood, be done away, and we be all transformed into a universe of Quakers? Shall we be Socinians? Shall all mankind be

Mormons? The answer to all such questions will be found in the answer to another:—Shall the Church, in that glorious future be *Presbyterian?* Or am I upholding an impracticable theory, that is to give place to one that cometh after it, and is to be preferred before it, because it was before it? This is a question entirely of order and of faith.*

As to the former, it occurred to me with great force, that the Presbyterian may become Episcopalian or Catholic, without the sacrifice of principle. The conditions of his own ecclesiastical existence oblige him to admit, that the Episcopal Church is a Church of Christ; that her ministry is a valid ministry; that her sacraments are valid and lawful sacraments; that, in entering her communion, he will still be in the Church of Christ; and that every Presbyterian on earth might return to her bosom to-morrow, without the slightest misgiving as to the validity of her ordination, sacraments, and discipline.

If it be said, that for a Presbyterian minister to submit to Episcopal ordination, would be to recognise re-ordination: I answer, that Presbyterians have never held ordination to be of so sacramental a character, that they should shrink from its repetition for the sake of a thing so holy as unity and brotherhood. It is known that the Genevan Church has, in several instances, laid hands on clergymen of the Church of England removing to Geneva; regarding this their act as of the nature, perhaps, of a local commission, such as it is pretended that Barnabas and Paul received at Antioch, to exercise their ministry in the locality and sphere to which they had come. There have been instances even in New England, where this species of ordination has been, in other days, conferred on ministers of the Church of England. And although this is not a valid vindication of Episcopacy, in imparting her orders to ministers returning to her bosom from other denominations: yet it has more than the force of the argument *ad hom-*

inem, because it takes the objection out of the mouth of the objector, by showing that Presbytery has really no conception of the matter that would render re-ordination itself either sacrilegious or sinful. But the whole reasoning, I admit, is intended to provide for an extreme case,—a case not likely to exist,—of a scruple based upon principle, against the repetition of a sacramental ordination; and the only inference we wish to draw from this mode of reasoning is, that the cause must be admitted to be good, which can cover apparent exceptions and actual extremes. For the sake then of Unity, the lost but priceless pearl of Christendom, I could see that the Presbyterians, and even the Presbyterian clergymen of the most straitest sect, might return to the bosom of the Church from which they went out, without the surrender of principle, and without a scruple of suspicion as to the validity of her ministerial functions; especially since the late controversy in New York, and the late numbers of the Princeton Review, have made it clear that the last stronghold of Old School Presbyterianism has surrendered to the Congregationalists, and that the sacramental character of ministerial ordination, through a line of ordainers reaching back to the Apostles, is for ever abandoned. And it is well! It will make the way the easier for your ministers and laity to come back into the Church. When your laity get to understand, that every five or seven good men may come together, form a congregation, and ordain one of their members as their minister; and that this ordination will be as valid as if the whole company of the Apostles had laid their hands upon his head; and when your clergy get to understand that this is all the inherent virtue, grace, or charm of *ordination:* they will find it all the easier to give up so cheap a luxury, and to return into the Church. The Church owes something certainly to Dr. Potts. His reasonings, and his cheapening the ministry, have already driven, at least three clergymen, that I have heard of, into the Episcopal Church. The Church will owe something also, we are certain, to the gentlemen of the Princeton Review, to which we look for similar results. "The authority to call the ministry is primarily in the whole Church. . . . The power belongs in all its vigor *to the people; and they can originate as valid a ministry as ever was made by Presbytery or Prelate.*"* Surely, after this, Presbyterians may return to the Church from which their fathers went out; and their ministers will be sure, in their sober second thought, to come back to Her for an unction that speaketh better things of their order and their honor, than the Princeton Review.

On the other hand, as to Churchmen surrendering Episcopacy, possibly some few might do it without the surrender of principle; but, almost universally, they feel a living confidence that in the Episcopacy are involved the preservation of the faith, the perpetuity of the ministry, the purity of the sacraments, the existence of the Church, and the hereditary title to the promises of Christ. A fundamental principle would be at once surrendered, and the heart would never know a moment's ease. They could not feel that they were in the old Church that had been from the beginning. But Presbyterians could recross the barrier which only their own hands have erected, and come back to the ancient Church, and still be sure that they were "God's husbandry," that they were "God's building." And the giving up mere *personal feeling* for the sake of doing all in your power to arrive at universal unity, would be "an odor of a sweet smell, a sacrifice acceptable, well pleasing to God;" and even the slight error would be forgiven,—if perchance it were an error,—ventured for the sake of binding the bleeding members of His Body upon earth together. Even parties in politics make concession for less noble ends; and there is a charm in the watchword, "Union *for the sake of* the Union."

* Princeton Review, 1844.

Then there was another question :—Does the faith that I have received from those before me and around me, hold out to me the hope that it shall be universal? Is it likely that the Westminster Confession of Faith shall be the faith of all the earth? Is it not too intellectual, too metaphysical, too extensive in its area? Is there not too much said in it, and said too positively, of the deep things of predestination, free will, foreknowledge, decrees, reprobation, personal election of angels, men, and infants, limited redemption, effectual calling, perseverance in grace? Be all this so—be these the secret pillars of God's everlasting throne, the hidden springs by which he moves the universe—whether they be or not, is not now the question: but, Are these points, which are so delicate and full of difficulty, and so unfathomably deep, requiring the highest metaphysical acumen either to believe or to defend them, are they of such absolute necessity, that they must be embodied and propounded to the human race as the symbol of the Christian faith? Is it likely, or even possible, that the whole world, "from the least to the greatest," shall reach the conclusions of the Westminster Assembly? The very question provokes DESPAIR! Calvinism can nowhere retain the ground that it has gained; much less can it make new advances, or add new territories permanently to its domain. It is said to be a fact that, while the population of New England has steadily increased, and has been doubled and quadrupled, the number of members of the Calvinistic congregations, diluted as that Calvinism is, is not greater now than it was a century ago: while innumerable *isms* have prepared her distracted communities to become, either a blind prey to the meshes of Popery, or an enlightened acquisition to a more ancient and Catholic Episcopacy.

In the now distracted condition of "those who profess and call themselves Christians," we need a creed for binding us together, that shall be infinitely simple. And what can we find, or what could we invent, that shall be more simple than the Apostles' Creed, the identical creed of the ancient Catholic and the present Episcopal Church? The mistake both of Rome and Geneva has consisted in prying into those things which are not convenient; binding the understandings of men with systems too minutely detailed, too tightly drawn, too metaphysically nice, and by consequence too difficult for universal agreement. The creeds of both are too large, too positive upon points never heard of in the Church's creeds before; and both are daring accumulations on the Ancient Faith: and to look at either—Trent or Westminster—one would feel safe in fearing *a priori*, that wherever they were imposed, well-informed minds would throw them off, and seek continually for a change; and that as creeds they *never could* be universally accepted. It is carrying legislation too far. It is despotism. Mind cannot brook it. Man will not bear it. Geneva was uneasy under the yoke, and broke it from her neck. Rome is uneasy too, and is breaking it from hers. Holland, Germany, New England, have done the same. But in England, and wherever Episcopacy exists, where man and mind have been free, the people are contented with the ancient faith, the yoke that is easy, the burden that is light, the happy medium between the too much and the too little: a faith worthy of the age of inspiration, and worthy the illustrious name it has borne from the beginning,—THE APOSTLES' CREED.

Nor is this merely an *a priori* apprehension. Look at the result. Fortunately for us, time has on both these systems made a long and fair experiment. Rome led the way; Westminster followed. Rome, for a thousand years, has been urging her never-settled and still accumulating creed upon the Christian world. Has she succeeded? No. From the utterance of her first dogma, claiming supremacy, to the publication of her last, by which the *sine labe concepta* is to be added to the honors of the Blessed Virgin by Pope Pius IX., and is to be incorporated as a new article into the Creed of Rome: she has been nobly and successfully resisted. Sixty millions of Catholics in the East, in communion with the sees of Constantinople and Jerusalem, disdained her pretensions from the very first, as they do still; while in the West, England, and even France, and Portugal, and Spain, contested, and still, to an important extent, contest, the encroachments; while millions of her followers are either ignorant of her real faith, or they hold it in convenient senses of their own, without any fear before their eyes of a whole universe of cardinals and popes. *Rome has made her experiment.* Intellectually—or so long as man shall reason, and morally—or so long as man shall enjoy the lights and rights of conscience, and religiously—or so long as men shall have the Holy Scriptures in their hands, it is impossible that all mankind shall embrace the tedious details of Romanism.

Equally marked have been the fate and the failure of Presbytery. Three hundred years it has run on, and the winds and the tides have been with it. Yet it has not achieved the destiny which its framers intended. It is farther from the goal than the day it entered, amidst the shouts of Geneva and Germany, upon its course. Its creed, like that of Rome, has required continual patching and refitting; and with every new piece inserted in the garment, the new hath taken from the old, and the rent hath been made worse. I am probably quite within the proper estimate in supposing that in the Presbyterian sects there are at this moment thirty millions of Unitarians, Universalists, and Pantheists, and that from fifty to one hundred millions who have received its Baptism have gone into eternity "denying the Lord that bought them with His blood." And, even in the last stronghold of Old School Presbyterianism perhaps, the man cannot be produced who would subscribe the "Confession of Faith" in the bold and manly sense intended by its framers. The whole body is in its opinions dismembered, and is dismayed at the results of its own experiment. There is not left in Europe, and perhaps scarcely here, a solid nucleus to the vaporous body; but in its eccentric orbit, whirling alternately through the extremes of heat and cold, it loses by evaporation in the high temperature of its revivals, and still further by contraction, as it passes next into the freezing aphelion of intellectual speculations. The denomination, which three hundred years ago was one, and which, from having been nursed in the Church, had caught the Church's accent, and answered the Congregational schismatics as a Church should do that stood as a giant oak which nothing but omnipotence itself could blight: we now behold rent and scattered, like the leaves of the oak in winter. She now presents no point of unity to her scattered and dejected members; much less, in the ears of the world without, can she raise among her legions the rallying watchword—We are one.*

* John Angell James may be regarded as a representative of Sectarism in England, and from an address of his, delivered last year before the "Evangelical Alliance," or "the friends of Christian Union," in Edinburgh, I make the following extracts:—

1. "It will be asked, what kind of Union it is that we are seeking and endeavoring to form; and to this question we reply, it is not an amalgamation of the different religious bodies, though even of this we need not quite despair, after what has lately taken place in Scotland—that land of secession and disruption, as it seems to be—in the coalition of two separate bodies of professing Christians."

Sectarianism, then, is incurable! The religious bodies are not to be amalgamated! But one might have supposed that at such a meeting, and for such a purpose, and in Scotland too, a Congregationalist would have passed by the opportunity of such a thrust at Presbyterian Scotland—"*that land of secession and disruption, as it seems to be!*"

The speaker proceeds—

2. "Much less is it the object of the Evangelical Alliance to create the real and essential unity of the Church of Christ; that has been arranged in the councils of Eternity. The will of man can neither make nor unmake this. We are, and must be, members one of another, even in spite of ourselves. There is but one Church; there can be but one. Wrangle as we will, we cannot wrangle away from each other. We cannot tear ourselves from each other, but by tearing ourselves from Jesus Christ, and, blessed be God, there is a power which will prevent this."

Calvinism cannot be kept out even from a "Christian Union!" "Arranged in the councils of eternity!" "We cannot tear ourselves from each other but by tearing

Thus have the results more than made good the bodings of the thoughtful and far-reaching minds of other days. Papist and Presbyterian have gone too far. Both have carried out

ourselves from Christ, and, blessed be God, there is a power which will prevent this." So, "wrangle as we will, we cannot wrangle away from each other." Is this the invisible Church, and the spiritual unity, or unity in spirit, that we hear of? Does it satisfy the longing heart? No, no; hear the same speaker again:—

3. "Our object, then, is not to *create* essential unity, but to *manifest* it—to make our union visible to the world. And what consistent Christian must not desire this? Who can look without deep concern upon the present state of the Christian Church, agitated by controversy, torn by faction, and rent by schism? Who can witness without grief her broken unity, her tarnished beauty, her shattered frame, her wasted energy? Who ought not to unite in repairing all this, to rescue Christianity from the taunt of the infidel, and Protestantism from the boasted triumph of the Papist?"

So spiritual unity is after all unsatisfactory. It must be made "*manifest*," and "*visible*," and "*Christianity rescued from the taunts of infidels.*" Mr. James is a sanguine man; but is he sanguine on this topic? Let him speak once more for himself.

"My reverend brother has cautioned us against idolizing our organization as an Evangelical Alliance. The warning is seasonable and salutary. We are not so to identify the cause of Christian union with this attempt to promote it, as to suppose that the former could not exist without the latter. This may not be God's method of bringing about the great object we have in view. He may not so far honor us as to accept our plan; still the cause will not ultimately fail. Another and a happier generation *profiting by our mistakes*, yet stimulated by our example, will take up again the subject, and do more and better than we have done," &c.

Yes, Mr. James, now you are right; it "may not be God's method of bringing about the great object you have in view." You can only know what that method is, by what you call "another and a happier generation," not however in the future, as you suppose, but in the past, when "they that believed were all of one mind;" not "profiting by your mistakes," as you express it, for they were the days of John, and Polycarp, and Irenæus, who never fell into such mistakes at all. But we are glad to see this Evangelical Alliance, albeit a sad *ignis fatuus*, that serves to pacify with an illusory hope, and to keep schism breathing a little longer. Sectarianism is got to be so intolerable to yourselves, that unless you can keep up some such hope, your people will be constantly returning to the unity of the Church which they have left behind.

But this Evangelical Alliance has given us some valuable hints of the spirit in which its advocates have gone about their work. The Rev. Dr. Patten, a Presbyterian divine of New York, crossed the broad sea to make, at one of its meetings, the following speech:—

"Some seem to be afraid that we are going by this Alliance to blow up the Church of England. If by blowing up the Church of England they mean that we are going to blow it into a great bubble or bladder, why, that is already done. But if they mean that we are going to blow it up *sky*-high, why, then we confess that we do expect to put that Church a little nearer heaven than it ever was before."

Strike on! The Church is the anvil, said a holy father, that hath worn out many a hammer.

too far the doctrine of development. Both have prescribed too much to be believed. Both have indulged too far in mingling philosophy with faith. Both have filled the continent of Europe with a skepticism that is but the natural goal of the human mind, when cut adrift from some dark dogma, abhorrent to reason, and incompatible with the nature of God. Both seem to have nearly run their course. Both have failed, after a fair experiment, to make any approach toward conciliation of parties and the restoration of Unity. And unless we can find some Witness sitting by, the while, in sackcloth, and preserving, as on a table of stone, the faith of the first ages: we must give up the heritage of God to the demon of discord and misrule, and mark the prayer of Him whom the Father heareth always, as *the unanswered prayer;* and His promise that the gates of hell should not prevail against His Church, as *the unaccomplished promise*. Forlorn is the hope that Presbytery offers, and dark is the alternative held out by Popery; for from them both we can gather but the one idea—that of A UNITY IMPOSSIBLE.

CHAPTER XIV.

A UNITY POSSIBLE.

STILL I sighed for unity. And I could sometimes see the bosom of my brethren swelling with the same emotion. A deep-seated conscience will cling to an idol that hath horns and hoofs, rather than be driven from its dim ideas of a God and of His worship. The inborn love of immortality, in the absence of the true idea, will picture its elysiums and its sensual harems sooner than quench the spark that thus flies upward from the heart. The heaven-born aspiration after Unity may be excused for seeking, in like manner, in the absence of the holy reality, to make up its loss by Articles, Associations, Alliances, Societies, Anniversaries, and Platforms, covering up with gauze the ugly disagreements of a hundred schisms;—the hearts of all parties appearing to warm and melt toward each other on a certain day in the year, as the blood of Saint Januarius is said to warm and liquefy in the vial before the eyes of the *believers* in Naples, as often as the martyr's anniversary returns. But it is no more like the beauty of Unity, than the ugly caricature which children draw of shadows on the wall is like the human face divine. As Frederick the First is said to have amused himself, during fits of the gout, in painting likenesses of his grenadiers; and if the picture did not happen to resemble the grenadier, Frederick painted the grenadier to the colors of the picture: so the sects, unable to present the world with a portrait of Unity, "that the world may believe," first disfigure the idea of Unity, and then paint over the face of schism, with its rents and scars more numerous than grenadier of a hundred fights could count, and ask the world to behold and admire the likeness! No, no; a temperance society, or tract society, was not the Unity for which my heart was breaking! I could see under the platform that there was a vacancy and hollowness; and the shout of an anniversary could not cause me to forget that it was a truce, and not a peace; a farce, and not a fact.* And as these got-up substitutes do not fill the heart, the resolution of Unity into an ethereal, invisible, spiritual, vaporous feeling, only serves to tantalize: like dissolving views under the combined agencies of magic lanterns, which amuse for the hour and pass away for ever. The invention is the invention of a *camera obscura*, and is resorted to only where the lights are extinguished, and the soul is dark.

* "Now, noble dame, perchance you ask,
How these two hostile armies met,
Deeming it were no easy task
To keep the truce which here was set,
Where martial spirits all on fire,
Breathed only blood and mortal ire.
By mutual inroads, mutual blows,
By habit and by *conscience* foes,
They met on Teviot's strand;
They met, and sate them mingled down,
Without a threat, without a frown,
As brothers meet in foreign land.
The hands, the spear that lately grasped,
Still in the mailéd gauntlet clasped,
Were interchanged in greetings dear.
Yet be it known,
Had bugles blown,
Or signs of war been seen,
Those bands so fair together ranged,
Had dyed with gore the green.
'Twixt truce and war such sudden change
Was not unfrequent, nor deemed strange
In the old Border-day."

Lay of the Last Minstrel.

I confess that on this great subject my soul was dark. For years of my Presbyterian ministry, like many of my brethren, I would have nothing to do with anniversaries and platforms. Are you opposed to these societies? Why do we never see you on the platform? or hear you among the speakers? or find you preaching in their cause?—were questions that gave me pain for years. I could not bear to tread over the hollow sepulchre that a platform covered;—beautiful without, but full within of hypocrisy and strife. I avoided the unions, because I contended for Unity. To me all this was like throwing so much dust into the ocean, to restore the Atlantis that may once have bound the continents together. The Atlantis of the ancients is gone! And until it be restored, the floating sea-weed will not tempt prudent men to tread upon the treacherous flooring.

I panted for a Unity—real, manly, visible, efficient—a unity that the world might see; in order, as the Mediator prays, "that the world might believe." I asked the watchmen that went about the city: "Can you tell me where unity dwelleth? and which is the way to the house thereof? Rome saith, It is not with me; and Geneva saith, It is not with me. Is it then hid from the eyes of all living, and kept close from the fowls of the air?" This I could not believe; for the idea of Unity shadowed on my heart, like that of God and Immortality and Heaven, must be referable to a substance or reality somewhere to be found: and Scripture and Antiquity said, We have heard the fame thereof with our ears. "O God, we have heard with our ears, and our fathers have declared unto us, the noble works that thou didst in their days, and in the old time before them." In the times of old, the Church was One; her creed was One; her government was One. We have seen who violated this unity: first Rome, then Geneva. But who has preserved the deposit intact? Is there anywhere a Church, still clinging to the creed and the discipline of those happy times, and beckoning the world back to unity again? O thou Guide of the wandering, show me the way!

Now Presbyterians, and even ingenuous Romanists, admit that the orders and sacraments of the Episcopal Church are at least so far valid as to be of themselves no barrier to Unity. If Pius the Ninth were of the same disposition with Pius the Fifth, he would acknowledge that Church to-morrow, with her creeds, her liturgies, her ministry, and her sacraments, as they are: provided only that she would bow her neck to his supremacy. Yet Romanism and Presbyterianism are agreed in getting rid of the restraints of the Episcopacy: the former, by the usurpation of the Popes; the latter, by the usurpation of the Presbyters. Both agree in nullifying the Episcopacy, while both concede the validity of its functions. Both acknowledge the creed of the Episcopal Church, while both have as singularly added the local adjudications of Trent and Westminster.

What is the creed of the Episcopal Church? "I believe in God, the Father Almighty," &c. It may all be written in less than twenty such lines as are now passing under the reader's eyes. It is called, and has been called from the beginning, "THE APOSTLES' CREED." There are reasons to think that it came from the Apostles' hands. It bears internal evidence that its framers were under a restraint of inspiration. It can hardly be imagined as within the range of possibility, that uninspired men should have been content with making such a creed as that. It can scarcely be conceived that the Apostles, while the New Testament was not yet written, would have left their converts in all lands without a summary or outline of their faith. Besides, the earliest fathers ascribe it to the Apostles. And wherever the Apostles or their helpers travelled, from Syria in the East, to England in the West, and away in Africa itself, this creed was known as the faith transmitted from the Apostles "*from the beginning.*" It was known in Churches where the Bible itself was not known. It existed, in fact, more than two centuries before the books of the New Testament were collected, examined, and received. Irenæus, the companion of Polycarp the disciple of St. John, after quoting this creed, declares: "This preaching and this faith the Church, scattered throughout the whole world, guards as carefully as if she dwelt in one house, believes as if she had but one soul, and proclaims, teaches, and perpetuates, as if she had but one mouth." The fathers that quote the New Testament as a collected and acknowledged symbol, belong to the fourth and the subsequent centuries; but the fathers that quote the Apostles' Creed belong to the second, and were born even in the first. And even then it was spoken of as the faith that *they* had been taught *in childhood*, and as the faith from *the beginning*. The Church hands it down to us, and tells us it is the faith dictated by the Apostles; just as it hands us the Gospels of St. Mark and St. Luke, and the Acts of the Apostles, and tells us that, although not written by Apostles, they were written under the eyes and dictation of Apostles. If we reject one, we may reject all. There was, then, a creed in the second century, known as universal, found everywhere, recited alike in all subsequent time, in Europe, Asia, and Africa, and even in the earliest age spoken of as the faith from the beginning; and it kept the Church at unity, through all its storms of fire and of blood, three hundred years. Where is the heavenly pearl? Is it lost or mislaid in the archives of the Vatican? Is it so buried under the rubbish of centuries that it cannot be found? No; there is a Church in America and England, on both the continents, and in a hundred isles, that can say with Irenæus in the second century, "This preaching and this faith the Church, scattered throughout the whole world, guards as carefully as if she dwelt in one house, believes as if she had but one soul, and proclaims, teaches, and perpetuates, as if she had but one mouth."

Again, what is this Church's Creed? "I believe in one God, the Father Almighty," &c., commonly called the Nicene Creed: at most a cautious explanation of the former; and, in fact, nothing more than a publication of the terms in which the Articles of the Apostles' Creed had been sometimes stated from the beginning. The fathers of the Council of Nice, in the year 325, did not attempt, because they did not think it either necessary or lawful, to protest against the wide-spread heresy of Arius in any terms, or words, or confessions, or creeds unknown to the Church from the beginning: but, as a mere mouth-piece or witness to a matter of fact, fell back on the Apostles' Creed, as explained and held from the beginning in the Apostolic Churches. In like manner, the Church of England did not deem it necessary or lawful to create new Creeds or Confessions of Faith, in order to protest against the corruptions of the Papacy: but, true to the spirit of 325, *fell back* on the Creed as then asserted to have been the faith from the beginning. Shall I say, then, that it betrays astonishing ignorance, or shall I more unkindly suspect that it proceeds from lack of Christian candor, that Presbyterians charge the Church with arrogance in dictating her faith to the world? So far is she from this arrogance, that this is the only point in which the Church has shown herself *timid.* She never *dared* to touch the faith of antiquity with one of her fingers. At Nice, in the year 325, she successfully resisted the overflow of the Arian heresy, by simply falling back on what was known to have been the faith from the beginning. And, *twelve hundred years* after, she as successfully resisted Rome, not by making confessions and creeds never heard of in the Church before, but by falling back upon the creed of Nice as received from the Apostles. She did not in either case raise the axe and the hammer against the image of Dagon: but only set up the ancient Ark of the covenant by his side, and Dagon straightway fell and was broken before the ancient symbol.

It is high time these facts were understood. The Assembly of Westminster, and the Synods of Dort and Geneva and Heidelberg, did have the "arrogance" to sit down, Bible in hand, and compile a creed. But *the Church* never imagined that she had authority to write one single word or syllable in the Christian Creed: but confined herself within her proper limits, as a mere Witness and Keeper, without mutilation or addition, of that which had been the faith "from the beginning."

We insist that this matter shall now be understood. Presbyterianism makes creeds. Popery makes creeds. The Church makes none. She would as soon think of making a Bible, as a creed. When the Reformation, whose "morning star" arose in England in the person of Wickliffe, called the Church of England to her feet, and made her signals that the day had dawned, and that there was a work for her to do: she did not take her Bible and sit down, as sects did then, and as individuals do now, gravely to look for a religion. She did not take a sheet of white paper, as did Calvin and Luther and the Presbyterian divines, and presume, or dare, to write one word upon it, as a creed. She found the paper already written on, and part of it written on from the beginning. She could distinguish the ancient from the new handwriting. She erased from it, for ever, what Rome had added; she left in its ancient type what had been from the beginning. She did not add. She did not take away. She did not alter. She wrote Articles, not in her Creed, but in another place, simply to explain what she had done. And once more she stood on the ground where Universal Christendom had stood, in one array, for six hundred years. She calls therefore her faith the Catholic or Universal Faith, and herself a Branch of the Catholic or Universal Church. It is the only Faith that ever was Universal; it is the only Church that can be shown to have been ever Universal. And as Popery itself has retained the Faith, but overshadowed it with additions, (just as Westminster and Geneva have retained it too, but encumbered it with dogmas hard to be believed:) we perceive that beneath the rubbish of the very Papacy still lies this guarded pearl, at this moment the Universal Faith of a Universal Church. The creed of Trent was never Universal. The creed of Westminster was never Universal. Neither was Popery. Neither was Presbytery. Yet, with all the manly and rightful Catholicity of the Episcopal Church, she has never ventured to *make a creed.* She confesses to the world, and denies not, but confesses that she is but an earthen vessel for a heavenly treasure; the humble Witness and Keeper of "the Faith once delivered to the saints:" that she would no more presume to touch that Ark of Testimony, to steady it when rocking over the rough places of the Arian heresy and the upheaving Reformation, than she would put forth her hand to tear down the pillars of heaven. The Apostles' and the Nicene Creeds—these are thy creeds, O thou Church of my understanding and my heart! Simple, but sublime; brief, but sufficient; so brief they are, that they may both be printed on the palm of a Christian's hand: yet are they so sufficient, that the demon of Arianism, in the first great conflict of the Church, went out howling from her presence; and Popery herself did them homage in flying before them out of England. It was a sublime spectacle—a multitude of priests and mitred heads assembled out of all lands, to hear and to bear the testimony of the Universal Church against the teachings of Arius; Europe, Asia, and Africa, all in agony for the result: yet the holy synod contented itself with saying, not what should be hereafter, but what *had been* from the beginning, in all places, the faith of the Church! Twelve centuries roll by, and again the mitred heads of an empire are in synod, and again the Church is in her agony: but she is again content to fall back upon the ancient faith, separating it only from the additions of Rome. Under the benign sway of this brief and simple creed, the Christian world was in one communion for six hundred years: and if the "thing that hath been is that which shall be," the Christian world may yet see fit to restrain themselves within the limits that this creed prescribes, or rather to walk forth into the larger liberty that this creed allows. It contains the essential faith, and nothing that is not essential: nothing of the worship of the host, or of dead men's bones, or of the immaculate conception, on the one hand; nothing of predestination, and limited redemption, and irresistible grace, on the other. Alas! why did Rome encroach upon the liberty of private judgment, when the ancient creed allowed it to range, and to reach different conclusions, on a thousand matters of individual opinion? And why did Westminster and Geneva follow in the footsteps of the Trentine bishops? Liberty! where will you go to find it? Not to Trent; she legislates on every thing, and leaves no room for private judgment. Not to Geneva; she legislates at equal length, with the same detail, on matters of mere opinion. As there were divines at Rome who "shut up the terrestrial body of Galileo in a dungeon, for asserting the motion of those bodies that are celestial:" so there were divines at Westminster who would hardly allow a man to be predestinated to salvation, unless he would consent that infants of a span long might, by the Father of mercies, be predestinated to perdition.

The case then, presented to my mind, was this. The "Christian world" is found under three general varieties—Papal, Presbyterian, and Episcopal. In point of doctrine, the creeds of Trent and Westminster are too detailed, too unwieldy, too metaphysical, too unlike the creeds held universally by the primitive Church, to afford the slightest reasonable hope that the world shall ever embrace them. The Episcopal creed, on the contrary, is the undiminished, unenlarged, unaltered, *verbatim et literatim* Creed of the first six centuries; the same Creed which Polycarp in Asia, and Irenæus in Europe, and Augustine in Africa, preserved as the very bond of Unity; which sixty millions of Oriental Catholics acknowledge to this hour; which we find imbedded in strong foundations under the rubbish of Rome itself; on which the Church of England fell back in her great battle with the Papacy; and for which both Polycarp and Cranmer, fourteen hundred miles and fourteen hundred years apart, perished gloriously in the fires.

Let me then go back, said I, beyond the times and the rise of Popery and Presbyterianism, when the whole company of Christian people on earth, with a wisdom that we find only in ages of inspiration, were content with these short and simple symbols, which so properly, and with such happy results, permit an infinite variety of opinion on minor matters, and safely leave ten thousand things to the varying influences of private judgment. Let me shake off, said I,—even if I myself believe them,—the inflated creeds of Westminster and Geneva, of Augsburg and Dort, of Trent and Rome, of Heidelberg and Saybrook; which all require of me more than all mankind can be expected to believe: and let me go back, with the Church of England and her daughters that already gird the globe, to the one Faith and the One Holy Catholic and Apostolic Church throughout the earth. They certainly hold out a reasonable hope of re-uniting the distracted world, on what is admitted by all sectarians, and by Papists too, to have been once, for whole bright centuries, the only Creed of Christendom. Within the spacious inclosure of this creed, the Methodist, as Mr. Wesley felt, may breathe with comfort; while an earnest liturgy will aid the loud amens and warm ejaculations of the people. Beneath this vine the Calvinist may dwell in quietness; for the Church has had her Augustines, and Henrys, and Scotts, and Topladys, and Huntingdons. In these wells of salvation the Immersionist too may bathe; for the Church has preferred immersion in her theory and in her rubrics, and the common substitution of sprinkling (said to have been originally resorted to in extreme cases) may have been an innovation of that Popery which has never feared to lay its hand upon the very sacraments. The foundations of this Church are wide; there is room for all—all who do not touch the short and simple faith. Some have in these days even questioned the divine right of Bishops: and yet have remained in her communion, rather than break the bond of Unity. In the times of old, there were good men who deferred their own and their children's baptism to a late period of life, for fear of sins that might, after baptism, grieve unpardonably the Holy Ghost imparted in that blessed sacrament: from which, perhaps, the extreme inference may be derived, that even the Baptist might have sat down quietly within the Church, for the love of the brethren, and for the sake of Unity, leaving his scruples to the influence of time; and there would have been none to harm him.

So long as men's minds are carried away with the undue magnifying of some small matter—immersion, election, rights of Presbyters—they are not in a position to see the force of this reasoning. We must rise higher, and yet higher, until we reach an elevation from which we may be able to see the entire Church—the past and the present—at once. With toil and tears did I climb up to that point of observation. I saw the Church nowhere so lovely as in the past, when her creed was shortest. To me the influence was overwhelming. Here is the only creed on earth that was ever universal. It is an outline of the essential faith. It came from the Apostles. *It is the great protector of the right of private judgment.* Its great principle—worthy of being written, not in letters of gold, but rather worthy of being written, as it was written, in the blood of the martyrs: "*in necessariis, unitas; in dubiis, libertas; in omnibus, caritas:*" "in things essential, unity; in things doubtful, liberty; in all things, charity:"—is ample as the universe. Let me then go back to the ancient things, said I, and repossess myself of the ancient name—older than Wesley, older than Presbyterian, older than Lutheran, Reformed, or Calvinist—ay, older than Roman. "*Christian* the name; *Catholic* the surname." On this foundation unity is possible; and on this alone is it *possible*. And on this rock still stands the Episcopal Church, inviting the world back to the "STATUS IN QUO ANTE BELLUM!"

Although I have written thus in seeming strains of hope, have I any expectation that these visions of brotherhood shall become, before long, a refreshing reality? Have I any hope that the Presbyterian bodies of Geneva, and Germany, and Switzerland, and Denmark, and England, and Ireland, and France, and Prussia, shall reconvene at Heidelberg, Geneva, Augsburg, Dort, London, and Belfast, and restore by acclamation to His brow, the Crown of Glory which they have taken from the Son of God? Have I a hope that the Conferences, and the Associations, and the General Assemblies of America, shall make overtures of return and reconciliation to the Ancient Church? No, none whatever. "There must first come a falling away"—that dark, chaotic, dismal period, which, although it must be short, is enough to make the good man tremble as he looks into the page of prophecy, now almost legible in the signs of the times. We believe, we know, we *see*, that Presbyterianism will fall—is falling—has, in nearly all lands, fallen already—from its hold on the skies through a Mediator; and is cast upon the earth, covered with the awful leprosy of Rationalism: and the only hope we cherish for this generation, is to persuade men who may have eyes, to *see* the flood that has already overflowed the fairest portions of the Presbyterian world, and will as surely overwhelm the residue, that *they* may escape with their sons and daughters into the Ark. The battle of the Church will not be fought with Presbyterianism, but with that brood of fancies which Presbyterianism hourly begets; perhaps not even with Rome, but with the frightful progeny that Rome, by the same process, engenders. Her battle will be with the great and terrible Antichrist, who shall appear when the vintage of the earth shall be ripe for him to gather. The shock must come, and the Church will not be unprepared. She is at this moment industriously girding on her harness for some mighty task, to which the spirit of prophecy that is in her is evidently calling her. She, who in the dark ages could maintain the faith, and in the eras of light could separate it from error, and amidst the change of the times can preserve it still intact, whether from the developments of Popery, or the wild progress of Protestantism: may look forward to the approach of Antichrist, and say, "The Lord that delivered me out of the paw of the lion, and out of the paw of the bear, He will deliver me out of the hand of this Philistine."

"That great day of God Almighty"—who does not see its dawning? Who does not hear the tread of Gog and Magog upon the mountains? Who does not see the banners moving, and hear the confused shout among the nations? Who does not see the towering head of Antichrist, rising "above all that is called God, or is worshipped?" O Sectarianism! thou hast no shelter "in the day that shall burn as an oven!" Alas! that day is one of thine own kindling! Thank God, he hath shown to one who is less than the least of all, the ancient foundations. I see their strength; I see their harmony; I see their Unity; I see their antiquity; I see their elevation above the light and darkness, the changes and chances of this lower sphere; I see a baptized world standing shoulder to shoulder for centuries upon them: I hope to see—although it may not be until the Lamb shall have wiped all tears from our eyes—a baptized world standing on them again!

CHAPTER XV.

CATHOLICITY.

I FIND that I have touched a chord endless in its vibrations; have uttered a word boundless in its meaning; have hinted a truth, bright, beautiful, holy; a truth that no man, cramped and hemmed in by an *ism*, hath seen or can see; a truth untrammelled by space or place; unlimited by duration or time; unaffected by chance or change; its presence, everywhere; its existence, always; its empire, all things, whether they be things in heaven or things on earth; itself, the image of the Universal Father: for, the moment we see it, and ask whose image and superscription it hath, it answers by its very existence—God's. But the Catholic idea—for this it is to which we have now come—would charm me too far away, and detain the reader too long, from the course of this narrative. I must therefore resist the temptation; but not without protesting, that my conversion has been less properly a conversion to Episcopacy than to Catholicity: certainly not to Episcopacy as sometimes drawn by our masters—high and beautiful and stately as the snows upon the summer mountains, but as cold and frigid as the eternal ice; high, dry, pompous, and freezing—an Episcopacy which is naked and cold because it is alone, (for how can a truth be warm alone?) and which, like Immersionism or Little-childrenism, is but the one idea—bald, naked, shivering, starving—of a narrow mind. I should rather say, that my conversion has been to that which the Episcopacy indicates as generally present with itself, and as certainly present nowhere else—in a word, as I said, to Catholicity; something for all times, for all places, for all intellects, for all hearts; breaking down the walls between temple and temple; forbidding the barriers between Christian and Christian; healing the breaches between man and man; denying the distinctions between rich and poor; refusing to know either Jew or Greek, Barbarian or Scythian, bond or free; feeding all on the one Bread; blessing for all the one Cup; shining with equal attractiveness on the child and the philosopher; bathing beggars and princes in the same waters; gathering all things back together into One; and thus realizing the great conception imbedded in the very word *re-ligion*,* binding all to each other again, and all once more to God: a Catholicity throbbing throughout earth and heaven with one pulse; beating, breathing, burning, bursting with one intention, one heart, one life; circling the earth with its sympathies; conquering the world by its determination; and weaving for the King when He shall return in His beauty with His spouse, a woof of hearts reaching back to the Apostles, and conveying in all its threads the electric fire first kindled at the Cross, and communicated to the Twelve.

This, I have said, is what a sectarian—isolated, and immured in an *ism*, or a one-idea—can never understand; how "all the Body," as St. Paul expresses it, "by joints and bands having nourishment ministered, and knit together, increaseth with the increase of God." Catholicity, like an affection or a passion, or rather like life itself, must be *felt*, and felt to be *ours:* else it can no more be understood (and I who have known it have a right to say it) than a severed branch can feel the circulation of the vine, or an amputated

* From the Latin *religo*—to *bind again.*

limb be warmed with the sympathies and pulsations of the body.

But though the secret of Catholicity is with her children, and her secret can never be imparted: yet it is pleasing to see that sectarians begin to understand *that there is something within the veil.* The "Advocate and Journal" has lately told it to the Methodists, and been candid enough to express satisfaction at the fact; the "Independent" has just discovered it to the Congregationalists, and speaks quite reasonably; and Dr. Nevin, in his chair, has but the other day enlightened the Lutherans with the information that Catholicity is a living energy: "deep-lodged," says Professor Nevin, "in the constitution of the age, and carrying in itself the gathered strength of centuries;" "possessing," says the Independent, "such fascination and power, that we do not wonder that some of the most manly intellects and purest hearts of the age have been captivated by its claims." Says Professor Nevin, "Protestantism, in its blind zeal and shallow knowledge, sinking the Church to the level of a temperance society, stripping the Ministry of its divine Authority, reducing the Sacraments to mere signs, turning all that is Mystical into the most trivial sense, and so exalting what is individual above what is general and Catholic, as to throw open the door to the most rampant sectarian license in the name of the gospel, can never, I repeat it, prevail against Oxford or Rome." Well, something has been gained; and although Catholicity is free-masonry to them that are without, yet we are glad to hope that we are no longer to be taunted with adhering to the mere dogma of a bald, pompous, lifeless, isolated, and freezing Episcopacy.

Who can wonder that, so long as such an Episcopacy was insisted on, the claim has never been made to appear even reasonable? Who can be surprised that Papist and Presbyterian, Baptist and Methodist, have fought against it? Whc can wonder that Episcopalians, exulting in the one idea, and making it the *only dividing thing on earth* between them and the "other denominations," have been taken to task by Mr. Barnes for their "position?" There are men, and there are bishops, who even now banish from the sanctuary the Cross, the symbol of *all* truth: but have a precious care to set up the Mitre the symbol of *one* truth. And why? Because, in their theology, *the mitre* is the only thing left to divide them in principle from the "other denominations;" and this the "other denominations" can never comprehend. But exhibit our Holy Church as preserving unimpeached and unimpaired the ancient faith, our worship as the daily and earnest utterance in which we join the souls under the altar, our unity as inviolable like the unity of the Holy Ghost, our sacraments as quickening instruments of grace, our Catholicity as binding the past to the present, the present to the future, man to his brother, and all to Heaven; and Episcopacy as *the sentinel at the door*, never mistaking the trappings of his office for the treasures of the palace—an Episcopacy above the whisperings and jealousies and heart-burnings and man-pleasings of an evil day, earnestly intent on guarding, not its own poor dignity, but the Church which God hath purchased with His Blood: and the world will cease to wonder that we contend for the Episcopacy, not as being the *one* truth which sectarians have not, but because it is the guard of a *thousand* truths, associations, sympathies, energies, and treasures which they can never have. An icy, barren dogma—a one-idea—a bald, narrow-minded, bigoted, high-low and low-church Episcopacy, the only thing preventing our fraternization with the sects?—with all my soul I would fight against it, too! The Church has groaned, and grown gaunt and ghastly, and has dwindled and disappeared from whole neighborhoods under such school-boy and contracted teachings.

It is a poor apology for such narrow views, that the Church

in this country has chosen to be called "Protestant Episcopal:" a name open, we admit, to misapprehension; but well intended, when well interpreted: PROTESTANT, against the doctrinal errors of either Popery or Presbytery; EPISCOPAL, against the usurpation of both Popes and Presbyters.

There are prudent men, however, who think it to be regretted that the Church in America did not take her name rather from her resemblance to antiquity, than from her contrast with Rome—Rome too much honored, they think, by the homage. Is Popery, they say, the pole-star by which churches are to steer? Is Popery the sun that is to fill all eyes, around which all sects, as planets struck from her body, are to roll and do homage, and by which the other bodies are to take their bearings, and measure their perihelions and aphelions, such and such a distance from the sun, and calculate each other's obscurations, penumbras, occultations, transits, eclipses, and number of digits immersed? Just as she was rising from her low estate, it may have promised the Church in this land some dignity and importance to assert herself *the champion* (for so far as I am aware it is the only body of Christians that has formally taken the *name* of "Protestant") now ready to measure weapons with gigantic Rome! But there are pure and prudent men who would rather have seen her measuring stature with antiquity, or faith with Scripture. Be this as it may, it is a most singular historical fact, that Evangelical Protestants in Europe are becoming embarrassed by the name.* Thus in the recent con-

* The beautiful prayer in the English Liturgy, "More especially we pray for *the good estate of the Catholic Church*, &c.," was altered in our Liturgy so as to read, "More especially we pray *for thy holy Church universal*, &c.," for the alleged reason, that persons not familiar with our service might understand the expression as identifying us with the Papists. Be this so, the change of phraseology has led to a still worse mistake, for on hearing the corrected prayer, strangers have sometimes asked whether we were *Universalists*. We live in an age of great intelligence in matters of religion!

struction of the great lever by which the new root-and-branch men are to uproot Popery from the earth, although the purpose was Protestant, yet they avoided the name, and called themselves the "Evangelical Alliance." "Protestants" would hardly have answered, for it would have let into the Alliance twenty Socinians to one "Evangelical." And the American branch of this very Alliance publishes a periodical in New York, entitled "Der Freie Deutsche Katholik"—"The Free German Catholic"—for among Germans the word *Protestant* would have meant *Infidel.* When I was a Presbyterian, at a hotel in Germany, in a mixed company at dinner, a debate arose between some Romish Priests and German Protestants, in which I was appealed to, and sided with the priests. "Why! are you not a Protestant?" inquired a German who sat near me. "No, sir," I replied; "I believe in God, the Father, the Son, and the Holy Ghost, and so far I am a Catholic." The celebrated Presbyterian orator and preacher of Lyons, M. Monod, said not very long ago in a speech before the Bible Society in Exeter Hall, that when he had been asked in his own country if he was a Protestant, he answered, "*No;* for a Protestant is a man that believes nothing. Yes, my lord," continued M. Monod, "that is the bad reputation we have got in France, in consequence of the very loose doctrines of the men of Geneva, which go to break down the glory of our Lord Jesus Christ; and hence, throughout France, they think that we Protestants have nothing any more that we believe." Even D'Aubigné is shy and sly upon this point, and puts in a disclaimer and a caveat in the first paragraph of his Preface to his "great work." "The history of the Reformation," he says, "*is altogether distinct from the history of Protestantism.* In the former all bears the character of a regeneration of human nature, a religious and social transformation emanating from God himself. In the latter we see too often a glaring depravation of first principles, the conflict of parties, the sectarian spirit, and the operation of private interests. The history of Protestantism might claim the attention of mere Protestants; the history of the Reformation is a book for all Christians, or rather for all mankind." We thank M. D'Aubigné for thus much candor; it is as much as we had any reason to expect. The rack must pinch when the martyr groans. He glories in the Reformation, but he is shy of Protestantism; he admires the throes of the mother, but is vastly cautious of acknowledging the child. So much for the well-meant name of "Protestant"—a name that the Houses of Convocation, when it was last proposed to adopt it in England, even then felt it a duty to repudiate; choosing rather to be called, like the Church of Corinth, or the Church of Ephesus, or the Church of Smyrna, or the Church of Thyatira, "the Church of England." The name of Protestant is a negation; it protests, it resists, it denies, it believes not, it means nothing. The name, as well as the operation of the system among sectarian Protestants, gives one the idea that its life is the result of conflicting forces acting in temporary antagonism, and must die when the antagonism ceases. So history shows. So our observation proves. A sectarian Protestant is never so devout, so grave, so earnest, so resolute, as in the task of pulling down, of making war, of *attacking*. Now the battle is against slavery, and now alcohol, and now Popery, and now against something else, and now against each other, and finally against its own standards. Its piety cannot live in the calm routine of life; its faith cannot settle down on known and tried foundations, but must be ever in the perils of controversy; its devotion seems to depend upon excitement, as the schoolboy's kite can rise only in a breeze, or as his top (says one) can be kept up only by whipping. Sectarian Protestantism, as a resisting force, can live only by antagonism; it is the storm-bird that cannot bear a calm, that loves the wild confusion of the whirlwind, and disappears so soon as the conflict of the elements is over. Even Monod and D'Aubigné have blushed!

Also the name "Episcopal," while it significantly enough condemns the usurpation of both Popes and Presbyters in riding over the conservative element of the Episcopacy, has nevertheless been open to misconstruction, and has made us a stone of stumbling to Dissenters.

Episcopacy! Episcopacy! Episcopacy! as if Bishop, Bishop were the first thing, the only thing, the every thing for which we contended. And it is not to be doubted that the popular title of the "Episcopal Church" by which we are known, has to some extent authorized the popular prejudice, that a naked, barren, haughty Episcopacy was the *summum bonum* of our creed, the all-in-all, essence and quintessence of our Church; and the iteration of a naked Episcopacy by controversial writers has filled the sects with prejudice. With regard to the relative importance of Episcopacy in the mighty circle of Catholic faith and grace, I should not fear to let Dr. Miller know that we have little fault to find with the reasonings of the "famous Jerome:" that it is but a part of the Christian priesthood; that in the acts of absolution and of the consecration of the Eucharist, a Bishop is no more than the equal of his Presbyter; that a Presbyter may absolve a Bishop, as a Bishop may absolve a Presbyter; that "*ordinatione excepta*" is the distinguishing mark of his Order; and that a Bishop is but one among many brethren, not so much the sensitive defender of his title, as he is the strong man armed to keep the treasures of the house of God.

This has been *the nature* of my own conversion—not to a name, to a bare Episcopacy, to a one-idea—but *to the Catholic religion*, to a thousand truths in one, to a thousand sympathies not born of earth, to a thousand thrilling associations with the past, to a thousand joints and bands that keep the weak from falling, to a thousand hallowed soul-stirring influences found nowhere else; to the Body of Christ, left by Him here when the Head went up, to say, to do, to suffer, what He left unsaid, undone, unsuffered, to "fill up that which is behind of the afflictions of Christ, ... for His Body's sake, which is the Church:" a Catholicity that covers all times, all places, all truths, all things in Christ. And here, as I have said, I would stay awhile, and build two tabernacles, one for the reader, and one for myself: for since I have burst the bands of sect and schism, the earth around me is a new earth, and the heavens over me are new heavens, and I see a universe unalterably radiant with truth, harmony, and love. But I must retrace my steps, and go once more into the plain below, and show the reader, if he will renew his company and sympathy, what things I have suffered besides, in coming to the heavenly Jerusalem.

CHAPTER XVI.

ELDERS AND DEATH-BEDS.

THOSE whom I knew when a boy as the "bench of elders" in a congregation, have latterly, among the Presbyterians, been dignified by the more august title of the "Parochial Presbytery." And the title may be well enough allowed; for their ministers, whether in Parish, Presbytery, Synod, or General Assembly, are on all questions—the fondest subtleties of theology, the dearest privileges of their order, the largest interests of the whole denomination—on a bare equality with their elders. If a minister be suspected of unsoundness in the faith, although the issue may depend on the nicest possible hair splittings of metaphysics, and the results may be more terrible to the accused than death itself: he must be tried, not by his peers, but by a court ascertained *in limine* to be incompetent to judge him.

Although I, for the moment, call their elders their laity, a controversy has lately sprung up among them, in which influential names have taken the ground, that the ruling elder is of the same order with the teaching elder or minister; otherwise, says Dr. Breckinridge, Presbyterians have after all retained the Prelacy: "one is preferred (*prelatus*,)" he says, "above the rest, and if this is not Prelacy," he asks, "what is it?" This dispute has grown out of the question (*proh pudor!*) whether ruling elders should impose hands jointly with the ministers, in ordination!—a question pronounced by a grave divine of the Old School to be "practically the question between a Hierarchical and a Presbyterian government:" "because," quoth he, "if the elders are of a different order from the ministers, then, with our deacons, we have three orders, or essential prelacy, in which one is pre-late or preferred above another." Call these elders, however, what they may—style them bishops, if they choose, and as some of them propose—the reader will see that the preaching bishop is overwhelmed in his parish by the number of the ruling bishops. And verily, by Dr. Breckinridge's showing, a poor bishop-ridden pastor, instead of having one Bishop to ride him, has from three to fifteen!

I had fifteen! They were the legacy of my predecessor, a divine of no mean authority; and I have still a recollection of the extent to which *some* of the ruling elders had a right good will to rule. They took the ground—and if I mistake not, the prevailing tone of the denomination would now bear them out—that the pastor, or teaching elder, is only the executive of the ruling elders. To give an instance: I saw proper to print a form of baptism and of admission to the communion, which was thought by some of the "parochial presbytery" to savor of Episcopacy, although it exhibited nothing more than the teachings of their own Confession; and accordingly an obstinate though abortive attempt was made to vote the pastor into a minority, and into the adoption of a form which one of them was actually at the pains to prepare, but which, on perusal, I assured them was no more consonant with the Confession of Faith in its theology, than it was with the English tongue in its grammatical construction.* Fifteen

* At this time, one of the deacons also took me sagely to task for requiring the parents, at Baptism, to teach the baptized child *the Apostles' Creed.* "And who knows," said he, "that it is the Apostles' Creed, or that the Apostles ever heard of it?" I replied, "The Confession of Faith, then, is mistaken!" "The Con-

ruling bishops! I had heard that the little finger of Puritanism was thicker than the loins of Prelacy. I had heard that poor Brown, the inventor of the Congregational theory, lived to repent in dust and sackcloth his surrender of the keys. I had heard that a minister in the days of Cotton Mather had said, "I fled from the Church of England, to escape the tyranny of my Lord-Bishops; but I was glad to get back again, to escape the tyranny of my lord-brethren." "For what is the deacon," says Mr. John Angell James, "in some of our dissenting communities? The patron of the living, the Bible of the minister, the wolf of the flock. In many of our churches the pastor is depressed far below him. His opinion is treated with no deference. His person is treated with no respect. In the presence of his lay tyrants, he is only permitted to peep and mutter in the dust." "I foresee," said Melancthon, "that unless we restore the government of Bishops, there will be hereafter a more intolerable tyranny than there ever was before." By the change that I have made, I find, for my own part, that instead of *fifteen* ruling bishops that thus were over me, not one of them capable of sympathizing with the sorrows and cares of the pastoral office: I am now under the mild sway of *one*, who is not an high priest that cannot be touched with the feeling of our infirmities, but who has drunk himself the pastor's cup, whose gentle counsels it is a privilege to seek, and whose mild rule it is, for Christ's sake, a pleasure to obey.

Especially in the administration of what Presbyterians once knew as "sealing ordinances," but now fritter down under the name of "rites," the preaching elder, or pastor, is the simple executive or agent, to carry out the decision of the ruling elders or bishops; and, as may be supposed, there

fession of Faith don't call it the *Apostles'* Creed," replied Mr. W. "Yes, sir, it does; if you will look again, you will see that it calls it *the Apostles' Creed*, and requires it to be taught to our children."

are cases in which this interference with the liberty of the pastoral office leads to consequences of the most painful nature.

A Quaker lady once resided in my parish, whom I never knew until I saw her on the bed of death. She was very anxious to be baptized; and, for myself, I was as heartily inclined to receive her into the congregation of the flock of Christ. But it being inconvenient, in a sick-room, to assemble the elders in order to hear her "experience," and it being cruel to think of subjecting the candidate to the agitations of so public a confessional, and as I saw that nature was fast sinking, and that what I should do for the dying lady must be done quickly: I endeavored to procure informally the consent of as many of the elders as I could conveniently find, and proceed to receive this lamb of Christ's redeeming to His fold. But with one consent they begged me *by no means* to administer the "rite," for fear a compliance should seem to attach an undue importance to "*a mere external.*" My own mind was clear; my heart was ready; O God, my heart was ready! Christ, I could not doubt, would allow the charitable work; the Father was waiting with the bright robe to put upon His child, and shoes for her feet to cross the dark river now gloomily winding through the vale, and a ring for her hand to claim a place withal among the children in her Father's house; and, in an agony which only the conjunction of repentance with the dying hour can produce, a blood-bought daughter asks, "What doth hinder me to be baptized?" O ye elders, and ye ministers of Presbyterian ism, is there aught in the Word of God that hinders? "He that believeth and is baptized, shall be saved;" "Except a man be born of water and of the spirit, he cannot enter into the kingdom of God;" "The like figure whereunto even baptism doth also now save us;" "According to His mercy He hath saved us by the washing of regeneration, [by

Calvin and other Presbyterian commentators allowed to be baptism,] and the renewing of the Holy Ghost;" "Having our hearts sprinkled from an evil conscience, and our bodies washed with pure water;" "Arise and be baptized, and wash away thy sins;" "Repent and be baptized, every one of you, for the remission of sins, and ye shall receive the Holy Ghost:"—thick and fast these texts came rushing to my mind. But against all these, and the entreaties of a dying penitent, came the stern mandate of a "parochial Presbytery," entrusted by the Westminster system with the responsibility of "admission to sealing ordinances." Yet Presbytery vaunts itself as being so wondrous "liberal," and endeavors to decry Episcopacy as "intolerant and exclusive." Be it known, then, that it is a canon of the Ancient Church, that the sacraments are *never to be withheld when requested by the dying.* Be a sacrament but a *straw*, if Presbyterians who once called it a *seal* will now have it so; the Church from the beginning has forbidden a *straw* to be laid in the way of a child's return: so careful is our Holy Mother lest she should break the bruised reed, or quench the smoking flax. As I returned to the lady, it seemed as if I could have given the world, if this necessity were not laid upon me. I I felt like one returning from a bench of Inquisitors. I had heard *de comburendis hereticis;* but this was a more exquisite invention *de angendis morientibus.* Heavy-hearted I went back to the chamber of the penitent. "Does any man forbid water that I should be baptized?" inquired the dying woman. As gently as I could let the awful words fall upon her ear, I told her she must die as she was. I saw her soul was dark. One that stood by wiped the death-sweat from her brow. But, endeavoring to satisfy myself that the tyranny of the rulers would excuse the sin on my part, and their ignorance extenuate it upon theirs, I endeavored to console the dying penitent with the assurance, that the desire of baptism was equivalent to its reception upon her part. But the painfulness and the sinfulness of that transaction, although done in ignorance, and many years ago, are things that, to this hour, and to the latest hour of my life, I shall never be able to think of without shame and sadness. I never turn *that street*, but the scenes of that occasion come picturing their horrid forms before me. I never see *that house*, without smiting on my breast, and saying, O Lord, forgive!

On the whole subject of administering sacraments to the sick and dying, there is among Presbyterians as profound an indifference as among the Quakers, and an unrelenting resoluteness in their elders and their ministers. I have known one of the most amiable of their pastors to withhold *the rite*, as Presbyterians now term it—*the right*, as an Episcopalian would say—of holy baptism from his own child, as it lay dying; although a prudent and judicious wife, whose counsels he was glad to hear on any other subject, begged, with a mother's earnestness, that the Shepherd's mark might be laid upon her dying lamb, as she was about to give it back into the Shepherd's arms. An infant is happily unconscious of these wrongs. But when an earnest penitent, in whose ears the awful hour of eleven is tolling, desires "to fulfil all righteousness:" the heartless refusal which will not "suffer it to be so" is an offence against humanity, and against all the liberties and rights of humanity redeemed, which only the most stern and intolerant of theories could ever have conceived.

There recently lived, in the city of Richmond, a well-known Presbyterian divine, who was sent for, not many years ago, to administer the communion to a sick member of his church, as determined to receive it, as the pastor was to withhold it. But when his parishioner, to unburden the pastor of his scruples in the matter, intimated the expedient of seeking the services of a clergyman whose Church delighted to allow "that most comfortable sacrament" to the sick and sorrowing, the good minister's scruples about fostering superstition were waived, and the communion was allowed. This, so far as I can recollect, is the only instance, save one, that I have known in this country, in which a Presbyterian, expressing a desire for "the children's bread"—a desire, I have good reason to suppose, much oftener felt than uttered--was allowed by his minister the *viaticum,* as the martyrs and dying believers used to call it, for the last journey. There has quite recently occurred a most painful case, in the northern portion of the city of New York, where an eminent Presbyterian divine, one, too, who has been a mouthpiece and exponent of the Presbyterian system, refused the children's meat to a young lady on her dying bed, who had begged for the crumbs as they fell from her Master's table. Her mother I had myself known as a child; the child I had known as a lamb in my flock, when I was myself a Presbyterian, and rejoiced was I to hear that she died with an appetite for the bread of life. Sirs, why do ye these things? Is the world so full of faith, that ye are afraid of exaggerating that faith into superstition? *Is it ever* a "superstition" to obey the commands of Jesus? Is it a "superstition" for a dying sinner to remember the commandment of a dying Saviour? If a man has neglected the Bible all his days, and on his sick-bed anxiously consults its pages: do you take it from him? If the giddy girl has all through life neglected prayer, and on the verge of eternity begins to lift her breaking heart to heaven: do you forbid her? If your parishioner, whom you have often, and in vain, invited to solemn converse with you on the things of eternity, seeks your counsels in the dying hour: do you refuse? Do you turn a deaf ear, and forbid these "externals" to a dying man, who needs all the aids and means that earth and heaven can devise to save him in the dreadful hour? Why, then, should you cast out the prayer of a dying soul, who says to you: "Sir, I have disregarded the commands of Christ, and some of those commands it is now beyond my power to fulfil; but there are others which I may yet obey: here is water, what doth hinder me to be baptized? Behold, here are bread and wine: what doth hinder me to lay my hand upon them, and take them to myself? Was not for me the Victim slain? Am I forbid the children's bread? See around me unbelieving companions; may I not leave my testimony in these solemn rites? And, behold, my prayers, how frail and filled with sin; let me but see with my eyes the bread lie broken and the wine shed forth, to plead with my offended Maker as a Pure and Undefiled Memorial, recounting to Him, for my soul, the griefs and tortures, the cross and passion of His Son! And behold my father, and behold my mother and my sisters, O may not I eat this Bread and drink this Cup with *them*, before I go hence and be no more seen?" Why do you cast out, I say, his prayer? Are the multitudes of your people, when they come to die, so anxious and busy concerning the things of Christ, that you must check their ardor, for fear of its growing into "superstition?" You hide from the eyes of the dying the mementos of the Saviour's passion, the symbols of the Saviour's pardon, for fear of superstition! Superstition! Do you call it superstition in a dying man to hug to his heart or press to his lips the Bible, the Bread, the Cup, the Minister, the *anything* that tells of Christ, of redemption, and of pardon? Superstition do you call it, also, if the Christian, all ripe for heaven, whose heart has many a time burned within him as the Blessed Master made Himself known in the breaking of Bread, longs in the dying hour, to go forth for the last time on earth to the place of meeting on the holy mount?

I have myself once lain, for many months, upon what was believed to be the bed of death; and, if I may dare to say it, like the Master Himself before He suffered, "with desire I desired to eat this passover." I anxiously debated with myself, whether I might hope to find a Presbyterian minister to give me "that Bread and that Cup." But as I felt myself too feeble to run the risk of refusal and perhaps rebuke, I requested an Episcopal clergyman to break to me the heavenly Bread: and richly did I enjoy the Blessed Sacrament; for, as the wounds of the Sacrifice lay open before me, I thought that I could read more clearly than ever the great mystery that my sins were covered. The withholding the Sacraments from the sick and dying, like the denying of Baptism to infants, is one of those crying wrongs and cruelties, which Popery in its blackest night has never dared to adopt among her penalties, and which it was reserved for Calvinism's heart to invent and Calvinism's hand to execute. Yet Calvinism, that has stolen its inheritance from the babe in its cradle, and practised robbery upon the dying, and pushed its sacrilege to the grave: has the courage and the art to raise in the crowd the cry of "illiberality" and "intolerance!" For myself, O my merciful Maker, let me die in a communion, that, when the chariot is at the door, and the appointed hour is striking, and the impatient steeds are waiting to convey me, will not withhold from me the traveller's Bread. O, in that hour, ye, my surviving friends, gather around me a company of the Catholic-hearted, to whom I may say: "Brothers, with desire I have desired to eat this Passover with you before I suffer. As for you, ye shall drink it again: but for me, I shall drink no more of this fruit of The Vine, until the day when I shall drink it new with you in the Kingdom of God."

CHAPTER XVII.

POPULAR LIBERTY.

I HAD often heard that Episcopacy was unfriendly to the just principles of human liberty. And I am free to say, "If it was so, it was a grievous fault." I should despise the religion that despised the poor. I should tread beneath my feet the faith that trampled under foot the rights of men. I am enthusiastic enough to ask,

> "Has earth a clod,
> Its Maker meant not should be trod
> By man, the image of his God,
> Erect and free?"

I looked therefore into the matter with no little jealousy, and, as the result of the most patient inquiry, must say, that I believe Episcopacy to be the true and tried friend of human liberty, and, in this land preëminently, *the great bulwark now, and the main hope hereafter, of REPUBLICAN FREEDOM.*

The charge that Episcopacy is anti-Republican and illiberal, has been of late years reiterated with new warmth by some who personally loved me once; and if I, who loved them in return, choose to place that church, to which my pure convictions have conducted me, on its defence before "the public," to which it has been cited by three of my classmates and by yet another of my bosom friends: I only pray my Maker that, in setting impartial truth before them, they may perceive in me one who loves them still.

There were two aspects under which I found it necessary to examine the subject: the civil and the religious; as there were two positions from which I could examine it with advantage: its theory, and its history.

By the light of other minds I came to see, in spite of all my prejudices, that the constitution of the Episcopal Church embodies the essential elements of the received definitions of political liberty. It is a maxim of English law, that "there is no liberty where the judicial power is not separated from the legislative and executive." According to President Jefferson, "the concentration of the executive, legislative, and judicial powers in the same hands, is precisely the definition of tyranny." "No political truth," says Chief Justice Marshall, "is of greater intrinsic value, than that the legislative, judicial, and executive departments should be kept separated and distinct; the accumulation of these powers in the same hands, whether of a few or of many, may be pronounced to be the very definition of tyranny." Accordingly, the Constitutions of the several States declare in effect, with that of Maryland, that "the legislative, executive, and judiciary powers shall be for ever separate and distinct;" so that, in the words of my own native Virginia, "neither shall exercise the powers properly belonging to the other, nor shall any person exercise the powers of more than one of them, at the same time." "No person," declares Kentucky, "or *collection of persons*, being of one of these departments, shall exercise any power properly belonging to either of the others." My author, to whom I owe these quotations, furnishes some others; but these suffice: and we may crown them with the farewell words of Washington, urging on the people of the United States "the necessity of reciprocal checks in the exercise of political power, by dividing and distributing it into different depositories, and constituting each the guardian of the public weal against invasion by the others. The consolidation of these powers in one," says Washington, at once the General, the Statesman, and the Churchman, "whatever the form of government, is a real despotism."

Now if these definitions had been framed expressly to exhibit the great fundamental principles in the structure of the Episcopal Church, they could hardly have done it more exactly. As far as things temporal and things spiritual may coincide, the lines of coincidence are strikingly exact. The fact will bear investigation, that, right or wrong, the Episcopacy of America is, with almost mathematical exactness, after the model of the Republic, with the more democratic provision that, whereas a President may veto an act approved by both houses of Congress, the veto power in Episcopacy can be exercised only by a majority of the Bishops. A Bishop can no more enact a law, than may a Governor. The entire college of Bishops is as powerless to do it, as would be a college of State Governors. A Convention, whether of a diocese or of the whole confederacy, can no more try a cause or act judicially, than a Legislature or a Congress. Throughout the Church the three powers are kept carefully and for ever distinct. And it is to be remembered, that the same separation of powers existed to a most wholesome extent in the Ancient Church, until the encroachments of the Papacy, taking advantage of dissensions or supineness in the churches around her, made vigorous and successful efforts to centralize them in the chair of St. Peter; a consolidation, against which the West protested long, and the whole East protested, and still successfully protests, as incompatible with the ancient liberties of the primitive Episcopal Church. And Popery is not the less a despotism because it is elective.

We do then allege, that according to the definitions by

Washington, Jefferson, and Marshall, the essence of despotism is covered up under the forms of Presbyterianism. Take first the purest form of Old School Presbyterianism. Its judicial act of 1837, separating from its communion sixty thousand communicants, was devised and consummated, under the pressure of high excitement, by the "*collection of persons*" known as the "General Assembly,"—at once Legislature, Judiciary, and Executive—from whose decision there is no appeal. There is but one Being in the universe to be trusted with such power: and even in the bosom of God, we have an Advocate with the Father; also the Holy Ghost the Comforter.

Take next the Methodists. The laity have neither representation nor voice in any of their legislative, judicial, or deliberative bodies. The preachers are as supreme as the priests ever were in the Papal communion. They hold the purse. They hold the sword. Let a man absent himself from the confessional of the class-meeting, without accounting for it, and see how the preacher's hand will straight lay hold on judgment! Let any member not pay his Peter-pence, or quota to the funds, and right soon will the cords of discipline find him. There is no escape! From the meanest member to the college-president, under the hierarchy of class-leaders, exhorters, local preachers, and circuit-preachers, the laity are under a surveillance *unknown to any thing on earth, except the Inquisition.* Scarcely may a female wear a ring upon her hand, a ringlet in her hair, or a bow upon her cap, without the censure of her lords spiritual. A congregation may humbly petition the so-called bishops in the matter, but have no more power to elect their pastor, than the writer or the reader of this narrative to elect one for them. Neither can a pastor go where he himself may wish, or remain with a flock ever so devoted to his person, for more than two years at a time—except by a rare "indulgence." The so-called bishop says to one, Go, and he goeth: and to another, Come, and he cometh: and to them all, Do this, and they do it. There is not an Apostolic bishop in the Church of God—no, nor even in St. Peter's chair—that assumes, in some of these respects, that interference with personal liberty which the so-called bishops of the Methodists exercise over their subjects. Musgrave of Baltimore has written a *quod erat demonstrandum* on this subject, (*quod vide,*) and the Princeton Review allows, that "the society of the Jesuits is the only one with which it is acquainted, that surpasses Methodism in the centralization of its powers."

Take, once more, the purer Congregationalists; among whom the company of communicants is at once Legislature, Judge, Jury, and Executive. Such a "collection of persons" enacts an arbitrary law, that your daughter shall not receive the communion, until she come under a vow to abstain from intoxicating liquors. This is no dream of the dark ages of Popery and asceticism and monkery. It is not a vow left optional, as vows are left to virgins under the Papal system. It is a vow, a vow for life, a degrading, unwomanly vow, submitted to, this moment, by several thousand congregations in the Presbyterian and Congregational communions. The rulers make the law, and the penalty is—excommunication! They who make the law stand particularly ready to enforce and execute it;—Legislature, Judge, Jury, and Sheriff, in a breath. No power on earth can interfere. There is no remedy for the indignant and dissatisfied, but the old one of secession and schism. I need hardly say, that Episcopacy knows no such interference with personal liberty. As to such surveillance and exaction, there is not an Episcopalian in the wide land that would tolerate them for one hour.

We assert, then, that in her constitution, the Episcopal Church is the only form of Christianity on this continent that is Republican and Free. It answers fully, it answers admirably to the converse of Mr. Jefferson's proposition, that the " accumulation of the Legislative, Executive, and Judicial powers in the same hands, whether of few or of *many*, may be pronounced to be the very definition of *tyranny*." And if this maxim of old English law, endorsed by Kent, and Story, and Marshall, and Madison, and Hamilton, and Jefferson, and the good Washington, be just: then Presbyterianism, in its varied forms, coincides so nearly with the definition, that I scarcely see room for laying down a hair between them. Ay, and the " tyranny" is felt. Sixty thousand felt it at a blow. A convenient act of legislation is thus converted into a judicial process;—summary, and without citation, and in the absence of the parties, without a collateral or restraining tribunal on earth to interpose its checks! No Episcopal convention in the country, no, nor all the assembled Bishops in the land, could so harm a hair of the head of the meanest layman.

But there is another thing to be remarked. In the first council at Jerusalem* the legislation was conducted by " the *apostles*, and *elders*, and *brethren*." But, in a Presbyterian synod or assembly, the *brethren* are excluded. Apostles or Bishops they avowedly have none. So that here is another centralization of power in the hands of the preaching and ruling elders alone. No Apostles above them, no brethren beneath them, to hold them in check! No layman, mere layman, can be admitted to the floor, *until he has been ordained an elder, and an elder for life.* Episcopacy, both here and in England, provides that laymen, in the purest and most unofficial sense, shall sit in her legislative councils. In England, Parliament legislates as the Church's laity. Even Popery, in its councils, has admitted the laity. But in Presbytery or Methodism you must be at least an elder; for otherwise you can have no more voice in the legislation of your church, than you have in the winds

* Acts, xv.

that blow above your heads. The Episcopal Church is, as far as we can learn, the only ecclesiastical organization on this continent, where laymen are represented at all. An elder, in the General Assembly, represents the elders, is even of the same grade or order (says Dr. Breckenridge) with the minister, and no more represents *the people* than does the minister. Even after the elders are in power, the people are not permitted to say which of them shall go to the Legislature; it is an election on the odious borough system which was so intolerable in England, with the additional aggravation that the electors are electors for life! Yet do but listen to the cry against Episcopacy, as being illiberal and anti-republican!

And I noticed yet one thing more, stamping Presbyterianism as anti-republican; which is, that its Legislatures convene and act as *one house.* In England, the Commons and the Peers act separately, and their action is submitted to the Crown. In America, the Senate and the Representatives legislate separately, and their legislation is submitted to the President. In Episcopacy, there are the same three branches of the legislative function; the Clergy and the Laity act in separate orders, and their action is submitted to the House of Bishops: the joint action of the three orders being necessary to an enactment, precisely as in the case of "the Apostles, Elders, and Brethren," in the council of Jerusalem. But in Presbyterianism, under all its forms, there is but one house, and the vote is on all questions taken but once for all; the "elders" are there, but neither the "apostles" nor the "brethren." Which then of these two is Scriptural? Which is Republican?

And as Episcopacy, so happily settled between the two extremes of anarchy and despotism, reflects in her fundamental law the great principles of human liberty: so, in her spirit and functions, there is that mixture of the liberal and the conservative, so necessary to ensure the perpetuity of a Republic. For to bring this matter home, now that our Republic is careering onward in the gushing tide of her prosperity, who that has eyes to see, or ears to hear, or a heart to fear, does not perceive that this very tide on which she bounds toward her destiny, may set her suddenly upon the rocks?

Is Republican Liberty in danger from the spirit of irreverence for authority? What better remedy than in the teachings of the Episcopal Church, not only conservative in their general tone, but inculcating as a divine and fundamental ordinance "fear to whom fear, and honor to whom honor is due," and reverence for "power as ordained of God," herself exemplifying in her own case this important principle of Christianity? Give her the children of the land; and, unlike the sects that look on division and disunion, even in religion, without compunction, she will train those children in a just reverence for authority, and in the admiration of unity and universal brotherhood, as being, next to redemption, the great revelation of the second Adam, who came to restore the oneness and integrity of the human family.

Or, be it that a danger to our glorious Republic is in the agitation of questions so bound up with the organization of society, that only the prudence of the serpent and the innocence of the dove can furnish their difficult and delicate solution: we see a fearful aggravation of the danger, not in reasonable and brotherly discussion, but in the well-known methods of Puritanism, which cannot even promote temperance without rending churches asunder, making harsh conditions of communion, laying its hand upon the awful cup of the Sacrament; and which cannot reach an alms to a slave without shaking the land with the ostentation of its trumpet, and which, having no power to imitate the Divine forbearance, would invoke the genius of the wild storm, to root up, in a night, trees that have been the growth of centuries.

Yes, we see clouds hovering in the distance, which the wand of the statesman may not be able to disperse. We hear invectives in the North, and murmurings in the South, which a Senate may not be able to conciliate. We feel a volcano trembling under our feet, which, if it burst, will blacken our bright Capitol to cinder. We see hands busy in designs which all Europe combined could not achieve against this fair Republic. But as the mouse, in the fable, gnawed the cable that had defied the strength of the lion; or as the despicable worm eats through the bottom of the ship at anchor, which had ridden out the wildest tempest of the sea: so may this Republic, parting its cable, at which Puritan fanaticism is at this moment gnawing, and letting in waters from causes operating in the dark, experience what more than one sectarian denomination—what even strong Methodism has already exemplified—the separation of the North and the South. The Church will not divide! You may expect it; you may desire it; a batch of Puritans or Romanizers may some day leave her: but by God's blessing, she will not divide; unity is her life; One Body, One Spirit; and should she have the keeping of the hearts of the people, when the storm shall descend upon the deep, she will go forth as her Lord upon the waters, and say, Peace, be still. If any thing is to save this Republic, it will be *Christianity*. If Christianity is to retain its power, it will be by its *Unity*. If Unity is to be preserved, it will be by *the Church*. And perhaps the day may come, when the Church shall be recalled, as she was to England, by a people weary of the endless tumults, disunions, and exactions of Puritan fanaticism, to pour oil upon the waves and heal the breaches of the nation.

No wonder that the "little one" has "become a thousand," and the *indotata virgo* the heir of the promise that "more are the children of the desolate than the children of the married wife;" and no wonder that the Church is gaining and growing among the friends of liberty and order in the land. No wonder that the pure hearts and polished intellects of our most brilliant statesmen have so often gathered to her standard, or (since the accusation I am refuting compels me to "this glorying") that in the single year of 1847, Chief Justice Spencer and Henry Clay, Chancellor Kent and Daniel Webster, all quite as competent in mind, and perhaps as cool in judgment, as either Dr. Potts or Mr. Barnes, have, without fear of doing danger to the liberties of the Republic, bent their knees at the altar of the Episcopal Church, given her their allegiance, and taken the cup of salvation at her hand.

The fact will bear attention, that the quiet ways of the Episcopal Church, her acknowledged dignity and manifest conservatism; her great principle of reverence, the negation of which is the chief danger in republican government; and her wholesome and tried stability as a solid sea-mark amid a sea of impulses and changes, with her own interior arrangements of order, propriety, and mutual restraints, constitute *the great desideratum*, and meet *the great danger*, and furnish the solution to *the great problem* of Republican Liberty and practical Democracy: while the harmony of her worship, the beauty of her sanctuary, and the unity of her body, will bind and blend together the millions of the people.

Although this is a subject on which we have perhaps no right to expect that the Bible should speak, yet we are not sure that the Bible has not spoken. God launched the Jewish nation on its new existence as a theocracy, almost another name for a Republic; and when, "to be like the nations around them," they desired a king, "he gave them a king in his wrath." But the great conservative element in that Republic while it lasted, as it was afterward the great check upon the monarchy, was the unity of its Church, and the Threefold Order of its Prelacy. This was the teaching of Moses; this was the wisdom of God: and this is the teaching of Episcopacy.

But there was another view in which a manly candor obliged me to regard this subject. We say to the infidel, as he boasts the sufficiency of the light of nature, How does it happen that your men, who have reasoned so eloquently of the unity of God, the spirituality of His worship, the excellence of repentance, the truth of immortality, and the certainty of the rewards of virtue, have all of them been born within the pale of Baptism? Think you, if your Tindalls, and Humes, and Bolingbrokes, and Gibbons, and Collinses, and Shaftesburys had been born among their red brethren of the western world, under the unintercepted blaze of the "light of nature," they too would not have been buried with their bows and arrows, and their hunting dogs and horns, to hunt in the forests of a future state, and with slaughtered servants to bring them wood and food and water in another world? We say to the infidel, Your writings bear too little likeness to the dreams of paganism, too strong a resemblance to the teachings of the Galilean Carpenter, to leave a doubt that you have stolen your fire from the altars of the Prophets, and lighted your tapers at the golden candlestick of the Apostles. And if the reasoning be just, we have equal right to say to the sectarians, Why is it that these embryo-empires of freedom, with which the earth is dotted, owe their beginnings and their being to an island in the sea, in which Episcopacy and Christianity have more power than in any portion of the globe? Why does the muddy Thames alone, from her unfailing urn, send forth these rivers of civil and religious freedom to the remotest lands, to make glad the wilderness? Why is it that a nation in advance of the nations, hemmed in as Palestine was to the ancient election, should be the torch-bearer in the car of freedom, rolling its golden circles over the western world; scattering from its wheels the light of liberty and progress over India and Burmah and China, and the East; kindling the beacon fires of redemption on the dark wastes of bleeding Africa, and driving back the cannibal and savage from the bright havens of Australia and the Isles? Where are Germany, and Prussia, and Denmark, and Holland, and Saxony, and where are their colonial monuments abroad, or their contributions at home, to the cause of freedom? The truth is, that England had been progressing for a thousand years in her advance towards freedom; and the States in Europe had been growing rapidly into the same ideas under the Papacy. At the last, liberty woke from her slumbers at the Reformation; and while, in consequence of schism and fanaticism, the nations on the Continent have been, ever since the Papacy was broken, retrograding into despotism without even the Papacy to hold, as it had done before, the secular power in check, the moderation of British Statesmen and Reformers secured for the world an asylum for liberty and for religion. Have any of the States of Germany, or Denmark, or Prussia, or Saxony, or Holland, presented the world with a model of constitutional liberty? As to Switzerland, it was a republic without the aid of Calvin, and has made little progress from that century to this. I have had as much trouble with my passport in Switzerland, as I had in Sardinia. In a colony of Denmark I have been cited to appear before rulers and governors, for baptizing a child of Presbyterian parentage; and I have known a clergyman, not long before, banished from the kingdom for a similar offence. And when it was reported to the authorities, that some forty Presbyterians had applied for confirmation in my parish, I received timely notice that the legal penalty of their reception, would be my banishment from His Majesty's dominions.

Civil government is nowhere more absolute than in Presbyterian States. Liberty dawned the second time on those empires a few months since, but day has receded again; and liberty, in the Presbyterian portions of the continent of Europe, is likely to be asserted only in a terrible crisis of infidelity and blood. Presbyterianism having failed to make those nations free, Socialism and Pantheism have stepped in to divide her laurels. If the same wild reform that succeeded at the Reformation on the Continent, had gotten sway in England, we have seen what would have been the fate of religion, and we may imagine now what might have been the fate of liberty. The only States in Europe where human rights are understood and allowed, the only States in Europe, which, like lofty light-houses, have looked in undisturbed composure on the angry and wild convulsions of the people in the political storm now sweeping over Europe, are Sweden and Great Britain; and the only States in Europe that have the primitive Episcopacy, and with it a virtual Republican liberty, are Great Britain and Sweden, the latter having the most liberal constitution and the largest liberty in continental Europe, allowing even its peasantry to be separately represented in its Congress.

So much for Episcopacy, the twin sister of human liberty. It were little to say, that her provisions and principles are in keeping with the great law of human progress; for her purposes in the creation of a universal Brotherhood, in which "no man shall count any thing he has his own, as long as he shall see his Brother have need," are as far above the sickly, sentimental theories of noisy and ephemeral philanthropists, as the heavens are higher than the earth: and all in a sense and a degree which sectarianism is too narrow to grasp, and which the Church can hardly be expected to accomplish, until the cold and shrill night-wind of schism is lulled, the waters of controversy have subsided, and the dove of peace shall brood upon the face of the deep.

CHAPTER XVIII.

LIBERTY OF WORSHIP.

THE reader may perhaps have heard of old Joyce Heth, who was exhibited in the Atlantic cities a few years ago, and brought great gain to her masters, claiming to be a hundred and sixty years old, and to have been the nurse of General Washington. I saw the old woman myself, and I saw *the documents* by which her pretensions were verified; thousands saw also and believed. In fact the poor old creature had heard the story so long, and had told it so often herself, and had heard so much about *the documents*, that she verily believed she was a hundred and sixty years old, and had been the veritable nurse of General Washington!

Now, like our heroine, Puritanism had told her own story so long, that not only had she begun to believe it herself, but until lately nearly every body else believed, on the strength of *the documents*, that Puritanism was the *bona fide* nurse and mother too of the great principles of civil and religious liberty. But the day has come, when the Pythoness herself begins to doubt the oracles, and they who use such curious arts may yet, like the writers of Ephesus, make a bonfire of their books.

As a boy at school, with Morse's Geography and New England Readers to enlighten me, I could imagine a company of "pilgrims" landing on Plymouth Rock, amidst the howlings of the winter storms, with no earthly end in view, but to find an asylum for the genius of "civil and religious liberty." When I was a child, I spake as a child, I thought as a child, I understood as a child. But what are the facts, which I know or notice now, and which I did not notice or know before?

First of all, my attention was called to the fact, which as a schoolboy I was not allowed to know, that the "Pilgrims," who landed on Plymouth Rock, in 1620, did not sail in the May-Flower from "their own native England," but from Holland, "where (to use their own words) they did quietly and sweetly enjoy their church liberties" for eleven good years, and where those who remained, enjoyed all the liberty they could desire, as long as they desired it; but where they soon got to be as restless as they had been in England, and, as a friendly writer was obliged to say, "their zeal began to languish for want of oppositions, and they grew tired of security in a place where they were without power and consequence." They came to America, no doubt, in part from religious motives; but it was to establish exclusively their own religion. And, as to the rest, Dr. Coit (to whom I shall owe the principal facts embodied in this chapter) has adduced documents of their own, to show that the "whale-fisheries," and the "fisheries of the coast,"* and "the exclusive trade from Nova Scotia to the southern parts of Carolina," and "the entire property of the soil besides,"—all secured by their charter from a British and Episcopal King,—entered about as much into their plans, as the whale fisheries of the North-West coast do now into the operations of New-Bedford Deacons, or the gold of California into the speculations of the multitudes now suffering and perishing to reach that country, some to get gold, some to extend commerce,

* The Puritans, it appears, very considerately advised their late friends, the hospitable Dutch, not to send their boats and ships to "the fisheries," for fear of capture by the Plymouth fishermen!

some to establish a political empire, and some to find new dominions for the Church of God. As the eyes of the world are this moment turning to the El Dorado of the Pacific, so in those days, the eyes of Europe were turned to America on the Atlantic, as the source of future wealth and aggrandizement, and the ships of all Europe were hovering about our coasts, as eagles gathering to their prey. It was *not* persecution that drove the Pilgrims to New England. The Pilgrims came from Holland; and, even in England, were not compelled to belong to the Church. What, then, was the great grievance? It was this. About two thousand ministers, and among them some Jesuits in disguise, entered the Church of England, raised the old cry of "Popery" against her forms, with a view to "revolutionize her," (as the Cincinnati divine I quoted in the early pages of this narrative, would say,) their vows of ordination sat loosely on them, for they took them intending at the time to break them; they threw aside the prayer-book, or mutilated and corrupted it, and sought to alter the whole framework of the Church; at last discipline became necessary, and the intruders were required to conform to the Church which had recorded their vows, or else to cease from officiating at her altars. This was the hardship. "They felt persecuted, because they were not allowed to persecute." And, says the Presbyterian "Quarterly" of Edinburgh, "they would not tolerate the Church, and taught, that if princes hinder those who seek for *the discipline*, they are tyrants both to the Church and ministers, and, being so, may be deposed by their subjects; thus completely," adds the "Review," "did Popery and Puritanism meet in the political deductions from their presumed infallibility." What they wanted, was plainly seen from the first; as it occurred thirty years afterward, when Charles was beheaded, an archbishop martyred, ten thousand ministers ejected from their parishes, and throughout the commonwealth forbidden to teach school for their living.

27

Persecuted out of England? *No, sirs!* In 1629, nine years after the "pilgrims" left Holland for "the fisheries" and the "exclusive trade," and the "sole right in the soil," Higginson left England with a fleet of eighty guns, and with stores of arms, and powder, and colors, and one hundred planters, and, on the eve of sailing, called all hands on deck of the ship Talbott, and said:—"We will not say farewell, Babylon! farewell, Rome! But, we will say, farewell, dear England! farewell the Church of God in England! We do not go to leave England, as separatists from the Church of England, though we cannot but separate from its corruptions; but we go to practise *the positive part of church Reformation in America;*" and concluded his address, "with a fervent prayer for the King, and Church, and State, in England." The next year, there was another embarkation of "pilgrims" on board the famous Arabella, when Winthrop and a large party of others, for the avowed purpose of "preventing misconstructions," addressed from her decks a long letter "To the rest of our brethren *in* and *of* the Church of England," in which they say,—"We desire you would be pleased to take notice of the principals and body of our company, as those who esteem it our honor to call the Church of England, from whence we rise, our Dear Mother, and cannot part from our native country, where she specially resideth, without much sadness of heart and many tears in our eyes; ever acknowledging that such hope and part as we have obtained in the common salvation, we have received in her bosom, and sucked it from her breasts. We leave it not, therefore, as loathing that milk whereby we were nourished there, but, blessing God for the parentage and education, as members of the same body, shall always rejoice in her good, and unfeignedly grieve for any sorrow that shall ever betide her, and while we have breath, sincerely desire and endeavor the continuance and abundance of her welfare and enlargement." Governor Hutchinson, in his History of Massachusetts, says, "This paper has occasioned a dispute, whether the first settlers of Massachusetts were of the Church of England, or not." When Chief Justice Story quoted this farewell letter of the "pilgrims," in a public lecture, a few years since, Dr. Coit tells us that he was present himself, and that a good Calvinist sitting near him, suspecting some unfairness in this statement by the Chief Justice, (who was known to be a Unitarian,) turned to him with some uneasiness, and wondered whether it could be so! *Quodcunque ostendis sic incredulus odi.* But the truth must come out. Authorities are consulted. Dr. Coit has found some curious MSS. that the world has not yet seen. Light increases. Stern historic truth, and that from the press of New Englanders themselves, begins to take the place of platform speeches and blind Homeric dinner-table rhapsodies. After a sharp and protracted controversy, the whole world is at last agreed that Joyce Heth was *not* the nurse of General Washington.

But was it not the persecution of Archbishop Laud and his King that drove the Puritans from England? *No!* we tell you, *No!* The Puritans emigrated to Holland in 1609, and to America in 1620; and Laud was not archbishop until 1633! As to the martyred Laud, it has been strikingly remarked, that he wrote against Popery after he became a Bishop, but that Mr. Cotton, of New England, wrote a book in favor of "The power of the Keys" and of "The Bloody Tenet" or the right to persecute, after he became a Puritan. The truth is, that the non-conformists never found fault with the Church of England for persecuting, but for persecuting "the discipline." And although it was the doctrine of the age, that the broachers of new opinions, unsettling society and endangering the quiet of the people, should be willing, like the first Christians, to prove their sincerity by meeting the penalties which society for its own safety had imposed: yet the Church of England used a moderation truly astonishing when compared with the measures of the Puritans.

With regard to this "freedom to worship God," which orators, and poets, and the Misses with the sweet guitar and the piano, tell us the "Pilgrims" came to establish on "the wild New England shore," let us look into "*the documents*;" for, as Socrates was not above observing, "a brass kettle will keep its sound a long time, unless one puts his hand upon it and stops it."

It is marvellous how the Puritans, in their abhorrence of Saint's days, delight to listen to the stories of the "Pilgrims," which have no counterpart save in the legends of Italian Monks recited annually to the awe-struck multitude. One can almost imagine certain minds in New England prepared now for the apotheosis of these heroes and "Messiahs" of the age, since at a New England dinner (1848) in New York, they *endured* without a shudder, the wretched *toasting*; —"Plymouth Rock! may it ever be, as it has ever been, *the Rock of ages*." From this Rock the orator strikes his fire, and even the divine looks to it for his inspiration; and in the wild delirium into which Puritanism has run out in Massachusetts, the Transcendentalism and Pantheism toward which it is restlessly careering, who can say that Plymouth Rock may not yet be adored as a development of the Divinity that sleeps in Nature until event or accident wakens It to life, and makes It the source of energy and inspiration to the world? "Glorious old Rock!" "Amid the peltings of the pitiless storm!" "Asylum of liberty!" "Freedom to worship God!" "Wilderness!" What a theme for the orator!

You have imagined, gentle reader, that, in the "asylum" which the "Pilgrims" reared, a man sat down under his own vine and fig-tree, and worshipped God according to the dictates of his conscience. Long did I think so too. And nothing but the casting the first stone at Episcopacy, and my own keeping with a hearty good-will the garments of those who did so, put me in the way of discovering that the Episcopalians were "more sinned against than sinning." For what are the facts?

In England a Puritan might rail to his heart's content against Churchmen as "Popelings," "Papists," and "Anti-christs;" but in Massachusetts it cost an Episcopalian *a flogging*, to call a Puritan a Brownist, and if one spake "irreverently of the Lord's anointed ministers" he suffered *fifteen lashes* and was cast into a *dungeon*. In England the Puritans had thought it hard to pay tithes of property within the parish; although they always bought the property at so much the less: but in Massachusetts, they compelled the Episcopalians and Presbyterians to pay taxes to Puritan worship, on estates in England and Scotland. Quakers were forced to attend their worship; and if, after doing so, they met for their own worship in private, their doors might be broken open; a thing, Lord Chatham said in the face of Parliament, the King himself could not do in England. "A Quaker could be apprehended without warrant, tried without jury, fined without mercy, incarcerated without bail, kept at silent labor, fastened in the stocks and in *cages*, exposed to scorn, hooting, and *filthy missiles*, and the disposition of his property rendered null and void. Men, women, and children could be stripped naked to the waist, stretched upon wheels, tied to a cart-tail, dragged through the public streets from town to town, and lashed as they went along, until they reached the limits of the settlement, where they could be set down and left among the wolves and bears in the howling wilderness; they could be branded with the letters R. and H., as Rogues or Heretics; their ears cut off, their tongues bored through with a hot iron; their bodies sold into perpetual slavery, or hung and left unburied for the ravenous beasts."

All this from "Pilgrims," whose greatest hardship in England, at the same time, was, that their ministers were not allowed to officiate at her altars, or to hold her livings, unless they would keep their vows and observe her ritual, and that their laity were fined *one shilling* if they did not attend the Parish church!

But these laws were a dead letter, will say the kind reader, intended only to frighten and keep "the other denominations" quiet. No, indeed! In 1658, three poor Quakers had their ears cut off. In 1659, several others were hung, and their naked bodies cast without covering into a shallow grave, and their friends forbidden to provide them shroud or coffin, or to deepen or fence their graves against the wolves. In 1661, yet others suffered, and among them an aged female, who was compelled to walk between two Quakers to the gallows, and was taunted and jeered along the road for the indecency, and perished amidst the hootings of the Puritans and the beating of their drums. And when the "profligate tyrant" Charles interposed the royal *mandamus* to stay this work of persecution in New England, the prisons were found crowded with fresh victims. Yes, there were martyrs to the cause of religious freedom on "the wild New England shore," but they were not Puritans. Soon history will bring them forth, and the world, as Heaven has done before her, will set the crown of martyrdom upon *their* brow, and not upon that of their relentless murderers.

But they were doing the same things in England, will say the inquiring reader? No! a thousand times, *No!* "The tyrant" Charles banished no Quakers, hung none of their preachers, confiscated none of their estates. In fact, the author of the "History of Maryland" declares, that "it will surprise the reader, at this day, after a minute search through the pages of the best historians of those times, when he finds considerable difficulty in discovering *one* solitary instance where a Puritan was either burnt as a heretic, or hung as a felon, for his religion." Let it never be forgotten, that in 1612, the last execution in England for alleged religious causes took place; and that in 1661, *fifty years later*, these sad events took place in Massachusetts. It was in 1661, that Leddra, a Quaker, after being chained to a log in an open prison through one of the coldest winters of that century, perished on the scaffold, appealing to God and to his mother country, which he reminded them knew no such laws, and crying with his last breath, "Lord Jesus receive my spirit!" Lord Brougham, albeit disposed to palliate the evils of Dissent, declares, that "long after the mother country had relinquished *for ever* the acts of persecution, they found votaries in the constituted authorities of the Colonies; and the *northern* States, at the end of the seventeenth century, exhibited the disgraceful example of that spiritual tyranny, from which their territories had originally served as an asylum." "Many," says Benedict, in his account of the Baptists, "were the oppressions and privations which *our* brethren suffered in this boasted asylum of liberty, *until the American war*." Not until 1834, were Church and State entirely separated by the Congregationalists of Massachusetts, or "freedom to worship God" consented to, as Roger Williams, the Baptist who was banished to Rhode Island, and the Presbyterians and Episcopalians, desired to make it in 1635, *two hundred years before*.

When we adduce such facts, and pile them one upon another until they reach the clouds, the Puritan apologist reminds us, that "it was the fault of the times and not of the men," and cries,

> "O blame not, as poor Harpool's crime,
> An evil of his evil time."

But by this claim on charity, they concede the point, and

plead guilty to the charge of uttering a miserable fable, when claiming that the Puritans established in New England "men's right to worship God according to the dictates of their conscience." They never raised this cry about "the evil times," until over and over we had exposed the fallacy of their pretensions.

But no; we will not let them off with this: we have pursued them to the gates; we now shall enter. We charge then, that it was the fault of the men, and not of the age in which they lived; and that, in the matter of civil and religious liberty, the Puritans here and the Presbyterians in Europe were *behind their times.* As lately as 1700, they enacted a law against the Roman Catholics, of arrest without warrant, of perpetual imprisonment, and of death. And as lately as 1774, they upbraided the Parliament of the mother country for the "Quebec Act," because it extended toleration to the Roman Catholics of a province, who constituted nearly its whole population. Nor let it be forgotten that Charles, to whom the Puritans gave the crown of martyrdom more than two hundred years ago, was anxious that his Parliament should pass an act of universal toleration, and that the Puritans defeated it because it would comprehend the Romanists. Nay, have we not seen, within the last fifteen years, not only the burning of convents and churches, but inflammatory appeals through the press, and even elaborate tracts and books, to prove foreign conspiracies against the liberties of the United States, with the avowed purpose of moving the government against the toleration of the Jesuits? So has Puritanism been ever behind the age in religious toleration. While New England soil was reddened with the blood, or blackened with the ashes of Quakers, witches, and Baptists, and red-hot irons might be thrust through women's tongues, and the cleft stick was employed to keep them still:

in Virginia and the Carolinas, there was felt neither fire, nor fagot, nor halter, nor axe, nor red-hot iron, nor even the cleft stick upon the tongue. And here I will turn aside to remind the reader that, while Presbyterians and Baptists and Quakers were in England free to "worship God according to the dictates of their consciences," the Episcopal clergy in *Scotland* were prohibited from officiating for more than four persons besides their own family, under penalty of *six months' imprisonment* for the first offence, and *banishment* for the second. A peer or freeholder, who attended such a service twice in one year, forfeited all his political rights! The Rev. Mr. Erskine, of the Episcopal Church, says, under date of 1750, "With such excessive severity were the penal laws exacted at this time, that Andrew Moir having neglected to keep his appointment at my house this morning, and following me to Lord Rollo's, we could not take his child into any house, but I was obliged to go under cover of the trees into one of the parks, and there baptize his child." About the same time, or somewhat later, a young Episcopalian from Connecticut, on going to Edinburgh to procure a medical degree, requested his host, the Sunday after his arrival, to tell him where he might find an Episcopal service or church. "I will show you," said his host; "take your hat and follow me; but we are watched with jealousy by the Presbyterians; do not come near me; keep me barely in sight." So following his guide at a distance, through the ins and outs and windings of some unfrequented streets, the stranger at length saw his host disappear suddenly into a dilapidated building, some five or six stories high, on the side of a steep hill; and following still the sound of footsteps into the fifth or sixth story, there "worshipped God according to the dictates of his conscience." This youth became afterward a shining light at our altars, and is known in our annals as BISHOP SEABURY—the apostle of America.* England, Scotland—Siamese-twins: England allowing "freedom to worship God;" Scotland (like Plymouth Rock—glorious old Rock!) denying it to the last!

But not only were the Puritans behind the Episcopalians, but they were behind the Romanists of their age and country, in the "freedom to worship God according to the dictates of conscience." Lord Baltimore and the Roman Catholics of Maryland, in 1642, opened their arms to the oppressed of all lands, and invited the Colonists of New England to settle freely among them, and become partakers of their liberty; offering them the undisturbed enjoyment of their religion, at the very moment that the laws of banishment and death existed in New England against themselves! The invitation was accepted; and what did the Northern advocates of the great principle of "freedom to worship God," as the poets and the pianos have it, do, when they were fairly warmed at these southern fires, to repay this hospitality? They served them worse than they had served the Dutch. They turned upon the hand that warmed them; and rattled, and sprang, and stung! Maryland knew no law for imprisoning and flogging Quakers until then; but with the Puritans came the law, and with the law came the fact, and the fair soil of Maryland was for the first time dishonored by religious flogging. Episcopalians too, and even the Roman Catholics who had invited the Puritans among them, were now excluded from the protection of the laws! These are the facts, and when the world shall be a little older, we doubt whether the man shall be found whom even a New-England Dinner shall be able to inspire with the temerity to say, that the "Pilgrims" landed on Plymouth Rock with the view of erecting an asylum where "men might worship God according to the dictates of their conscience."

* The father of Bishop Seabury was once a Congregational preacher, but crossed the sea to obtain a better ordination.

Yet Edward Everett once said in an oration, (for an oration may sometimes have the merits of a poem, and an orator enjoy the poet's privilege of drawing on his imagination,) "Notwithstanding, we are indebted to them for two great principles; one of which is the separation of Church and State." Now it is known to thousands of living men, that in Massachusetts, and at Plymouth Rock itself, Church and State were not entirely separated until 1834, long after every trace of such a connection had been obliterated and forgotten in every other portion of the land. Even Judge Story, a man whom we have already found in advance of his age and his neighbors, declares that "*the fundamental error* of our ancestors, an error which began with their settlement of this colony, was a doctrine which has since been happily exploded, I mean *the necessity* of a union of Church and State; *to this they clung as to the ark of their safety.*" My own proud State, Episcopal Virginia, began her career with the right (as to all religious differences) of universal suffrage, whereas about the same time (1646) in Massachusetts, "no one could be tried, for life or limb, for name or estate, but by those of their own (Puritan) communion, and no man in their Plantation could vote as a freeman, unless a member of the Congregational Church." Episcopalians, and the Westminster Presbyterians and Baptists, petitioned again and again for an equality of rights, or at least, that they "might be freed from the heavy taxes imposed upon them, and of the impressment made of them, their children, and their servants, into the wars." As late as 1739, Mr. Vinlay, a celebrated Presbyterian divine, was arrested and carried from town to town, *as a vagrant*, until beyond the limits of the colony; when he went to Episcopal Virginia, and was permitted to preach unmolested. Much the same was the fate of the celebrated Mr. Tennent.*

* **Mr. Chapin says, "*Puritan* Massachusetts and *Puritan* Connecticut had their religious establishments. But *Roman Catholic* Maryland never had any, nor any test**

In England, if a Puritan absented himself from the parish church, he was fined *one* shilling; while at the same moment, in New England, if an Episcopalian were absent from Puritan worship, he was fined *five* shillings, and *forty* shillings a month for non-conformity to the Congregational Establishment; and, if he were incorrigible, the law said *death!* And while in Massachusetts the fine was *five* shillings, in Plymouth (glorious old Rock!) the penalty was *ten!* Right truthfully hath it been said, "The little finger of Puritanism shall be thicker than the loins of Prelacy; Prelacy hath chastised you with whips, but Puritanism will chastise you with scorpions." Why, a man who kept Christmas or any holyday of the Episcopal Church, or who denied the right of the Commonwealth to compel attendance on Puritan worship, was fastened by his heels in the stocks; and toleration was preached *against* from the pulpit, as "a sin in rulers that would bring down the judgment of God on the land." Judge Story says, "In this exclusive policy, our ancestors *obstinately persevered, against every remonstrance, at home and abroad.*" Not only were numerous letters written them from their friends in England, in the first instance, "to guard against too great a deviation from the Episcopal Establishment," but Sir Harry Vane, then in England, addressed in 1645 a letter to Governor Winthrop, warning him against these intolerant measures, "lest the Congregational way teach its opponents here [in

acts, except in the time of Cromwell. *Quaker* Pennsylvania never had any. *Baptist* Rhode Island never had any. *Episcopal* Virginia and *Dutch Reformed* New York never had any. *Episcopal* South Carolina and *Presbyterian* New Jersey never had any. Episcopal Virginia had a religious establishment, but it was given up in 1785. The principle of a religious establishment was first given up in Connecticut in 1818, and in Massachusetts in 1834. One cannot avoid the conclusion drawn by Mr. Tyson, that 'if all the colonies had been peopled by men of similar views and policy with those of New England, it may be doubted whether the Anglican form of religious freedom, now our presiding and guarding genius, had ever descended, to crown the happiness or bless the social charities of the present United States.'"

England] to extirpate and root it out from its own principles and practice." Sir Richard Saltonstall wrote them an earnest admonition, that "these rigid ways have laid you very low in the hearts of the saints in England;" to which they of New England made answer, "God forbid our love for the truth should be grown so cold, that we should tolerate such errors." Judge Story says that, in 1676, five-sixths of the people were disfranchised by the influence in New England of the ecclesiastical power, and as late as 1731, the poor Episcopalians were still petitioning for *the right of suffrage.*

Perhaps the reader will discover, in these facts, a reason why Churchmen were, some of them, slower than some of their neighbors in siding with the Revolution. If the War of Independence had been against the Dutch, would any man have thought marvel that the Dutch ministers in New York should have been the last to yield to the alternative of garments rolled in blood? And is it to the discredit of Episcopalians, that they were the last, (albeit they *were* often the first,) to take up arms against their brothers? I trow not. And would such a fact be an ill augury for the peace of the Republic and the joy of the world,—if all should be henceforth of one Lord, one faith, one baptism,

"Brethren in one glorious host,
Men whose brows were bathed and crossed?"

And are we to deem it a discredit to the Episcopalian clergy that they sometimes suffered exile, and surrendered their livings, as the nonjurors had done before, rather than violate the solemn oath of allegiance taken at their ordination? But Episcopalians, it must be admitted, had good reason to fear that a successful revolution might reduce them to a slavery worse than the first. Puritanism, it must be remembered, was the established religion in New England. The first Episcopal parish in New England dated from 1629, (a fact showing that the "Pilgrims" were not all "Puritans," as the speech on the ship Talbott and the letter from on board the Arabella have already indicated;) but it was not until 1743, one hundred and fourteen years after, that St. Peter's in Salem was allowed to have an organ, and not even then, until the question had been submitted to the vote of a tumultuous town-meeting! Episcopalians knew too, that it was now one hundred and twenty years since Dr. Murray had been appointed Bishop of Virginia,—an appointment that had been defeated by the Puritans; that every subsequent effort for the same end had been in the same manner frustrated; that it was openly avowed in the Eastern States, as one motive for the Revolution, that it would prevent the introduction of Episcopacy; and when Episcopalians remembered that, while as yet under the protection of the crown itself, they had paid in Plymouth (glorious old Rock!) ten shillings a head for each absence from Puritan worship, and as lately as 1731 had been petitioning in Massachusetts for the right of suffrage, and that, fifty years after death by fire had been for ever abolished in England, it was still known in Boston; when they recollected too, the irruption of the Puritans into Maryland, and the floggings that even there they inflicted on men's consciences, we cannot certainly affect surprise if some of them felt some little misgiving about the consequences of a revolution. Franklin did something to pacify these fears, by declaring the opinion, in his "*Cool Thoughts*" published before the Revolution, that "this event [the introduction of a Bishop] will happen neither sooner nor later, for our being, or not being, under a royal government." In spite of all this, there were Churchmen who felt the wrongs done to the colonies, and the greater wrongs done to themselves, by a government that had allowed the Episcopal settlements of the south, with all their intelligence and opulence, to be deprived of the Episcopacy and their essential apostolic character, for now a hundred and fifty years. And if the North furnished for that Revolution the iron, the South contributed the tow and the fire; and while Washington, nursed at the Church's breasts, kindled in the camp the fires on his country's altar, the Venerable White, chaplain to the first Congress and afterward Bishop of Pennsylvania, kindled in the same cause, the fires on the altars of his country's God.

CHAPTER XIX.

LIBERTY OF PRIVATE JUDGMENT.

There is, as I have shown in a former place, a species of liberty, so called, which Presbyterianism originally had no intention to encourage, but to which, in her downward tendencies, she inevitably conducts; and against which, as Antichristian, Episcopacy irreconcilably protests. She protests against levelling down the sublime mysteries of religion to the intellectual grasp of every sewing girl; every text of Scripture to the exegesis of the washerwoman; the Church of God to the dignity of a temperance society; the Priesthood to an office made and unmade by the hands of men; Government to a social compact that parties may dispense with at their will; Sacraments to a place beneath the mystery and power of masonic symbols; the ancient severities of repentance to a spasmodic agitation, lasting sometimes not an hour; the majesty of divine worship to a weekly off-hand prayer: and a thousand like things, that strive to leap the intellectual space between finite and Infinite, strike at the crown of Jesus, and sink the redeeming God into a feeble man. Saint Peter and Saint Jude, in concert, warn us against "dreamers," that should come "in the last time," or under the last dispensation, who, having "denied the Lord that bought them," shall "despise government, and shall not be afraid to speak evil of dignities;" who, "with feigned words make merchandise of men," "waves of the sea, wells without water, clouds carried about by the winds, wandering stars," "speaking great swelling words of vanity," "murmurers, complainers, promising men liberty."* "Religious liberty," as the phrase is, and as some men count liberty, is not the liberty of religion, but the liberty of *ir*religion, to assert itself, and obtrude itself into all places and companies with its whole execrable brood of profane and licentious fancies. The moment you call it to order on the score of reverence, or of common decency, you are considered as impertinently interfering with religious liberty; so that, in portions of our land, in companies where the reverence and deference of Catholicity are out of the question, in the stage-coach, at the hotel, at the dinner-table, in the ship at sea, one can scarcely, in mixed companies, get through the day without submitting to undue and ill-mannered flings at the dearest object of his faith and hope. One has said, that "if you wish to think a little, you may be an Episcopalian; if you wish to think a little more, you may be a Presbyterian; if you wish to think a little more, you should be a Congregationalist; and if you wish to think as much as you please, you must be a Unitarian." Now this chain itself indicates the power of thinking; and yet, poor man! if he would but "*think a little more*," he will see, that of this *stuff* the infidel, pantheist, atheist, may each one weld and add his potent link to this portentous chain! "Having heard that it is a vastly silly thing to believe every thing, some persons get the idea that it is a vastly wise thing to believe nothing."

Reason is the mind's eye or telescope, for the perception of truth; nor is it any more necessary that the mind should comprehend the truth perceived, than that the mountains or the stars should be compressed into the lenses of the eye or of the telescope. The medium through which reason discov-

See Jude and 2 Pet. ii.

ers truth, is light—the light of nature, and the light of revelation; but reason can no more create these lights, than the eye or the telescope can create the light of day. In the truths that reason arrives at by the light of nature, we travel from link to link along the chain, until we come into individual contact with the conclusion: in the truths that we perceive by revelation, we skip the chain; we bound across the intervening gulf; we see the bright object in the heavens; we admire; we adore; we have no means of reaching it. The Christian religion descends upon the earth. It finds reason on the throne, and demands her allegiance. Produce your credentials, replies the haughty mistress. If I do not works, none other ever did; if I speak not words, none other ever spake; if I live not a life, none other ever lived; if I die not the death, none other ever died; if I rise not again as none other ever rose; if I ascend not to heaven to show that from heaven I came; believe me not: is the answer. Reason until your heads shall burst, to prove that I am to be believed at all; *then* yield me up the right to say for you, what you are to believe and what you are to do. Let the child reason its little self to death, to know whether this is the mother that bare him; although a mother's voice and hovering love will, in the very dark, strike conviction to its heart: but once having satisfied itself that she is its mother, let it honor her with faith and obedience to the death. Reason, if you will, till a thousand suns go down, whether the heavenly Jerusalem, "the Lamb's wife," "the Mother of us all," is the "Faithful and True Witness" left by Jesus upon earth to "fill up that which is behind" of His teachings and His sufferings: then follow Her, to the prison and the cross. Reason if you please, till the lamps of night expire, that it is safer to believe what the universal church of God believes, than to imagine that your own unaided reason can decide where all the individual reasons round you differ and have differed ever; or reason, if you please, until the world grows old, to prove that it is more likely that God's guiding Spirit would "lead into all truth" the universal company of His elect, than that He should send that Spirit to guide you alone into the truth, when you have cast yourself on the ocean of conflicting doctrines with the rash hope that a miracle would interpose to save you! Yes, saith the Church; reason at the threshold: but let it be once for all. Establish the claim; let faith and obedience follow. Be not for ever learning, and never coming to the knowledge of the truth. Do not reason, and reason, and reason, against each article and particle, and fight every inch of your unwilling way to heaven, and look to "irresistible grace" to force you on. Establish the mother's claim; you can know Her by Her voice and very look, for they speak to the heart: let reverence follow. There is truth in the saying,

> "Quand l'homme commence à raisonner, il cesse de sentir,"

as a child that will reason and face down his parent at every trivial turn, will shortly cease from reverence, obedience, and filial affection. I would not for a universe of gold risk my salvation on the deduction of my "private judgment," unless I could be sure of the repetition for my benefit of the alleged Alexandrine miracle. The Jews have a tradition that when the Seventy in Egypt translated the Old Testament into Greek, for their brethren who had lost the Hebrew tongue, each translator was immured for a long period in a private cell, and when the seventy-two translators at the expiration of the time were brought together, it was found that, word for word, they had all by divine guidance made the same exact translation. Now if earnest and devout men could come forth from their closets where they expect individual guidance, and speak the same thing, even on the awful question of the Divinity of Jesus, and on the thousand questions in which individualism has split them up, we might believe that like the Seventy they were guided by one Spirit. But they differ; they for ever differ; they differ world-wide. One makes Jesus a man; another makes Him a God: one brings infants to His blessing; another keeps them back: and so they differ and will differ ever. Sooner would I this night leap from the vessel's decks into the boiling sea, in the expectation that in answer to prayer I might drift safely to shore: than plunge from the floorings of the Heavenly Ark, into a wild sea of sects, and expect Him to uphold me in the waves.

O, I have seen men's heads reel, and their feet stagger, and their bones wrecked along my path, from this intoxicating doctrine, and I thank God that He has put strength into my arm to fling from me for ever this cup of sorceries and sorrows. I have seen the mischief it has done. I do well to be heart-broken and angry. I have had many dear ones in life, whom tears cannot recall from the grave, whose feet have slidden on these slippery places. I have trodden over the dark sepulchre of millions, as I have shown before, who in the intoxicated hour have lost all upon the giddy wheel of "private judgment." I will not taste the cup. I see reasons to make me fear. When Cyrus was a boy, acting one day the part of cup-bearer to his grandfather Astyages, it was observed that, before handing the cup to the king, the little fellow did not taste the wine. "You forgot to taste it!" said the king. "No," said the child, "but I was afraid there might be poison in the cup; for whenever the lords of your court drink from it, I see that they become noisy and quarrelsome, and even yourself when you drink, forget that you are a king!" How can we say, Drink freely, drink deeply, when we see the whole ultra-Protestant world either "noisy and quarrelsome," for ever disputing and wrangling, or else slumbering its death-sleep after its excesses? I have seen another story that may illustrate this danger:—"The Caliph of Bagdad having lost his way in the chase, and entered the hut of an Arab in a fainting state, the latter deemed it an occasion when he might transcend the requisitions of the Koran, and set wine before his guest. Mahadi did not hesitate to drink, and soon began to tell his host that he was one of the chief servants of the Caliph, and would not forget his hospitality. Whereupon the attentions of his host were redoubled; and Mahadi having again drank freely of the wine, began presently to say, 'I must tell you, my friend, confidentially, that I am the favorite of the Caliph's household, and in return for your kindness, he will load you with his favors.' The wild Arab, now kissing the seam of his guest's robe, set all the luxuries of his hut before him, and begged him not to spare the wine if he found it to his taste. By degrees, Mahadi ceased to require pressing, and taking the old Arab's hand, said to him, 'My good friend, in wine is truth, and your hospitality obliges me to confess to you, that I am the Caliph himself, and as Caliph I confirm to you the promises I have made.' The child of the desert now took up the wine and marched towards the door. 'Where are you going?' asked the Caliph; 'I am going to remove the wine,' said the son of the desert; 'for after the first draught you said you were a servant of the Caliph; at the second, you were his confidential favorite; at the third, you were the Caliph himself; *now I know not what to believe;* but I fear, if you should drink again, you will declare that you are our Great Prophet!'" Alas! the stripling Cyrus and the wandering Bedouin saw, from the same cause, the same effect. And how many millions, since the intoxicating cup of private judgment was put into their hands, with the wild Arab, may say, "*I know not what to believe;*" first, Jesus was God; then he was an eternal emanation from God; then he was a creature higher than the angels, and created before them; then he was one of the angels; then he was nothing more than man. First, the Bible was inspired; then only a portion of it was inspired; then only the words of Jesus were inspired; then there was no inspiration at all. Once Jesus was alone Messiah; now He was but one of a succession of Messiahs, who have already appeared, or are yet to come. First, there were three that bare record in heaven; then there was but One; now there is None, save the Spirit of Nature, whose highest development is Man; and the apprehension of the Arab that his guest would declare himself next the Great Prophet himself, has had its terrific counterpart in the discovery, that Man is the highest impersonation of the Divinity of Nature waking into consciousness; and that while every thing else is God in its degree, Man is the God of gods. Thus with its unbounded "right of private judgment," Presbyterianism, where its course is run, has torn up the foundations of Christianity; and the whole Protestant world, seeking one negation after another, is now reduced to the condition of the child of the desert,—"*I know not what to believe.*" There is no Mother to teach; faith is at an end; reverence is no more; unity is gone; the great business of the sanctuary is supplanted; and where the Regulator is wanting,

> "'Tis with our judgments as our watches, none
> Go just alike, yet each believes his own."

As there are men in the state who imagine that it interferes with their *liberty*, to be obedient to law; as there are men in society who think it an interference with their liberty, to be compelled to maintain their offspring; as there are parents who think it an interference with their children's *liberty*, to teach them the fear of the Lord; as there are ruined youths who have thought it an interference with their *liberty*, to be required to obey their parents; as there are men who deem themselves not free, so long as government and property are in their way: so among Christians there are men who deem it an interference with their *liberty*, to be bound by the uniform voice of the Church. I can almost imagine that, in the hands of a Genevan watchmaker, a thousand watches might be set going without a regulator, and all practical utility be sacrificed to the singular caprice, that it would interfere with their liberty to put it in their power to go right. A man is held not to be free, if he believes the truth: and by parity of reasoning, a man is not free, who is compelled to believe that three times three are nine; nor a mathematician free, who cannot escape the fact, that the three angles of a triangle are equal to two right angles; nor a Christian free, unless he be allowed to deny and betray his Master; nor a Catholic free, unless he can be brought to depend more on his own private judgment as to what was taught in the Church eighteen centuries ago, than on the testimony of that Church herself! This world is a probation for the passions; ought it not consistently to be a probation for the reason? There are men who teach, that if you will but read the Bible and seek God's aid by prayer, He will infallibly guide you into all truth! But the first thing we notice is, that God has punished your temerity by distracting you amidst a thousand conflicting doctrines, and has punished his own child by leaving him to doubt—yes, since they would not believe the testimony of His Church, leaving *millions* to *deny*—the Divinity of His Son! Can any man believe, that He who never gives a stone when His child asks bread, would suffer this, if this teaching were true? Does it not rather look like the only method left in the wisdom of God, to bring a distracted world back to the teaching of the Church: precisely as He left the heathen of old to stumble on, and feel the insufficiency of reason, and the necessity of a Revelation, before He gave it? Here the Mother of us all—the Lamb's Bride—steps forth, and, protesting against the harlot's words of flattery with which the heart of her child might be too easily seduced, cries, My child, the waters are deep, and the storm is wild; the wind is high, and the night is dark; the sea is covered with the wrecks, and your bark is frail: stay, stay, my child, within the ark, and take your portion with its ransomed ones; "lean not unto thine own understanding; for it is not in man that walketh to direct his steps."

If order be incompatible with liberty; if reverence be irreconcilable with freedom; if obedience be derogatory to the dignity of human rights: then is Episcopacy now and for ever at war with liberty. If it be slavery to believe what is true; if it be slavery to chain the passions in arriving at conclusions; if it be slavery to do studied and formal homage to the Parent whose goodness is equal to His power; if it be slavery to obey the powers that are ordained of God; if it be slavery to listen to a Witness who was there from the beginning: then is the true Catholic a slave.

But no! In this sad world where man by sin has forfeited so much, it is well to remember there are divinely chartered liberties and rights, which the Church only hath preserved, and which Presbyterianism has now many a day trampled under foot. Episcopacy in her first synod at Jerusalem had elders—and she has them still—apostles, and brethren: Presbyterianism concentrates all in one order, and has excluded both the apostles and the laity. Episcopacy, even in monarchical England, has a branch of her legislature in a Parliament of laymen: Presbyterianism, in republican America, admits no laymen to her councils. Episcopacy distributes the three powers of government, Executive, Judicial, and Legislative, as the forms of constitutional liberty require: Presbyterianism consolidates them in one. Presbyterianism attempts to bind her followers by a confession of faith so extended, that it covers the whole ground in divinity with finespun dogmas, and leaves no room for innocent diversities of judgment; so that when diversities arise, the body explodes:

all this, Episcopacy affirms, is unphilosophical, unscriptural, unprimitive, incompatible with the variety of men's minds and modes of thinking, and an insufferable abridgment of human liberty; and she gives you, instead, her simple and ancient Creed, which can be written on your thumb-nail, and tells you that for the rest you may believe *salva fide* as you please; and whereas Presbyterianism may lengthen, or shorten, or alter, or amend its creeds to-morrow, the Church guaranties to you the ancient Charter, and tells you that no bishop nor nation of bishops upon earth can any more make a Creed, than they can make a Bible, or a God. Strict Presbyterianism teaches you, that you are by nature fast bound in misery and iron; that a decree of Omnipotence holds you; that you can no more reverse your destiny, than you can reverse the poles: the Church touches your fetters, and they fall; and as she bids you go and work out the destiny that under a Covenant of universal Grace brightens in the distance,

> "Hark! the roused captive spurns his heavy load,
> And asks the image back that Heaven bestowed;
> Warm in his heart the glow of freedom burns,
> And as the slave departs, the man returns."

Presbytery teaches you that there are millions of such captives, for whom Christ never died: the Church says, Away with the un-Godlike thought, by which ye cause our "brother to perish for whom Christ died." Presbytery insists, that the Holy Ghost, in His saving acts, is imparted only to the elect: the large-hearted Church cries out, in the language of the Apostles, "Repent, and be baptized every one of you for the remission of sins, and ye shall receive the Holy Ghost." Presbytery leaves little to an enlightened and generous conscience, but by a vast system of exaction and surveillance, extending even to drinks and dress and social recreations, is an omnipresent task-master, binding burdens that Episcopalians would feel degraded to carry for a moment: but the

Church, substituting for this "love of law" Her "law of love," throws an enlightened and generous conscience with free-breathing, unaffected ease, upon the great Christian principles in which it has been reared. Presbyterianism seals up your lips in the house of God, and suffers you to be only a silent listener in the high act of worship: the Church unseals your lips, and restores you, not in poetic fiction and sentimental song, but in delightful fact, "the freedom to worship God." Presbytery, shutting up the wounds which Christ left open, and from which gushed forth not the blood only, but the blood and water, takes away the birthright of your child if you have sinned, and bids it begone from the waters where its birth-sin may be washed away: the Church, like a gentle mother, says, "Bring thy son hither; it is the purest sacrifice the wide earth now has to lay upon the altar; I baptize him in the name of the Father, and of the Son, and of the Holy Ghost; and I charge you to remember that henceforth he is a child of God, a member of Christ, and an inheritor of the kingdom of heaven." Presbyterianism next gives over even the child it has baptized, to the tender mercies of the world, until it may please God by his "irresistible grace" to bring back the prodigal: but the Church, like the rightful mother, will not thus wrong and rob the child of Her womb; but with affectionate solicitude recalls it to her altar, to be confirmed in its bright inheritance, and receive on its young head and heart the baptism of Her second blessing. And in the hour of death, when the powers of darkness hover around and make their last dread effort with you, and when Presbytery listens coldly to your cry, "I thirst;" and, less merciful than the heathen soldiers at the cross, refuses to touch your lips with the wine and myrrh: the gentle Mother is by your bed, wiping with Her napkin the death-sweat from your brow; and, giving you the heavenly supper, leaves you with a sweet "Good-night!" to close your eyes upon the world.

That, as Presbyterians, you may not have observed the gradual steps whereby these encroachments on your liberties have been established, or that you are now insensible to the loss, one after another, of your rights secured to you once in the ancient Charter of the Church, only adds melancholy force to a melancholy fact. You have worn the chains so long that you do not feel them; and in this respect you are in the condition of the Papist, who does not care for the "liberty" to read the Scriptures, the "right" to receive the cup in the Holy Eucharist, or the "freedom" to worship God in a language he can understand.

Thus was I dislodged from my position, Number One, in which I had fortified myself at Princeton;* and these were the obvious reasonings that drew me on toward a Church, at once Catholic—Reformed—and Free; itself the best solution I could find of the mighty problem, of which the terms are Law and Liberty—Obedience and Freedom.

* See page 43.

CHAPTER XX.

HYPOTHESES.

I CAME now to the question of the *Episcopacy.* Some have employed their pens upon it, appearing to deem it the main matter at issue between the Church and the sectarians. Already I have said that I do not so regard it. We think that truth, grace, redemption, are all equally in peril; and the crown of our Lord's Divinity, and the blessed Mystery of His Cross, are wildly hazarded upon the die. I have sufficiently detailed the facts which too well support this terrific charge.

But, if the chaff be necessary to defend the unripe grain from blight and frost; if the rind be necessary to contain the mellow juices of the fruit, and advance them to maturity; if the shell be necessary to preserve the kernel from decay; if the body be necessary to retain the soul, and be the channel of her functions while doing her errand in this terrestrial sphere; if, in a word, Eternal Wisdom has imposed upon Itself a uniform law to protect every thing in nature with a covering, and to lock up the life of every thing inexplicably in its appropriate corporeal form: then is Christianity a rational and philosophical reflection of the Divine Wisdom, only when it holds in indissoluble union the Spirit with the Letter, the Grace with the Sacraments, the Promises with the Priesthood, the Realities with the Symbols, the Gospel with the Church. With this explanation, therefore, Episcopalians believe that, as the Church is essential to the preservation of the Faith, so is the Episcopacy essential to the preservation of the Church.

The broad fact stared me in the face that, certainly at a very early age, the Church was in all places under an Episcopacy. In Palestine and Syria, in Armenia and India, in Greece and Italy, in France and England, in Spain and Africa, from Antioch to Canterbury, from Asia Minor to Abyssinia, over three continents, and in all the islands of the sea, the Church was everywhere Episcopal. It was the age of piety, the age of miracle, the age of martyrdom, while the kiss of peace yet bore witness to the heart's purity, and the saints in humility stooped down and washed each other's feet. Yet in this age of truth and danger, there was, in every city and island and town, one, and one only, who was known as the chief pastor or bishop of the place. We never read in antiquity of more than one such person in a city at a time: James in Jerusalem; Clement in Rome; Ignatius in Antioch; Polycarp in Smyrna; Irenæus in Lyons; surrounded by their Presbyters and Deacons. And when the fires of martyrdom blazed high and bright, there was in every city and town *one*, known alike to Christian, Jew, and Pagan, as the chief shepherd, who must first unbind his girdle and lay down his life for the flock. Thus, in defiance of considerations almost enough to have extirpated Episcopacy from the Church, unless it had been an ordinance of Christ which they durst not violate, or even for a time conceal: Episcopacy existed wherever the Church existed, and the world has been again and again challenged to produce one single church in all Europe, Africa, or Asia, which in the first, the second, the third, the fourth, the fifth, or the sixth century, was for one moment Presbyterian. When Presbyterians demand of Episcopalians a chain of Bishops from 1850 back to the days of the Apostles: Episcopalians produce it—link after link, name after name—back to the hands of St. Thomas in Syria, St. John in Ephesus, St. James in Jerusalem, St. Mark in Alexandria, St. Peter and St. Paul at Rome. But when Episcopalians ask of Presbyterians to produce, not a succession of churches reaching beyond Luther and Calvin and a gulf of a thousand years, but one poor, single, solitary church in a world-full of Churches, that in the first, or the second, or the third, or the fourth, or the fifth century, was bona fide *Presbyterian:* they return the writ with the *non est inventus;* it cannot be found!

I recollect well that, with this view of the matter, I began to suffer an uneasiness that subsequent investigations served only to increase. It struck me forcibly, as arguing the Apostolic origin of Episcopacy, in the same manner that the universal worship of Jesus, in the earlier ages, demonstrates His Divinity. It is distinctly in my memory, that the Professor of Theology, at Princeton, introduced a brilliant Lecture on the Divinity of Christ, with these words: "It is a strong presumptive proof of the Divinity of Christ, that the Church Catholic has held it from the earliest ages." Now we require but the *mutato nomine* to say: "It is a strong presumptive proof of the Apostolic origin of the *Episcopacy,* that the Church Catholic has held it from the earliest ages." Nay, in favor of Episcopacy, the argument, like the testimony that supports it, is unbroken: whereas, in its application to our Lord's Divinity, the Unitarian exultingly adduces the Ebionites of the first century, the swarming sects of Gnostics in the second, and the mighty multitudes of Arians in the third and fourth, all crying out against the doctrine as an innovation or corruption. Could Presbyterians produce, in favor of their pretensions, one tithe of the outcry in the first four centuries against Episcopacy, that Unitarians can produce against the claim in the same centuries of our Lord's Divinity: they would make the land ring again with the protest and the clamor that Episcopacy had thus elicited in the first, second, third, and fourth centuries. But, on the subject of Episcopacy, there is no clamor. There is not a voice to break the silence. The Christian world reposes for at least three unbroken centuries of piety, miracle, and martyrdom, under the undisputed watch and rule of the Episcopacy. This was the phenomenon; and, by attempting to account for it, Presbyterians acknowledged it.

One of my earliest misgivings in this matter, was a secret and increasing dissatisfaction with the prevailing explanation of this phenomenon, among the Presbyterians around me, and their singular method of accounting for "the rise and growth" of Prelacy in the primitive Church. It would not have answered to suppose, that it was introduced violently into the Church, or in any great degree against the wishes of the people or the clergy: for the absence of all clamor or outcry, or even notice of the event, precludes the hypothesis. When the Bishop of Rome usurped but the smallest beginnings of power unknown to the pre-existing church, the whole East cried out in a rebuke of thunder; a standard that was never struck, was raised against him in Bohemia and the Alps; every nation in Europe contested, for a while, the growing usurpation; France would not submit, but on conditions that to this day are dear to the Gallican Church; even Austria and Spain protested loudly and long; while England surrendered last, and to the last retained much of her ancient independence, and in fact never, formally and legally, by authoritative act of either Church or Parliament, surrendered to the domination of Rome. The smallest change in ecclesiastical administration is sure to be noted on the pages of the fathers. Scarcely can a bell-ringer or a candle-snuffer, a sub-deacon or an acolyte, be introduced to complete the service of the sanctuary: that the event and the date are not set down in history. Yet, if the Apostles left the Church on three continents Presbyterian, not only did it become Episcopal in one hundred years over the entire world: but not a writer of antiquity has told us when or where, or by what means the change took place, or who effected it, or that such a change took place at all. When or where was it that some tall commanding intellect arose, and, setting one foot on the sea and one on the dry land, with a voice that reached and overturned three continents and shook the islands of the sea, lifted his hand and said, Wherever Apostolic Presbyterianism hath been, there let a human Episcopacy be hereafter? Fair must have been his form, winning must have been his countenance, and sweet must have been the music of his tongue, methinks, to persuade three continents at once, and at one stroke, to destroy an institution so lately left them by the inspired Apostles, and at the same time to agree throughout the world that not one word should be said about the matter, either to extenuate it, to account for it, or so much as to record it! Presbyterianism, child of the Apostles, and first love of the martyrs, nurtured and held dear wherever the feet of the Apostles trod, died, and was buried, and neither foe nor mourner on the earth either shed a tear or exulted at its death, or raised a slab to say to the passer-by how long it lived, or when or where it died! This was a fact that embarrassed me much, so soon as I was brought by other causes to a state of mind that compelled me to lend it my attention. When, in the sixth century, Rome sent Augustine and his companions into England to convert the Anglians, they found a Church in her beauty, using the ceremonial of the Oriental Christians, claiming parentage from the successors of St. John; also tracing her annals to the very person of St. Paul, and adorned with a hierarchy that, two or three centuries before, had sent its Prelates to the councils of Arles, Sardica, and Ariminum. When Buchanan made his journeys to the East, he found in the clefts of the rocks and the fastnesses of Syria, the remnant of the disciples of St. Thomas, a simple and frugal flock, claiming descent from Israel according to the flesh, for thirteen centuries cut off from the Christian world: but hugging to their hearts a beautiful liturgy, erecting the simple cross upon the altar as the sufficient expression of their faith, evincing their ancient and Jewish origin by retaining the thank-offerings, the sacrificial lamb, and the circumcision of the Jews, and having and holding in reverence the order and office of the Bishops. When Dr. Wolff, whose benevolence in seeking the outcast races of the earth has been equalled only by his courage in conquering the obstacles that resisted his will, and who has exemplified the self-denial of the Gospel as few have illustrated it since the fathers and Apostles of his race first fell asleep, was led to remark that, in the whole circuit of his travels, Greek or Armenian, Coptic or Syrian, every thing Christian and bearing traces of antiquity, had everywhere its triune priesthood of Bishops, Priests, and Deacons: it suggested a thought that ripened into conviction, and led him like a child, though late in a career of usefulness and fame, to seek a Deacon's Orders at a Bishop's hands. In fact, Episcopacy needs no other argument than its universality, at a time and in circumstances that make that universality a simple impossibility *if*, at the death of St. John, the Universal Church was Presbyterian.

But something must be done; if we let it thus alone, the world will go after it; in the absence of any outcry or remonstrance, or even record of the overthrow of Presbyterianism, can we not follow up the supposition that it *was* overthrown, by *another* supposition that shall explain to the people *how* it was overthrown? Yes, say the scribes and champions of Presbytery, a happy thought now strikes us; let our soldiers and fighting men say, when questioned closely by the people about the disappearance of the Presbytery, and of its sepulchre, and of the stone that marked the place where it lay: that while the Presbyterians slept, the Episcopalians came somewhere in the darkness, between the first and fifth centuries, and stole it away! And the thing happened on this wise. The Moderators of the Presbyteries, through compliment to their discretion, piety, or age, were permitted to hold their office from one sitting to another; at length the office came to be considered permanent; until at last, these "Standing Moderators" took the name of Bishops, while the rest of the clergy were notified to keep the name of Presbyters; and what occurred at Rome, occurred at Alexandria; and what happened at Alexandria, happened at Canterbury; and in fact, every city and town on the three continents presented the same phenomenon. But where it began, and when it occurred, we have no means of knowing, for we tell you that the thing took place while the Presbyterians slept! This is the supposition of Doctor Miller. As a student at Princeton, I as innocently believed as though I had seen it with my eyes, that could I have time to go into the libraries of the Seminary, and to turn over the folios of the fathers that lie there in undisturbed repose and dust, each with its virtual inscription, *Requiescat in pace*, I should have seen, on many a page of earliest antiquity, a venerable company of pastors sitting in Presbytery with supreme and equal jurisdiction, and a "Standing Moderator" putting the question simultaneously to every church under the sun, "As many of you as agree to the resolution, that I shall hereafter be invested with the title and prerogative of Bishop, while the rest of you shall be my Presbyters, will signify it by saying,—Ay; and they of the contrary will say—No;" and that all the Presbyteries throughout the world, from Tartary to England, and from Abyssinia to Asia Minor, gave their voices in the affirmative; and came to a second resolution, that none of their historians or writers should ever say one word about Presbyterian parity, or so much as let posterity know that it had ever existed: this, perhaps, for the honor of Presbytery, which had worked badly, and which they would bring under the motto, *De mortuis nihil nisi bonum.* Imagine, then, my surprise, on finding that all this was *supposition*, without the shadow of historical authority, and that the Fathers do not say one word about Moderators, standing or sitting, temporary or permanent. These "Standing Moderators" are a standing proof, therefore, of the fertility of the imagination, when roused by the necessities of the case to a particularly striking effort. The universality of Episcopacy, and the universal silence over which it reigns, are awkward facts to deal with; and though we may wonder that some better hypothesis has not come to the relief of Presbytery, yet, on reflection, it will be seen that this is as rational, perhaps, as any other that could have been invented. I shall never forget the embarrassment of a fellow-student at Princeton, and the mirth he created for his class at one of their recitations, when the Professor asked him whether the story of the Jews about the disappearance of the Body from the sepulchre was not very lame; and asked him further, whether he did not think they might have gotten up a better story? "I think they might," said the youth. "Well, what would *you* have said?" asked the Professor, whose playful manner by this time indicated that the catechumen was getting among the breakers. There was an awful pause; the poor young man (albeit certainly not under thirty) could scarcely maintain his perpendicularity in the midst of his dilemma, but throwing his weight first on one leg, and then on the other, and seeming to feel very dubious himself whether he was on his legs at all, at length, by a peculiar conformation of his countenance, made signal to his class that the Jew had fairly outwitted the Gentile, and had told the best story that the case admitted of.

But this hypothesis of the Presbyterians is lame in another particular. It does not account for the disappearance of the "ruling elder," or for the acquisition by the Deacons of the right to baptize and preach. For herein, said I, is a marvellous thing: one Presbyter in every city in Christendom gets to be Bishop; and two other results, requiring contrary causes to produce them, simultaneously take place; the ruling elders are supplanted and annihilated, and live not again until a thousand and five hundred years are finished; and yet the Deacons are promoted from an inferior service to an Order in the Ministry. Let the Presbyterian give us, if he can, the *rationale* by which these three results were simultaneously produced: one of the Presbyters in every church on earth becomes Prelate; the ruling elders in every church on earth are annihilated; the Deacons in every church on earth are elevated over the heads of the elders to an order in the ministry. The three phenomena are to be fairly met and covered, which they can never be by this *montes-parturiunt* hypothesis of "Standing Moderators." We look therefore to Presbyterianism for a more satisfactory solution, some happier afterthought:—I say afterthought; for such hypotheses were never resorted to, until the dilemma began to be severely felt. Necessity proverbially is the mother of invention. Say ye, "His disciples came by night, and stole Him away, while we slept." Say ye, "While the Church reposed in simple and unsuspicious piety, the Bishops came and stole away our rank and our prerogative, and stole away our elders and our deacons, and we know not where they have laid them." So this saying is commonly reported among the Presbyterians unto this day. But to me, when I understood its terms, it seemed a story more difficult to swallow than that which told of disciples stealing a body without noise or stir, or waking up the sleepers upon guard: for not only has the Presbyterian body disappeared, without stir or noise, but the same event has occurred in every city on the globe, and even the sepulchre is stolen too, and the stone from the door, where we might have seen that for certain the body had lain. In the one case we can say, as it is a Jewish story, *credat Judœus;* but in the other we know not what to say, and shall simply add to it, *Non ego!*

The universality of Episcopacy in the early ages, when there were heretics innumerable who would very gladly have disputed an authority which visited them so often with the stern exercise of a discipline not very easy in those days to bear, and yet which they submitted to without questioning the Bishop's rights: is an argument strong men have admitted to be stronger than they. Baxter, Le Clerc, Bucer, Beza, Casaubon, Blondel—all in the Presbyterian ranks—have yielded to it as *the unanswerable argument.* Luther and Calvin lamented the loss of the Episcopacy, and professed the intention to restore it when it should be practicable. Luther, like the Methodists, unable to get upon his own terms the genuine, adopted for the time being a spurious Episcopacy, which is still perpetuated in the Lutheran communion. Calvin declares, "If the Bishops so hold their dignity, that they refuse not to submit to Christ, *no anathema is too great* for those who do not regard such a hierarchy with reverence and the most implicit obedience." Blondel, the learned Presbyterian, says, "By all we have said to assert the rights of Presbytery, we do not intend to invalidate *the ancient and apostolical constitutions of Episcopal pre-eminence,* but that wheresoever it has been put down or violated, *it ought to be reverently restored.*" This argument of universality was one with which even Grotius could not grapple, as a Presbyterian, and therefore, with a candor equal to the gigantic stature of his mind, he says, "To reject the supremacy of one pastor above the rest, is to condemn the whole ancient Church of folly or even of impiety." Grotius was as familiar with antiquity and with its monuments and fathers, as the child with his alphabet and toys. Yet Grotius says, "The Episcopacy had its commencement in *the times of the*

Apostles. All the fathers, without exception, testify to this. The testimony of JEROME alone [Doctor Miller's famous and favorite witness in behalf of Presbytery!] is sufficient. The catalogues of the Bishops, in Irenæus, Socrates, Theodoret, and others, all of which begin in the Apostolic age, testify to this. To refuse credit, *in a historical matter*, to so great *authorities*, and so *unanimous* among themselves, is not the part of any but an irreverent and stubborn disposition. What *the whole Church* maintains, and was not instituted by councils, but *was always held*, is not with any good reason believed to be handed down by any but *Apostolic authority.*" It will be observed that Grotius makes it a strong point, that Episcopacy had existed as a fact from the beginning, and was never "instituted by the authority of councils." In this respect it stands on the same footing with infant baptism. No council of the Church ever commanded infant baptism; it was a universal custom from the beginning. If, in the third century, or even in the second, a council had enjoined infant baptism, or female communion, or the observance of the Lord's Day, it would have justly created suspicion at this day, that these were innovations at the time, unknown, or certainly not universal, in the pre-existing Church. But councils and fathers and catalogues all speak of the Episcopacy as universal already, and coeval with the Apostles. No one once speaks of Presbytery as ever existing in the Church. Episcopacy did not come in while the soldiers slept. The soldiers were awake and at their posts, throughout the long chain of défences which they were set to guard. Clemens at Rome and Ignatius at Antioch, the former mentioned by St. Paul to the Philippians, and the latter a companion of the Apostles, and both of them Bishops, and consequently martyrs; Irenæus the Bishop of Lyons, and the disciple of Polycarp Bishop of Smyrna and friend of St. John; Tertullian in Africa, in the lifetime of Irenæus; and from them onward, a chain of witnesses through all the earlier centuries, testify, as Grotius allows, not only to the universality of the Episcopacy, but to the fact that it was settled "by Apostolic authority." His strong language is—yet not stronger than the fact—that "*all* the fathers, *without one exception*, testify to this." And we do not wonder that so great a man as Grotius recoiled from the thought that "all the fathers, without one exception, testify to" falsehood! Yet he saw the other horn of the dilemma, when he declared that "to reject the superiority of one pastor above the rest, is to condemn *the whole ancient Church* of folly, or even of *impiety*," and "to refuse credit, in a historical matter, to so great authorities, and so *unanimous among themselves*, is not the part of any but an irreverent and stubborn disposition." Thus was my own mind shaken, nor could the far-fetched supposition of "Standing Moderators" moderate at all the misgivings I began to suffer.

But I understood my right as a Presbyterian too well, not to exercise my "private judgment" in the matter, and seek a theory for myself; and for some time after I had seen the philosophical fallacy and historical nonentity of the hypothesis of "Standing Moderators," I was content to remain a Presbyterian, on a theory that to me appeared at first, to harmonize the several phenomena alluded to before: the appearance of the Prelate, the disappearance of the Ruling Elder, and the absorption of the Deacons into the Orders of the Clergy. My idea was, that the truth lay somewhere between the two systems of Presbytery and Episcopacy; that the former had unduly abridged, and that the latter had unduly expanded, the respective powers of pastor, elder, and deacon. I took the liberty of *supposing* that there were originally in in every congregation, by advice of the Apostles, a pastor, a bench of elders, and a board of deacons. Keeping this synagogue theory in view, I in the next place *supposed*, that in the absence of the pastor, an elder might have been allowed to pray, exhort, baptize, and discharge other functions of the pastor; which being allowed, it was then easy to *suppose* that the deacons also, coming into contact with the sick and dying, might have shared in certain cases the ministerial offices, an inference that the preaching of St. Stephen, and the ministration of baptism by St. Philip, two of the seven Apostolic deacons, appeared to justify. Then I had only to *suppose*, (for I had seen something like it in my own denomination,) that in cities and towns the pastor might have sent his elders out into destitute neighborhoods, to collect the more distant converts into new congregations; and that thus, by degrees, the ruling became the teaching elder imperceptibly, while the pastor became naturally overseer, bishop, or chief pastor of the whole circle of congregations. This accounted also, I supposed, for the small extent of the early dioceses, and the great number of the Bishops. This theory appeared to me also more plausible than the hypothesis of "Standing Moderators," and seemed to harmonize the facts, and to lie more clearly within the principles that govern human conduct, by allowing pastor, elder, and deacon, simultaneously, to enlarge each his appropriate sphere, and, by mutual compromise and mutual connivance, to further in each other the expansion of their several prerogatives. I *supposed* that the pastor might have said to his elders and deacons, "Make me your Diocesan, and I will make you into orders of the ministry, and give you certain districts of my Diocese." The difficulty did not then occur to me, how such a metamorphosis could have taken place in every parish under Heaven, when as yet there was no possibility of collusion by electric telegraph, and the Christians of those unenlightened times did not communicate across sea and land by the aid of necromancers, mesmerizers, mysterious knockers, and clairvoyants. But a grave objection to my theory, as I soon began to feel, was, that it was an afterthought, a strained and labored device for getting rid of palpable historic testimony. And though I managed for a time to pacify (for I cannot say to satisfy) myself with some such theory floating in dim outline through my troubled mind, yet it did not last me long. History was silent as the grave about any such expansion of prerogatives, and the hypothesis would never have existed but, like the "Standing Moderators," *ex necessitate rei.* Besides, my theory conceded Prelacy in principle, by allowing that, on ever so small a scale, there was a chief pastor, a council of elders with the inherent right to administer the word and sacraments under his direction, and an order of deacons permitted under certain limitations to baptize and preach. Besides, if my hypothesis were allowed, it would fasten upon modern Presbytery the very usurpation charged against Episcopacy, of abridging the ancient powers of the elders and deacons, and engrossing all ministerial prerogatives in the person of the pastors; so that Episcopacy, by allowing ministerial functions to the three orders, would be, after all, in fact and principle, the very Presbyterianism that was *supposed* to have existed in antiquity. Moreover, the theory did not harmonize with the historical fact, that there was but *one* bishop to a city, although, like Alexandria, or Antioch, or Jerusalem, or Rome, it may have reckoned its disciples by myriads. Yet thus it was that I fought conviction off, by flying, like the infidel, from one crude hypothesis to another; lending too, like him, a more willing ear to a cavil or a doubt, than to a compact and universal body of unbroken evidence. The demonstration returned upon me more overwhelmingly than ever: There, said I, is the universal fact, attested by universal history, and universally accounted for by the writers of the times as Apostolic in its origin; a fact which the fathers nowhere argue, but everywhere set down as a fact before their day, a fact from England to India, a fact reaching to the Apostles. No other fact in history is so variously and well attested. Every doctrine of Christianity was disputed in its turn: but the Episcopacy was never disputed. Ebionites, Gnostics, Arians, all fought to the death against our Blessed Lord's Divinity: but against the Bishops there were none to fight. Perpetually was the Church kept busy in defining and guarding the traditions and faith against every species of innovation and heresy; but there was a subject in which all were agreed, a tribunal from which none appealed, a fact which none at any time contested—Apostolical Episcopacy. We produce a chain of witnesses for the Episcopacy back to Clement, (the companion of Saint Paul,) in his Epistle to the Church at Corinth. We produce a chain of Bishops, name after name, back to St. Mark, St. Peter, St. Paul, and St. John; and if you will go to the foot of Mount Lebanon they will exhibit to you still the succession of their Bishops back to St. Thomas on his way to India. We produce a universal Church quietly reposing for centuries under the rule and guidance of the Bishops, as the centre of unity, the channel of benediction and grace, the antitype of the Old Testament Prelacy, and the type of heavenly things. And in return for all this demonstration, the like of which is to be found for no other doctrine, fact, sentiment, or usage upon earth, we ask you to produce *one single witness* from the first, or the second, or the third century, to intimate that such a thing as Presbyterianism ever lived; one—only one—*one* Church, that, in the first, or the second, or the third, or the fourth, or the fifth, or the sixth, or the seventh century, was bona fide *Presbyterian.* Show us *but one,* and we will lay down our pen.

CHAPTER XXI.

A FALSE ISSUE; OR, THE PHANTOM GIANT.

It is no part of my design to discuss at length, the particular question which many both within and without the Church have too long regarded as the only point of essential difference between the Churchman and the Sectarian. Were this with me the main point of difference, I should here lay down my pen, or suffer it to write but two words more, to say with all the fervor I could throw into a prayer—*Perish Episcopacy!* Never could I make *that* the one-idea which should separate me from the sects around me, and yet assimilate me to them by magnifying a one-idea into a cause of denominational distinction. I should without effort drop the miserable with from my arm "as a thread of tow when it toucheth the fire," and reach to brother Barnes not the left, but "the *right* hand of fellowship."

Time has been, however, when the government of Bishops was, in the ears of Dissenters, the main note of discord among "the notes of the Church." In many other things Dissenters once spake the Church's language, and sang the Church's song, and the Church listened with delight to the distant, though broken, echoes of her own voice. But the hour is coming, yea, is already come, when the widening departures of the sects have demonstrated, at terrific cost, that the whole circle of evangelical truth is in controversy. So long, therefore, as the mystery of the Trinity shall be the deep and solid archway over which a sinner's path to heaven must lie; so long as the Crown of the slain Man of Calvary shall be so bright that not even "the brightness of the Father's glory" can excel it, and only the Cross can vie with it in beauty; so long as the Blood of the Lamb shall be the sole hope in the universe, of restoration to the Divine favor; and the Holy Ghost, proceeding from the Father and the Son, the sole power in heaven or earth to effect our restoration to the Divine image; so long as the enunciation of Faith shall be more sublime than the stammerings of reason; and the ministry, and word, and sacraments, and alms, and prayers, and fasts, shall be the medium for the operations of grace; so long as sin shall be vile, and hell dark; or a Saviour precious, and heaven bright; or the soul immortal, and the resurrection and the judgment certain: so long we must value the Episcopacy as earth's great Antipas, and heaven's living and faithful Witness. And if the evil time has been when Churchmanship was a proud enigma, and another name for bigotry, and an intolerable one-idea: the good time has come when, to relax it by playing into the hands of vacillating sects, is to play false to the ancient Faith and to the Crown of "the Ancient-of-days." For two reasons, however, I shall but briefly touch the particular dogma of the Episcopacy. One is, that so long as Hobart, and Bowden, and Burscough, and Cooke, and Onderdonk, and Leslie, and Perceval, and Richardson, and Kip, and Wilson, are accessible to the popular reader, and the Fathers of a pure and early church may be consulted by the student, Episcopacy asks no defence from one who is less than the least of all. My other reason is, that since Churchmen do not regard it as by any means in itself the main question at issue, I do not wish to give it an enlargement that may convey to the reader the impression that I have, myself, any such idea. But inasmuch as I must give a faithful narrative, this part of the subject is not to be entirely passed over.

Nothing was now in the way of my returning with entire satisfaction to the communion of my forefathers, but the repudiation of my Presbyterian ordination. For the reader will bear in mind that I was a Presbyterian of an olden school, and never for one moment regarded ministerial ordination as a matter of mere ecclesiastical convenience or propriety. That it was getting to be so regarded, by the controlling spirits of my own communion, was itself the circumstance that more than any other made me unhappy, and awakened my suspicion that, so far as this matter was concerned, there must be something wrong. I had regarded my office with awe, and my brethren as "ministers of Christ and stewards of the mysteries of God," and it was more than I could bear to hear, in the words of the Princeton Review, "that the people can *originate* as valid a ministry as ever was made by Presbytery or Prelate." If the people, I said, may impart to me the right to preach the gospel of the Son of God, and to administer His holy sacraments, and to "remit and retain sins," which the Confession of Faith recognizes as their high prerogative: then the people must have that right themselves, and the ministry is all superfluous. If, moreover, they have the unbounded right of "private judgment," and the Bible alone be a sufficient guide: they have no need, that I can see, of a Church or ministry to teach them. If the sacraments are nothing more than mementos of past events, their commemorative virtue is as good in the hands of the people, as of one on whom the people have laid hands: for if there be no charm in the hands of a Bishop, it will not be pretended that there is any in the hands of the people. If the people may authorize me to preach, I must furthermore preach the preaching that they bid me. In vain should I remonstrate,

"Who ever saw in all his days,
Sheep lead their shepherd out to graze?"

The people, as the source of power, would justly answer me,

"Though you are now in pastor's chair,
Consider, sir, who put you there;
Surely, as Shepherd, you must know
'Twas we, the flock, that made you so;
And must the thing created claim
O'er its creator power supreme?"

No, no! Fearful is this utterance of the oracle at Princeton. Who is not reminded by it of the "ancient gainsayers?"

KORAH AND HIS COMPANY.	PRINCETON REVIEW.
"Ye take too much upon you, seeing *all the congregation* are holy, and the Lord is among *them;* wherefore lift ye up yourselves above *the congregation* of the Lord?"	"The power belongs in all its vigor to *the people*, and *they* can originate as valid a ministry as ever was made by Presbytery or Prelate."

And a fearful door does this open for the people to fulfil that which is written, "The time will come when they will not endure sound doctrine, but shall heap *to themselves* teachers, having itching ears." That time has come. The people can be now accommodated to their heart's content, and set up teachers and preachers to teach and to preach just such teaching and preaching as the people please.

What floodgates hast thou opened in these latter days, O Presbytery, to a Socinian, Universalist, and Pantheistic *ministry!* While the imperishable Priesthood proclaims "the sound doctrine," "as it was in the beginning, is now, and ever shall be," whether men will hear or whether they will forbear; while, amidst all the sorceries of Rome and the mysteries of her iniquities, thou wilt find no pulpit so mysterious in iniquity as to entertain a preacher who should be so much a "man of sin" as to deny the Divinity of Jesus, the redemption by the Cross, the Trinity, or the final perdition of the ungodly; while these everlasting truths are so securely guarded that not even a Deacon is allowed to serve at table till he have first been "set before the Apostles," and *they* have "laid their hands on him:" thou, O Presbytery, hast proclaimed that *the people* have the unbounded right of private judgment in these matters, and the prerogative besides "to *originate* a ministry as valid as was ever made by Presbytery or Prelate!" Interrogate thyself, O Presbytery, whether, if Satan had two things to ask thee for, thou couldst have better pleased him than by granting these: first, that the people should have the right to choose their own religion; and, secondly, that they should create a ministry to preach it!

I have been more than surprised to find a Presbyterian champion, professedly of the olden school, seizing with such eager grasp upon a weapon which had long lain rusting on the field where the Presbyterians of former days had wrested it from the hands of the Independents. I allude to the famous supposition of the company of Christians cast upon a desert island. "It will be time enough to provide for the case when it occurs," said Doctor Miller to the class of which I was a member. And better still is the answer of Doctor Lathrop, which I shall quote, but not yet. But Doctor Potts and the Princeton Review succumb completely to the Congregationalists, in advocating the power of the laity to "originate" a ministry. Well did Doctor Wainwright answer, that if the wrecked company, having lost their last Bible, should engrave on leaves of trees such parts of it as they could imperfectly remember, to be transmitted to their posterity: would not their more fortunate descendants be bound to receive the unmutilated Scriptures, if a bright sail in the horizon should afterwards convey to them the authentic Word? And ought not a ministry "originated" in the same manner, to give place, when times should be more favorable, to the ancient and authoritative Priesthood? I recollect that a Unitarian adduced this very argument to a parishioner of mine, to convince him that *baptism with sand* was as valid as baptism with water, because, forsooth, the occasion for its ministration *might* arise in the *desert!* On the same principle, a vegetable instead of bread, and water in the place of wine, may be substituted in the most Holy Sacrament, because there might be neither bread nor wine upon the desert island. And it is a sad fact that the Puritans, in former times, presumed to celebrate the Lord's Supper with beer, and milk, and ale, and other drinks, for fear the people should lay too much stress upon a *mere external.* Mr. Delavan informs us, too, that wine has been dispensed with in a thousand dissenting congregations in America! The only answer that the supposition above stated seems to deserve, is, that whatever you may write upon the leaves of trees is not the Bible, where the true Bible may be had; that baptism with sand is no baptism, where the baptism with water may be gotten; and that the ministry set up by the people is no ministry, where the ministry transmitted from Christ may be enjoyed. A desert island! The ancient order of God's kingdom to be uprooted, because, in your judgment, it does not meet the necessities of a desert island! Sirs, do you not perceive that you are borrowing, as is not uncommon with you, from the armory of the infidel? He tells you, God has left many of His children upon lonely isles for ages without your Bible or your ministry, and therefore their present priesthood is sufficient, and your ministry and Bible are unnecessary. He tells you that even a better than Socrates may live in heathen lands, walking uprightly in the light and following the best voices of nature: and shall a better than Socrates be doomed because he never heard of the Messiah to come? And must the pious Jew, who lives according to the precepts he has imbibed at his mother's breast, and rejoices in the light of *his* revelation, and who, perhaps in the heart of Asia, has never heard of a Messiah already come, must he perish? Is the Unitarian, in every conceivable circumstance, to go down to swell the lamentations of the lost? Sirs, take back your supposition of the "desert island;" it savors not the things that be of Christ. Your men might be all drowned as well as your ministers, and the women escaping from the wreck be compelled to institute *a female ministry.* It is nothing but a silly cavil, that would stand as well against any other truth of our most holy faith. It is, *mutatis mutandis*, the standing cavil of the infidel against all Christianity: that, like the Apostolic succession to your forlorn Christians, there are millions who cannot hear of Christ, and therefore Christianity is not essential. And you, my good friends, my former brethren of a better school, however you may be pressed for an answer to more solid reasonings, do, for our old acquaintance's sake, let the desert island alone, and leave the Congregationalists, by the right of discovery, to provide water for its baptism, wine for its communion, and men—or (if all the men be drowned) women—for its ministry.

No alternative was left me now but to face the question of the three-fold order of the Ministry, and of the claim to absolute Apostleship by the present Episcopal bishops. It was to me none other than the great question of the succession, not to a throne of time on earth, but to a jurisdiction reaching beyond earth and time, and to keys which open and shut the everlasting gates.

In pursuing this inquiry, a multitude of facts, of which the following may serve as an example, forced themselves on my attention.

First fact: The faith, separated for any length of time from the Episcopacy, disappears; as a spirit, parted from its body, returns from the world to the bosom of God. The Episcopacy, therefore, which never surrendered the faith, may not absurdly claim to indicate "the church of the living God, the pillar and ground of the truth."

Second fact: The histories of three hundred years have shown, that a church once separated from the Episcopacy undervalues the great principle of unity, or an incarnate Saviour dwelling by His presence and adorning by His spirit a visible, external, and imperishable Body; and would suffer that body to be dismembered and scattered to the winds: just as the human clay, when no longer animated by the principle of life and unity, falls into fragments and is dissipated into vapor. It is not therefore to be believed that, if the element of the Episcopacy present a check to this amazing evil, it should in the wisdom of God have been overlooked in the organization of His Church.

Third fact: The Lutherans in Europe, and the Methodists and Mormons in America, as well as other sects, have done homage to the Episcopacy, by engrafting on their own organizations the government by superintendents, bishops, or superiors; and even the Presbyterians and Congregationalists, finding their denominations inefficient, on the principle of ministerial parity, when they rouse them to exertion and action, assume invariably an artificial organization with agent, secretary, or other officer, to be found always at the headquarters of the society, emancipated from the pastoral tie, well acquainted with the field at different and distant points, the mouth-piece and source of life to the association, essential to its unity, harmony, concert, strength, confidence, action, and success. If there be force, therefore, in analogy, the central influences so effectively exerted by the Apostles in their lifetime were no more intended to die with the men, than the dissenting missionary and Sunday-school societies at Boston and elsewhere, intended that the excellent Evarts, and Wisner, and Cornelius, and Armstrong, and their brethren of the same order anywhere, as Heads of these societies, should fall into their graves without successors.

Fourth fact: The Episcopacy was no part of the outcry and battle-cry in the Reformation. Neither Luther nor Calvin, neither reformer nor reforming synod, had one word to say against it. The Church of England, with her noble and undaunted bishops, was the admiration and the envy of the continental reformers, who lamented the necessity they supposed themselves under, of advancing farther and faster than the continental bishops would approve; and who agreed, with Calvin, that "no anathema was too great" for those who should refuse allegiance to a pure Episcopacy.

Fifth fact: For years subsequently to the reformation from Popery, the men of learning among Presbyterians were ready to acknowledge, with Grotius, the early, universal, and Apostolic institution of the Episcopacy; and this concession, it is worthy of remark, ceases to be made only when antiquity ceases to be a study.

Sixth fact: The lovers of antiquity, the readers of the Witnesses and Fathers and Councils of the earliest ages, and of the contemporaries and companions of the Apostles, are, so far as we can learn, believers in the divine gift of the Episcopacy. Who has ever known a man made a Presbyterian by reading the early and unmutilated records of the Church? Who requires to be told that sectarians are compelled to thrust into a corner the writings of the Christian fathers?

Seventh fact: Of the many hundred ministers who have broken the sectarian spell and returned into the Church, all tell the same story: that to a careful re-examination of Scripture and "attendance to reading," they attribute their conviction of the Scriptural claim of the Episcopacy. Episcopacy, therefore, from the same high ground with Christianity, bears, and demands, and courts, and urges, and challenges investigation in what court you please, provided all her witnesses be present. This is strong presumptive proof that she rests on "the foundation of the Apostles and prophets."

Eighth fact: The Episcopacy is in harmony with the order of the natural world; just as every other great truth of the kingdom of God finds itself reflected in the mirror of nature, even as it is beautifully echoed in nature's voice. "No man hath seen God at any time;" but we may see the gems of His robe twinkling on the firmament by night, and the glance of His eye kindling on the sun by day, the dust of His feet sweeping by us in the clouds, and the obediences to His will in the motions of the universe. The mystery of the ever blessed Trinity we may not comprehend: but we may observe a mystery of trinities in the air above us, in the light around us, in the operations of nature, and in man who was made in the image of God. The bright and blessed resurrection of the just may elude our philosophic grasp: but the bird emerging from a putrid egg, and the butterfly uprising from an ugly worm, both soaring to the skies on gorgeous wing, tell by their flight and song that our flesh shall rest in hope, and come up bright as the day, buoyant as the air, and swift in its motions as the electric fire; or else that the meanest seed hath a dignity above man, having "power to lay down its life and power to take it again." The great principle of the atonement which I accept as a believer, I cannot repudiate as a philosopher: for the mighty fact of vicarious toil and suffering to save others from suffering and toil, is interwoven with all the orderings of Providence. And thus it is with every truth of Revelation: if we had the keys, we might unlock them all in the hieroglyphics of nature; even hell casts its cloud upon the earth, and heaven lets down on us its prophetic ray. So I could see the principle of the Episcopacy in the unities and harmonies around me. In all the analogies of nature I could see no such thing as individualism. The things of earth are all controlled by a controlling centre in herself; the earth and planets, with their satellites, move in the spheres assigned them round their lord, the sun; the sun and his peers roll steadily around a still loftier throne; thrones and dominions and principalities and powers revolve in their turn around some starry centre; and the bright hosts of an unmeasured universe roll round some vast metropolis, perhaps, the capital of God. For the sake of unity and order, a family is provided with its head; the families of a city require their magistrate; the cities of a state their governor; and the states of a continent their president. In the world of action every company or corporation has its presiding officer; every merchantman on the wave its master; every fleet upon the seas its admiral; every army its general. This very argument to subordination is magnificently set forth by St. Clement, the companion of St. Paul, in his admirable Epistle to the restless and schismatical members of the Church at Corinth. There is to every thing a central point, from which every thing depends. Even Presbytery cannot shake off the principle; it would not dream of appointing two secretaries of equal power to its great societies, two pastors equally supreme over a flock, two moderators at a time to one of its assemblies. Thus I perceived all nature, the moment its active elements are put in motion, does homage to the principle which the Episcopacy recognizes, of subordination and obedience.

Ninth fact: It struck me as strong presumptive evidence that the ministry of the Church was to be Episcopal, that under the theocracy, or what in modern language we should almost call republic, the Jewish priesthood was by divine direction made One in essence, but Three in the distribution of its powers, and to all ages a monumental witness to the Holy Trinity. When Korah and his company, ministers of the inferior order, rose up against the prelate of their people, the earth, at the commandment of the Lord, opened her mouth, and they went down alive into the pit. It is certainly in keeping with these facts, that Episcopacy exhibits the unity of the ministry in the trinity of its orders; and it is hardly to be wondered at, that earnest men were formerly reminded of the Angelical glory, as they saw the Deacons ministering around the Priest, and the Priests circling about their Bishop, and the Bishops, Priests, and Deacons, arrayed in white robes, waiting on their Lord, as satellites about the Sun of Righteousness. But there the fact remains, broad as the light of day, that *God did establish Prelacy*, and did vindicate it from the levellers in the company of Korah, by a portentous and terrific miracle.

Thus did a multitude of independent and collateral facts continually force themselves on my attention—although my space does not allow me to prolong their record—which show Episcopacy to be the only theory that can explain and harmonize them all. I now began to see in the venerable locks of Episcopacy something that looked like strength; and mistaking the Samson of Israel for the Goliath of Gath, I said in my haste, "Let me look again into my scrip for the smooth stones which I took from the brook at Princeton." So I took out another, which was

NUMBER TWO.* "It is now *conceded* by all the most *pious* and *learned* Episcopalians throughout the world, that Bishop and Presbyter are terms of the same meaning in the New Testament; that Bishops are called Presbyters, and Presbyters are denominated Bishops: the setting of Bishops over Presbyters is, therefore, with a thousand *ergos*, a usurpation."

Doubtless I shall have readers who will hardly understand that the form in which this proposition is current among

* Page 43.

Presbyterians, gave me the impression—the real, *bona-fide*, large-as-life impression—that this had been the grand point in dispute. Even Dr. Potts, treading in the steps of his predecessors, finds it impossible to get out of the fog. The learned Divines have occupied themselves for years in proving what a school-boy with his Greek Testament and Lexicon, can discover in fifteen minutes! But this seems to be their way. When we "contend earnestly for the Faith once delivered to the saints," they have the faculty of making the impression that it is only *the Episcopacy* for which we battle; and when we come to that Episcopacy, as the least among the imperishable truths to be preserved, they would make it appear that we are contending that the *word* Bishop in the New Testament signifies more than the *word* Presbyter, and as much as the *word* Apostle. However sincere they may be in wishing to get the world to think so, or even in thinking so themselves: "one thing is very clear," as the child of Erin said, "they are all very much in the dark." The miserable sophism—for it hardly rises to the rank of a sophomorism—that all *the more learned and pious* Episcopalians now concede that Bishop and Presbyter are convertible terms in the New Testament, is to most of them the end of controversy: the citadel has been surrendered, say they, the outposts will soon fall. To this, I imagine, it is mainly owing, that Episcopacy is not a subject of investigation in their course of studies; and to this it is owing, I suppose, that subsequent *investigations* of the question really at issue, have drawn away so many from the pulpits of Presbytery to the altars of the Church.

Yes, I imagined that Episcopalians, in harness and shield and buckler clad, had been breathlessly battling this point for three hundred years, until now, in the era of steam, and electricity, and Greek, they could "kick against the pricks" no longer. It gave me no very exalted opinion, I must confess, of the learning of the Episcopalian clergy; for if they were such animals as not even yet to know that in the Greek Scriptures the term *Presbuteros* was *toto cœlo* as good and "weighed as much" as the term *Episcopos*, then, spite of their groaning shelves of classic and patristic lore, I deemed there must, notwithstanding, be

> "*About* the shelves
> A beggarly account of empty"

noddles. I knew indeed that the noble universities of the Church of England had, now and then, produced their men of learning, who might have grasped the annihilating proposition: but it was easy to suppose that they continued in the Church, through an Erastian deference to the civil magistrate, or out of veneration for the ecclesiastical element in their national greatness, or, mayhap, out of regard to their seven principles, as John Randolph would have called them—viz., the five loaves and two fishes. I knew also that men of mind and learning had appeared in the Church of America, capable of rising to the dignity of this discovery: but then I could account for their presence in the Episcopal Church by the force of habit and association, or, perhaps, of some foible-fondness (for great minds are wont to have their foibles) for a flowing surplice or swelling organ. It was also rumored among us at Princeton, that a batch of young divines in that celebrated school, who, at a certain epoch, had found their way into the Episcopal Church, had not taken the step so much from conviction, or because they wished at all to lift the heel against Presbytery, as out of bowels of compassion for a sister Church, into whose system it was desirable to infuse a more evangelical leaven, and that even the professors, when consulted on the subject, had applauded the motive and acquiesced in the measure; so that when accident threw me, a few years afterwards, on a homeward voyage from Europe, into company with one of these now Right Reverend graduates of Princeton, it was with no little surprise I heard him declare, that if he had been able, by any possibility, or by any moderate violence to the light then thrown into his inner man, to remain in the Presbyterian communion: no conceivable motive short of the stern bidding of conscience could have drawn him from it.

Gentle reader, you may imagine my surprise on discovering that I had been led into a fog, and had been all this while pursuing a phantom. "Presbyter and Bishop designate the same office!" It was certainly humiliating to discover that Episcopalians had never denied it, and had no motive to dispute it, and that all this while I had been fighting "as one that beateth the air," and although looking on with both my eyes, I had never detected the sleight-of-hand (-writing) by which Presbyterian authors had contrived to wrest the Scriptural argument from its proper basis, and set it on a pedestal of straw.

Know all men, therefore, to whom these pages shall come, that Episcopalians have never disputed that Bishop and Presbyter were the words in use to designate the pastoral office. But as the pastoral office still remains among Presbyterians, although they may not call their pastors by the name of Presbyter or Bishop; and as among Episcopalians too, the pastoral office abides, although they also have dropped the name for it of Bishop, and have adopted that of Minister, or Presbyter, or Rector: in like manner, Episcopalians contend that the Apostolic office is perpetuated also, although, like the pastoral, it may now be known under the different appellation of Bishop. As the pastors did not require so many names to designate their office, they went afterward by the name of Presbyters: while the successors of the Apostles, "not thinking themselves meet to be called Apostles," adopted the humbler name of Bishops, which, by consent, was to be thenceforth entirely theirs. How beautifully Theodoret, the Syrian Bishop and disciple of St. Chrysostom, who lived in the fourth century, has transmitted to posterity this fact. "The same persons," he says, "were in ancient times called indifferently, Presbyters or Bishops, at which time those who are now called Bishops, *were called Apostles.* But shortly after, the name of Apostles was left to such as were Apostles in the strict sense, and then the name of Bishop was given to *those who before had been called Apostles.*" The same may be found in the pages of Clemens Alexandrinus, Hilary, Chrysostom, and even of Doctor Miller's "famous Jerome." And that this motive did operate, and was natural to the breasts of holy and humble-minded men, may be gathered from the language of Saint Paul himself, who, feeling himself "less than the least of all," exclaims, "*I* am not meet to be *called* an Apostle." Suppose Saint Paul had followed out this inward shrinking of his heart, and had asked his brethren everywhere to call him Presbyter or Bishop: would he have been, for his humility, any the less an Apostle? Was Saint John any the less an Apostle, because he never took the name, but always styled himself "the Elder?" And are the *successors* of these men any the less their successors, because, feeling unworthy to be clad in their mantle, and choosing to leave an illustrious title to those who could have no equal after them, they contented themselves with the more modest name of Bishop? —the Presbyters being able to spare it for them, as they did not require for themselves the two-fold name of Presbyter and Bishop. Or if the successors of the Apostles had taken, in humility, as even Paul and the lowly-minded John *did* take, the name of Presbyter or Elder, and had left the name of Bishop to the pastors: how could such an arrangement of *names* have ever affected the vested powers of the Apostolic office?

At this distance of time we may suppose, that if the successors of the Apostles had claimed and retained the name as they did the office, this war of words could never have arisen, nor these fogs and mists have dimmed the Presbyterian vision. There is a very similar case, familiar to the Hebrew student, involving, however, much greater injury to the cause of truth. The Jews to this day, and from time immemorial, have felt it almost wrong to pronounce or to translate "the Great Name," (JEHOVAH.) Their most ancient commentators, the Chaldee Paraphrasts, some of whom flourished before the Christian Era, always substitute the title "Lord," wherever Moses had employed the Name "Jehovah." From the same motive, the Septuagint, before the era of Christ, always translated the Great Name by the word Κύριος, or Lord. Now the writers of the New Testament, who quote usually from the Septuagint, in applying both these phrases to Christ, have distinctly proclaimed the LORD or the WORD of the New Testament to be the JEHOVAH of the Old. Yet this change of *names* has greatly weakened the evidences of the *fact* in the understanding of the English reader. Had the name JEHOVAH been made over unimpaired and unaltered from the Old Testament to the New, in the sundry passages which speak of Jehovah in the Old Testament, and in the New are applied to Christ under the equal but ambiguous name of LORD, it is difficult to see how His Divinity could have ever been questioned without setting aside entirely the authority of the Bible. And if the earlier successors of the Apostles had retained their name, and left the Pastors to be called Bishops or Presbyters, or Presbyter-Bishops, at the beginning, we should in all probability have heard the trump of Gabriel, before we should have been startled by the name of Presbyterian. The word Lord, used at the time to designate inferior dignities, falls infinitely short of the awful import of the name Jehovah; as the name of Bishop, used once to designate an inferior office, falls short of the clear import of the name Apostle: and thus on both hands the *prima facie* argument is weakened by which the Lord of the Apostles is shown to be the Jehovah of the Prophets, and the *Bishops* of the present Church, the *Apostles* of the primitive. Sadly has the Protestant world suffered through this over-reverence of the Jewish fathers, and this over-humility of the Christian. As a result of the latter, three-fourths of the Protestant world have been made Presbyterian: and as a consequence of the former, three-fourths of the Presbyterian world have been made Unitarian. But as the devout scholar will not suffer the crown of Jehovah to be wrested from His brow, by a scholastic play on Greek or English words: so a true scholar, familiar with antiquity, will not suffer the mitre to be trodden in the dust by a repetition of the unmanly quibble. *Under the surface* of the New Testament, the name of JEHOVAH is the name of Jesus; and both *under* and *on* its surface, I could see that the name of APOSTLES is the rightful name of those whom we call Bishops.

This I shall presently show. In the mean time, as to this idle talk that "all the more learned and pious Episcopalians now *concede* that Presbyter and Bishop are convertible terms in the New Testament," give me leave to say, that Episcopalians deny that their learning compels them to *concede* it; but they are willing with all modesty to affirm, that their humble measure of learning does not permit them to *debate* it. And I would suggest to Presbyterian debaters, if they regard their literary reputation, never again to descend to this hackneyed and childish bandying of *words*, which, to those who perceive that it is no part of the question, appears so exceedingly beneath the controversialist and the scholar, or is at best a literary sleight-of-hand, right cleverly metamorphosing the issue, or taking away one and substituting another, while skilfully diverting the eyes of the spectators. That our Saviour is called Lord, a name in itself ambiguous and applying to lords many, is no reason with me that He is not "THE LORD of lords;" or that Apostles in gentleness of mind have called themselves Presbyters, is no evidence to me that they held no higher rank; or that their successors chose the modest name of Bishops, is no proof to me that they were not successors of the Apostles. The noble spirit of that single act proves that they were most worthy to be the successors of the Apostles; for if "through ambition" they had usurped the *office*, they would through ambition have usurped the *name:* but if through humble-mindedness they felt unworthy of the *office*, they would have then felt—as they did feel, and as even St. Paul declared himself to be—unworthy of the *name*. Besides, the fact that the name of Bishop was early and universally surrendered to them, and from the earliest ages applied no more to any inferior dignity, is as strong a proof of their Apostleship, as it would have been of our Lord's Divinity, if the Church in all lands had agreed never again to call any inferior or created being by the name of LORD. But if this arrangement of the ancient Church is unpalatable to our Presbyterian neighbors, and they dislike the bargain: let them take back the name of Bishop, so that hereafter it shall mean nothing more than pastor, and let the Bishops take back their ancient name of Apostles, and let our Blessed Lord have back His ancient and awful name Jehovah; and Presbyterianism and Unitarianism, the parent and the child, will die and disappear together.

Thus fell to the ground this breastwork of sand. Thus vanished in a trice this man of straw. Episcopalians disclaim him. Presbyterians made him, and therefore we consent to his annihilation by Presbyterian valor.

And thus ended my first pitched battle with the giant. I fought him in a field he never trod: yet I was sure I saw him in his greaves of brass, sitting and eyeing me from above the ramparts. And although I noticed at the time that it was a little foggy, yet, as all my neighbors declared that he was there, and that that was his grand entrenchment, and that they had heard him muttering that Bishop was a greater *name* than Presbyter, I sent my Number One, the smooth stone from the brook at Princeton, upon its destined mission, and felt not a little disconcerted to see it pass smoothly through the shadow without striking. Whereupon the fog lifted, and the apparition vanished!

Do then, Gentlemen, forbear this exhibition of your Greek. If you are disposed to come to the question, I will now turn a leaf, and give you the opportunity to meet *the true issue*, as I was compelled to encounter it myself. The phantom-giant has vanished; but there is a real live Giant a little further on.

CHAPTER XXII.

THE TRUE ISSUE.

We are not to forget that the more respectable Presbyterians of a school now nearly extinct, maintained for a while that the Apostles imparted all the ministerial prerogative of their Order to the Presbyters or Parish ministers, who were to be, in all essential matters, their lineal and legitimate successors, in a descent that should never be interrupted or lost. Among those respectable persons was Dr. Lathrop, who, although a New England Congregationalist, has left the following testimony:—"A ministry in the Church was undeniably instituted by Christ; introduction to the ministry in the apostolic age being by prayer and imposition of hands by Elders. The usage was invariably, and without a single deviation, continued as long as the sacred history affords any light. No provision is made for cases of necessity, or for the renewal of the ministry if it should happen to cease; [we shrewdly suspect that the Dr. intended here a sly allusion to the 'desert island;'] we have an express promise from Christ, that He will support His Church and be with His ministers *always, even to the end of the world.* It is by no means necessary that we should prove an uninterrupted succession; we have a right to presume it until evidence appears to the contrary. If any say the succession has failed, the burden of proof must lie wholly on them. Let them, from incontrovertible history, show us the time, place, and manner, in which it terminated; who the laymen that ordained them; and where was the scene of the transaction. Until we have this information, we rely on the promise of Christ, in the sense in which we understand it." I have quoted this language of Dr. Lathrop, because it most accurately expresses the views I held as a Presbyterian myself, although they are now repudiated by Dr. Potts in behalf of the Presbyterian denomination generally.

As the opinion here advanced, that the Apostles imparted all their official rights to Presbyters or Elders, was founded principally on single passages, which for example say, "The Elders which are among you I exhort, who am also an Elder:" it is proper I should show how I was compelled, like Dr. Potts, although from different premises, to surrender the "tactual" succession, as he calls it, through a long line of Elders. And although I had rather do this in English than in Greek, yet as my endeavor, in the last chapter, to get a word in edgewise among learned men, has wrought me somewhat into a Greek mood, I shall venture to dabble a moment longer in Greek names and synonyms. For if the Elders be regarded as the true and legitimate successors of the Apostles, because the Apostles call themselves Elders: we shall find, by looking into the Greek, that the argument will carry us farther than is convenient, and therefore that the Presbyterians are quite prudent to recede from their old position. On looking into the Greek, I found that in several places* the Apostleship is called a *Deaconship;* and that in another† the Apostle exclaims over the sin of calling disciples by the name of men, "Who then is Paul, and who is Apollos, but *Deacons* by whom ye believed?" and that on two other occasions‡ he calls the Apostles *Deacons.* If then the fact that the Apostles call themselves Presbyters, proves that the

* Acts, i. 17, 25; xx. 24. † 1 Cor. iii. 5. ‡ 2 Cor. iii. 6; vi. 4.

Presbyters are their successors: the fact that they more frequently call themselves Deacons proves that the Deacons have equal claim to be their successors too, especially as their order was instituted before that of Presbyters, and made illustrious in the preaching of St. Philip and the martyrdom of St. Stephen. The argument therefore of the olden Presbyterians was good for nothing, because, as I have shown, it proves the Deacons to be, even more than the Presbyters, the successors of the Apostles. But though this mode of reasoning has proved too much already, yet it would prove even more; for our Blessed Lord is, in one place* called "Apostle," and in another† "Bishop," and in another‡ "Deacon," (see the Greek;) and it will not be alleged that this gives any ground for presuming an equality of jurisdiction or of order. Gentlemen, is it not time to cease this foolish babbling about "convertible terms?"

In fact, I perceived the utter irrelevancy and inadmissibility of this reasoning, long before I ceased to be a Presbyterian; and therefore did not retain it among the "smooth stones from the brook." For, in the green season of youth, I had analysis enough in my mental organization to perceive, that the lower was covered by the higher, and the less comprehended of the greater: that the Lord might significantly enough be called Apostle, Bishop, or Deacon, as he washed the feet of his disciples; that an Apostle might be styled Presbyter or Deacon; and in like manner a Presbyter be called a Deacon: the greater, in each instance, comprehending all the less. At the same time, I saw that there was no confusion of order, or mixture of prerogative; for in the New Testament, a Deacon is *never* styled a Presbyter; a Presbyter *never* called an Apostle; and an Apostle *never* designated by the Master's name: but Apostles, Presbyters, and Deacons, all serve in distinct and harmonious Orders around their Lord.

* Heb. iii. 1. † 1 Peter, ii. 25. ‡ Rom. xv. 8.

And on observing more attentively, I found the Apostles sometimes in the actual office of the Presbyter, consecrating the Eucharist; and sometimes (especially before the Deacons were ordained) in the capacity of the Deacon, administering baptism, (although at other times St. Peter only "commanded them to be baptized," and in the Church at Corinth, St. Paul scarcely consented to baptize at all:) but I could never find a mere Deacon usurping the consecration of the Holy Eucharist, nor a mere Presbyter presuming alone on the ordination to the holy ministry. It cannot surely be worth while to notice the resort had to the incident at Antioch,* where "certain prophets," acting by inspiration, laid their hands on Barnabas and Saul and sent them on a special mission; for we read afterward† that they returned "to Antioch, from whence they had been recommended to the grace of God for the work which they *fulfilled*;" and St. Paul says most distinctly that he was made an Apostle, "not of *men*, neither by *man*," and he had in fact been an Apostle *ten years* before the transactions at Antioch. The necessity of resort to such an incident, may convince the reader how entirely the theory lacks the countenance of Scripture.

When Presbyterians perceive therefore that, if the Elders be the successors of the Apostles, the Deacons must be their successors too: they take back this move upon the board, and, contrary to all the rules of ingenuous debate, make another —in the opposite direction. But let them take back the move! They tell us now that the Apostles had *no* successors; that the Apostolic office *died out* with the twelve original incumbents; in fact, that the whole doctrine of lineal and tactual succession, whether in the line of Presbyters or of Apostles, is useless and absurd: since "the power belongs in all its vigor to *the people*, and they can *originate* as valid a ministry as ever was made by Presbytery or Prelate." Though I myself

* Acts, xiii. 1-3. † Acts, xiv. 26.

repudiated, as a Presbyterian, the latter part of this proposition, yet I adhered to the former, viz., that the Apostolic office had died with the first Apostles, and that the only succession was of Presbyters to Presbyters. So here I put my hand into my bag again, and took out another smooth stone, which shall I call

NUMBER THREE. "The Apostles were twelve, and this number was never meant to be increased. They have therefore no successors. They saw the Lord, whom their pretended successors have not seen. They wrought signs and wonders, which their pretended successors cannot do. They were individually inspired, which their pretended successors are not. Therefore their pretended successors 'say they are Apostles and are not, but do lie,' and are 'not Apostles but Apostates, not Pastors but Impostors, not Prelates but Pilates.'"

According to the terms of this proposition, an Apostle is one who (1) has seen the Lord, (2) can speak with tongues, (3) can work miracles, and (4) has the gift of inspiration. But on turning to the New Testament, I soon began to notice (1) that devout women, and about five hundred brethren at once, had seen the Lord after he was risen; and although St. Paul appeals to them as living witnesses, of the resurrection, surely they were not all Apostles! I read in another place (2) that the disciples of St. John the Baptist, when St. Paul had baptized them with a Christian baptism, and had laid his confirming hands on them, as also Cornelius and his friends, and also a confused multitude in the Church of Corinth, spake constantly with tongues: but it will hardly be supposed that these were all Apostles! I saw again (3) that the disciples at Ephesus, and the four daughters of Philip, and certain who came from Jerusalem to Antioch, especially one Agabus, were all inspired; some of them foretelling events which even to Apostles had been unknown, and which had much to do in shaping their course, and giving direction to the counsels and destinies of the whole Church: yet who will say that these were all Apostles? And yet again I saw (4) that the deacons, Stephen and Philip, and their brethren, filled Jerusalem and Samaria with the fame of their stupendous miracles; and that the scattered Presbyters spoken of by St. James, could raise the sick by anointing them with oil: yet surely these were not all Apostles! One thing is therefore certain, either that the elders, and deacons, and lay men and women were Apostles, and that thus there was a multitudinous succession: or else that having seen the Lord, speaking with tongues, working miracles, and being inspired, were never the marks by which to distinguish an Apostle from a deacon, from a presbyter, or even from a lay man or woman. All the facts on the face of Scripture tend to the same point. When St. Paul writes to a Church—for example to the Church of Corinth—it is not to speak with tongues that he intrudes: for he says to them, "Though I speak with the tongues of men and of angels, and have not charity, I am as sounding brass or a tinkling cymbal." It is not to dazzle them with the splendor of miracles, that he interferes: for he declares, "Though I could remove mountains and have not charity, I am nothing." It is not to tell them that he exclusively had seen the Lord: for he appeals to five hundred witnesses of the great event. It is not to utter prophecy or convince by inspiration: for in all these gifts the Church at Corinth was already itself illustrious. Nor was it to impart the holy supper; nor was it to baptize; nor was it to preach the gospel merely: for Corinth had her Eucharist and established ministry already. But it was to assert a jurisdiction, an "authority," "a power which the Lord had given him;" to tell them that sinned, and all other, that "if he came he would not spare;" to deliver one particularly, who had sinned, "unto Satan for the destruction of the flesh, that the spirit might be saved;" to declare his "forgiveness" and restoration of the penitent to a place and hope among the faithful; to enjoin the weekly offertory for the saints, as he had "given order in the Churches of Galatia;" and to assert the right as to "the rest" of their affairs, to "set them in order when he should come." Miracles, tongues, inspiration, having seen the Lord—what are they all, but incidental circumstances, which might or might not exist in the person of the Apostles, as they might or might not exist in the persons of the presbyters and deacons?

But it is not enough that this proposition should be loose and unscriptural in its terms; it must be urged by comments that make it painfully profane. So respectable a Presbyterian divine as engaged Doctor Wainwright in the controversy that did the Church such good service a few years since, would like to see the Bishop who "could tell of a disease cured, sight restored, a fractured limb healed, or a discourse in an unknown tongue delivered, by any of those upon whom he has laid his hands. The Apostles wrought miracles," exclaims this learned author! "they could take up serpents and drink any deadly thing without harm; but what Prelate would be hardy enough to try the experiment upon himself, of taking a dose of poison? Prussic acid would be, I doubt not, as fatal to Doctor Doane as to Doctor Wainwright."

I am not able now to lay my hand on a copy of Tom Paine, or of Voltaire, or of Rousseau; for this sort of language I think I have met with almost verbatim in one or other of those writers. Let me remind the reader of the passage to which this controversialist so flippantly alludes.* "These

* We have already had occasion to remark the want of reverence which is at once one of the most potent causes, and one of the most terrible results, of the experiment of separation from the ancient Church. "We did not owe God any money; we did not rob the treasury of heaven; Christ therefore did not pay any debt of ours," exclaims the learned and evangelical Doctor Edwards. "God knows," "the Lord knows," "on God's earth," "under God's heavens," and phrases with the words "cursed," the "devil," "hell," &c., flippantly brought in by

signs shall follow *them that believe:* In my name shall they cast out devils; they shall speak with new tongues;

the many platform divines, have called forth the notice and reprobation even of a wounded secular press. "How the minister did 'cuss' to-day!" is a just criticism I have heard more than once upon the preacher; nay, I have heard an educated Presbyterian preacher reprove the slothful as "too cursed lazy," and another promise the spiritual that their very eyes "should be so filled with the Holy Ghost as to look all hell out of countenance." How far the Sectarian pulpit, by its familiar use of such language, is responsible for the frightful profanity and blasphemy that darken our land, is a question I desire not to answer, but take the liberty of asking. Certainly, it contrasts much with the sparing use of such terms in the preachings of Apostles and of the Blessed Master! At a late May Missionary Anniversary in New York, a learned and Rev. Professor from Cincinnati, presented the following:

"*Resolved*, That the valley of the Mississippi is a part of the territory between 'the great river and the ends of the earth,' which belongs to Jesus Christ by especial grant from Almighty God, and that Jesus Christ must have it!" Such language would have turned the faces of an Episcopalian audience pale! A recent Plymouth dinner in New York, it appears, could suggest the "sentiment," "Plymouth Rock, the Rock of Ages!" The Editor of the New York Evangelist, a scholar and an evangelical divine, on the principle of Sectarianism maintaining one truth (in this instance, the atonement) "at the expense of other truths," indulges in the following wild strain against the Unitarians: "What is the example which the sufferings and death of Christ afford? An example, if unexplained by any other circumstances, 'the most frightful and disgusting the world ever saw.' If this were Christ's object, 'he has most miserably failed.' He never manifested any extraordinary exemplary deportment. His *anguish* and *cries*, his *bloody sweat* in the garden, and his pitiful cry on the cross, seem to be entirely unmanly. The desertion of his friends and the cruelty of his enemies, 'he might have borne with far greater composure.' Many of his 'followers in all ages have endured much sorer evils than he experienced, with 'far more apparent magnanimity and self-possession.' So far from setting an example of patience and self-possession in the hour of suffering and trial, 'he might be commended to the example of some of his own followers.'" O my Blessed Saviour! How long, how long? Brethren of the Church, why will you seek alliances with the downward system, and put your hand within the hand of sects upon the precipice?

"Prussic acid" and "fractured limbs" and "discourses in an unknown tongue" are but the genteeler utterance of the same irreverent spirit. But to show that the most gifted and brilliant minds are fated to be borne helplessly along this tide which sweeps all the old sacred landmarks before it, read the lecture of Dr. Cox, a divine known as widely to fame in the dissenting world, as any in America. I can give but a few extracts, together with the demonstrations of applause they elicited from his audience. (Scene, a meeting-house in Broadway. Time, 1844.) After alluding to the Puritan Dinner, Mr. Choate's oration, and the controversy then pending between Drs. Wainwright and Potts, this divine, as reported by the press, proceeds: "In his opinion, the words 'a Church without a Bishop, a State without a King,' deserved the same immortality with the Star-spangled banner, or

they shall take up serpents; and if they drink any deadly thing, it shall not hurt them; they shall lay hands on the

even 'Yankee Doodle.' [A round of applause.] There was no more reason why men should be ridden by churchmen 'booted and spurred by the grace of God,' than that they should admit that they were born 'with saddles on their backs,' for monarchy or aristocracy to ride. But he meant to keep his temper while he treated 'this eminently satanic' dogma as it deserved . . . for all the afflicted communities which believe in it, must 'fall with the devil.' . . . The word Bishop only meant an overseer; as simple, uncrosiered, unmitred, unfrocked, as Paul was 'when he left his cloak at Troas!' [A roar of laughter from every part of the house.] . . . The unchurching dogma placed such quarantine on all Christians, except the Prelatists, as to render it actually only 'a case of smuggling' if they ever got into heaven at all. [The audience roared again with merriment.] The Doctor then read from a commentator on the Romish notion of the Eucharist, in which the '*quid et ubi*' of the Body of Christ was discussed. The 'quiddity' of it [great laughter] troubled them much. As to 'where' it was, there was a difference of opinion; but most agreed it was in 'the imagination.' . . . Monsieur Talleyrand, after a life of any thing but clerical purity, 'was greased in his extremities' and became 'reconciled to God.' [Loud laughter.] That was unction without function, with a witness. [Roars of laughter.] He did not wish to make his audience laugh, and vindicated his irony by referring to passages of Scripture where that mode of treating sacred things was adopted. 'Where two or three are gathered together in my name, there am I in the midst of them, and when Christ is present, he should like to know how many deacons, priests, bishops, popes, and cardinals it takes to make a quorum. How many do they count Christ? [Laughter.] Rowland Hill, though he died only a deacon, to which '*primus gradus*' he was kept by that Church because he was too evangelical, had more religion than all the rest of the English clergy put together. Three-fourths of them all were Puseyites, and he did not know how many more would be so by the arrival of the next steamer. [Laughter.] The tendencies of their clergy were towards Oxford; and the tendencies of Oxford were towards Rome; and the tendencies of Rome were towards —— but look in the book of Revelation. [Laughter.] . . . He told a humorous anecdote about 'kneeling at the Eucharist,' which stirred greatly the mirth of his audience. This genuflection in the sacrament, was an idolatrous observance, originally paid to the bread, which was held to be the very body of Christ. And hence arose the term now in common use, of 'hocus-pocus,' a corruption of '*hoc est corpus*,' 'this is my Body'; and this (said the Doctor) is the origin of 'all this curvature on marrow bones.' [This, adds the Reporter, was the most successful hit yet made by the reverend lecturer. The audience were literally 'convulsed with mirth.' Perhaps, however, 'the droll allusion to Paul's missing garment,' was somewhat more cordially applauded.]"

But I cannot proceed with this any further. My soul revolts, my heart is sad, and every bone in my body cries out with fear. "Yankee Doodle," "unfrocking an apostle," "greased in his extremities," "booted and spurred by the grace of God," and such like things, might all have been endured: but the blasphemy about "the quiddity of the Body of Christ," the kneeling at the awful Eucharist, practised universally one thousand years before transubstantiation was invented,

sick, and they shall recover."* "These signs shall follow *them that believe.*" I have known two highly intelligent Presbyterian laymen, who, by "private interpretation" of this and other passages, became almost atheistical, and revelled for years in the reading of Voltaire and Paine: but who are now walking hand in hand humbly and happily "in the fellowship of the *Apostles.*" The wild blasphemer on the streets may now catch from solemn divines the exulting demand, not that these signs should follow in the steps of Bishops, but that they should "follow *them that believe.*" Not the right of the Apostolical succession, gentlemen, but the "*articulus ecclesiæ stantis vel cadentis,*" the great doctrine of Justification by Faith, you have now cast before the feet of swine: for "these signs shall follow *them that believe.*" Am I dreaming? Or has a Presbyterian and dignified divine, schooled neither at Geneva nor at Berlin, neither at Belfast, nor at Harvard, but at Princeton, challenged a Bishop to drink *prussic acid*, that the world might at once believe or scorn? Look well what company you are now in! "What works we have heard done in Capernaum, do here in thine own country." "If thou be the Son of God, cast thyself down from hence." "If he be the King of Israel, let him now come down from the cross, and we will believe him."

Had it been an infidel, baffled in his reasonings and taking counsel of his passions, I could in silence have suffered him to rail and wag the head. But as it is one of "the scribes and elders" that has cast the same in our teeth, our common

yet here most ignorantly charged to that invention, and ridiculed as "curvature on marrow bones," and the terrific blasphemy of "hocus-pocus" alleged to be derived from the awful words—not of Rome, remember, but of Jesus—"*hoc est corpus,*" this is my Body; and the "roars of convulsive laughter" responded by the multitude: all these things cause me to yearn, with every affection of my soul, to shield my blessed Saviour from the hootings of a populace, for whom His own example must teach those who "reverence the Son" to pray, "Father, forgive them; they know not what they do!"

* Mark, xvi. 17, 18.

Christianity requires me to speak in her defence. A pure and virtuous generation then, desire no miracle to draw them into close alliances with truth and virtue. Miracles have never been demanded but by "an adulterous and sinful generation." They have never, in the wisdom of God, been deemed necessary, except for gross and unenlightened minds, and in periods of dark and deep corruption: and when they have answered this temporary purpose, they. pass away. When Moses claimed to be a Lawgiver, and Elijah a Reformer, a degraded people asked and were allowed a sign. When One came claiming to be "equal with God," a people incapable of appreciating truth and goodness, demanded that he should work the works of God. When it was alleged that the Holy Ghost descended invisibly in Baptism, it was proper that outward evidences should be at first allowed, in the descending "dove," the nightly "wind," the cloven "flame," and the gift of "tongues." When it was alleged that a new measure of grace was vouchsafed in Confirmation, it was well that palpable and audible proof should be allowed, as in the converts of Samaria, and the disciples at Ephesus, when St. Peter and St. John had laid hands on the former, and St. Paul on the latter. When it was alleged that grace upon grace was imparted by the unseen Comforter to the believer, as he rose to the higher functions of the ministerial office, it was expedient that He should indicate His gracious Presence, as He did, in the humblest deacons at Jerusalem, by tongues and inspiration, and the gifts of healing. All this was done, that the Church in all ages might believe, that the Holy Ghost is ever flowing forth at her prayer, in these appointed channels; and that the cheering promise "as thy days so shall thy strength be," might accompany her children as they passed on to the higher callings of the Christian life. The miracles, once wrought, are her perpetual credentials, the seal and stamp of Omnipotence impressed, once for all, upon the vocations and offices she bears. She no more asks to see them again, than an ambassador from human courts would ask to see the act renewed by which his sovereign's seal was stamped on his commission. There it is. It cannot be counterfeited. It is not the office: but it beareth witness of the office, that its acts are valid and authoritative. It is enough. The wise shall understand. The elect shall believe. "A sinful generation seeketh after a sign, but there shall no sign be given it."

Albeit, the Church is not without her "signs following." Korah and his company went down alive into the pit *for rising up against the Prelacy.* The leprosy of Socinianism pursues the generations of Presbytery under all suns and climes; and, sirs, you cannot shake the poison from your skirts! These are the only "signs" that shall be given you. We do not ask Bishop Doane to take the "dose of poison" or to drink "prussic acid:" Jannes and Jambres might ask the same. But the long line of Bishops "have kept the faith," which they who have quitted "the fellowship of the apostles" have been unable to do. "Lo, this is the finger of God." The deadly poison has been proffered to the lips of the Church and of her Bishops: but they who have had by inheritance the discerning of the spirits, have perceived that death was in the cup. Once ye imagined that ye had consigned the evil spirit of Socinianism, with the body of Servetus, to the fires: but as ye stood around the stake, the evil spirit leaped from the flame, and overcame you, and prevailed against you! "Jesus I know, and His Apostles I know; but who are ye?" From the pinnacles of your temples in Geneva and Belfast, and Boston and Berlin, we have in grief unutterable seen you cast headlong the Lamb "that did not resist you:" but the Church, as a good angel, hath run and "borne Him up in her hands!" As the keeper of the strong Tower built in the midst of the Vineyard, she has preserved the Crown of her Lord untouched by the thieves of Berlin and Geneva; and the crown-jewels of His kingdom safe from the burglars of Belfast and Boston. Ask not then, to see a father of the Church take "prussic acid;" as "that fox" desired to see some miracle done by the Master: but amidst the endless distractions of Dissent, look about you for the more "infallible sign" which the Great Master Himself hath given us, even the succession and unity, "*that the world might believe.*"

As logically might you reason that a Deacon is not a Deacon, because he does not work the works of St. Stephen; or that an Elder is not an Elder, because he does not anoint and raise the sick as did the Elders of St. James; or that Believers are not Believers, because they do not show the signs promised to "follow them that believe:" as that Apostles are not Apostles, because they do not the works of St. Peter or St. Paul. While your doctrine of individualism requires these signs to follow you, as individual believers: *our* doctrine of the One Body makes these demonstrations as much ours as they were those of the believers in the Apostles' times. We no more ask to see these miracles attend each individual, succeeding to his lawful predecessor in the Apostolic chain, than we should ask to see the Holy Dove descend in open day on each copy of the Scriptures, as it emanated from the press in the line of its predecessors back to the original manuscripts of Moses and Matthew. Do then desist from this unmanly and atheistic quibbling!

We beg the reader to pardon this digression. Purged of its profanity and stripped of its irrelevant appendages, the proposition will stand simply thus: "The Apostles were twelve. Their number was never meant to be increased. They have therefore no successors."

The Rev. W. D. Snodgrass, Doctor of Divinity, and an Old School Presbyterian, in his "Discourses on the Apostolic Succession," as late as 1844, thus states the proposition in capitals:—"THEIR NUMBER WAS DEFINITE AND SPECIFIED—there were only TWELVE—and this number was not to be increased—Jesus said, Have not I chosen you *twelve?* And *the twelve* was the name by which they were constantly known. They were to have *twelve thrones*—are compared with the *twelve tribes* and with the *twelve foundations* of the city. Here we are transported, not only to the end of time, but to the visions of eternity. Earth has passed away, and there is no more sea—and still the number is only TWELVE!" Really, Doctor, this is *almost* as logical as, "In the beginning God created the heavens and the earth"—but not one word, my Brethren, of his creating Bishops!

The Apostles without successors? Where is the Master's promise, "Lo, I am with you alway, even unto the end of the world?" This was a promise made to *Apostles*, and to Apostles *only*. Examine it minutely, if you will: "UNTO THE END OF THE WORLD." This same evangelist had said in sundry places, "The harvest is *the end of the world;*" "so shall it be in *the end of the world;*" "what shall be the sign of thy coming, and of *the end of the world.*" This phrase in all instances designates distinctly the Day of Judgment, or the end of the Dispensation of Grace. Here then is Jesus on the mount in Galilee. It is the parting scene. The cloud of shining ones is on the air, approaching to receive Him. No more, till He shall come to judgment, shall we behold His face or hear His voice on earth. Master, what words of comfort wilt Thou leave? To whom shall we look up when Thou art gone? See Him "lift up His hands" that virtue may go forth from Him to the Eleven. See now His lips opening to speak. Hear now His last words in this dark world to His Apostles: "*Lo, I am with you alway, even unto the end of the world.*" But scrutinize the parting promise, if you will, with a freezing and jealous criticism: "*Alway*"—*πάσας τὰς ἡμέρας*,—*all the days* of the world unto its very end. *Not even for a day*, so long as the world shall stand, shall your venerable line be interrupted. And now, if you think that there has been at any time an interruption, we beg you to tell us when and where. Who were the last in the old line of the Apostles, and who were the first in the line now claiming to succeed them? Show us, if you can, that one single link has failed in this long chain through eighteen centuries. *You cannot do it!*

The Apostles without successors? No, Sirs! We can produce the long and truthful catalogue of their successors, reaching back at Alexandria to St. Mark, at Antioch to St. John or St. Peter, at Jerusalem to St. James, at Rome to St. Paul and St. Peter, in Syria to St. Thomas, at Canterbury, in "a three-fold cord not quickly broken," to St. Paul and St. John and St. Peter. The existence of these catalogues, in nations which had had no mutual intercourse for centuries, is as reliable evidence as are the genealogies kept by the Levitical priesthood of the ancestry of the Messiah himself, as traced through Joseph and Mary. One seems absurd to the infidel: the other may seem absurd to the Presbyterian. It was not to meet the cavils of Dissent that these catalogues were kept. They were but the natural records of the Society. A thousand years before Calvin and Luther were born, holy men, deemed worthy of the crown of martyrdom, recorded, on the open page of history, these catalogues of a then bright and unbroken and uncontested succession. Even the Syrian Church, so early and Jewish in its origin as to have incorporated and to this day retained among her rites the circumcision, the slain lamb, and the first-fruits, of the Jewish faith: will show you, in the inaccessible fastnesses where she dwelt alone and has not been numbered with the people, nor even been known to her sister churches for fifteen hundred years, a long line of Bishops back to St. Thomas. Rather than the line should be broken, men were found willing to bridge the threatened chasm by throwing their bodies into fire or flood, to perfect the chain and connect the future with the past. And now, as you believe the flowers of the field to be, each in its line, the legitimate successors of the originals as they bloomed first from the Creator's hand, although you are quite unable to trace the succession back to the miraculous beginning; or as you are sure that the line of believers has never failed in happy succession back to the disciples who first sat at the Master's feet, although you are entirely unable to trace the holy line through the centuries gone by; or as you know the Bible to be a true copy of a copy of another copy still, back to the inspired pens of Moses and Matthew, although you are equally unable to trace the lineal succession: so are we certain that the present Bishops or Apostles are the rightful successors of Apostles who succeeded others, in unbroken chains, back to the hands of the adorable Master. And a miracle is no more necessary to prove Bishop Doane an Apostle, than to drink prussic acid with impunity would be to prove Dr. Potts a *believer;* or a voice from heaven saying, "Let the earth bring it forth," to prove the lily of the field to be the work of God; or the Dove descending from the sky to prove our Scriptures to be a true successor, in unbroken line, to the Greek and Hebrew scriptures indited by the Holy Spirit. To us the Master's promise is the end of doubt. To you, and to the world, we produce the uninterrupted testimony of the Church, and in lands ever so remote, the unfailing chain of names from the beginning to this present; besides the signs following of Unity and an unalterable Faith.

The Apostles without successors? No, Sirs! As we find the early Church full of Deacons, whom we believe to have succeeded to the office of the inspired and wonder-working Deacons at Jerusalem, although the Master made them no promise to perpetuate their order, inasmuch as He ascended into heaven previously to their existence; or as we find the early Church full of Presbyters or Elders, and believe them to have inherited the office of the wonder-working Elders in the days of St. James, although as Elders they could have had no promise of their perpetuity from Christ, who returned to the Father before their ordination: so when we find the early Church illustrious in lofty names claiming and tracing their succession in unbroken line to the Apostles, and even declaring schismatics to be separated from Christ because separated from "the fellowship of the Apostles, shall we doubt that these holy men were the legitimate inheritors of Apostolical prerogatives? The whole world, Catholic and heretic, acceded to the claim; no heretic we read of, however chafed and galled by his Bishop's excommunication, was heretical on this one point. It is not Doane and McIlvaine and Meade and Ives putting forth this claim in the nineteenth century; nor Cranmer nor Latimer nor Ridley nor Jewel in the sixteenth: but Augustine and Cyril in the fifth, Chrysostom and Basil and Ambrose and Gregory in the fourth, Firmillian and Cyprian in the third, Irenæus in the second, and Clement and Ignatius and Polycarp in the first, all asserting, in easy and natural language, as if it was understood by all and disputed by none, that they succeeded to the jurisdiction of the Apostles. It is the six early and general Councils of the Church, at Nice, at Constantinople, at Ephesus, at Chalcedon, and twice again at Constantinople, numbering in all 1628 Bishops, besides local and provincial Councils almost innumerable, not legislating the Apostolical succession into existence, but recognizing it as a fact already universally taken for granted. And I cannot refrain from again adducing the concession of the very learned Grotius, who says: "All the fathers without exception testify to this. . . . The catalogues of the Bishops in Irenæus, Socrates, Theodoret, and others, all of which begin in the apostolic age, bear witness to the same. To refuse credit in an historical matter to so great authors, and so unanimous among themselves, is not the part of any but an irreverent and obstinate disposition. What the whole Church maintains, *and was not instituted by councils*, but was always held, is not with any good reason believed to be handed down by any but apostolical authority." It may be very well, gentlemen, for you who have lost the Apostolical Succession, whether accidentally or by cutting yourselves away from it, now to denounce it (so did not your fathers) as a cumbersome and inconvenient appendage to the body ecclesiastical: but still we have noticed that the Lutherans and Methodists have begun to re-admire the cumbersome excrescence, and have fastened on to their bodies the artificial fixture of this same appendage.

The Apostles without successors? Let us open the New Testament and see. The writings of this book were not ascertained or collected for three hundred years after the Church had been in vigorous operation on three continents. The earliest Epistles were written thirty years after the Church was organized; and those to the seven Churches in Asia upwards of fifty years after the ascension of Christ. I shall not therefore find in it directions for the organization of the Church; but I may find in it allusions to a state of things, in that respect, already settled. In like manner I shall find no commandment to keep the first day of the week, to baptize infants, to worship Jesus as the only God, to hold the Trinity as the foundation of the faith: but if the first day of the week was known and venerated, I shall find allusions to the day, not to be mistaken; if Jesus was worshipped as God, I shall find language that cannot be explained on any other theory; if the Trinity was held as the foundation, I shall meet with expressions that harmonize with the sublime and blessed doctrine. In fact, these incidental references to well-known facts are stronger demonstrations than direct and studied and dogmatic definitions, which are never resorted to so long as the facts are admitted; and which, in the Church, were never employed on any subject until the facts began to be disputed. Hence, in the councils of the Church, and all her legislation, and in the Scriptures, there is no strong, dogmatic order to enforce Episcopacy, because (as Grotius observes) the great fact of Apostolic Succession was already universal, like the observance of Sunday and the baptism of households. You might as well reason that the Scriptures leave the worship of Christ, and the observance of Sunday, and the communion of females, and the baptism of infants, open questions: as say (and we have heard Presbyterians say) that they leave the government of the Church "an open question." On the contrary, on all these subjects the Apostles must have established a precedent one way or the other *before* they wrote the Scriptures, and we have no right, without a new revelation or a prohibition in the New Testament which was *afterwards* written, to depart from their orders. It would be a very suspicious circumstance indeed, if St. John, writing in the year 96 to the seven Churches of Asia, should exhort them to set over them an *apostle* or *angel*, for this would imply that *hitherto* they had been *Presbyterian:* but if he had long previously placed over each of them an angel or apostle, (as Tertullian tells us the beloved and venerable Polycarp was placed by him over the Church of Smyrna,) then each Epistle to the Angel of each Church is in perfect keeping with the fact. Let us now see, if this evidence of allusion to existing facts do not demonstrate the Episcopacy, in the very best way possible; as it does the observance of Sunday, the baptism of infants, or the universal worship of Christ. I shall now repeat the issue as it was now presented to my mind:—If it was intended that the twelve original Apostles should have successors in their office, it is quite probable that the appointments would in some instances have been made before the New Testament was written, and I may therefore reasonably expect to find in it occasional allusions to the Apostolic office in the persons of others, and incidental language or phraseology difficult of explanation on any other theory. I may even find Epistles written to men as they were about succeeding to Apostolic powers. Now is this the fact? Episcopalians say it is. Let us see.

I had been, I must confess, not unfrequently struck, in reading the New Testament, with a glimpse of official powers assumed by the Apostles, entirely aside from their miracles and tongues and witnessing the resurrection. I determined, therefore, to read attentively large portions at a time, to satisfy myself whether these allusions to a state of things already existing in the Church, justified the claims of Presbytery, of Popery, or of Prelacy. And before I laid the Scriptures down, I became overwhelmingly satisfied that both Popery and Presbytery entirely fail to account for and harmonize the ecclesiastical phenomena on the face of Scripture. Up to this time—nor do I believe my case to have been singular in this respect—I had never in my whole life condescended to read (except as quoted into hostile writings) a single word in defence of the Episcopacy.

"The twelve," "the twelve apostles," "the twelve apostles of the Lamb,"—"figures cannot lie,"—the number was manifestly "twelve,"—not one more—not one less: it was the "*Presbyterianismi stantis vel cadentis articulus.*" But if I chance, said I, to find that the Bible recognizes even one over and above this number, then must the superstructure fall with the foundation.

I suppose the household phrase "the twelve," had something to do in suggesting this mode of reasoning. But how unreasonable would it be, because we read of "the twelve patriarchs,"* to suppose there were no others invested with

* Acts, vii. 8.

this venerable name? Or, because we read of "the seven,"* nearly thirty years after the ordination of the Deacons at Jerusalem, that "the seven" were to be the only Deacons in the universal Church? Therefore, as we read of "the patriarch Abraham," and of "Deacons" innumerable: and the appellations "patriarch" and "Deacon" were restricted neither to "the twelve" nor to "the seven:" so we may find, upon inquiry, that "the twelve" is but a designation which attached to the first Apostles, as "the seven" was a designation of the first Deacons. Therefore "to the law and to the testimony."

"Now the names of the twelve Apostles are these:

1. The first, Simon who is called Peter,
2. And Andrew his brother;
3. James the son of Zebedee,
4. And John his brother;
5. Philip,
6. And Bartholomew;
7. Thomas,
8. And Matthew the publican;
9. James the son of Alphæus,
10. And Lebbæus, whose surname was Thaddæus;
11. Simon the Canaanite, called also Zelotes,
12. And Judas Iscariot."

One of these soon perished; but the office he had borne was not to perish with him. Immediately upon his death, the Eleven, after solemn invocation of the Divine direction, chose *Matthias* to take the place of Judas. Dr. Miller himself says of this transaction, "When Judas fell by transgression, measures were immediately taken to appoint another, thus showing that *a succession in the ministry* was to be kept up." Notice the Doctor's language, "a succession in the *ministry*." Mark the language of Scripture, "that he may take part of this ministry and *apostleship*;" and again,

* Acts, xxi. 8.

"he was numbered with the eleven *apostles*."* Here then, on the very first page of ecclesiastical history, it is evident that one of the twelve *had a successor*, and in circumstances that seem intended to establish the fact of an imperishable succession in the line of the Apostles. There are considerations that give force to this opinion. Forty days had elapsed since the vacancy had occurred. During those forty days our Lord was "going in and out among them, speaking of the things pertaining to the kingdom of God;" and if we examine the nature of these interviews, we find them mainly occupied with the powers of the ministry; the sacraments; and the Church, or "the kingdom of God." Yet all this while that "He went in and out among them," He did not appoint a successor to Judas; but as soon as He ascended, his Apostles entered into the election. No reasonable man can imagine that they proceeded *proprio motu* to this important act. No man can suppose that the Lord had taught them that their number was never to be increased, or that, when the reapers should fall one by one in the field, their girdle and sickle should descend in no instance to another. It is evident that, if the Eleven were Presbyterians when the Master left them, it would no more have entered their mind to ordain a successor to an Apostle, to clothe him with equal prerogative and dignity, than to elect and ordain a successor to the office of the Master. And there is no escaping the conclusion, except on the rationalistic ground taken by Dr. Snodgrass, that the whole thing was wrong, and was owing to the "characteristic precipitation of Peter." We stop then to renew our list.

1. Simon Peter.
2. Andrew.
3. James, the son of Zebedee.
4. John,

* Acts, i. 25, 26.

5. Philip.
6. Bartholomew.
7. Thomas.
8. Matthew.
9. James, the son of Alphæus.
10. Lebbæus or Thaddæus.
11. Simon Zelotes.
12. Judas Iscariot.
13. Matthias.

The charm is broken. Thirteen is said to be a fatal number. Certainly it is fatal to Presbyterianism.

But we turn a few leaves further in the record, and find a new and shining light added to the constellation of "the twelve," which, it was alleged, was no more to be increased than the signs of the zodiac. A vulture with uplifted talon pouncing on the fold, is transformed into a lamb; a scoffer into a believer; a reviler into a preacher; a tentmaker into an Apostle: and Saul, once "breathing out threatenings and slaughter against the disciples of the Lord," now writes his name, "Paul *an Apostle* of Jesus Christ." Unless then St. Paul, as the eleven would seem to have done before, misapprehended the fact that the number of the Twelve was not to be increased, we must here increase our register to fourteen. Fourteen Apostles—genuine, *bona fide*, large-as-life Apostles—one of them succeeding to an Apostle deceased, and another added as the growing exigencies of the Church required it. If it be alleged that Paul was miraculously called to be an Apostle, we answer that Matthias was chosen by the agency of the Apostles, without the least intimation of a miracle. And if it be alleged that, at the election of Matthias, St. Peter said, "Of these men which have companied with us all the time that the Lord Jesus went in and out among us, beginning from the baptism of John, unto that same day that He was taken up from us, must one be ordained to be a witness with us of His resurrection:" it is evident that St. Paul did not company with them one hour of that time. Nevertheless, as broad and complete a mantle falls upon Matthias and Paul, as upon the original "Twelve."

And there is yet another. Barnabas is twice called an Apostle, and is continually spoken of in terms that preclude the idea of his being any thing less. His name is constantly associated with that of St. Paul; and generally takes the precedence, where the two are named together. If the brethren at Antioch send relief to the Church in Judea, they do it "by the hands of *Barnabas* and Saul."* "*Barnabas* and Saul returned from Jerusalem, when they had fulfilled their ministry."† "The Holy Ghost said, Separate me *Barnabas* and Saul."‡ He is sent forth with Paul on apostolical journeys.§ Barnabas is dispatched to Antioch, as one of superior dignity to the "prophets and teachers" already there; just as Peter and John were sent to the converts of Philip in Samaria. Considerably further in the history,‖ we find Barnabas undertakes an earnest dispute with Paul, remonstrating against his severity on Mark, "and the contention was so sharp between them, that they departed asunder one from the other;" which is unintelligible as an occurrence between a mere Presbyter and an inspired Apostle: especially if our reasoning with the Romanists be just, that Paul's taking Peter publicly to task, and "withstanding him to the face," and rebuking him "before them all,"¶ justifies the conclusion that St. Paul was not a whit behind the chiefest of the Apostles. At Lystra, *Barnabas* is taken for the chief divinity, and Paul for the inferior. The holy synod at Jerusalem "kept silence, and gave audience to *Barnabas* and Paul;" where, as usual, Barnabas takes pre-

* Acts, xi. 30.
† Ib. xii. 25.
‡ Ib. xiii. 2.
§ Ib. xi. 22, 30; xiii. 4.
‖ Ib. xv. 39.
¶ Gal. ii. 11, 14.

cedence. The same synod speak in their letter of "our beloved *Barnabas* and Paul, men that have hazarded their lives for the name of our Lord Jesus Christ." Again,* "when James, Cephas, and John, who seemed to be pillars, perceived the grace that was given unto me, they gave to me and *Barnabas* the right hand of fellowship, that *we* should go unto the heathen, and *they* unto the circumcision." Nor is this the only intimation in this chapter of the footing of perfect equality with the other Apostles on which St. Barnabas stood. But, say you, "We must have further evidence; we should like to see the place where Barnabas is *called* an Apostle." Well, you shall see more than you have asked: you shall see *three* such places. Read carefully this passage,† "Have *we* not power to eat and to drink? Have *we* not power to lead about a sister, a wife, as well as *other* [Gr. the rest of the] *Apostles*, and as the brethren of the Lord, and Cephas? Or I only and Barnabas, have not we power to forbear working?" Can any man in his senses, or out of his senses, tell us why Barnabas, who is not mentioned again in the whole Epistle, should be named in this connection, unless he were an Apostle as well known as St. Paul, and as well entitled to the support of the Church at large? Turn now to another place:‡ "The priest of Jupiter . . . . brought oxen and garlands, and would have done sacrifice with the people. Which when the *Apostles*, Barnabas and Paul, heard of, they rent their clothes," and so on. Turn again to yet another text:§ "But the multitude of the city was divided: and part held with the Jews, and part with the *Apostles*," [Barnabas and Paul.] We are told too that Barnabas and Paul went to Antioch, and Cyprus, and Salamis, and Perga, and Antioch in Pisidia, and to Iconium, and Lystra, and Derbe, and again over the same ground, and back to the

* Gal. ii. 9.
† 1 Cor. ix. 4-6.
‡ Acts, xiv. 12-14.
§ Acts, xiv. 4.

other Antioch, "confirming the disciples" and "ordaining elders in every city," while the subordination of the other clergy is recognized in the fact that throughout this tour, they had John, whose surname was Mark, *for "their minister.*"* I have adduced this tedious array of facts and phraseology, to show how thoroughly the Episcopacy is interwoven with the whole texture of the New Testament, and to save the trouble of going, in other cases, into the same details to show the apostolical pre-eminence of others, of whom like language is continually held. It is time to amend the catalogue.

1. Peter.
2. Andrew.
3. James, son of Zebedee.
4. John.
5. Philip.
6. Bartholomew.
7. Thomas.
8. Matthew.
9. James, son of Alphæus.
10. Lebbæus or Thaddæus.
11. Simon Zelotes.
12. Judas Iscariot.
13. Matthias.
14. Paul.
15. Barnabas.

I once asked an excellent Presbyterian divine, (who was taking me pleasantly to task for my conversion to the ancient Faith,) how he could maintain that the Apostles had no successors: when scarcely had our Lord left them to carry out His will, before they set about apostle-making, and made Matthias as the thirteenth Apostle? What think you, Episcopal reader, was his answer? Why, precisely that which

* Acts, xiii. 5.

Dr. Snodgrass gave in his book two years afterwards: that the Apostles acted prematurely, and made a mistake; because they were commanded (as he interpreted it) to remain quietly in Jerusalem until they should receive instructions from on high. Very well. Go on. But, Gentlemen, if a thirteenth Apostle puts you thus to your wit's end, what will you do with the *fifteenth?* Remember, we have now *fifteen!* Poor Barnabas of Cyprus! I found thee a sorry son of consolation in the hour of need! And in vain did I fly to Jerome, for JEROME made Barnabas the equal of Paul; saying of Titus, that *he* had "*not yet* attained to the same rank (*eundem gradum*) which *Barnabas* held, and Paul."*

The charm by which "the Twelve" had held me being now broken, I felt less interest in contradicting the claims of others to the apostolic dignity; for if there might be fifteen Apostles, there might now, for aught I could see or care, be fifteen hundred. So, turning to Scripture† I found it said, "Salute Andronicus and Junia, my kinsmen, and my fellow-prisoners, who are of note among the Apostles, who also were in Christ before me;" and I could not for my life perceive that either in Greek or English the passage would bear any other straight-forward, above-board meaning, than that Andronicus and Junia were *Apostles.* If St. Paul, after placing Timothy and Titus over the churches of Ephesus and Crete, had written to the good people in those places, "Salute Timothy and Titus, who are of note among the *Presbyters,*" I trow we should not soon have heard the last of it. When we say that Washington was of note among the Presidents; or that Augustus was of note among the Emperors; that Herodotus was of note among Historians; or that Homer was of note among the Poets; that Stephen was of note among the Deacons; or that Peter was of note among the Twelve: the whole world at once perceives our meaning. To

* S. Hieron, Comm. on Gal. ii. † Rom. xvi. 7.

the silly cavil that Junia may have been a woman, it is sufficient to say, that Luther and Calvin both make the name (in the nominative) Junias; that the learned Grecians, Robinson and Stuart, allow it to be the name of a man; and that Calvin* admits that "Paul himself, indeed, in one place giveth this name to Andronicus and Junias, whom he saith to have been notable *among the Apostles.*" Even Neander allows them the title of Apostles, in a "secondary" sense. And the fact related of them, that they had been carried off to Rome, and had preceded St. Paul in their imprisonment, as they had done in their conversion, is certainly an intimation that they had filled important spheres, and had been conspicuous offenders in the eye of the heathen law. If they were Apostles, the language is such as we should have expected St. Paul to use. If they were not, Junia must be changed into "Julia;" or Apostles must here mean "messengers;" or some other device must be resorted to, to explain a natural and graceful salutation! And this is our position all along: that the entire New Testament finds a natural interpretation, only on the hypothesis that the Church was Episcopal, and that any further conjecture requires forcings and twistings and strainings innumerable.

In like manner, I found Epaphroditus called the Apostle of the Church at Philippi.† "I supposed it necessary to send to you Epaphroditus, my brother, and companion in labor, and fellow-soldier, but your messenger" [in the Greek, your *Apostle*]. And St. Paul uses just the language that we should expect from him toward his equal: "*my* brother;" "*my* companion in labor;" "*my* fellow-soldier," "but *your* Apostle;" "he longed after you all, and was full of heaviness, because ye had heard that he had been sick;" "receive him therefore in the Lord with all gladness, and *hold such in reputation.*" This is addressed too, not only to the saints at

* Instit. B. iv.

† Philipp. ii. 25.

Philippi, but "to the Bishops and Deacons;" and it is to Presbyter-Bishops and Deacons that he says of Epaphroditus, "*my* brother and companion," and "*your* Apostle;" and again, "receive him in all gladness, and hold such in reputation." Toward the end of the Epistle, too,* he apostrophizes some one, and probably Epaphroditus, in terms ("True yoke-fellow") that appear to recognize Apostolical equality. *Germanus dictus est nomine qui erat Compar officii*, says Jerome. Here then was another Apostle on my hands. I went for consolation to sundry of the Fathers: but the Fathers with one voice insisted that I must leave it as St. Paul had left it, for Epaphroditus was the Apostle of the Church at Philippi. Theodoret, an accurate writer of the fifth century, replied, to my inquiries, that "Epaphroditus was called the *Apostle* of the Philippians, because he was entrusted with the Episcopal *government*, as being their *Bishop;* for those whom we *now* call *Bishops* were more anciently called *Apostles*." What could I do? I remembered, after some misgiving, that there was a Father contemporaneous with Theodoret, who, according to Dr. Miller, would give me comfort, if any of them could. But even JEROME spoke out to me in his rude, blunt way:

"Paulatim vero, tempore procedente, et alii, ab his quos Dominus elegerat, ordinati *Apostoli;* sicut ille ad Philippenses sermo declarat, dicens, Necessarium existimavi Epaphroditum fratrem, co-operatorem, et commilitonem meum, *vestrum autem Apostolum*, et ministrum necessitatis meæ, mittere ad vos. Et ad Corinthianos de talibus scribitur, Sive Apostoli ecclesiarum, gloria Christi."

"But by degrees, in process of time, *others also were ordained Apostles*, by those whom the Lord had chosen; as that passage to the Philippians declares, which saith, I supposed it necessary to send to you Epaphroditus, my brother, my companion in labor, and fellow-soldier, *but your Apostle*, and he that ministered to my wants. Also to the Corinthians it is written concerning such, 'They are the

* Philipp. iv. 3.

Apostles [in our English version "messengers"] of the Churches, and the glory of Christ.'"

Accordingly I gave it up, that Epaphroditus was an undeniable Apostle.

The next that troubled me was St. James. Soon after the martyrdom of James the brother of John, by King Herod, another James makes his appearance, and becomes conspicuous in the Church of Jerusalem. He sends forth an Epistle General "to the Twelve Tribes which are scattered abroad." He closes the debate in the venerable council of "Apostles and Presbyters and Brethren" in Jerusalem, by a final and authoritative judgment, "Wherefore my sentence is, that we trouble not," &c.; on which Luther (approved by Neander) remarks that the Apostles, after a frank discussion, in which Peter and others took part, were willing to leave the decision to James, as a generous-minded man, and the representative of the Jewish interest. The brethren who bore the decisions of the Council to the Churches, are afterward thus spoken of by St. Paul:* "For before that certain came [not from those Apostles and Elders, but] from JAMES, he [Peter] did eat with the Gentiles." Again; St. Paul says, "JAMES, Cephas, and John, who seemed to be pillars;"† thus allowing, throughout, the precedence to St. JAMES. When St. Peter went to the house "where many were gathered together praying," and declared how the Lord had brought him out of prison: not finding St. James among them, he said, "Go, show these things to JAMES and to the brethren."‡ And twenty years afterward, when St. Paul and his company visited Jerusalem: "the day following, Paul went in with us unto JAMES, and all the Presbyters were present."§ And it is remarkable that, up to the ordination of the Deacons and the settlement of the Church in Jerusalem,

* Gal. ii. 12. † Ib. verse 9. ‡ Acts, xii. 17. § Ib. xxi. 18.

St. Peter had always taken the lead: but from that time he gives precedence, in every thing relating to that Church, to St. James. Moreover, all antiquity agrees that this James was Bishop of the Church at Jerusalem; as Clement of Alexandria, at the close of the second century declares: "After the ascension of Christ, Peter, James, and John did not contend for the honor of presiding over the Church at Jerusalem, but, with the rest of the Apostles, chose James the Just to be the Bishop of that Church."

Now this James, according to St. Paul, was an Apostle: for "other of the *Apostles* saw I none, save James the Lord's brother." But, on further inquiry, I saw reason to suppose that the James here mentioned was not one of "the Twelve." Many Presbyterians and Congregationalists are of this opinion. Neander, who would not easily allow it, as it weighs heavily against his exceedingly loose ideas of ecclesiastical rule in the primitive Church, is, nevertheless, constrained to allow that "the question is one of the most difficult in the Apostolic history; "and a doubt, admitted by an author of Neander's views on a point like this, is almost equivalent to demonstration. That this James was not James the brother of John, is clear: for he is spoken of in the Acts for twenty years after that Apostle's martyrdom. And that he was not James the son of Alphæus, appears from the following among many reasons: (1.) It may be doubted whether one of "the Twelve," who had received a commandment from the Master's lips to "go into all the world, and preach the Gospel," would have been content to spend the thirty remaining years of his life in Jerusalem. (2.) This James is called "our Lord's brother," and St. Matthew,* *after* naming the two Jameses among the Twelve, represents the *Jews* as saying, "Is not his mother called Mary? and his *brethren*, *James*, and Joses, and Simon, and Judas? And his sisters, are they not all *with us?*"

* Matthew, xiii. 55, 56.

(3.) In the last half-year before our Saviour suffered, his *brethren* urged Him to quit Galilee, and return to his *disciples;* and St. John adds, "For neither did His *brethren* believe in Him." (4.) Before this, we are told by three of the Evangelists, that when Jesus was in a house with his *disciples,* "His mother and His *brethren* stood without." (5.) St. Paul speaks of "the other Apostles, and the *brethren* of the Lord," as different individuals."* (6.) In St. Matthew,† we read of "Mary the mother of *James* and Joses" as witnessing the crucifixion, and in St. John,‡ we find at the Cross "Mary the wife of Cleophas" with the two other Maries: so that they who make this James to have been one of "the Twelve," are obliged to make the Cleophas of St. John the Alphæus of the other Evangelists, and to suppose that St. Mark has called the same person by these different names. (7.) In the Book of the Acts,§ after naming "the Eleven," St. Luke informs us that "*These* all continued with . . . . Mary the mother of Jesus, and with His *brethren.*" (8.) There seems a special design in distributing the three titles, "James the son of Zebedee and brother of John," "James the son of Alphæus," and "James the Lord's brother." (9.) The character of this James, as being so singularly ascetic, and a Nazarite from the womb, does not comport with the reputation that "the Twelve" had borne among the Pharisees. (10.) And as it is so much easier and more natural to confound this James with James the son of Alphæus, than to separate them, the very fact that so many of the ancients did distinguish them, is very good evidence that the persons were, in fact, distinct. Clemens of Alexandria, in the age next to that of the Apostles, declares, as we have seen, that "Peter and *James* and John, did not contend for the honor of presiding over the Church of Jerusalem, but with the rest

* 1 Cor. ix. 5.
† St. Matt. xxvii. 56.
‡ St. John, xix. 25.
§ Acts, i. 14.

of *the Apostles* chose *James the Just* to be the *Bishop* of that Church." Once more in my despair, I sought refuge in the ever "famous JEROME," but once more the unfeeling Presbyter repulsed me, saying, in his commentary on the passage, "Other of the Apostles saw I none, save James the Lord's brother:"

"Quod autem, exceptis duodecim, quidam vocentur Apostoli, &c. . . . . Paulatim vero, tempore procedente, et alii ab his quos Dominus elegerat, ordinati Apostoli, &c.," as before quoted.

"But that others besides the twelve may be called Apostles, &c. . . . . But by degrees, in process of time, *others also* were ordained Apostles by those whom the Lord had chosen, &c.," as before quoted.

And equally little consolation did I find in turning to his biographical account of James, who, he says, "after the passion of the Lord, was immediately ORDAINED by the Apostles, the Bishop of Jerusalem," (post passionem Domini, statim ab Apostolis Hierosolymorum Episcopus ordinatus;) and that he governed (rexit) the Church of Jerusalem for thirty years. And elsewhere Jerome calls this James "*the thirteenth Apostle.*"

Really this was too bad. I asked for bread, and he gave me a stone. I could hardly believe my eyes. But there it was, most unmistakably conceded, that the Twelve were but the pioneers and ordainers of a whole host of Apostles. And now my catalogue runs thus:

1. Peter.
2. Andrew.
3. James, brother of John.
4. John.
5. Philip.
6. Bartholomew.
7. Thomas.
8. Matthew.

9. James, the son of Alphæus.
10. Lebbæus or Thaddæus.
11. Simon Zelotes.
12. Judas Iscariot.
13. Matthias.
14. Paul.
15. Barnabas.
16. Andronicus
17. Junias.
18. Epaphroditus.
19. James the Just, the Lord's brother.

Even if the last were one of the twelve, I was very little better off: for all the ancients, to a man, had allowed that, agreeably to the usages of the Primitive Church, he *might* have been a layman, converted about the time of our Saviour's passion, elevated *by ordination* to the Apostleship. And, whoever he was, all concurred with Jerome in giving him a fixed Diocese, for thirty years, over the Model Church of Jerusalem; and a local authority to which even Peter and Paul did homage.

If in the Church there was a man likely to be promoted to the Apostolic Order, it was the admirable youth, who, from a child, had known the Holy Scriptures—the companion and bosom-friend of St. Paul. Accordingly we find Timothy in due time an Apostle, as it is written, "When WE might have been burdensome, as the *Apostles of Christ*."* For the phrases, "our *hearts*"† and "our own *souls*,"‡ show that St. Paul speaks for Silvanus and Timothy, as, in fact, he seldom speaks in the singular number in any part of the Epistle, and not at all until the nineteenth verse of the second chapter. And this explains why Timothy is associated with St. Paul in writing six of the Apostolical Epistles, in some of which the authoritative tone is distinctly made use of in the plural

* 1 Thess. ii. 6. † Ib. verse 4. ‡ Ib. verse 8.

form. And wherever he is named, in these or the other Epistles, it is in a way that is easiest explained on the supposition that he was raised to the Apostleship, and for that reason entitled, as much as St. Paul, to the support and obedience of the Churches. And when to all this I came to add the Epistles to Timothy himself, and to superadd the voice of all antiquity, it expresses less than I felt, to say, that I had no longer the shadow of a shade of doubt. From the time of his settlement in the Church of Ephesus, we never find him absent from his charge, except on the invitation of St. Paul, to visit him once more before he suffered. Leaving then out of view his previous high relations to other Churches, what was the nature of his charge at Ephesus?

Now, if the Epistles of St. Paul to Timothy were written to an Apostle, we may reasonably expect to find in them still further intimations of Apostolic prerogatives and powers. Let us see.

In Chap. i., after the salutation, his first words are "I besought THEE to abide still at Ephesus, when I went into Macedonia, that THOU mightest *charge* some that they teach no other doctrine:" thus devolving on Timothy the function that would otherwise have belonged to himself, if he had not been called away elsewhere. "*This charge* I commit *unto thee*, son Timothy, according to the prophecies which went before *on thee:*" intimating that the vocation to his present work had been an event grave enough for the interposition of prophecy.

In Chap. ii. he instructs him carefully concerning the nature and subjects of the prayers or liturgies of the Church to which he was now sent; and also how the women should behave in private life, and in ecclesiastical assemblies.

In Chap. iii. he "charges" Timothy, at considerable length, with regard to the proper qualifications of the inferior Bishops: "A bishop must be blameless, the husband of one wife, vigilant, sober, of good behavior, given to hospitality, apt to teach, ... one that ruleth well his own house, ... not a novice, ... must have a good report of them which are without." He then charges him with equal care respecting those to be admitted Deacons, and respecting their wives and children, and recommends their promotion when they "have used the office of a deacon well."

In Chap. iv. he reminds Timothy of the sad prediction of the Spirit, that "some should depart from the faith, giving heed to seducing spirits, and doctrines of devils;" and charges him to put the brethren in remembrance thereof: and adds, "These things COMMAND and teach."

On the subject of discipline and of provision for the poor, he recommends in the next chapter moderation and prudence, towards old and young, male and female, married and unmarried. After some directions, relating apparently to useful institutions, giving employment to females in the Church's service, and also to the subject of marriage, he says concerning another matter that Timothy must look after, "*Let the Presbyters* that rule well be counted worthy of double honor, especially they who labor in the Word and doctrine;" for "the laborer is worthy of his reward." But "against *a Presbyter* receive not an accusation, but before two or three witnesses;" and, "them that sin *rebuke before all, that others also may fear.* I CHARGE thee before God, and the Lord Jesus Christ, and the elect angels, that thou observe these things, without preferring one before another, doing nothing by partiality. LAY HANDS SUDDENLY ON NO MAN."

In Chap. vi. he gives directions concerning the duties to be required by servants; and, after a renewed allusion to false teachers, and some counsels pertinent to the occasion, he exclaims once more, with great solemnity: "I give thee charge in the sight of God, who quickeneth all things, and before Christ Jesus, who before Pontius Pilate witnessed a good confession; that thou keep this commandment without spot, unrebukeable, *until the appearing of our Lord Jesus Christ.*" And yet once more, when we had thought that all he had to say was said, his full soul bursts again with its anxieties: "O Timothy, keep that which is committed to THY trust!"

Again, in a second Epistle, he says to Timothy, "Stir up the gift of God, which is IN THEE by the putting on of MY hands;" "Hold fast the form of sound words, which thou hast heard of me;" "That good thing which was committed unto THEE keep by the Holy Ghost which dwelleth in US;" "The things that thou hast heard of me among many witnesses, *the same commit* THOU *to faithful men*, who shall be able to teach others also;" "Of these things put them (the Presbyters) in remembrance, CHARGING THEM before the Lord that they strive not about words to no profit, but to the subverting of the hearers." Then, solemnly recurring to the perilous times they were to look for, he exclaims again, "I charge thee therefore before God, and the Lord Jesus Christ, ... preach the Word; be instant in season, out of season; reprove, rebuke, exhort, with all long suffering and doctrine; ..... do the work of an evangelist, make full proof of THY ministry. For I am now ready to be offered, and the time of MY departure is at hand."

Thus with his dying hand the venerable St. Paul delivers up the keys to a successor in his office. What single thing was there that St. Paul could have done in the Church at Ephesus, which Timothy is not here instructed to do? And pray where is it that mere Presbyters, so often addressed in other Epistles, ever received any such injunctions as these?

Timothy is sent to Ephesus to ordain Presbyters and Deacons. Yet, for years before, the Church there had its Presbyters; and, what is yet more singular, although we have a discourse of St. Paul's, addressed to them when he sent for them to meet him at Miletus, as recorded at considerable length in Acts xx., yet in that address—that solemn address, that parting address to the Presbyters at Ephesus, "hanging on Paul's neck, and sorrowing most of all that they should see his face no more"—he says not a word about "charging," "reproving," "rebuking," or "receiving accusations against" each other, even although he told them, "Yea, of your own selves shall men arise, speaking perverse things, to draw away disciples after them;" and again, "I know that after my departing, shall grievous wolves enter in among you, not sparing the flock." There is here not one word concerning *discipline*, as there had been none concerning *ordination:* but only, "Take heed unto *yourselves*, and to the *flock*, ... to feed the Church of God, which He hath purchased with His own blood." But when these evils begin actually to appear, and these wolves commence their havoc of the fold, and Timothy is sent to them, because St. Paul cannot go: it is with the anointing oil, the rod, and the sword. The question has been well put, Had these Presbyters the same power to "receive an accusation against" Timothy, that he had against them? or to "rebuke" him, that he had to rebuke them? or to "charge" Timothy, "that he teach no other doctrine," even as he had "by prophecy" and "the laying on of Paul's hands," to "charge" them?

These Epistles to Timothy require such interminable straining and forcing, into a sense so entirely non-natural, in order to get rid of the Episcopal prerogative, that some more skilful Presbyterians, who have felt the pressure, and who can, *à la* Hudibras,

——— "divide
A hair 'twixt south and southwest side,"

have fallen on the expedient of allowing Timothy a delegated authority to act temporarily in the place of Paul, as a sort of *tertium quid*, or intermediate thing between the Presbyters at Ephesus and the Apostle.*

Very well, have it so if you will: half-presbyter, half-apostle; it can do no harm. It still makes Timothy a Bishop and Paul the Archbishop; or, if we must call the Presbyters of Ephesus Bishops, it makes Timothy the Archbishop, and Paul the Patriarch. We care not by what name you call him—Priest, Presbyter, Bishop, Suffragan, Superintendent, Ruler, Governor, Evangelist, Missionary, Moderator, Primus Presbyter, Apostle, Assistant of the Apostle, Messenger, Prelate, Angel, Antistes, Princeps, Præses, Præpositus, Archon, Proestos, or Præfect, (as Calvin styles James in the Church at Jerusalem,)—*call him by what name you please;* write it in Latin, Greek, or Hebrew; read forward, read backward: it comes to the same thing; Timothy succeeds to the prerogatives and powers of Paul—Paul now in irons at Rome, "his course finished," "the time of his departure at hand"—and Timothy to act henceforth "*until the appearing of Jesus Christ,*" not by delegation in the place of an absent, but by succession in the place of *a deceased Apostle.*

Turn we to the ancients? They call Timothy an "Apostle;" and the Fathers, to the number of ten or twelve, name him as the successor of St. Paul in the Church at Ephesus. The words of the "famous" Jerome are, "*Timotheus a Paulo*

* This Apostle-splitting, so to call it, reminds me of an anecdote with which Dr. Miller used to point his caution to our classes, against too fond an exhibition of our powers of strained and rigid exegesis. A Doctor of Divinity, it appears, occupying a Professor's chair in a literary institution, entered into one of those elaborate discussions which are sometimes heard from sectarian pulpits, to ascertain how many evil ones there were that passed out of the two men among the tombs, into the herd of swine; and, after a long dissertation on the military tactics of the Romans, he came at last to the conclusion that, as the Roman Legion contained six thousand four hundred and seven men, and as the "legion" of evil ones was divided between the two men among the tombs, there must have been just three thousand two hundred and three and a half devils in each man: in consequence whereof, the learned Divine went afterward, among the beardless youths of the place, by the name of "Doctor Split-devil."

Ephesiorum Episcopus ordinatus;" and in his commentary on Philemon, Jerome makes not only Timothy, and Silvanus, and Sosthenes "Apostles," but *inspired* equally with St. Paul in writing the Epistles under their joint names! Theodoret calls him "the Apostle of the Asians." Eusebius, the great historian of the Church, declares, "It is recorded in history that Timothy was the *first* Bishop of Ephesus"—over the Presbyter-Bishops, be it remembered, who were there before him. On this passage Dr. Bowden, in great good humor, takes Dr. Miller to task for one of those innocent mistakes to which the latter is so singularly prone, in translating the ἱστορεῖται of Eusebius by the *free* rendering, "It is *reported!*" The idea that Eusebius—who lived within two centuries of the Apostles, who sat in the council of Nice assembled out of all the world, who had access to all the writings of his predecessors, who obtained a special order from Constantine that the records of all the churches in the Empire should be furnished him for the compilation of his history—the *idea* that Eusebius should have said of an event so recent and necessarily so well known, "It is *reported* that Timothy was ordained Bishop of the Ephesians by Paul!" Is there no limit to new discoveries in Greek?

It will be now less necessary to go over the same ground with regard to Titus. In the Epistle to him, immediately after the salutation, we find the Apostle beginning precisely as he had done to Timothy.

TO TIMOTHY.	TO TITUS.
"I besought THEE to abide still at Ephesus, when I went into Macedonia, that THOU mightest charge some that they teach, &c"	"For this cause left I THEE in Crete, that THOU shouldst set in order the things that are wanting, and *ordain Presbyters* in every city, as I had appointed THEE."

Now in Crete there were a hundred cities. It lay in the path of St. Paul and others in their frequent journeys westward. St. Paul had been there at least once, for there he left Titus. There were Cretans among the first who heard the Gospel on the day of Pentecost. The very phraseology, "that thou shouldest *set in order the things that are wanting*," shows that churches had been founded. The whole drift of the Epistle shows that there were Churches there, and Churches infested already with Judaizing and false teachers. Nor do I know any man but Dr. Miller who has been hardy enough to ask *proof* that there were Presbyters in the Churches of Ephesus and Crete before this time. I care not, except for the credit of common sense, whether there were or not. For here is the dilemma. If there were Presbyters in Crete before, Paul, a remarkable observer of professional propriety and etiquette, slights them entirely, and leaves his friend Titus among the Presbyteries of Crete for the purpose of ordaining. Dr. Potts, I trow, would take it for an ill-mannered thing, if the Presbytery of Philadelphia should send a man to ordain elders in the cities of New York. Or, if there were no Presbyters in Crete, still the one man Titus is left, in the place of the one man Paul who cannot stay longer, to "ordain elders in every city," and to "set in order the things that are wanting." Either way, Titus represents and succeeds the Apostle.

St. Paul then charges him, as he had done Timothy, to ordain as Bishops or Elders only such as he may find "blameless, the husband of one wife, having faithful children, . . not self-willed, not soon angry, not given to wine, no striker, not given to filthy lucre; but lovers of hospitality, lovers of good men, sober, just, holy,—temperate, holding fast the faithful Word." As to false teachers, he tells him that their "mouths must be stopped," and "a man that is a heretic, after the first and second admonition, REJECT." The body of the Epistle, very like those to Timothy, is occupied with charges respecting "aged men," "aged women," "young women," "young men," "servants," "the powers that be," and the local " magistrates."

Now this pre-eminence of Titus in Crete is confirmed by the fact of his having on other occasions represented St. Paul, during the absence of that Apostle from some other Churches. Thus, twice he was sent to Corinth; and St. Paul says of him,* "His inward affection is more abundant toward you, whilst he remembereth *the obedience of you all, how with fear and trembling ye received him.*" Again, in the next chapter,† "We desired Titus, that as he had begun, so he would also finish in you the same grace also;" and again,‡ "Thanks be to God, which put the same earnest care into the heart of Titus for you;" and again,§ "whether any do inquire of Titus, he is *my partner* and *fellow-helper* concerning *you:* or our brethren be inquired of, they are THE APOSTLES [Gr.] of the Churches, and the glory of Christ. Wherefore show ye to them, (*i. e.*, to Titus, Luke, &c.,) and before the Churches, the proof of your love, and of our boasting on your behalf." And all this in so famous a Church as that of Corinth, renowned for its tongues, its prophets, and its pastors.

Accordingly we find the whole regiment of Fathers allowing Titus the rank in Crete which we have seen them with one consent give to Timothy at Ephesus. In commenting on the second chapter of Galatians, where St. Paul recounts his visit to Jerusalem with Barnabas, having Titus also with them, and where James, and Cephas, and John, gave to him and Barnabas the right hands of fellowship, the "famous" JEROME, whose name our old Presbyterian habits oblige us to write always in capitals, remarks:

"Sed Tito, qui cum eis erat, dextras non dederunt; *necdum* quippe ad eam mensuram perve-

"But to Titus, who was with them, they gave not their right hands; for he had *not yet* attained

* 2 Cor. vii. 15.
† Ib. viii. 16.
‡ Verse 6.
§ Ib. 23.

nerat ut possint ei Christi mercimonia ex æquo cum majoribus credi; et eundem tenere negociationis locum quem Barnabas tenebat et Paulus."	to that measure that the interests of Christ should be intrusted to him equally with his superiors, and that he should hold the same rank of administration which Barnabas and Paul held."

I noticed too, that St. Paul settled Titus in Crete with these high powers, as he had done Timothy in Ephesus, when now his race was well nigh run, and he was about to loose his girdle and lay down his staff.

And my attention was called, as the "famous" JEROME's had been a thousand years before me, to the further fact, that when St. Paul requested Timothy to leave his charge awhile and come and visit him, he sent Tychicus to Ephesus;* and when he desired Titus to do the same thing, he sent Tychicus to Crete;† it would appear to take their places in their absence: "When I shall send Artemas unto thee, or Tychicus, (called by Neander, Paul's "missionary assistant," and by Calvin, "the Bishop of the Colossians,") be diligent to come unto me."

And yet once more, Silas or Silvanus, (for they are but two forms of the same name,) is a New Testament Apostle. In Acts xv., he and Judas are called "chief men among the brethren,"‡ and "prophets,"§ as Barnabas and Saul had been on a former occasion. He was, with Paul and Barnabas, charged with "the decrees" of the Synod of Jerusalem;‖ and of his own will remained at Antioch,¶ "confirming the brethren." In the occurrences at Philippi,** he is constantly mentioned as the equal of St. Paul. In the following chapter the same equality is still preserved. In another place†† he is associated with St. Paul, and takes precedence of Timothy. In

* 2 Tim. iv. 12.
† Tit. iii. 12.
‡ Ib. verse 22.
§ Ib. verse 32.
‖ Ib. verses 22, 25, 27.
¶ Ib. verse 34.
** Chap. xvi.
†† 2 Cor. i. 19.

another,* the same circumstance occurs, with the additional importance that his authority is added in the address of the Epistle; and in another,† Paul declares both him and Timothy to be, equally with himself, "APOSTLES," ready to impart not only the gospel, but also "their own souls," when they "might have been burdensome [marg., *used authority*] as THE APOSTLES OF CHRIST." Again, in 2nd Thessalonians, we find Silas or Silvanus uniting with St. Paul and Timothy, in the Epistle wherein they say, "that ye both do, and will do, the things which *we command* you,"‡ and "now *we command* you, brethren, in the name of our Lord Jesus Christ, that ye withdraw yourselves, &c."§ And again, "that we might not be chargeable to any of you; *not because we have not power*, but to make ourselves an ensample unto you to follow us."‖ I marked especially the language, "When we might have been burdensome as THE APOSTLES OF CHRIST."

In my despair I appealed once more to JEROME. But Jerome, on the passage "or our brethren be inquired of, they are the Apostles of the Churches, and the glory of Christ," says further:

"Silas quoque et Judas ab Apostolis Apostoli nominati sunt."	"Silas also and Judas are called Apostles by the Apostles."

In the same manner the passage just quoted undeniably includes St. Luke, who went with Titus to Corinth, "the brother whose praise is in the gospel throughout all the churches; and not that only, but who was also chosen of the churches to travel with us;"¶ the author moreover of a gospel, and of the Acts of the Apostles, albeit himself not by any means one of "the Twelve:" And to this agrees also the language of antiquity. Once more then the Catalogue:

* 1 Thess. i. 1.
† 1 Thess. ii. 6, 8.
‡ Chap. iii. 4.
§ Ib. verse 6.
‖ Ib. verses 8, 9.
¶ 2 Cor. viii. 18, 19.

1. Peter.
2. Andrew.
3. James, the son of Zebedee.
4. John.
5. Philip.
6. Bartholomew.
7. Thomas.
8. Matthew.
9. James, the son of Alphæus.
10. Lebbæus, or Thaddæus.
11. Simon Zelotes.
12. Judas Iscariot.
13. Matthias.
14. Paul.
15. Barnabas.
16. Andronicus.
17. Junias.
18. Epaphroditus.
19. James, the Lord's brother.
20. Timothy.
21. Titus.
22. Silas.
23. Luke.

It is really not the most pleasing thing in the world to confess one's former ignorance:

> —— Durum est
> Quæ juvenes didicere, senes perdenda fateri.

I did once believe that the Apostolic office had perished with St. John, and that the Twelve had passed away without successors: nor can I give a better apology for my mistake, than that I had never thought the subject of sufficient importance to compare attentively Scripture with Scripture, considering time more profitably employed in hunting for confirmations of "the decrees of God, whereby for his own glory he hath foreordained whatsoever comes to pass;" and that "none are redeemed by Christ but the elect only;" and that "by the decrees of God, for the manifestation of his glory, some men and angels are predestinated unto everlasting life, and others are foreordained to everlasting death," and that "those men and angels, (I still quote the Confession of Faith,) thus predestinated and foreordained, are particularly and unchangeably designed, and their number is so certain and definite, that it cannot be increased or diminished." A merciful God forgive me, that some of the time thus wasted was not employed in finding the foundations of the Church's ancient unity, and peace, and triumphs! Then, too, had I been spared this confession. For so soon as my investigations were directed to this point, I found the number of the original "Apostles" just doubling on my hands, and that almost exclusively in the path of St. Paul.

I desire it to be remarked, that in the foregoing catalogue I have confined myself exclusively to such as are distinctly *called* in the New Testament "*Apostles*," and to whom antiquity allows both the name and the prerogative. There are other individuals named in the New Testament, as "companions," "fellow-soldiers," "fellow-laborers," "fellow-helpers" of the Apostles, but not distinctly *called* Apostles, yet whom the early fathers speak of as "Apostles," or as successors to apostolic functions; such as Dionysius the Areopagite, at Athens; Gaius and Aristarchus, successively at Thessalonica; Archippas at Colosse; Antipas at Pergamos; Crescens in Gallia or Galatia; Euodius at Antioch, (succeeded by Ignatius;) Linus and Clement at Rome; Mark, Judas, &c., &c. These I have excluded from the catalogue, meaning to admit those only who are called "Apostles" *in the Scriptures.* If exception be taken to St. James, on the ground that he may have been one of "the Twelve," he can very well be spared:

although, if the original Apostles were to have no successors, it is utterly unaccountable how others have been so intermixed with "the Twelve" that it was difficult even in ancient times to see the difference, and also how antiquity should have ever entertained the question whether this James had not been a layman up to the time of the Master's death.

Of course, in this inquiry, I could not overlook the seven Epistles addressed by St. John to "THE ANGELS OF the Seven Churches." The words Angel and Apostle, both meaning "Messenger," are much more nearly synonymous than the names of "Presbyter and Bishop." And if the unusual metaphor of "the Synagogue of Satan," occurring twice in these Epistles, indicate an allusion to the Jewish Synagogue, in which the chief officer or overseer was sometimes called the Angel: St. John may have had special reason for transferring this title to the Rulers of these Churches. Moreover, these "Angels" are expressly affirmed by the ancients,* to have been individually the Presidents, Rulers, or Bishops of those Churches. But, more than all, St. John addresses them as holding the keys of discipline, and as being responsible for the teaching allowed in their respective Churches. For example, the Angel of the Church at Ephesus, said by some of the ancients to have been Onesimus, (although by others supposed to have been Timothy,) is thus addressed, and with the highest commendations: "Thou hast tried them which say they are apostles and are not, and hast found them liars;" and if a man can be tried only by his peers, we must allow the trier to have been himself an Apostle. And in the Epistle to the Angel of the Church at Smyrna, (agreed by all the ancients to have been Polycarp,) how affecting are the allu-

* Especially by Irenæus, who was personally acquainted with Polycarp, the one at Smyrna; and by Ignatius, who names Onesimus as the one in his time at Ephesus; and by the reliable Eusebius, who was familiar with the very earliest histories; and by others down to the famous JEROME inclusively.

sions to his poverty and piety, and to the mournful persecutions about to befall his flock, and to the "crown of life" to which he was shortly to pass through the fires. So also to the "President" of the Church at Pergamos, he writes: "because thou hast there them that hold the doctrine of Balaam, ... so hast thou also them that hold the doctrine of the Nicolaitanes." Again to another, "Thou sufferest that woman Jezebel, which calleth herself a prophetess, to teach and to seduce my servants." I could not resist the evidence, taken in connection with the powers of Titus, and especially of Timothy in one of these very Churches, that these Angels—call them, we say again, by what name you will—were individuals, as responsible as ever St. Paul or St. Peter was for the condition of their churches, and for the doctrinal purity of the teachers. Doctor Mason's flaming capitals, in which he quotes the phrase "shall cast SOME of YOU into prison, that YE may be tried, &c., &c.," to show that the Epistles are addressed to Presbyterians, is really too puerile to be considered. St. Paul, in his Epistle to Titus, says, "Grace be with you all;" Ignatius, in an Epistle written at this time and to this very Polycarp, speaks at first in the singular number, using among others that beautiful expression, "stand THOU firm as an anvil when it is beaten:" but knowing the maxim of antiquity, "Ecclesia in Episcopo," he breaks out at last, in like manner, in the plural strain: "Labor YE one with another; strive together; run together; suffer together; let NONE of YOU be found a deserter; . . . . be long suffering towards EACH OTHER." And Dr. Mason himself, writing to a brother minister in Philadelphia, might very well in these days have allowed himself to say: "Do send sound men to the next Assembly, for we hear with sorrow that *some* of *you* are tinctured with the new divinity." This miserable quibbling, to which Blondel, and Cartwright, and Beza, and Grotius would not listen, is certainly, to our mind, altogether less manly than the bold suggestion of the "evangelical" Neander, that these Epistles are addressed to Angels, in allusion to an Asiatic superstition that Angels presided over certain districts and provinces; or his still bolder hypothesis that John the Apostle never wrote these Epistles at all!

It is unnecessary to pursue the succession further. Here is the catalogue, so far as we have gone:

1. Peter.
2. Andrew.
3. James, son of Zebedee.
4. John.
5. Philip.
6. Bartholomew.
7. Thomas.
8. Matthew.
9. James, son of Alphæus.
10. Thaddæus.
11. Simon Zelotes.
12. Judas Iscariot.
13. Matthias.
14. Paul.
15. Barnabas.
16. Andronicus.
17. Junias.
18. Epaphroditus.
19. James, the Lord's brother.
20. Timothy.
21. Titus.
22. Silas.
23. Luke. All these are called "Apostles;" to whom add,
24. Onesimus, or "Angel of the Church at Ephesus."
25. Polycarpus, or "Angel of the Church at Smyrna."
26. Successor of Antipas, "Angel of the Church at Pergamos.

27. Carpus, or "Angel of the Church at Thyatira.
28. "Angel of the Church at Sardis."
29. "Angel of the Church in Philadelphia."
30. "Angel of the Church of the Laodiceans."

"Well, really!" will exclaim the Presbyterian, "according to this, Apostles were not so rare on the earth as I had supposed." No, gentle reader, they were not so rare as you have been led to think; for these we have found in the path of the succession of only St. Peter, and St. Paul, and St. John. How many more might, then, have been added to the list, if St. Luke had given us a record of the Churches planted by the rest of the Eleven!—for, besides Peter, and James, and John, not one of the original Twelve (Jude perhaps excepted) is again noticed in the Scriptures after the day of Pentecost. We must take the "Acts" of these as an example of what was done by the others; and, in fact, uninspired records of other churches (as in the Church of Syria, only discovered three centuries ago) have come down to us, in which the very same state of things is shown to have existed. No indeed! The apostolic office entered into the very constitution of the Church. "God hath set some in the Church; first, Apostles; secondarily, prophets; thirdly, teachers;" "and he gave some Apostles; and some prophets; and some evangelists; and some pastors and teachers,"—till when? "Till we all come into the unity of the faith."

No! Apostles were not so scarce as we have heard. How absurd the question, "Are ALL Apostles?" if it were a conceded thing that there had never been but *Twelve!* How absurd the charge* that "such are false apostles ...... transforming themselves into the *Apostles of Christ*," if the Corinthians understood that no new Apostles of Christ were ever to be known! How absurd the boasting of St. Paul,†

* 2 Cor. xi. 13. † Gal. i. 1, 17.

that he was "an Apostle, not *of men*, neither *by man*," "neither went I up to Jerusalem to them which were Apostles before me," if no such thing were known in the whole world as one's being made an Apostle by "*those that were Apostles before* him!" What earthly meaning will they attach to the declaration,* "Thou (the Angel of the Church at Ephesus) *hast tried* them which say they are *Apostles*, and are not, and *hast found them* liars,"† if it was understood, in the primitive Church, that the Apostles were to have "no successors?" The Angel of the Church at Ephesus had simply to say to any such intruder: "Sir, Peter is dead, and Paul is dead, and every body knows that *the Apostles* are *all* dead, save the beloved John. Whom makest thou thyself? Surely thou art mad! The Church is Presbyterian! THE APOSTLES, every body knows, HAVE NO SUCCESSORS!" Just as soon might men present themselves within the spiritual charge of Dr. Potts, or Mr. Barnes, or Mr. Boardman, claiming to be Apostles: as within the bounds of the "Moderator" of the Presbytery at Ephesus!

Alas! now I was fairly driven out from my position Number Three, which involves in fact the true issue between the Sect-makers and the Church. Thirty Apostles rising up in the path of but three of the Eleven! Or, if the seven in Asia, who had power to try "false apostles," are to be omit-

* Rev. ii. 2.

† Among my classmates who have assailed the Church, is the Rev. Mr. Boardman, of Philadelphia, who chose this, I am informed, as the text of his Discourse to his congregation on this subject. To me it is one of those proofs—the more unanswerable as it is less intentional—that Apostles, both true and false, were so numerous as to create the necessity of caution, discrimination, and discipline. Can Mr. Boardman imagine that men rose up in Asia about A. D. 95, claiming to be Apostles, when all the Apostles that were ever to exist, were dead, save one? If I were preaching in reply to Mr. Boardman, I should desire no better text than this of his own selection. I never saw the sermon. I can well suspect, however, that he took care not to tell his "people," that a claim to the apostleship was tried at Ephesus so late as A. D. 95!

ted, because they have instead of Apostle the title of angel: then here were at least twenty-three; all, most distinctly, called by the very name APOSTLES; receiving such deference as Peter and Paul and John received; and sent to the Churches with power to ordain, to rule, to receive accusation against, and to silence the inferior bishops; all antiquity, too, for more than three hundred years, taking the same view of a transmitted "apostleship;" and not a heretic, writhing under an apostolical anathema, venturing to question it, until the days of Aërius; Episcopacy as universal as the name of Christ; and so great the number of the true Apostles, that "false" ones cross their path, and even are able, like their predecessor Judas, to do mischief in the churches. It was the first time I had searched the Scriptures thoroughly upon this subject; and this was the result. I saw it written with a sunbeam, that the number of Apostles was to be increased, and *was* increased, both by accession and by succession. If the apostolic office was thus to perish: much more that of Elders and Deacons, as the Quakers more justly reason, because *they* had no promise nor injunction of perpetuity. But the promise of Christ is gloriously redeemed in an Apostolic Office, meant to be as perpetual as the most Holy Sacrament.

"Lo, I am with you alway, even *unto the end of the world.*"

"As often as ye eat this bread, and drink this cup, ye do show the Lord's death, *till he come.*"

So also it is written to Timothy, "The same commit thou to faithful men" . . . . "that thou keep this commandment *until the appearing of the Lord Jesus Christ.*" If the Presbyterians are right in casting off the perpetuity of the Apostles, the Quakers, as I have said before, are much more right in casting off the perpetuity of the inferior ministry and the sacraments, as being necessary only in the elementary condition of the Church, to set it going. But delightful it is to know that, for the first three hundred years, in which all other facts, not excepting the Divinity of our Blessed Lord, were ruthlessly subjected to wild discussion: there was one fact, not only not contested, but not even discussed*—the succession in the line of the Apostles, unbroken, perpetual, and ever offering to the Christian world a tangible starting-point for the recovery of ancient unity and peace and love; vindicating at the same time the ways of God, who has been consistent with himself in transferring to the Gentiles the Prelacy which he had established and preserved among the Jews.

ADDENDUM.

It cannot be supposed that I overlooked St. Paul's saying to Timothy, "Neglect not the gift that is in thee, which was given thee by prophecy, with the laying on of the hands of the *Presbytery:*" for I felt for a long time concerning it, like the old lady, who was always satisfied with the sermon, if it had only in it "that sweet word *Mesopotamia.*" But to be grave:

The learned Grotius declares he "would not allow himself to adduce this passage in proof of the custom, [of the Presbyters laying on hands with those of the Bishop,] because Ambrose [Hilary] and Jerome, among the ancients, and Calvin, the chief of the moderns, interpret Presbytery here to mean *the office* to which Timothy was promoted." But let it mean the collection of persons that laid on hands: and even then, the Apostles are called Presbyters, so several of them acting together might well be called a Presbytery. And

* Dr. Miller himself says, "No Father of the Church, for the first three hundred years, ever discussed the question of the Prelacy:"—*admitted.* And again, "Jerome at the close of the fourth century, was the first to *discuss* the question of parity." We beg the Doctor's pardon. Aërius, who denied his Lord, was the first known to the Church, who cavilled at the Episcopacy.

so Ignatius, in their day, uses the word: προσφυγῶν τῷ εὐαγγελίῳ ὡς σαρκὶ Ἰησοῦ, καὶ τοῖς Ἀποστόλοις ὡς πρεσβυτερίῳ ἐκκλησίας—fleeing to the gospel as to the flesh of Jesus, and to the *Apostles* as *the Presbytery of the Church*." I could find the word in but two other places in the New Testament,* in both which it means the highest ecclesiastical court known to the Jewish Church; and St. Luke and St. Paul, being companions, and the only persons that use the words at all it seems to point to the highest ordaining power in the Christian Church. Add to these considerations, that Paul the Apostle was certainly himself one of that Presbytery, for he says,† "Stir up the gift of God, which is in thee by the putting on of *my hands*." Observe, moreover, that St. Paul ascribes no virtue whatever to "the hands of the Presbytery:" for he says, in the passage, "the gift that is in thee, which was given thee (διά) BY *prophecy*, (μετά) WITH the laying on of the hands of the *Presbytery;*" and, in the other, "the gift of God, which is given thee, (διά) BY the putting on of MY hands." The virtue is in the one ascribed solely to the "prophecy," and in the other solely to "*the hands of Paul.*" That this transaction was accompanied *with* the hands of others—whether Apostles or Presbyters, consenting to the act of the consecration—is of no consequence whatever. St. Paul was to Timothy precisely what Timothy was to be to others in Ephesus—the ordaining power, the *sine qua non.*

"But," say you, "Timothy is called an 'Evangelist.'" So is Philip the Deacon; was Timothy, then, only a Deacon? St. Paul says, indeed, "Do the work of an evangelist:" but please to read on, "make full proof of thy ministry, (Gr. *deaconship.*)" Thus you play upon words, until you reduce Timothy to a Deacon! Why not go a little further and say, with the "evangelical Neander," that there is little evi-

* Luke, xxii. 66. Acts, xxii. 5. † 2 Timothy, i. 6.

dence that St. Paul ever wrote this first Epistle to Timothy at all? Or else take ground with the Rev. Edwin Hall, a recent assailant of the Church in Connecticut, who says very learnedly, on the passage, "For this cause left I thee in Crete, that thou shouldest ordain elders in every city," that the word *ordain* "in the original has no possible reference to any ceremony or mode of ordination," being the same word that is used in the passage, "By one man's disobedience many were *made* sinners:" whereupon the learned Sectarist exclaims, "There is no more reference to a mystic ceremony of ordination in the case of Titus, than there is of a mystic ordination to make men sinners."* So Mr. Hall would revive the Levitical priesthood in the Church: for if men must be "made ministers" precisely as they are "*made sinners*," I see no other way than, as it was among the Jews, by genealogical descent. Gentlemen, go on! All this harms not the Church.

Nor did I overlook the passage† alleged by Dr. Miller as a notable record of a Presbyterian ordination: "When they had fasted and prayed, and laid their hands on them (on Barnabas and St. Paul,) they sent them away." Now mark the learned Doctor! "*This*," says he, "*is the most ample account of an ordination to be found in the Scripture;* and it is an account which, if there were no other, would be sufficient to decide the present controversy in our favor." I accept the challenge. In that very passage, Barnabas and Paul are said, before this "ordination," to be "prophets and teachers" already, "ministering to the Lord:" so that if Paul and Barnabas were ordained a *second* time by the other three prophets, it must have been to a higher office than that of either "prophet or teacher." And the argument, in the mouth of a Presbyterian, is suicidal: for it makes Paul and Barnabas to be Apostles, ordained as such by the hands

* See Chapin's excellent reply, "Puritanism not Protestantism."

† Acts, xiii.

of men acting under the express instruction of "the Spirit;" and these Presbyterian "prophets" are commanded by revelation to *add two more* to the number of the Twelve! A fine day's work for Presbyterians! Those "primitive Presbyterians" seem to have discovered very early that the Church required more than Twelve Apostles! *We* have no objection to this view. But the truth is, the context declares they were called to a specific "work," which they "fulfilled" and "returned to Antioch, from whence they had been (not ordained, but) commended to the grace of God for *the work* which *they fulfilled.*" Moreover, St. Paul had been an Apostle eight or ten years before this transaction at Antioch, and expressly and solemnly reiterates, that he was an Apostle, "not of man nor by man," nor even did he go up "to them that were Apostles before him;" so that if he was now "ordained," it was to *something higher than the apostolic office* which he held before. Let us beware, lest, in escaping from the three orders, we may run into a *fourth;* and make "Peter and Paul," for the circumcision and the uncircumcision, the founders of the Papacy! Really, we think that Dr. Miller's "ordaining" St. Paul after he had been ten years an Apostle, entitles him to rank with Mr. Hall, who would have Bishops "made" as men are "made sinners!" If it had been true, that Paul and Barnabas were, by this transaction, ordained to the Apostleship, we should have no reason in the world for disputing it: for the parties concerned were "prophets," and, by usage since the days of Adam, "prophets" could, under inspiration evidenced by suitable signs, make and unmake Priests, Kings, and Empires; and even an infant-prophet, like Samuel, could pour upon the hoary head of a High Priest, a blessing or a curse. Do let "the prophets" at Antioch send the two Apostles forth on a short mission with their blessing, without making it out "*the most ample account of an ordination to be found in Scripture!*"

CHAPTER XXIII.

NUMBER FOUR; OR, PRESBYTERIANISM AMONG THE FATHERS.

WHAT was there to oppose this array of Scripture? The Fathers of the Church? Who can tell? We know the restlessness of human nature. Scarcely were the thunders or the trumpet on the mountain hushed, when Korah and the Levites of the lower order said to the Prelate-Priests: "Ye take too much upon you, ye sons of Aaron, seeing all the congregation are holy, and the Lord is among them!" Nor would it have been strange, if the severity of discipline under which the Bishops held the church and clergy in early ages, and to which modern times furnish no approximation, should have caused the like murmurings of discontent. But no. For three hundred years of piety and miracle and discipline, there was not a voice raised, within or without the church, against the Episcopacy. Aërius—"the madman," as he was called in his own times—was the first to assail it, under the specious, but till then unheard-of, play upon the words "Presbyter" and "Bishop;" a *ruse* which Theodoret instantly met, by reminding the faithful that those who, in humility, were now called Bishops, had been in earlier ages called Apostles. Nor is it strange that the man who denied the Divinity of the Master, should have sought to cast the Master's servants out of the vineyard. No, Gentlemen, no; you cannot father your new faith upon Jerome! Aërius, of the band of Arius who betrayed the Master, is, in respect of the Episcopacy, the father of you all!

I left Princeton, as sure that at least Augustine, and Hilary, and Jerome, and Cyprian, were Presbyterians at heart, as that Dr. Miller was. And if they were not, it certainly was not the Doctor's fault, who did his very best, by every *ex post facto* art, to *make* them so. It mattered not that these men lived four and five hundred years after Paul and Peter and John. They were men of learning; and, what was more, they were Fathers; and with me, as with Mr. Hall, a Father was a Father, without regard to his age. As soon therefore, as I could, I furnished myself with the best Benedictine editions of these Fathers; that, under the far-reaching shadow of my Presbyterian vine, I might regale myself, in the years to come, on their record of its planting by apostolic hands. Accordingly I read these Fathers, and—O ye stars and light! finding *them* Episcopalians, whither should I fly? Sermons upon sermons, commentaries on commentaries, Epistles on Epistles, heaps upon heaps:—will there be no end, said I, to this testimony for Episcopacy? Not more surprised could I have been if Cyprian and Augustine, mitred and crosiered, and Jerome with cowl and scowl, had stood in their winding-sheets before me, to protest, one and all, against the slur for now two hundred years attempted to be cast upon their memories.

But what did these men *mean*, say the pupils of Dr. Miller, by those famous passages *against* Episcopacy, so indelibly impressed upon our memory? So the Socinian inquires, What did inspired men *mean*, by representing our Lord as not knowing the judgment day? What did Paul *mean* by saying, "I have no commandment of the Lord, yet I give my judgment;" "I suppose, therefore;" "I speak by permission, not by commandment;" "the rest speak I, not the Lord;" "I think also that I have the Spirit of God?" Just as the infidel pounces upon certain passages, and separates them from the rest of Scripture; or as the "Little-children Baptists," or "Mormons," or "Glory-Alleluia Brethren," or "Universalists," or "Perfectionists," or "Live-for-evers," or "Predestinationists," fasten on certain texts, isolating them from the whole tenor and drift and spirit of Scripture: so Blondel, and Mason, and Miller, and Potts, seize upon *the word* Presbytery or *the word* Bishop, in writings inspired; and, in writings uninspired, fasten upon certain passages, which, if they prove any thing Presbyterianish, prove that some of the Fathers entirely forgot, at times, that they had written quartos and folios teeming with the opposite doctrine! Even the humble writer of these pages would feel it an injury done to his memory, if hereafter, in order to make it seem that the Churchmen of this day held the Episcopacy in little esteem or reverence, it should be alleged that, in a chapter on Catholicity, he alluded (but it was pain and grief to him) to sentinels at the gates who admired more, and defended with more zeal, the trappings of their office, than the treasures of the palace; and that he avowed, if the Episcopacy were all that separated him from the sects around, he would cry, with all the earnestness he could throw into a prayer: *Perish Episcopacy!* And so I would; for, without judging another man's servant, *in me* the absurdity would be exceeded only by the wickedness of pretending agreement with the sects around me in "all that was evangelical and essential," and yet withholding the hand of fellowship because they did not agree with me about *the rank* of the servants at the door! If the treasures were safe without them, what should I care about the sentinels? Yet this is the way in which the memories of these Fathers have suffered. Read their writings for yourself, and do not rely even on an earnest "*Perish Episcopacy*" hunted up out of ten or twenty volumes, with "a hound's scent, that can smell further than it can see."

A man who can say, with Dr. Miller, of the transaction at Antioch, that it is "the most ample account of *an ordination* to be found in Scripture," when St. Paul had been an Apostle many years before, and over and over denies that he was made an Apostle by the hands of men;—this, moreover, to students and Christians who have the Bible in their hands: such a man is certainly quite competent to the task of metamorphosing Jerome, Augustine, Hilary, and Cyprian, or even Irenæus and Ignatius, into Presbyterians; at least to the satisfaction of students and people in whose hands the writings of these fathers *never were, and never will be, seen.* If they do these things in a green tree, what will be done in the dry?

Poor Augustine! Little did he dream that a delicate *tour de phrase* in a private letter to Jerome would, after the lapse of a thousand years, be construed into a concession that a Bishop had no prerogative of right above a Presbyter! The compliment runs thus:

"Atque identidem rogo, ut me fidenter corrigas, ubi mihi hoc opus esse perspexeris. Quanquam enim secundum honorum vocabula, quæ jam Ecclesiæ usus obtinuerit, Episcopatus Presbyterio major sit, tamen in multis rebus Augustinus Hieronymo minor est; licet etiam a minore quolibet non sit refugienda vel dedignanda correctio."

"And indeed I beg that you would from time to time correct me, when you see plainly that I need it. For although, *according to the titles of honors which the usage of the Church has now** *established*, the Episcopate is greater than the Presbytery† [here Dr. Snodgrass inserts the words, "*not by authority of the Scriptures*"]: yet in many respects Augustine is inferior to Jerome; though correction from any manner of inferior ought not to be avoided or disdained."

* The word *now* (not *jampridem*, nor *jamdiu*, but *jam*) signifying that these titles were *recent*, is omitted by Dr. Miller.

† In the Lecture Room at Princeton, the words here inserted, according to my notes, are "Yet it was not so in the Apostles' days!"

Now what were the high-sounding "titles of honors" thus heaped upon the Bishops in the times of Augustine? Let us turn to the passage, and we shall find the following explanation. Augustine had written to Jerome a friendly remonstrance, respecting some interpretations upon holy Scripture from the pen of that learned Presbyter; and, through the carelessness or malice of the bearer, the letters were seen in Italy, and their contents divulged to the injury of Jerome. Whereupon Jerome wrote a characteristic letter to the Bishop; at which the poor Bishop, who was both as innocent and ignorant of the affront as a child unborn, was exceedingly perplexed. A second letter came. A third. Shorter and sweeter the missives grew, as time went on, and the *amende honorable* was not forthcoming from the bewildered Bishop. But Jerome covers up the bitterness of his indignation with the honeyed words, "your Holiness," "your Blessedness," "most happy Pope," or "Father," and the like. Meantime the solution of the mystery reaches Augustine:—the bearer of his letter had blazoned it by the way, in Italy. And now he writes to Jerome an explanation, in the most soothing terms he can employ. But, forasmuch as he cannot reciprocate the honorary "titles" by which *the usage of the Church* had "of late" distinguished the Bishop above the Presbyter: yet, very naturally and very sensibly and very delicately too, he compliments the Presbyter to whom he was writing, as being in many things superior to himself. And pray what does all this prove? That a Bishop was no better than a Presbyter? Nay, it proves only that Augustine was a *gentleman;* and so endowed with no mean qualification for his office. Yet this is all, so far as I can hear, that the sectarists of the last three hundred years have been able to extract from *sixteen huge folio volumes* of a Father who, speaking of Aërius, who was the first to reject the Episcopacy, says:

"Aëriani ab Aërio quodam sunt, qui, cum esset Presbyter, diluisse fertur quod Episcopus non potuit ordinari; et in Arianorum hæresim lapsus, propria quoque addidisse dogmata* nonnulla, dicens—Presbyterum ab Episcopo nulla differentia debere discerni."

"The Aërians are from one Aërius, who, when a Presbyter, is related to have taken it hard that he could not be ordained a Bishop; and, falling into the Arian heresy, is reported to have added also some dogmas* of *his own*, saying that a Presbyter ought not to be accounted in any respect different from a Bishop."

And poor Chrysostom! I have thy pardon, too, to crave, for having believed that, through the two-leaved gates of thy golden mouth, there came forth once a word to betray the unity of the Episcopacy, into the hands of a schism yet future by twelve hundred years. I was told by one whom I believed, and who received it by oral tradition, I suppose, that thou hadst said, about the year of Grace 400, that "They (the Bishops) *have gained the ascendency* over the Presbyters only in ordination, and *in this they have defrauded them.*" But thy words had fortunately been written down; and, on looking at them for myself, I found that thou hadst never uttered such a thought, neither came it into thy mind. Thy words were, "In the laying on of hands alone have the Bishops been above the Presbyters, and in this only do they seem to have the pre-eminence:"—γαρ χειροτονίᾳ μόνῃ ὑπερβεβήκασι, καὶ τούτῳ μόνον δοκοῦσι πλεονεκτεῖν τοῖς πρεσβυτέροις. And this is the very essence and quintessence of our claim: *that the laying on of hands* (for the word χειροτονία includes more than ordination) is the grand prerogative lodged with the Bishops. Yet this is all that art and learning have been able, these three hundred years, to rake up for Presbytery, out of ten ponderous tomes of the great Bishop and orator of Constantinople. But though we have done with the testimony,

* Epiphanius, of the same age, calls this dogma of Aërius, *Dogma furiosum et stolidum—a wild and crazy dogma.*

yet it may amuse the reader to see two translations of this passage from the same pen.

DR. MILLER'S PRINTED LETTERS ON THE CHRISTIAN MINISTRY, 1807.

"In ordination alone, they (the Bishops) have *gone beyond* the Presbyters." [Nothing said about the original.]

LECTURE ROOM VERSION, PRINCETON, JAN. 7, 1831.

"They (the Bishops) *have gained the ascendency* over the Presbyters only in ordination, *and in this they have defrauded them—defrauded*, πλεονεκτεῖν—the same word used in the Bible, Let no man *defraud* his brother."

Really, here is an exegesis worthy of Mr. Hall, the discoverer that the word used for ordaining *Bishops* is the very same word used for making men *sinners*. And both are admirably on a par with the exegesis of the grave Divine who says, that all Paul meant by saying to Timothy, "Lay hands suddenly on no man," was to caution him *never to strike a man in a passion:* proving his interpretation in the usual way, too, by "comparing Scripture with Scripture;" for it is written in the same Epistle, and also in the Epistle to Titus, that a Bishop must be "*no striker!*" *Quod erat demonstrandum.*

Surely, had Chrysostom been a Presbyterian, we should have had some glimpse of it in his commentary on the expression, "with the laying on of the hands of the Presbytery:" but there he says, "The Apostle here speaks, not of Presbyters, but of Bishops; for Presbyters did not ordain a Bishop." Chrysostom, by the by, to recall the subject of the last chapter, is one who styles Timothy "The Apostle and Bishop of Ephesus;" and speaks of Ignatius as succeeding St. Peter in Antioch, and as being "worthy of so large a principality; for how great must we suppose his virtue and wisdom to have been, to be intrusted with the rule of so renowned a city, and the government of a people numbering two hundred thousand men!" Also, upon the passage,* "With the Bishops and Deacons," Chrysostom asks, "How is this? Were there many Bishops in one city! By no means. But he calls the Presbyters by this name." So that if this renowned Bishop was a Presbyterian, all the Episcopalians of the nineteenth century are Presbyterians: for they believe with Chrysostom that Bishop and Presbyter designated the pastoral function, during the period that "Apostle" designated Episcopal.

Poor Theodoret, too, about A. D. 440, in a commentary on 1 Tim. iii. 1, had said, "The Apostles call a Presbyter a Bishop, as we showed when we expounded the Epistle to the Philippians. . . . . For, as I said, of old they called the same men both Bishops and Presbyters." Another hint, say you, of Presbyterianism? Wait one moment. He says we must turn to his commentary on the Philippians, which runs thus: "Epaphroditus was the Apostle of the Philippians, because he was intrusted with the Episcopal government, under the appellation of *Apostle*, ... that those who, although in the order of Presbyters, were called Bishops in the beginning, *should be subject to him.*" But this reference is unnecessary. Dr. Miller chose to end his quotation with the words, "*Of old* they called the same men both *Bishops* and *Presbyters.*" What could be more conclusive? But, Sirs, not quite so fast. I will not trouble you to turn to the commentary on Philippians to which Theodoret refers you: I only ask you to read *six lines further on* in the very passage Dr. Miller has undertaken to quote. Theodoret indeed does say, "Of old they called the same men both Bishops and Presbyters:" but, only six lines further on, he adds: "For those, as I have said, whom we now call *Bishops*, were in old times called *Apostles;* but, in process of time, the name of Apostle was left to those who were in the strict

* Philip. i. 1.

sense Apostles, [sent personally by the Saviour,] and the name of Bishop was restrained to those who were anciently called Apostles; thus was Epaphroditus the Apostle of the Philippians, Titus of the Cretans, and Timothy *the Apostle* of the Asiatics." Yet this passage, only six lines further on in the very same paragraph, as also the one to which Theodoret so expressly refers the student to prevent any misconception of his meaning, are kept by Dr. Miller both out of his "Letters" and out of his "Lectures!" Is it any wonder that the students of Princeton make zealous Presbyterians? How could it be otherwise?

And poor Hilary, to you also must I make apology, for *imputing* to you, in my Calvinistic days, a sin that was certainly *not yours*. It may have been good Calvinism in me to do so, but I am ready to acknowledge that it was not fair play. You said (or so I heard) that "In Egypt, even to this day, in the Bishop's absence the Presbyters ordain." Who can wonder that I was a Presbyterian, when so conclusive a testimony, escaping the vigilance of monks and mitres for a thousand years, now burst its cloistered sepulchre to bear witness to the truth? But did Hilary say it? What *did* he say? He said exactly this:*

"Denique, apud Egyptum, Presbyteri consignant, si præsens non sit Episcopus."	"Finally, in Egypt, the Presbyters sign or seal, if the Bishop be not present."

Every body knows that *ordino* is the Latin word to express the act of *ordination*. Its use for this purpose is universal. On the contrary, it is doubted whether the word *consigno* was ever employed, in any single instance since the world began, to express the act of ordination. Moreover, we believe that for two centuries sectarians have been looking for a passage in antiquity where this word has such a meaning,

* Hilary, the Deacon, as the learned are generally agreed: not Hilary, the Bishop.

and, so far as I remember, they are not yet able to produce it. Besides, is ordination so trifling a matter, that it is not worth while to wait till the Bishop could be "present?" And are we to believe that Hilary could have supposed that Presbyters in his day ordained in Egypt, when he must have known that, even prior to the Council of Nice, a Council in Alexandria itself had formally pronounced the ordinations of one Colythus to be *no* ordinations, and his Presbyters to be *no* Presbyters, because it was discovered that Colythus was but a Presbyter himself, having never received due Episcopal consecration?—for the Council are careful to explain that they do not depose these men as Presbyters, on the ground of schism; but merely make it known to the Churches that, Colythus being only a pretended Bishop, the persons he pretended to ordain were neither now, nor ever had been, Presbyters. What was it then that the Presbyters of Egypt did, in the absence of the Bishop? Perhaps they absolved returning penitents, an office usually allowed to the Bishops. Perhaps even Cyprian, in his exile, had allowed them to do so at Carthage. Perhaps they gave tickets of readmission, under the Bishop's name and *seal*, to those who had lapsed in time of persecution. Perhaps in the Bishop's Cathedral, or Basilica, they gave the solemn benediction in the Bishop's place. Or, I am willing to admit that, possibly, in the Bishop's absence, the Presbyters *confirmed*, for it may *possibly* be that the Church in Egypt fell, in this respect, into a usage of the present Church of Rome, practised in our own day, in Porto Rico and elsewhere, where political motives have, at times, prevented the residence of a Bishop. But, let *consignant* mean what it may, we are yet to see the first passage in antiquity where it signifies to *ordain*. We are strongly of opinion that it has reference to "trifles light as air." The passage (too long to quote) is a commentary on Ephesians, iv. 11. "He gave some, Apostles; and some, Prophets;

and some, Evangelists; and some, Pastors and Teachers, &c." "The Apostles," he says, "are the Bishops—Apostoli sunt Episcopi; the Prophets, expounders of Scripture; the Evangelists are the Deacons, &c. For in the Bishop are contained all the other orders: because he is the first priest, that is, he is the Chief, or Prince of the Priests; and he is also the Chief Prophet, and Evangelist, &c."* Why does Dr. Miller omit this from the beginning of the passage he pretends to quote? Hilary goes on to say that "after churches were established, things were settled otherwise than at the beginning, for the sake of order." Why not tell us, Doctor, what these awful innovations are? Hilary tells us thus: Philip did not demand a long probation of the Eunuch, or interpose a period of fasting; but baptised him on the spot: the Church now requires a probation and a fast. Paul and Silas did not require time, in the baptism of the jailor: the Church at the present time requires a delay. Peter had no deacon to assist in baptising Cornelius and his house, for as yet the deacons were but seven. "And here it is," adds Hilary—but we cannot consent to go on further with Dr. Miller's version only; we place our own more literal translation by its side.

HIS.†	OURS.†
"And here it is that the Apostle's writings do not in all things	And hence it is that the writings of the Apostle do not in all

* "Nam in Episcopo omnes ordines sunt, quia Primus Sacerdos, hoc est, Princeps est sacerdotum, et Propheta, et Evangelista, et cætera."

† "Ideo non per omnia conveniunt scripta apostoli ordinationi quæ nunc in Ecclesia est; quia hæc inter ipsa primordia sunt scripta. Nam et Timotheum Presbyterum a se creatum Episcopum vocat, quia Primi Presbyteri Episcopi appellabantur, ut recedente eo sequens ei succederet. Denique apud Ægyptum Presbyteri consignant, si præsens non sit Episcopus. Sed quia coeperunt sequentes Presbyteri indigni inveniri ad Primatus tenendos, immutata est ratio, prospiciente concilio ut non ordo, sed meritum crearet Episcopum constitutum multorum sacerdotum judicio, ne indignus temere usurparet, et esset multis scandalum." It will be observed that the sentence about Egypt abruptly breaks the progress of the passage, and the unity of the writer's idea respecting the succession to the Episcopate, of the Presbyter next in order. Besides, it is nearly the identical

agree to the present constitution of the Church; because they are written under the first rise of the Church—for he calls Timothy, who was created a Presbyter by him, a Bishop, for so at first the Presbyters were called;* among whom this was the course of governing the Churches, that as one withdrew, another took his place; and in Egypt, even at this day, the Presbyters ordain in the Bishop's absence. But because the following Presbyters began to be found unworthy to hold the first place, the method was changed, the Council providing that not order, but merit, should create a Bishop."

things agree to the present order of the Church; because they were written *amidst the very beginnings* of the Church. For he calls Timothy, who was created a Presbyter by him, a Bishop, (for the First Presbyters were called Bishops;) so that, on his departure, the *one following* [or *the next in order*] should succeed him. Finally, in Egypt, [the words "even at this day" are an interpolation by the Doctor] the Presbyters sign, [or seal, or absolve from censure, or *confirm*, if you please; but it nowhere means ordain,] if the Bishop be not present. But because the Presbyters *next following* [or *next in order*] began to be found unworthy to hold the Primacies, (Primatus,) the method was changed, the Council providing that not order but merit should make a Bishop, who should be appointed by the judgment of many priests, lest one unworthy should rashly usurp the office, and become a scandal to many.

Now what does all this amount to? Simply, that the Egyptians had changed the old-fashioned way of obtaining a successor to the Episcopate. In old times, he says, the

passage in a fragment once attributed falsely to Augustine: "Nam in Alexandria et per totum Ægyptum, si desit Episcopus, consecrat Presbyter." Whether Hilary be the author of *this* fragment or not, Presbyterians could make no use of it, and indeed, I believe, do not adduce it: for, supposing it had a reference to ordination, it says *consecrat Presbyter*, not *consecrant Presbyteri.*

* So Dr. Miller renders it; or, more literally, "for so the first (*primi*) Presbyters were called." This, then, was another of the *innovations*, that those who were once called Apostles, now went by the unassuming name of Bishops, by which even Presbyters were called at first.

Presbyter next in seniority (of age or orders) succeeded to *the primacy :* but because the next in order was often unfit, a council decreed it should be determined by election. Now to all this add: "*Finally—Denique*, (an important word, overlooked by Dr. Miller,) in Egypt, the Presbyters (if you please) *confirm* if the Bishop is not present," and it makes another of *the innovations* practised by the Church in Egypt! Here is the list of these *innovations :* 1. The candidate for baptism must submit to a probation; 2. He must perform an alloted fast; 3. A Priest has now-a-days a deacon to assist him at baptism; 4. A Bishop is no longer called by his ancient title of Apostle; 5. Nor a Presbyter called Bishop as of old; 6. The next oldest Presbyter does not succeed to the Episcopate, as he did formerly in Egypt; 7. A Layman is not now permitted to baptise; 8. *Deacons* no longer preach; 9. *Finally*, (*denique—to conclude, in fine, finally, lastly*—say the lexicons,) in Egypt, if the Bishop be absent, the Presbyters bless, absolve, consecrate the Chrism, confirm —no matter what—it is the *denique*, the last and worst of the innovations! But even in Egypt—land of the old magicians, land of Jannes and Jambres—they never dreamed that Presbyters could make a Bishop. Dr. Miller leaves out the word *finally*, and inserts, "even at the present day." We have seen Dr. Miller's omission too of the commencement of this passage, that *Bishops are the Apostles.* But among Hilary's alleged *innovations*, Dr. Miller takes care not to notice another, viz.: that in his days the Deacons did not preach; although he had before quoted the fact that as "Bishops were Apostles," so Deacons were and ought to be Evangelists or preachers! Certainly if Presbyterians, who stop the mouths of their Deacons, are satisfied with the passage they have found, we, for our part, are quite delighted. In St. Paul's days, "Bishops were called Apostles," and in the days of St. Peter, "Deacons preached!"

But you have only had the Doctor's translation: now take his comment. I ask the *candid* reader to judge between the comment and the fact.

COMMENT.

"In this passage . . . . Hilary declares that Presbyters, even then, sometimes ordained; and that the reason of their not continuing to exercise this power was, that many of them being unfit to be trusted with such a power, it was taken out of their hands, as a prudential measure, by the authority of the Church."

FACT.

In this passage Hilary says not one word about Presbyters ordaining; and declares that their confirming (if it was so much) in the Bishop's absence, was an *innovation.* He thinks, too, that the reason why the next Presbyter in order did not now succeed to the Primacy was, that thus unfit men sometimes obtained the "Primacies:" which indicated the expediency of resorting, in case of vacancy, to an election.

The Princeton "Professor of Church History and Government," adduces also Hilary's commentary on 1 Tim. iii. 8, which we will compare with Hilary himself.

DOCTOR MILLER.

"Hilary affirms—'The ordination of Bishop, and ordination of Bishop and Presbyter, is one and the same.' Could he possibly have said this, if they had been different orders, and had received a different ordination?"

HILARY.

"After the Bishop, the Apostle proceeds to the ordination of Deacons. Why? Because the ordination of Bishops and Presbyters is one; for *each is a Priest. Every Bishop is a Presbyter, though every Presbyter is not a Bishop; nor was it lawful or allowed*—neque enim fas erat aut licebat—*that an inferior should ordain a superior; for no one can give what he has not received.*"

Fain would I here take leave of Hilary. But Dr. Miller, in his last book of 1835, prepared expressly as a permanent work for the Presbyterian Tract and Sunday School Society, says, on page 57: "Ambrose, in the fourth century, in his commentary on the Ephesians, expressly declares that, in his day, the Deacons ordinarily were not authorized to preach." Now, who would suspect, Dr. Miller, that this quotation is from the commentary of Hilary, and from the very passage in that commentary* which we were but now considering? *Then* you rightly called the writer *Hilary*, now you call him *Ambrose!* This, however, we may forgive; it has not misled us.† But how shall we forgive your adducing this passage as a proof that the Deacons were not generally authorized to preach until after the days of Hilary: when Hilary declares, that their not being allowed to preach then, was an *encroachment on their rights*, and one of the nine or ten *innovations* he speaks of in the Church, alleging, out of Scripture, that Philip the Deacon was a *preacher*, and that "Deacons were *Evangelists!*" Can we wonder that Princeton has made Presbyterians? Or that Presbyterians have made dumb Deacons?

Very queer quotations these of the Doctor's! But no matter: Hilary must serve them one more good turn before they can let him go. They have done their best to make him out an enemy to the Bishops; why not also prove him to be a friend to ruling Elders? Here is the proof! "Wherefore," says Hilary, on 1 Tim. v. 1, "both the Synagogue, and afterwards the Church, had *Elders*, without whose counsel nothing was done in the Church; *which order*, by what negligence it grew into disuse, I know not, unless perhaps by the sloth, or rather the pride of the teachers, while they alone wished to appear something." This passage made on me

* Ephes. iv. 2.

† That these commentaries were attributed to Ambrose falsely, has been established within 300 years, Erasmus leading the way; and they are now commonly credited to Hilary, the Deacon. How does Mr. Miller quote them as from Ambrose in his *last* book, when in a former one he was correct? Is he going backward in his learning?

a strong impression. "Synagogue!" "Elders!" "Which *order!*" "Grown into *disuse!*" For years I believed the tradition. At length I turned to the passage, and, as usual, found that the clew to its meaning had been omitted in the quotation. It is on the injunction to Timothy, to treat "old men as fathers, young men as brothers, the elder women as mothers, the younger as sisters." It begins: "Apud omnes gentes utique honorabilis est senectus," &c. "Among all nations old age is held in honor. Whence the Synagogue, and afterwards the Church, had its old men, (not Elders, *not Presbyters*, but elderly persons, seniors,) whom it was usual to consult. Which—not "*which order*," as Dr. Miller renders it, but—which *custom of taking advice from the aged* had been laid aside." A sort of church-wardens, perhaps, of whom even still one is commonly that highly respectable individual, "the oldest inhabitant," at that time dispensed with! Or, it may have been a council of advice, both of laymen and Presbyters: a council which all the Bishops of the Church in this country enjoy, and which is often composed of the aged and wise. But the idea of turning these old gentlemen into "*Elders*" and calling them an "order," is really laughable.

These may suffice as examples of the strange things which I formerly credited, on *traditions* handed down from Salmasius and Blondel to the present race of Presbyterians. Indeed, I once believed of the world-renowned Irenæus, born twenty-five years before the death of St. John, and Bishop of Lyons, that "while he held this station," (so says Dr. Miller,) "he was the bearer of a letter from 'the Presbytery of Lyons to Eleutherius the Bishop of Rome,' in which the Presbyters call him their *brother* and *colleague!*" The Doctor says that Irenæus took the letter, when he was sent "on some special ecclesiastical business to Rome." But what was this "special business?" Let us see. A frightful persecution rages at

Lyons. The blood of the martyrs dyes the streets. Pothinus, *their Bishop*, has just received the crown of martyrdom, at the age of ninety. His Presbyters, as was done in the case of Ignatius and of Polycarp, instantly send news of it to Asia and Phrygia; and by Irenæus, their "brother and colleague," to Rome. It was not until the Church at Lyons could take breath, that this disciple of Polycarp, who was in turn the disciple of St. John, was, *after his return* from Rome, ordained the successor of Pothinus! When will our Presbyterian Divines learn to be accurate? So, likewise, I believed on a modern tradition, (for the traditions of Presbyterianism, like those of Popery, are extremely modern,) that Cyprian, the renowned Bishop of Carthage, had called a very worthy man named Numidicus, "*a ruling Elder*," and had promised to promote him to the office of "teaching Presbyter." But the words of Cyprian are, "Promovebitur quidem, cum Deus permiserit, ad *ampliorem locum* suæ religionis"—not to a higher, *but a wider place*, or field, or sphere. And, to prove that this is so, Cyprian in this very Epistle declares that he is commanded by revelation to add "*the Presbyter* Numidicus to the roll of the Presbyters of *Carthage;* that our numbers, which the lapse of some Presbyters hath lessened, may be replenished with such glorious priests—*gloriosis Sacerdotibus*." So my ruling Elder turned out to be a glorious Priest! And a right *glorious Priest* he was! For, while the Presbyters of the city were cowering before the executioner, and their ranks were thinning out, partly by martyrdom, but more by apostasy: he, an obscure and humble country-Presbyter, came to the notice of his Bishop, as one who, by his exhortations, had sustained numbers of martyrs while they were burned or stoned to death; and had seen, unshaken, his own wife committed to the flames; and who, after being roasted and stoned himself, was left for dead, when his daughter discovered him under a pile of stones, and, by her courage and her skill, brought him back to life. No wonder Cyprian desired such piety to shine in a "wider sphere!" Nor is it, at the same time, wonderful that the young men at Princeton believe in ruling Elders!*

This is about as far as I ever went in believing the strange things that are handed down at Princeton concerning the Fathers. I do not think I ever believed that the General Council of about two hundred Bishops which condemned the heresy of Nestorius, numbered "six thousand Bishops;" or (the fact so well authenicated, says Dr. Miller) that St. Patrick, a Bishop sent under the auspices of the Pope of Rome to Ireland, ordained "three hundred and sixty-five Bishops or pastors, and "three thousand ruling Elders;" or that a single metropolitan had "six thousand Bishops" under him; or, that "the Bishop of Antioch, or Rome, or Carthage, even until the fourth century, was the pastor of a single congregation," although I did not then know that, at the end of the *third* century, Dioclesian destroyed *forty Churches in the city of Rome;* and that Rome, in the middle of the same century, had forty-six Presbyters, fourteen Deacons, above fifteen hundred poor, supported from the offerings, and an innumerable multitude of people, that aided or sustained many other Churches in different cities, even as far as Arabia and Syria. Nor did I know that in the "parish" of Constantinople there were at the same time sixty Presbyters; and in the "parish" of Carthage a large number, for many of them cowered before the persecution, and Cyprian, himself afterwards a martyr, names eight that were yet celebrated in the list; and, in the passage concerning Nu-

* "Who, sir," says Dr. Bowden, in a colloquy with Dr. Miller, "informed you that there were ruling Elders in Carthage?" "Cyprian, Ep. 39." "Go on, sir, if you please:" "Cyprian, writing to his Presbyters, and Elders, and people,"—"Stop here one moment; that is not the address of the Epistle. It runs thus—'Cyprian, to his Presbyters, and Deacons, and to all the people, his brethren, sendeth greeting.' You add *Elders*, which is not in the address. This is not quite fair. I am sorry you should have had recourse to it, but I will put it to the account of those things *quas inuria fudit.* Now, this being corrected, proceed."

midicus, he speaks of replenishing the "*copiam*, or abundance," of his Presbyters with such "illustrious priests," and says that the persecution was so terrific, that every day "thousands" of cards were issued by the confessors and martyrs for the reconciliation of those who had lapsed; and another writer says, that when the persecutor entered Carthage, about A. D. 240, he found there *Episcopum et maximam turbam clericorum*—"the Bishop and a very great crowd of clergymen:" all in addition to the fact that we find recorded accidentally, not long afterwards, the very names of the Cathedral and seven of the principal churches. Bishops of a "single congregation," Gentlemen? Surely you cannot be in earnest! Still, I see that, in close quarters, it is the only shift you can make. "Six thousand Bishops in a province," when you wish to show that a Bishop had only a single congregation; and, in the next breath, "but one congregation in all Constantinople, or Rome, or Carthage," when you have to show that each congregation had its Bishop! What can be the origin of this fanciful idea?* With Lord King, towards two centuries ago, it seems to have weighed considerably, that a Diocese was, in the language of the Fathers, called a *parish*—παροικία. He seems not to have observed, until Sclater drew his attention to the fact, that the Greek word *diœcesis* (diocese) was rendered by the Latin *parochia* (parish); that Jerome so renders it himself; that Augustine speaks of the town of Fussula, though forty miles distant from Hippo, as belonging to his "*parish*;" and that even in later times the Venerable Bede says, "*the province* of the Southern Saxons belonged to *the*

* Perhaps, as Sectarians are satisfied with their ordained ministers, without inquiring who ordained the first that started out: so writer takes from the writer before him this story, without asking the question, "Where did it come from?" As this particular tradition is traceable to Lord King, so nearly all their other abbreviated quotations from the Fathers may be seen in King and Blondel. A quaint old writer, nearly two centuries ago, speaks of "Salmasius, who writ on this subject before Blondel, and whose steps Blondel most-what treads in."

parish of Winchester." All this trifling about "a single congregation" in the capital cities of the Roman Empire, as "the utmost result of all the labors of the blessed Apostles, and martyrs, and confessors, for three hundred years together," was nauseating even to my youthful stomach. Why, Sirs, you are shaking hands, as we have shown you is your wont, with the Jew and the Infidel, who have always insisted that the number of Christians was despicably small, and that Christianity was utterly powerless to make any impression on the masses, until the accidental conversion of Constantine threw into the scale the argument of the sword. But we excuse you! You have never read Tertullian, in the age succeeding the Apostles, who declares to the Roman magistrates that, even then, the Christians were "nearly the majority in every city;" that "though we are of yesterday, yet your cities, and islands, and forts, and tribes, and armies, and even senates, and courts, and palaces, are filled with us. Your temples only have we left you free. Should we go off from you to climes unknown, you would be amazed at your desolation, and have more enemies than subjects left you." You have never read the accurate Eusebius, who tells you that in "all the cities and villages," at the close of the apostolic age, "there was the greatest multitude of thronged and crowded assemblies, like heaped-up grain upon a barn-floor." But certainly you have read the account, in Scripture, of the vast numbers in the Church at Jerusalem, where "three thousand souls" were added "*in one day*," and the Lord yet "added to the Church *daily* such as should be saved;" and yet again, "the number of *the men* was about five thousand," and "believers were *the more* added to the Lord, *multitudes* both of men and women," and "*still* the Word of God increased, and the number of the disciples *multiplied in Jerusalem greatly*, *and a great company of the priests* were obedient to the faith." *You* say that James, the brother of the Lord, was one of the

Twelve: think you that one of the Twelve, a brother of the Lord, would have remained for thirty years in Jerusalem to minister to "*a single congregation?*" Nay, says St. James himself, twenty years afterward, "Thou seest, brother, how many thousands (in the original, *how many myriads, or tens of thousands*) of Jews there are which believe." But you had rather reïterate the slander of the Jew and the Infidel, that, after three centuries of fanatic toil, there was "but a single congregation in Alexandria, or Rome, or Carthage, or Constantinople," than give the Catholic Church her rightful argument for the Episcopacy, from the multitude of her parishes.

This, then, is your dilemma: if there was but a single congregation in Constantinople, why *sixty Presbyters?* If there were sixty, or even thirty congregations, why the *one Bishop?* A new idea strikes you! He was the "Standing Moderator of the Presbytery." "Standing Moderator?" "Yes!" Let us try how this "new reading" harmonizes with an historical fact. The "Moderator" of the Presbytery of Rome dies about the year 250. The event produces a marked sensation in the Churches, far and near; and, in due time, sixteen "Moderators," from the Presbyteries around, assemble in Rome to "make" a "Moderator" for the Presbytery of Rome! "Why would not the forty-six Presbyters at Rome," asks Dr. Bowden, "have done the business?" Really, bad as it is, I think you had better stick to your first hypothesis, even at the expense of an old and unanswerable argument for our holy religion—"That for three or four hundred years there was but one congregation even in Rome itself!" Crowd into it the forty-six Presbyters, and the fifteen hundred widows and poor supported by its alms, and the large offerings sent to the Churches of Phrygia and Asia: still it is a better story than the other. People do not read Eusebius, or Cyprian, or Tertullian. Students of theology do not look into the fathers.

Only stick to it that, for three hundred years, there was but a single society of Christians in a city; that the blood of the martyrs was *not* the seed of the Church, fertilizing its soil and multiplying its harvests, but that it fell on our altars, extinguishing their fires! Go on telling the story: a great many will continue to believe you.

Irenæus, who was an infant in the latter days of St. John, is another to whom I must make reparation. Let one quotation suffice,* since they are all of them of the same nature. "Obey those *Presbyters* who have the succession, as we have shown, from the Apostles, who, with the succession of the *Episcopate*, received the [undoubted] gift of truth according to the good pleasure of the Father." Here Dr. Miller stops. Irenæus proceeds: "*But those who keep aloof from* THE PRINCIPAL SUCCESSION, *and have gatherings elsewhere*, (quocunque loco,) hold ye in suspicion, as of evil report, or as heretics; or schismatics, proud, self-pleasers; or as hypocrites, doing this for gain or vain-glory." Irenæus then compares them to Nadab and Abihu bringing strange fire to the altar; to Korah, Dathan, and Abiram, "sundering and destroying the unity of the Church." We see now *why* the Doctor stopped where he did. But take even the words the Doctor quotes: Irenæus does not say, "Obey *the Presbyters*," but "Obey *those* (*his* presbyteris) Presbyters who have *the succession* from the *Apostles*," in contradistinction to all and any others. For Irenæus, arguing in another place† against Presbyters who taught strange doctrines, which they alleged had been confided to them secretly by the Apostles, declares that, "If the Apostles knew secret mysteries which they communicated to the perfect, separately and secretly from the rest, they would by all means have committed them to *those* to whom they committed *the very Churches;* for they would have *those* irreprehensible and perfect, whom they

* Lib. IV. cap. 23. † Lib. III. cap. 3.

left as their *successors*, handing over to them *their own very place of supremacy*," (magisterii.) We remind you again, that Dr. Miller's quotation of this passage leaves out this sentence. Irenæus then goes on to say that Linus succeeded the Apostles at Rome, then Anicetus, then Clement, then, Evaristus, Alexander, Sixtus, Telesphorus, &c., to Eleutherius, the twelfth in the Apostolic line. Then follows a similar rebuke to Presbyters "who *have gatherings elsewhere*." The whole thing then amounts to this: that those Presbyters pretended (as others do now) to have discovered some great secret hidden from mankind before, and derived directly from the inspired Apostles; and Irenæus meets them with the answer, that such secrets, if any existed, must have been confided to *those* Presbyters to whom they delivered "*the very Churches*," (ipsas ecclesias,) and "*their own very place of authority*," (suum ipsorum locum magisterii;) such, says Irenæus, as was *Linus*, mentioned in the Epistle to Timothy, and *Clement*, who saw and conversed with the Apostles: delivering to them, not the Episcopacy that Presbyters held in common, but "*the Episcopacy of administering the Church*," (episcopatum administrandæ ecclesiæ.) So then, Doctor, your Presbyters holding gatherings elsewhere, are over and over exhorted to return to the unity and line of *those* Presbyters who received the *succession from the Apostles*, and with it their "*very*" and "*own*" place of "*authority*." Very good advice! Will the gentlemen at Princeton take it?

If rest be sweet to the weary, I should rejoice here to rest. But there are two other ancient writers to whose memories my former imputations did an injustice, that must now be atoned for. One is at the beginning, the other at the end, of the period covered in this chapter. One is Ignatius; the other, Jerome.

In the year of Grace 1835, Doctor Miller prepared, "by particular request," for "The Presbyterian Tract and Sunday

School Society," a third work, entitled, "Presbyterianism the truly Primitive and Apostolical Constitution of the Church;" in which, after quoting Theodoret only, and him but once, on the Episcopal side, and accompanying the quotation with the remark, "No one doubts that, in Theodoret's time, Prelacy had obtained a complete establishment," he goes on to say:

"It is very certain that the Fathers who flourished nearest to the Apostolic age, generally represent Presbyters, and not Prelates, as the successors of the Apostles. Ignatius, in particular, who was contemporary with the last of the Apostles, expresses himself again and again in the following language: 'The Presbyters succeed in the place of the bench of the Apostles;' and again, 'In like manner, let all reverence the Presbyters as the Sanhedrim of God, and college of the Apostles;' and again, 'Be subject to your Presbyters as to the Apostles of Jesus Christ, our hope.' And once more, 'Follow the Presbyters as the Apostles.' Which shall we believe, Ignatius or Theodoret?"

Is it to be wondered at, that the students at Princeton are satisfied with Presbyterian ordination? Do, young Gentlemen, allow your eyes to look farther than your ears hear, and be at the trouble for once to see what Ignatius did really say! But let us first of all ascertain exactly when Ignatius lived: for you may be misled if you are not careful. One of your latest writers, the Rev. Edwin Hall, says of Ignatius that "*he comes too late by a whole hundred years*," to have any thing to say of the primitive church! We send him, for correction, to Dr. Miller, who confesses that Ignatius "was contemporary with the last of the Apostles," having been, in fact, made Bishop of Antioch by them in the year 70, and having thus exercised his Episcopate for about *thirty years* before the death of St. John. Now for the quotations!

THE IGNATIUS OF PRINCETON.	THE IGNATIUS OF ANTIOCH.
1. "The Presbyters succeed in the place of the bench of the Apostles"—said to be declared by Ignatius "again and again."	1. Ignatius never wrote such a passage in his life. Its author was a "venerable father" who flourished at Princeton toward the middle of the nineteenth century.
2. "In like manner, let all reverence the Presbyters as the Sanhedrim of God, and college of the Apostles."	2. "In like manner let all reverence *the Deacons as Jesus Christ; and the Bishop as the Father; and* the Presbyters as the Sanhedrim of God and college of the Apostles." (Ep. to Trall. sec. 3.) The words here italicized the Doctor did not see.
3. "Be subject to your Presbyters as to the Apostles of Jesus Christ our hope."	3. "*Do nothing without your Bishop, even as ye are wont; also* be subject to your Presbyters, as to the Apostles of Jesus Christ, our hope; in whom if we walk, we shall be found in Him. *The Deacons also, as being the ministers of the mysteries of Jesus Christ, &c.*" (Ep. to Trall, sec. 2.) Again I have put in italics the words that escaped the Doctor's notice.
4. "Follow the Presbyters as the Apostles."	4. "Follow *your Bishop, as Jesus Christ did the Father; and* the Présbytery, as the Apostles; *and reverence the Deacons, as the command of God.*" (Ep. to Smyrneans, sec. 8.) Poor *Bishops and Deacons,* still not noticed by the Doctor! And if any person will show me in Ignatius the passages that, Dr. Miller says, represent a Bishop as "THE PERSON *by whom all marriages were celebrated,*" who was "to be PERSONALLY *acquainted with all his flock,*" or, "to take notice WITH HIS OWN EYE of

those who were absent from public worship," I promise to commit this work, as an atonement, to the flames, and to present to the Seminary at Princeton a complete and handsome series of the Fathers of the first ten centuries.

Now, kind reader, I have a thing to show you that is somewhat odd. On page 53 of the same work, Ignatius is brought forward again, in the following passage:

"With respect to the testimony of Ignatius, early in the second century, who is commonly regarded and resorted to as the sheet-anchor of the Episcopal claim, we could scarcely wish for a more distinct and graphic description of Presbyterianism than his Epistle represents as existing in all the Churches which he addressed. Ignatius speaks expressly of a Bishop, Elders, and Deacons existing in every worshipping assembly which he addressed. Is this the language of Prelacy? So far from it, nothing can be plainer than that this language can be reconciled with the Presbyterian system alone. Presbyterians are the only denomination who have, in every worshipping assembly, a Bishop, Presbyters or Elders, and Deacons."

Now what are we to make of this? In the former place, he quotes Ignatius as proving that the *Presbyters* or *Pastors* were the successors of *the Apostles;* but now he says, "Presbyterians are the only denomination who have in every worshipping assembly a Bishop, *Elders*, and Deacons." Well done! On page 47, it is *the Presbyters* that succeed the Apostles: on page 53, the very same word, in the very same passages, is translated *Elders;* and we have a Pastor with his *Elders* and Deacons "in every worshipping assembly."*

* Ignatius, by the by, says not one word of "any worshipping assembly;" his Epistles are to *Churches*:—one, for example, to the Church of Ephesus, a Church

Certainly these Presbyters of Dr. Miller's remind one of the bats: when the cat comes, each of "the bench" of bats cries, "You mistake, sir, I am not a mouse;" and, when the hawk comes, "I am not a bird." This dexterous somerset with Ignatius, our Princeton Divine has performed in another way, to which a venerated Bishop has already invited attention.

THE DOCTOR'S LETTERS ON THE MINISTRY.	THE DOCTOR'S LETTERS ON UNITARIANISM.
"That even the shorter Epistles of Ignatius are unworthy of confidence, as the genuine works of the Father whose name they bear, is the opinion of many of the ablest and best judges in the Protestant world."	"The great body of learned men consider the *shorter* Epistles of Ignatius as, in the main, the real works of the writer whose name they bear."

There is a similar feature in the lecture delivered to the class at Princeton, January 5, 1831.

FORMER PART OF THE LECTURE.	LATTER PART OF THE LECTURE.
"Says a zealous advocate for *Prelacy*, in the 'Christian Observer,' the Epistles of Ignatius are so studied and contrived to prove the three orders, that we cannot receive one word of them without suspicion."	"If principle would allow me, I should contend earnestly for their genuineness, because they speak most decidedly in Presbyterian language of the Bishop or *Pastor*, the bench of *Elders*, and the *Deacons*."

Really this is "hot and cold out of the same mouth." When Professor Stuart denied, in opposition to the Fathers, that the Son of God was "Begotten before all worlds," he remarked that "we may climb on the shoulders of the fathers *and see farther than they did;*" to which Dr. Miller replied, that it is "not so easy for pygmies to climb upon the shoulders of giants." Yet, when it suits our Doctor,

which, in St. Paul's time, had Presbyters that *preached* and "fed the Church of God."

"the fathers are not to be trusted." Poor Ignatius! The manner of his martydom seems to have but foreshadowed the mercilessness with which he should again be mangled in the last days, and fragments be torn from him, and made a spectacle to angels and to men. We admit, that these are fragments of Ignatius: but they are not Ignatius!

See how Mr. Powell, an English "Wesleyan Minister," as he writes himself on the title-page of his work, thus boldly avowing in the outset the fearful principle, "I of Paul, and I of Apollos, and I of *Wesley*," see how he severs member from member, and holds them aloft as the body and soul of Ignatius. The capitals are Mr. Powell's. In the right-hand column Mr. Powell's "select fragments" will be found in brackets [ ].

THE MANGLED IGNATIUS.	THE TRUE IGNATIUS.
I. "The Deacon is *subject* to the *Presbyters*, as to the LAW of JESUS CHRIST."—Ep. to Magn.	I. "Seeing then that I have been thought worthy to see you by Damas, your godly and excellent *Bishop*, and by your worthy *Presbyters*, Bassus and Apollonius, and by my fellow-servant, Sotio, [the Deacon,] in whom I rejoice, because he [is subject] to his Bishop as unto the grace of God, and [to the Presbyters as to the Law of Jesus Christ."]

The words in brackets, picked out and put together, make up Mr. Powell's quotation. This Epistle was written to the Church of Magnesia, in Syria, from Smyrna, where Ignatius tarried for a brief space, on his way to a martyr's crown. Here he saw "the Apostle Polycarp," and hither the neighboring Churches of Asia sent their Bishops, Presbyters, and Deacons, to take their last farewell of him. The Church of Magnesia sent Damas, their Bishop; Bassus and Apollonius, their Presbyters; and Sotio, their Deacon. Ignatius even *names* them, and exhorts the Magnesians not to "despise the youth of their Bishop," and to "submit themselves to him, yet not to him but to the Father of our Lord Jesus Christ, the Bishop of us all." Who could have believed that an *unjesuitized Christian* could have represented the above as being the sense or sentence of Ignatius? Yet this is but the beginning. Let us go on.

THE MANGLED IGNATIUS.	THE TRUE IGNATIUS.
II. "The PRESBYTERY preside in the place of the council of the APOSTLES."—Ep. to Magn.	II. "Study to do all things in a divine concord; your *Bishop* presiding in the place of *God*, and your [*Presbyters* in the place of the council of the *Apostles*,] and your *Deacons*, who are most dear to me, being entrusted with the ministry of *Jesus Christ*."

This Epistle it is, too, that speaks of "your most worthy Bishop, and the well-woven spiritual crown of your Presbytery, and your godly Deacons."

THE MANGLED IGNATIUS.	THE TRUE IGNATIUS.
III. "Be ye subject to your *Presbyters* as to the *Apostles* of Jesus Christ, our hope."—Ep. to Trall.	III. "Do nothing without your *Bishop*, even as ye are wont; also [be ye subject to your Presbyters, as to the Apostles of Jesus Christ, our hope.] . . . . In like manner, let all reverence the *Deacons*."

This Epistle also was written from Smyrna, whither the Trallians had sent Polybius their Bishop, (actually named in the Epistle,) to greet the martyr on his triumphal way. And the martyr begs them, "Remember in your prayers the Church of *Syria*," as, in his Epistle to the Romans, he calls himself not the pastor of Antioch, but the *Bishop of Syria*, saying, "Ye can do me no greater favor than to suffer me to be offered up to God, now that the altar is prepared; that when ye shall be gathered together in love, ye may sing praises to the Father, through Christ Jesus, that he hath vouchsafed that a *Bishop of Syria* should be found to call him from the east unto the west;" and again, "Remember in your prayers *the Church of Syria*, which now enjoys *God for its Shepherd instead of me.*" Pray, why could not the Presbyters of Antioch get another "Moderator?" In Sec. 3, of this Epistle to the Trallians, he speaks of himself as a "condemned criminal," yet "commanding as an Apostle—"* ὡς ἀπόστολος. "But," he adds, "I refrain myself, lest I perish in my boasting."

THE MANGLED IGNATIUS.	THE TRUE IGNATIUS.
IV. "Let all remember the *Presbyters* as the *Sanhedrim of God*, and COLLEGE OF APOSTLES."—Ep. to Trall.	IV. "Let all reverence the *Deacons* as *Jesus Christ;* and the *Bishop* as the *Father;* and the [*Presbyters* as the Sanhedrim of God, and College of the *Apostles.*] Without these there is no Church." He then speaks of their Bishop Polybius, who had come to "rejoice with him in his bonds," whose "mildness" and "love" should provoke their "reverence," for his very "look is instruction, and his gentleness is power."
V. "See that ye follow the *Presbyters* as the *Apostles.*"—Ep. to Smyrn.	V. ["See that ye all follow] your *Bishop*, as Jesus Christ followed the Father; [and the *Presbyters* as the Apostles;] and rever-

* In Sec. 4, of his Ep. to the Romans, Ignatius says, "I command you not as Peter and Paul did. They were Apostles, I, a condemned man; they were free, but I hitherto a servant. But if I shall suffer, I shall then be free," which seems to us an Ignatian method, borrowed from St. Paul, of asserting his Apostleship. (See Jerome's testimony of this "ecclesiastical Prince," and "Bishop of Asia," and Chrysostom's "Apostle of Asia."

ence the *Deacons*, as the command of God. Let no one do any thing of what belongs to the Church, separately from the Bishop.

This Epistle was written after Ignatius had passed through Smyrna, and had arrived at Troas; and, together with his Epistle to the noble Polycarp, their Bishop, is full of indirect allusions to the relative powers of the officers of their Church, whom he had seen and known and learned to love. Thus he says, "Your prayer is come to the Church of Antioch which is in Syria; whence being sent in chains, the fittest ornament of a servant of God, I salute all the Churches, not as though I were worthy to take my name from that Church, being the least among them. . . . . It is fitting, and for the honor of God, that your Church should appoint some worthy delegate, who, being come as far as Syria, may rejoice with them, in that they are at peace, and are again restored to their former greatness, and *have again received their proper body*." Perhaps the Presbytery had elected a "Moderator!" History tells us, however, that the successor of Ignatius was Heros. But to proceed: "Send some one from you with an Epistle," says Ignatius, "to congratulate them upon the calm which hath been given them of God, and that through your prayers they have now attained a harbor." Again, to Polycarp he writes concerning the person to be sent into Syria, "Grace be ever with him, and with *Polycarp who sends* him." So Ignatius rejoices that the Church at Ephesus had sent their "Bishop" Onesimus to meet him on his way; and this from Ephesus, which in the days of Timothy had its plurality of Presbyters—"your renowned Presbytery," as Ignatius calls them. And that there may be no mistake about the rank of these Presbyters, he uses, in the Epistle to the Philadelphians, the expression, "some, Bishops; and others, *Priests* and Deacons;" speaking of the different grades of persons sent by the Churches in Syria to meet and greet him on his way to martyrdom.

But to return to Mr. Powell. After holding up these dismembered fragments to the "Wesleyans," Mr. Powell adds, with all the coolness imaginable, "*all the above passages are from Archbishop Wake's translation.*" How to deal with such a statement we are entirely at a loss. Yes, they are "*from* Archbishop Wake's translation," that is, a few words picked out "from" entire sentences: but, as we have seen, they are not Ignatius! Rather than put forth such spurious things to guide the awakening world to the ancient church of God, would we lay down, upon a chart, safe bays and harbors where there were rocks and shoals, or cut pieces out of coin and stamp them with the value of the whole. We are sorry to see the Methodists re-issuing this book, of which we have given the errors of *but one half-page!* Never mind. Enlightened Methodists, as well as Presbyterians of other names, are discovering the cheat. Mr. Powell felt compelled to say something, and full-length quotations would not suit his purpose: felt compelled, we say, for the Wesleyans, in a late annual report in England, represent that the number of their ministers and members had *fallen off* the previous year, and a single Bishop (of Salisbury, I believe) had received applications (as I myself heard when in England about that time) from some seventy Wesleyan preachers, for a better ordination.

Where is this to end? How are we to account for misrepresentations that would dishonor even a Jesuit? The mildest explanation we can think of is, that modern traditions have supplanted all recurrence to the originals, one dissenter quoting from another back to Lord King; while it is not even known that he was answered, silenced and, it is believed, converted, by the admirable work of Sclater. Though we cannot say the times of this ignorance are past, yet the necessity for it no longer exists; for an accurate translation of the Epistles of Clement, ("whose name was in the book of life,") of Polycarp and Ignatius, (disciples of St. John,) and of the work of Justin Martyr, may now be had, in a single small volume, at a trifling expense; and, to the Christian and scholar, they present most pleasing and precious treasures* of literature and piety, some of them having been read for generations in the primitive Church, along with the sacred writings, and being excelled, in richness and beauty, only by the prophets and evangelists. Gentlemen, read them. You will look back upon the time thus employed, as among the best-spent hours of your life. These admonitions to adhere to the Bishops, Presbyters, and Deacons, as the expression of the Church's unity, are the least part of these Epistles, poured by the wayside from the bosom of a man on his way to be offered up at Rome. To the Churches in the East he addresses these earnest exhortations† to purity and unity, in *the unity of the altar and of the ministry*, because the Gnostics had everywhere corrupted that purity and threatened that unity: but to the Church of Rome, not so disturbed, or else too remote for him to know its circumstances, he does not introduce the subject. To the rest he names it, and in strains how musical. "Your renowned Presbytery (Ephesus) is fitted to the Bishop, as the strings are to a harp; so that, in your concord and harmonious love, Jesus Christ is sung; and every single person among you makes up the chorus; that all being in concord, ye take up the song of God in per-

* Particularly the Epistle of Clement to the Corinthians, which, in its style and majesty and force of reasoning, singularly resembles St. Paul's Epistle to the Hebrews; and this, perhaps, has suggested to Neander the idea, that the Epistle to the Hebrews was written by some one bearing, to St. Paul, the relation borne to Luther by Melancthon.

† These have been alleged as reasons to suspect the authenticity of the Epistles: but to my mind they are evidence of their genuineness; for we have reason to suspect, from the Epistles and Gospel of St. John, that, in the Eastern Churches, the Gnostics had already begun their work.

fect unity, that He may hear you and perceive that ye are members of His Son." And again, (to the Magnesians,) "With your most worthy Bishop, and the well-woven spiritual crown of your Presbyters, and your godly Deacons; that so there be among you a unity both in body and in spirit." You have indeed a treat before you, if you are yet to read these incomparable writings. How delightful to hear men speak who spake with Peter and Paul and John, and on whom the mantle of those Apostles fell!

Thus it has been my office, as it has been of others—in humble measure like the task of the pious ones who gathered up the bones and fragments of the venerable martyr when the wild beasts had made their meal—it has been our office to bring back into their places the scraps and fragments torn out of the heart and body of this renowned Apostle, and exhibit the symmetry and beauty of the true Ignatius once more. When this noble martyr and "Apostle," as Chrysostom calls him, was loaded with his chains at Antioch, he sweetly styled them "his spiritual jewels, and the most fitting ornaments of the servant of God." And even as he progressed further in his journey, "Now," said he, "I begin to be a Disciple; the nearer to the sword, the nearer to God." And to prevent the brethren at Rome from unseasonable officiousness in attempting to rescue him, he says, "Do not hinder me, nor love my flesh, for then I shall again have my course to run; for when the wild beasts shall be my sepulchre, then I shall be Christ's disciple; when I shall be with the wild beasts, I shall be with God." But I trow that his mighty heart would have sunk within him, to see the unity of the Church broken as it is now, and as he himself predicted; and the dreadful work promoted by mangled half-sentences out of those writings in which his last breathings were for the unity of the Church, in the unity of her Altar and her Bishop.

One act of justice more, and I have done. Men had told me that Jerome was at heart a Presbyterian; and I believed it, until I asked him, and he told me a thousand times, "No." But, as in Scripture, there are statements seemingly at variance with fundamental doctrines elsewhere clearly inculcated: so in Jerome there may be passages, apparently varying from the truth of the Episcopacy running through all his writings. He wrote toward the year 400. His famous Epistle to Evagrius (or, according to the Benedictine edition, to Evangelus) runs thus, in the translation of Dr. Miller, which we accept so far as it goes; desiring the reader to notice that he stops precisely where Jerome comes to the gist and marrow of the matter. To make this evident, we shall enclose in brackets the parts quoted by Dr. Miller, to which we shall add the omitted parts of the Epistle.

EPISTLE OF JEROME.

"We read in Isaiah, that 'The vile person will speak villany.' [I hear that a certain person has broken out into such folly, that he prefers Deacons before Presbyters, that is, before Bishops; for when the Apostles clearly teach that Presbyters and Bishops were *the same*, who can endure it, that a minister of tables should proudly exalt himself above those at whose prayers the body and blood of Christ is made?* Do you seek for authority? Hear that testimony, 'Paul and Timothy, servants of Jesus Christ, to all the saints in Christ Jesus that are at Philippi, with the Bishops and Deacons.' Would you have another example? In the Acts of the Apostles, Paul speaks thus to the Priests† of one Church, 'Take heed to yourselves, and to all the flock over

* *Conficitur.* I find the phrase elsewhere, *conficere chrisma.* To say "made," may not, therefore, convey the sense intended.

† Not Ruling *Elders*, by the bye, as the Doctor a while ago made them out, in the Epistle of Ignatius to the Ephesians. Do make them one thing or the other. Are they ruling *Elders*? Or are they *Bishops*?

which the Holy Ghost hath made you Bishops; that you govern the Church which He hath purchased with His own blood.' And lest any should contend about there being a plurality of Bishops in one Church, hear also another testimony, by which it may most manifestly be proved, that a Bishop and Presbyter are the same: 'For this cause left I thee in Crete, that thou shouldst set in order the things that are wanting, and ordain *Presbyters* in every city, as I have appointed thee. If any be blameless, the husband of one wife, &c. For a *Bishop* must be blameless, as the steward of God.' And to Timothy, 'Neglect not the gift that is in thee, which was given thee by prophecy, by* the laying on of the hands of the Presbytery.' And Peter also, in his 1st Epistle, saith, 'The Presbyters which are among you I exhort, who am also a Presbyter, and a witness of the sufferings of Christ, and also a partaker of the glory that shall be revealed; to rule the flock of Christ and to inspect it, not of constraint, but willingly, according to God;' which is more significantly expressed in the Greek,—Ἐπισκοποῦντες, that is, superintending it, whence the name of *Bishop* is drawn. Do the testimonies of such men seem small to thee? Let the evangelical trumpet sound, 'the Son of Thunder' whom Jesus loved much, who drank the streams of doctrine from our Saviour's breast: 'The *Presbyter* to the elect lady whom I love in the truth.' And in another Epistle, 'The *Presbyter* to the beloved Gaius, whom I love in the truth.' But that one was *afterwards* chosen,† who should be set above the rest, was done [Mr. Powell here foists in the words 'after the Apostles' times,' and puts '*after*' in italics] as *a remedy*

* Gr., *with.* Jerome makes it also *the gift of prophecy;* both of them careless quotations.

† If this be insisted on, the quotation from Hilary, about Egypt, must be given up; for Hilary tells us the ancient usage there was for the *next* Presbyter to be made Bishop, and that the resort to an *election* was never had until a Council ordered it, to prevent abuses.

against schism; lest every one, drawing the Church of Christ to himself, should break it in pieces. For at Alexandria,* from Mark the Evangelist to Heraclas and Dionysius the Bishops thereof, the Presbyters always named [perhaps *nominated*] one, chosen from among them and placed in a higher degree, *Bishop.* As if an army should make an Emperor, or the Deacons should choose one of themselves whom they knew to be most diligent, and call him *Archdeacon.*"]

DR. MILLER.

And a little afterwards, in the same Epistle, he says, [But stop, Doctor! Why do you skip? Go straight on, as *we* do in the opposite column. *We* are not afraid of Jerome: are you?]

JEROME CONTINUED.

"For what doth a Bishop do, ORDINATION EXCEPTED, which a Presbyter may not do? Nor is the Church of the city of Rome to be considered one, and the Church of the whole world another. Gaul, and Britain, and Africa, and Persia, and the East, and India, and all the barbarous nations, worship one Christ, keep to one rule of faith. If authority is desired, the world is greater than a city. Wherever there is a Bishop, whether at Rome or at Eugubium, whether at Constantinople or at Rhegium, whether at Alexandria or at Tanis, he is of the same validity (*meriti*) and of

* Jerome says, "Presbyteri semper unum ex se electum, in excelsiori gradu collocatum, Episcopum nominabant." Dr. Mason produces an "analogous passage" from Cæsar's Bridge over the Rhine, "Tigna bina sesquipedalia paulum ab imo præacuta, dimensa ad altitudinem fluminis, intervallo pedum duorum, inter se jungebat," and thinks that if Cæsar did the *sharpening* and *measuring* as well as *joining*, the Presbyters did the putting the Bishop into a higher degree, and talks of "the hands" of Cæsar. Now, as we doubt whether Cæsar ever worked a beam of that bridge at all with his own hands, so we doubt whether the Presbyters ever touched their Bishop's head to ordain him. We believe ourselves that the peculiar phraseology implies that the Presbyters in Egypt only *nominated* (*nominabant*) their Bishop; while the election, as well as the rest of the proceedings, was consummated by the Bishops.

the same priesthood. Neither the power of wealth, nor the weakness of poverty, can make a Bishop more exalted or more depressed; but *they are all* SUCCESSORS OF THE APOSTLES. But you say, How is it that at Rome a Presbyter is ordained on the testimonial of a Deacon? Why do you cast up to me the custom of *one city?* Why do you justify this paucity, [of the deacons,] out of which has arisen a disdain for the laws of the Church? That which is scarce is the more sought after. In India penny-royal is more costly than pepper. The paucity of the Deacons causes them to be held in honor; the multitude of the Presbyters causes them to be despised. But even in the Church of Rome, the Presbyters sit, and the Deacons stand; although, as disorders increase by degrees, I may have seen a Deacon, in the absence of a Bishop, sit among the Presbyters, and at domestic feasts give benediction to the Presbyters. Let those who do this, too, understand that they do not well; and let them hear the Apostles, 'It is not meet that we should leave the word of God to serve tables. Let them know why Deacons were appointed; let them read the Acts of the Apostles; let them remember their rank. [Presbyter and Bishop: one is the name of age; the other, of dignity. Whence, in the Epistles to Timothy and Titus,

Here Dr. Miller resumes the quotation: ["Presbyter and Bishop; one is the name of age; the other, of dignity. Whence, in the Epistles to Timothy and Titus,

there is mention made of the ordination of Bishop and Deacon, but not of Presbyter, because the Presbyter is included in the Bishop."] Here the Doctor again dropped the quotation, as he would a live coal; the "*Apostolical tradition*" in the other column will explain why.	there is mention made of the ordination of Bishop and Deacon, but not of Presbyter, because the Presbyter is included in the Bishop.] He who is promoted, is promoted from less to greater. Either then let a Deacon be ordained out of a Presbyter, that a Presbyter may be shown to be less than a Deacon, into whom he grows up from something small: or, if a Presbyter is ordained out of a Deacon, he should know that he becomes meaner in emolument, but greater in Priesthood. And that we may know *the Apostolical traditions taken from the Old Testament, that which Aaron, and his sons, and the Levites were, in the Temple: that let the Bishops, and Presbyters and Deacons, claim to be, in the Church.*"

The reader has now before him *the entire* Epistle—no thanks to the Presbyterians! Pray, why did the good Doctor omit the words, "What does a Bishop do, ORDINATION EXCEPTED, that a Presbyter may not do?" and resume his quotation further on? Did he see it? He must have seen it: for, on the very next leaf in his "Letters on the Ministry," he says, "Some zealous Episcopal writers have endeavored to destroy the force of these express declarations of Jerome, by quoting *other passages*, in which he speaks of Bishops and Presbyters in the current language of his time; for instance, *in one place*, speaking of that pre-eminence which Bishops had *then* attained, he asks, 'What can a Bishop do, that a Presbyter may not also do, excepting ordination?'" "For instance, in one place?" "*Other* passages?" No, Sir! The words are in *that very Epistle.* Nay, they are *the very next words* in that Epistle! If a Jesuit had written thus, we should have felt a glow of shame for the ill-concealed evasion. But we must forgive the Doctor, and reserve all hard feeling for those who not only represent this as "another passage," but leave out of it the words, "*ordination excepted.*" The last writer guilty of this, is Dr. Eddy of Newark; whose book, after doing the Church good service in New Jersey, was wisely bought up and *suppressed.*

"In like manner," proceeds the Doctor, "in *another* place" ["*another* place?" No, my dear Sir! In *the same place*, right on before your eyes in *the very same argument*— Proceed!] "Jerome makes *a kind of loose comparison* between the offices of the Christian Church and the Jewish Priesthood; these passages, however, furnish nothing in support of the Episcopal cause; Jerome, when writing on *ordinary* occasions, spoke of Episcopacy as it *then stood;* but *when he undertook explicitly to deliver an opinion respecting primitive Episcopacy, he expressed himself in the words we have seen;* and to attempt to set vague allusions, in opposition to such express and unequivocal passages in which the writer professedly and formally lays down a doctrine, reasons at great length, and deliberately deduces his conclusion, is as absurd as it is uncandid." Why then, Doctor, did you not save yourself the imputation of being "uncandid and absurd," by letting your readers and your classes see, if not the "reasons" at their "length," at least "the conclusion he deliberately deduces," and to which he comes in the last words of *this very argument:*—"*That which Aaron, and his sons, and the Levites were, in the Temple: that let the Bishops, and Presbyters, and Deacons claim to be, in the Church.*" Call ye this "*a kind of loose comparison,*" or "*a vague allusion,*" or a "*passage in another place* where he is not called to speak of the system established by the Apostles?" Nay, it is the very cap-stone to the argument. A Deacon at

Rome alleges the inferiority of Presbyters to Deacons. Jerome is roused. He uses sundry arguments to put the assumption down: 1. Presbyters "make (*conficiunt*) the body and blood of Christ," just as well as a Bishop. 2. They and the Bishops went anciently by the name of Presbyters, and *vice versa.* 3. Even Apostles call themselves Presbyters, (a poor argument, because the Apostles *still oftener* call themselves *Deacons;* thus, "Who then is Paul, and who is Apollos, but ministers (Gr. *Deacons*) by whom, &c.") 4. At Alexandria, it had been the custom from the first, for the Presbyters to elect a Bishop, not from among the Deacons, but out of their own order—a thing to which Deacons are incompetent. 5. This argument the Doctor does not notice; it proves too much (for *him*); "What does a Bishop, *ordination excepted*, that a Presbyter may not do?" If a Bishop may preach, bless, absolve, do pastoral duty, consecrate the awful mysteries: so may a Presbyter; all—all *except ordination;* for the Presbyters were set first over the Church, reasons Jerome, and one need never have been placed over them, if "schism" could have been otherwise avoided, and unity preserved. 6. This argument the Doctor also passes over, as irrelevant to *his* purpose; but it is a capital one, and one that we should expect a Jesuit, indeed, to omit, (for it is death to the supremacy of Rome,) but why the Doctor? The argument is this: Let not this *Roman* Deacon carry his head so high, presuming on the pride of the great city, and the countenance of *his Bishop;* for whether at Rome, or Constantinople, or Alexandria, or elsewhere, powerful or feeble, poor or rich, the Bishops are all equal, for "THEY ARE ALL THE SUCCESSORS OF THE APOSTLES!" Jerome's 7th was also good: that when Deacons are promoted, they are promoted to be Presbyters; but it were absurd to say Presbyters should be *promoted* to be Deacons. But of Jerome's 8th and last argument, the Doctor could not see the point *at all; the "apostolical* tradition," that "*what Aaron, and his sons, and the Levites were, in the Temple: the same let the Bishops, the Presbyters, and the Deacons claim to be, in the Church.*" This is the conclusion of the whole matter; with this ends the Epistle. I have produced it entire, because I do not remember to have seen it entire elsewhere; and, mutilated and mangled as I had always seen it, it appeared to me "conclusively in favor of the Presbyterians." When I opened Jerome, and found that the passages which Dr. Miller told us were to be found "in another place," "where Jerome speaks of Episcopacy in the ancient language of his day," were, in one case, *the very next words* to his own quotation from this Epistle, and, in the other, were the conclusion and last words of the argument: I could hardly have been more astounded had I seen the heavens above me spanned in blazing letters with Jerome's "Ordinatione excepta," or if Aaron and the whole tribe of Levi had appeared in "white linen," to announce the correctness of Jerome's "tradition," that they were but predecessors of the three Orders in the Apostolic Church!*

* There is a singular fragment, placed among the writings of Augustine, (although not his,) and by some ascribed to Hilary the Deacon, on account of words in it almost *verbatim* the same with those of Hilary respecting the Presbyters in Egypt, which is so much more like this letter of Jerome, that to me it seems reasonable to assign it to his pen. It has the remarkable title, "Concerning the boasting of the Roman Levites." The following is a synopsis:—

"Falcidius, a *Roman Deacon*, presuming on the wealth and power confided to his office, dared to sit among or above the Presbyters"—"temerity"—"presumption"—"audacity to make servants equal to their masters—Levites, messengers and burden-bearers of the temple, hewers of wood and drawers of water, equal to the priest! Deacons are not made of Presbyters, but Presbyters of Deacons, the higher including the lower—a Presbyter was, in the times of Timothy, called a Bishop; and a Bishop is but the Primate-Presbyter. (*Primus Presbyter*,) that is, Highest Priest (*summus sacerdos*)—a Bishop calls Presbyters his *fellow* Presbyters or Priests. Then follows the case in Egypt, if the Bishop be absent, a Presbyter (*consecrat*) performs acts of consecration—not *ordains;* for then it would have been in the plural, *Presbyteri consecrant.* Then the objection, Why is a Presbyter ordained by

But there is one passage more from the works of Jerome.* After showing, as in the Epistle to Evangelus, that Presbyter and Bishop were at first interchangeable titles, he proceeds: "And before that, by the instinct of the Devil, there were parties in religion, and it was said among the people, I am of Paul, and I of Apollos, and I of Cephas: the Churches were governed by the common council of Presbyters. But *afterwards*, when every one thought that those whom he baptized were rather his, than Christ's, it was determined, throughout the whole world, that one chosen from the Presbyters should be set above the rest, to whom all the care of the Church should belong, that the seeds of schism should be taken away." Jerome then adduces the same text as in his Epistle, and proceeds: "these things I have written to show that, among the ancients, Bishop and Presbyter were the same. But *by little and little*, [*paulatim—by degrees*,] that all the seeds of dissension might be plucked up, the whole care was devolved on one. As, therefore, the Presbyters know that by the *custom of the Church* they are subject to him who is their President, [*præpositus fuerit*—who has been set over them:] so let the Bishops know that they are above Presbyters more by the custom of the Church, than by the true dispensation [or literally, *disposition*] of Christ; and that they ought to rule the Church in common, imitating Moses, who, when he might alone have ruled the people of Israel, chose seventy, with whom he might judge the people."

the concurrence (*obsequio*) of the Deacons? is met by saying, that a man in the ranks is not made equal to the General of an army, simply by the fact that the army express their consent by their acquiescence, (*obsequio*.)" It seems scarcely possible that different pens could have written these two arguments; at least they are productions of the same period, and make good the often repeated argument of Jerome, that Bishop, Priest, and Deacon are the High Priest, Priest, and Levite of the Church: an argument first used by Clement, ("whose name is in the book of life,") in that most admirable and sublime Epistle to the Corinthians, which Presbyterians are not allowed to see.

* Com. on Tit. i. 5.

Although this is merely the opinion of Jerome respecting the manner in which Bishops came to be set over the Presbyters, yet I am quite disposed to adopt it, and every part of it, as my own. As God did not give the world a Revelation until the world was made to feel the want of it; as He did not send a Saviour, until the condition of the world made it painfully necessary: so it was part of the same wisdom to delay the distribution of Orders in the Church, until the Church, by severely suffering from the want of them, should be prepared to welcome and appreciate the gift. Our Lord did not ordain Deacons in advance, as if the treasury were to be the great subject of concern at first: but his Apostles ordained them when the revenues of the Church became burdensome, and the complaints of the poor made it expedient. Presbyters, though prior in dignity to the Deacons, came after them in point of time: but not so much by the Lord's personal direction, as by the subsequent direction of his Apostles, when believers were multiplied in every city, and could no longer be safely left to the irresponsible charge and instruction of each other. It is the law of the Kingdom of Grace, that the want shall precede the provision. And now, with travelling Apostles, and fixed pastors and Deacons, the Church might have been left to grow and fill the earth. But the "seeds of dissension" soon sprang up among the Presbyters themselves, and that these seeds might be choked in the germ, one of their own number was set over them as a Bishop. Thus, if Dr. Miller had read this very commentary on the last chapter of the Epistle to Titus, he would have seen the explanation, that the Apollos there mentioned was "the Bishop of Corinth," and was the same Apollos who is spoken of in that passage to the Corinthians, Every one of you saith, I am of Paul, and I of Apollos, &c.; who, "*on account of the dissensions at Corinth*," had retired to Crete, but was about now to return, on the pacification of his Church by the letters of

Paul; and that Zenas was also "an Apostolical man," charged with the same work with Apollos, of building "*the Churches*;" moreover, that Titus, another "Apostolical man," must not come to Paul, until he should send Artemas to take his place," or Tychicus to be his "*successor*." By-the-bye, to these "Apostolical men," or companions of St. Paul, Jerome, on the next leaf,* attributes the inditing, in part, of St. Paul's Epistles; for so he accounts for the association of Sosthenes, Sylvanus, and Timotheus, with St. Paul, in writing them: not only, says Jerome, "that the Epistles may have *more authority*," but because there was "no emulation among THE APOSTLES; Paul very gladly inserting in his Epistles whatever the Spirit suggested to the others, thus exemplifying his own command to the Corinthians, that if, while one prophesied, the Spirit revealed any thing to another sitting by, the former should hold his peace." This is going rather far, Doctor, with regard to these "Apostolical men!" Can you keep company with "famous JEROME?"

Dr. Miller says, that the phrase "I of Paul, and I of Apollos, &c.," is applicable to all periods, and does not settle the question whether it was "half a century or two centuries before the 'whole world' came to an agreement on the subject." Surely Dr. Miller never read Jerome to the end of the Epistle, in which the dissensions at Corinth, and the return of Apollos, the Bishop of the Corinthians, to his distracted flock, are mentioned in conjunction. So, at Ephesus, "grievous wolves" had rent "the flock;" some "had turned aside to vain jangling, without understanding what they said, or whereof they affirmed;" and, in this emergency, Timothy is set over them. In Crete, also, were "many unruly and vain talkers and deceivers, whose mouths must be stopped, giving heed to Jewish fables." "Under these circumstances," says Dr. Miller, "Paul sent special missionaries"—call them so,

* Comm. on Ep. to Philemon.

Doctor, if you please—"immediately empowered by a person of acknowledged authority . . . . to curb the unruly, ... to repress the ambition of those who would thrust themselves into the ministry; to select and ordain others of more worthy character, and, in general, to set in order the affairs of these Churches." In relating these "circumstances," the Doctor, having elsewhere argued that there were, *perhaps*, no Presbyters in Crete or in Ephesus before, incautiously adds:* "*The ministers residing there* were probably themselves involved in disputes and animosities, and therefore could not be considered suitable persons to compose tumults and settle differences."

Really this is as well said as we could have said it ourselves; and Jerome, and Dr. Miller, and Dr. Miller's pupil, are at last all of the same mind: that, if Presbyters had been either more or less than men, there never would have been reason "throughout the whole world" to set a Presbyter, or, as the Doctor calls him, "a special missionary," above the others. So there never would have been *Deacons*, if the Church could have done without them, or there had been no poor; no *Presbyters*, if there had been no jangling among the laity; no *Apostles*, if there had been no heathenism; no Saviour, if there had been no sin; no Revelation, if there had been no ignorance. It is one of the beautiful ways of God: evening before morning; chaos before order; sin before redemption; the want before the provision; and, if you please, Presbyters before Bishops. So Jerome thought. So I think too. So things go still. It is "*by degrees*" that the Church of England sends forth her Bishops to preside over her Church collected from the heathen. It is "*by degrees*" that our own dioceses are provided with their Bishops. It was "*by degrees*" that the United States obtained Bishops at last, after nearly two centuries of opposition from the Puritans. It was "*by degrees*" that Deacons and Presbyters were established, in one

* Letters, p. 103.

place after another, by the Apostles. Why, Doctor, it was "*by degrees*" that the world was made! No one ever dreamed that a Church "booted and spurred by the grace of God," as Dr. Cox reverently says, sprang from the brain of St. Paul or St. Peter—Bishops, Presbyters, and Deacons, all complete —any more than that the world sprang perfect and finished from the hand of God at once. If long geological cycles must elapse before the one can become fit for the abode of man: so a few years were necessary to rear, in its beauty, the spiritual temple that was to become the dwelling-place of God and of the Lamb!

Finally, I have found what previous Episcopal writers on this subject have not, I think, noticed: the explanation of this phrase "*by degrees*," out of the Commentary of Jerome himself.*

PAULATIM vero, tempore procedente, et alii *ab his quos Dominus elegerat ordinati sunt Apostoli;*	BY DEGREES, (or as Dr. Miller might say, "by little and little,") *in process of time,* others also were ordained Apostles *by those whom the Lord had chosen;*

"as in that passage to the Philippians, *Epaphroditus your Apostle;* also to the Corinthians, *They are the Apostles of the Churches;* Silas also, and Jude, are called Apostles by the Apostles." Here we have not only this same word, "*by degrees,*" which Presbyterians spread over *five centuries;* but it is hampered by the phrase "*in process of time,*" implying more deliberation still: yet, "by degrees, in process of time, others were ordained Apostles" not five hundred years after but "*by those whom the Lord had chosen,*" such as Epaphroditus, Silas, Jude, &c.† The Episcopacy being introduced

* Comm. on Gal. i. 19.

† "In process of time," is also the very expression used by Theodoret, of the period when the first Bishops of the Church began to lay aside the name of Apostles.

"as a remedy against schism," is no more an objection to Episcopacy, than that Deacons were introduced "as a remedy against" poverty, or Presbyters "as a remedy against" ignorance. Even the Scriptures of the New Testament themselves were introduced "by little and little," and were not all received or collected for *three hundred years:* yet which of you will therefore deny the authenticity or the inspiration of the Bible?

I have now gone over all the important "testimonies of the Fathers in favor of Presbyters," that I had once relied on for the demolition of Episcopacy. What I have said of my own venerable preceptor Dr. Miller, might as truly have been said of others "who had writ upon this subject before him, and whose steps the Doctor 'most-what treads in:'" as well as to those who, since the Doctor, have "most-what" trodden in his steps. But I have pursued this course, because Dr. Miller has been, by reason of his other virtues, too much relied on in his marvellous quotations of the Fathers; and also because I feel it a most grievous wrong, that I have been, by this very reliance, personally misled and confirmed in my separation from the ancient Church.

It is evident that the Presbyterian student knows no more of the true teaching of the Fathers, than he does of the writings of Confucius or the doctrines of the Shaster. If the day ever comes when the Fathers shall be read, and it shall be seen how Clement took the story from St. Paul, and Ignatius from St. Peter, and Polycarp from St. John, and these reached hands to Irenæus and Tertullian and Justin, and these again to others, all consenting in the existence of the Episcopacy everywhere, all testifying to "one Altar," "one Church," "one Priesthood:" we may begin to hope that schism, with its forked tongue, and hundred hands, and ugly scowl, and cloven foot, will fly from the Christian sanctuary. Laymen, women, and children among the sects, will not read the admirable Epistles of Clement, Ignatius, Polycarp, and others, on whose heads the Holy Apostles, in awful ordination, laid hands that had embraced the Lord: so long as they who profess to "sit in Moses' seat" have neither the curiosity nor taste to read them. Do, gentlemen, begin with Ignatius! When you have read Ignatius, you will long to read Polycarp. When you have read Polycarp, you will read "the great and admirable" Epistle (as Eusebius calls it) to the Corinthians, by Clement, St. Paul's "fellow-laborer, whose name is in the book of life." When you have read this magnificent Epistle, resembling so much in dignity and style the sublime Epistle to the Hebrews, that some have regarded Clement as the composer of it under St. Paul's dictation, while your own Neander goes farther, and thinks it was written by one who stood in the relation to St. Paul that Melancthon did to Luther: you will desire to learn more, if indeed more shall be wanting, to cause you to admire the harmonies of the Church, and restore you to the unity and brotherhood, which, though lost in the first Adam, had been restored in the Second, until schism crept into the new Paradise, and did what sin had done in the old. And as the Apostles wisely waited, in some instances, not ordaining resident Apostles or Bishops in the Churches until the evils of division had become incurable, and competent men had ripened for the office: so again, in the wisdom of God, the mischiefs of schism, growing more intolerable and terrific every hour, may be the appointed precursors of a unanimity with which, "throughout the whole world," the lovers of ancient truth shall become the admirers of ancient order, and there shall be One Fold as there is One Shepherd.

CHAPTER XXIV.

PRACTICAL TEACHINGS.

"As when a hungry man dreameth, and behold he eateth, but he awaketh, and his soul is empty; or as a thirsty man dreameth, and behold he drinketh, but he awaketh, and behold he is faint:" so I must confess that, while among the Presbyterians, I had longings and cravings, which the dogmas of my faith could never satisfy. They know it. Their divines know it. When they have attempted to vindicate the ways of God in the decree to give sin existence, they have often confessed that, while they sought to satisfy the people, they have not felt satisfied themselves. When they have smoothed over the tenet of personal election quite to the satisfaction of the hearers, I have heard them acknowledge that, beyond and behind all this, they themselves saw an unbridged and unfathomable gulf. When they represent the sufferings of Christ as "*satisfaction*" to the "*vindicatory justice*" of God, intended to "*appease*" God's wrath toward our unhappy race; and those sufferings as of equal commercial value with the sufferings of the elect to all eternity: these are terms in the proposition from which I know that they often, in their heart of hearts, instinctively shrink. If they extend to all mankind this substitute of "so much suffering" for "so much sin," they are hampered with the objection, Why should a just God exact this suffering twice, once from the innocent, and once from the guilty? If, to escape the embarrassment, they adopt the new New England heresy, that the sufferings of Christ were merely "an exhibition" of God's hatred of sin "by inflicting pain on an innocent Person:" the exaction bears still more the appearance of a wanton and vindictive determination. No wonder the mind revolts. No wonder New England falls back into Unitarianism, or any other *ism* that will cling to the Creator in His rightful character as the universal Father. On these and a thousand cognate points, there were moments when my soul was dark; nor did the day-star dawn into my heart, until I came within the Spirit's sphere of the teaching of the ancient Church.

Calvinism sees no purpose of the Incarnation, but that the Son of God should *suffer*. No other purpose seems to occur to the mind of Calvinism, than to "satisfy" an offended God, and placably dispose Him toward our unhappy race. Here the light of the Catholic religion bursts into my sepulchre! I wipe the cold sweat from my brow, and emerge from the darkness of suffocation, in which the corroding chains of Calvinism held me.

"God manifest in the flesh!" Not simply man, but made "in the likeness of men" and "in fashion as a man:" for "the Word was made flesh;" God was made man; the Divinity-Humanity; the GOD-MAN; the "Second Adam" or generic MAN, comprehending the race; as the First Adam, or generic Man, comprehended the same race before. "The first Adam [or the first MAN, as the name signifies] was made a living soul," and through him the human race became partakers of his natural life; "the last Adam (or MAN) was made a quickening Spirit," imparting new life to that race again. As the race was a unit in Adam, so it was a unit in Christ; and the Church, like the race, existed as a whole, before it existed in its parts. To speak nearly in the words of others:—"In

Him human nature—elevated by conjunction with Divinity, perfected by the discipline of self-denial and suffering, having subdued temptation, freed by death from all that is corruptible, rendered incorruptible by the resurrection, glorified by His ascension—this redeemed Humanity, by the power of the Divinity with which it is inseparably united, passes over (as did the principle of natural life from the first Man) to the members of the second Man, as the principle of their regeneration and perfection. The last Adam (or Man) is made a quickening Spirit—a Spirit of regeneration, righteousness, sanctification and resurrection: for, 'if the Spirit of Him that raised up Jesus from the dead, dwell in you, He that raised up Christ from the dead, shall also quicken your mortal bodies by His Spirit that dwelleth in you.' What Christ is in Himself, He becomes in us," and, in all that He did, it was not the individual person, but the new, the second, the generic MAN that did it—we in Him, and He in us. The presence, moreover, of the second MAN in heaven, is a continual recommendation of us to God's mercy, as a pledge, to God and all His angels, that they in whom He dwells, by His "quickening Spirit" passing over from His Body into ours, shall in like manner be presented in heaven free from the defilements and deformities of sin. When the members of the universal Church now worship, in the earthly sanctuary, their worship is exalted far beyond all sectarian conception, because the second MAN, the High Priest of the universe, is passed into the heavens to appear for us in the Presence of God, and to offer for us, and with us, and within us, by a Humanity from which every thing on which sin had fastened is purged, a worthy and boundless worship. And as "we in Him" do worship in heaven, so "He in us," an energizing principle carried over into our "mortal bodies," by his Spirit that dwelleth in us, worships and is worshipped in the earthly house. And as the mere form of man, in which Christ came, cannot fill all things in heaven and earth at once: so we are now "baptized into Christ," "baptized into His body," "and are members of His body, of His flesh, and of His bones," as truly as we were of the first Man; that we might be "His Church, which is His Body, the fulness or *pleroma* of Him that filleth all in all." His bodily presence is in heaven; it is no mystery; it is no calamity; the world has the loss made up: His *members* are on the earth—everywhere and always—which He, in the body, could not have been. They are His eyes to look around and weep with them that weep; His feet to go from scene to scene of want and sorrow; His hands to distribute bread among the poor, and be laid in blessing on the heads of little ones; His ears to hear the cry of distress along the wayside; His lips to teach, console, absolve, and save, and bless the healing waters, and the life-imparting cup: in a word, they are, in Him, Prophets, Priests, and Kings, "a royal Priesthood," to perpetuate the fasts, the prayers, the teachings, the life, the alms-deeds, the sufferings, that He began on earth; yea, to "fill up that which is behind of the sufferings of Christ, for His Body's sake, which is His Church." And when sectarism shall pass away, and the Church again feel that She is but the universal presence of the Body of Christ—"the fulness of Him that filleth all in all"—how shall the tear of sorrow gladden into joy, and the desert blossom as the rose!

Our adorable Lord did not teach all who were to be taught, nor feed all who were to be fed, nor heal all that were to be healed, nor comfort all that were to be bereaved, nor bless all babes that were to be blessed, nor say all that was to be said, nor do all that was to be done, nor suffer all that was to be suffered, for the world's redemption: for "I," said one of His members, "fill up that which is behind of the sufferings of Christ, for His Body's sake which is His Church." Christ, as the second Adam, soon went out from

Himself into the Twelve, the seventy, the hundred and twenty, the three thousand, the universal Church, to multiply and replenish the earth. But the Church was in the Twelve before it was in the seventy; and it was in Christ before it was in the Twelve. This blessed Union, whence is derived our Life through the "quickening Spirit," is one of *the lost pearls* of Sectarianism. For more than a gloomy century, Sectarianism has lost the illustrious doctrine of the Incarnation in its power, arrays the Son of God in a body, with terrific ceremony, expressly and solely for the scaffold: and cannot understand how all Humanity was sanctified in Him by meritorious deeds and sufferings, by prayers and fasts, by vigils and victories; and from its second Adam has inherited the universal principle of life. It regards Christ, not as the Second Man, but as an isolated person, alike isolated from God and men, appeasing the former, and "purchasing" the Holy Ghost to be sent, distinctly from himself, and for a separate work, to the elect. No Calvinist on earth can tell you why Christ *fasted:* only His Body that perpetuates His fast can reveal to you the secret. No Calvinist on earth can tell you satisfactorily what meant *the awful conflict* with the devil: only the Church can impart to you this heavenly knowledge. No Calvinist on earth can tell you why Christ *must be* an infant, and pass through all the stages of humanity up to the final triumph: only the Church can explain the blessed mystery. Calvinism asks of Christ only his manly form, to "bathe the sword of justice" in His Blood: the Catholic religion requires that form to embrace all the states and conditions of humanity, that it may sanctify them all, and become an energizing principle of life and renovation to them all. Sectarianism begins therefore with the full-grown man, to effect his regeneration: the Catholic religion begins, where redemption in the body of Christ began, with "*the infant of days.*" Sectarianism commences by imparting *knowledge:* the Catholic religion begins, where its race began, by imparting *life.* Andrew and Peter and Matthew received the germ of *life,* so that they left all and followed Him, before they were *taught:* and the Twelve received the direction, "Go, teach (a word badly translated, and literally signifying to *disciple*) all nations, *baptizing* them in the name, &c., *teaching* them to observe all things, &c." This was the natural order in the first Man Adam; life first,—knowledge and improvement afterwards; and this is the order in the second Man; life first, then faith and progress. Life *must* come before knowledge and faith, else were our children not saved. "The Word was made Flesh, ... and in Him was Life, and the Life was the Light of *men.*" And as the infant lives, before it is born: so is this Life "the Light of every man that cometh into the world." As, by the natural birth, the previous natural life is introduced into a new condition, more favorable to its development: so, in the washing of regeneration, each human being is born again, or brought, by Baptism, into the more congenial sphere of the Spirit's operations, and the more immediate energization of the Body of Christ through the "joints and bands" which "knit" it together and "minister nourishment." Our second Adam, when baptized in Jordan, in the name of Humanity at large, received a pledge and measure of the Spirit, and the element of victory in the future conflict in the wilderness; and this life, in our individual baptism, is born again into conditions more favorable to its progress and its growth. In the lands of Paganism, we eat with the woman of Canaan the crumbs from the children's table; and where the energizing dews of baptism fall, we are only more positively "a holy nation," and come within the Body of Christ, the peculiar sphere and presence-temple of the Spirit. The Church is not made *first* of individuals: but proceeds from a Unit, and destroys individuality and separatism by drawing all things to itself. "The communion *precedes* the reception." The "preventing grace" is prior to all knowledge and to all faith. There cannot be even faith, without grace; and this glorious "predestination to the adoption of sons" in a new and sinless Adam, is a predestination of all your "infants of a span long" to salvation, from which they can only fall as a fruitless branch may wither from its vine. Light breaks on my path! Away with your cold and freezing dogmas!

Dr. Alexander, of Princeton, in a work already quoted, remarks that the simple reason for believing that *all* baptized infants are not born again, is, that they give no evidence of such regeneration. I confess that my own observations in life lead me to a very different conclusion. I find no such "fruits of the Spirit" in adult years, as I see in new-born babes. Such things, in babes "totally depraved" and without renovating grace, could never have been! They are soon made gentle and meek and generous, readily forgiving and presently forgetting, reposing on your word, not filled with envy, and evil-speaking and suspicion, and unbelief and jealousy and selfishness, as your grown-up regenerated men are: and all this, in a great degree, before instruction; proving "the *life*-principle" to precede the principle of knowledge and faith. Treat your "regenerated" *men*, as you treat these babes in Christ; tell *them* they are not regenerated; keep *them* from the sacraments, because their selfishness, and skepticism, and doubts, and avarice, and heart-burnings, prove them "totally depraved:" and mark in them the result of that terrible experiment you make upon your children, teaching the little ones that they are the children of the devil, born to sin in the first Adam, and not born again to grace in the second! No, Sirs! You cannot find the child that gives no sign of spiritual life, or the baptized and trained child that does not give those signs affectingly and delightfully. See its little eyes bathed as you tell it of the Child in the manger! See its little heart swell and break, as you tell it the story of the Cross! See how it sleeps in perfect faith in the keeping of its God! See how it sorrows when you tell it, it has wounded its Lord! See how it forgives, and asks its playmates to forgive! Not regenerated? What, Sirs, can you mean? See your regenerated man in his experience-meeting, vaunting his recent gorgeous conversion! He "does not care any more what man can do or say; he could lie down and let the world tread on him; he is born again:" but do that man an injury, and put him to the trial! He "has parted joyfully with all for Christ, and grieves that he has not a thousand worlds to devôte to the service of his Lord:" go, ask that man to part with one poor shilling for an orphan passing by, and put his vaunted love to its proper test!*

But now, do our little baptized child a wrong: does his momentary passion settle into sullenness and hate? Bring to *him* your little crape-covered orphan, or tell *him* that that orphan's mother is in yonder cottage, pale with hunger and want: and he will put into that orphan's hand the last far-

* The orphan may still want for bread, but your "regenerated" soul will sing above the rest, at the next high-wrought meeting:

"How happy are they,
Who the Saviour obey,
And have laid up their treasure above!
What tongue can express
The sweet comfort and peace
Of a soul in its earliest love!

"I rode on the sky
Freely justified, I,
Nor did envy Elijah his seat!
My soul mounted higher
In a chariot of fire,
And the moon it was under my feet."

thing he has on earth !* No, no ! it is the teaching and example of Sectarism that smothers the love-born evidences of regeneration in your children. You have *another* reason for believing they are not regenerated. You hold that a child once "regenerated" can never "fall from grace"—a reason that of course has no weight with us—and we fall back, and invite the world to fall back with us, upon the Mother-hearted bounties of the Catholic religion.

As little could I say that I was satisfied with the Calvinistic mode of teaching doctrines that are true. The Trinity is so held as to sever the sympathies and interests of the Father and the Son; the Father exacting the utmost farthing from the Son; the Son in turn *claiming the purchase* of His blood; the Spirit acting independently and separately from the life-imparting Flesh of Christ, and a boon *earned* after all, by dint of *suffering:* all tending to drive the popular mind to Tritheism or to alienate it into Unitarianism. The Atonement, too, is preached entirely apart from our incorporation with Christ and His assumption of our common Flesh, as a naked, stern, commercial, *quid pro quo* transaction, that has driven all New England, and whole communities on the continent of Europe, into a denial of the mediation. The Spirit's influences, too, instead of being preached as a "quickening Spirit" passing over from perfected Humanity in the second Adam into all his children, are distinguished into "common" and "special," the latter for the elect, the former for the commoners of the human race; imputing to the Divine mind a "respect of persons," and together with the semi-miraculous, transubstantia-

* Lines that your "regenerated" man has never learned, are already graven on his little heart:

"The Scripture saith, the poor and sad
Are types of God the Son,
And he who makes their bosoms glad,
Makes glad the Holy One !"

ting descent in "regeneration," fretting the world into a denial of the precious mystery.

So with Repentance. Instead of an enlightened, earnest, life-long sorrow—weeping, not to obtain forgiveness, but rather, with Mary at His feet, because we are forgiven—Sectarian teaching has produced the wide-spread impression, that Repentance is a feeling worked up to a high pitch, perhaps, at some animated meeting; succeeded, in the same hour it may be, by peace or transport: whereby the world now understands that the penitent is, in a perverted sense, "the Lord's free man," enjoying too often a "liberty" to do what the world's veriest slave would feel to be disreputable. Who ever sees these sudden bursts of penitence making a man sorry, as a baptized child is sorry, for the injuries he has done or is doing to his neighbors? Who has ever known the sins of the tongue to be retracted by one of these glowing conversionists? Is not the spiritual pride it generates an absolute barrier to the possibility of *retraction* and *reparation:* although these are essential parts of repentance as the Catholic religion teaches it? A sudden burst of sorrow; a lightning-flash of joy; and the repentance is done: and is all the more genuine for the suddenness of its coming, the shortness of its stay, and the abruptness of its departure. In the days of Bunyan and Baxter and Flavel, these two experiences, which have always gone by odd names, were denominated "law work" and "grace work." In those days, the Pilgrim was kept in terror under the overhanging mountain for three or four or five long years, before he was admitted to the "gracework" of finding "peace and joy in believing:" but in these times of speed and steam and electricity, the motions of the Spirit are so concentrated and controlled, that a single "meeting" is quite sufficient to "get through" the experiences both of "conviction" and "conversion;" the worst man living performing the life-long offices of penitence and satisfaction to the wronged, in the ebullitions of an hour!

So likewise with Faith. Calvinism, I know, does not in theory, but I as well know that it does in practice and effect, separate and put asunder the works and the faith that God hath joined together. One might suppose that every doctrine of Christianity was faith; that every precept of the law was faith; that every fruit of the Spirit was faith; that every duty toward God or man was faith; that every virtue to fit us for the skies was faith: whereas it is, like repentance, but one of "the first principles of the doctrine of Christ," from which we are to "go on unto perfection." Revivalism begins and ends too much with faith. I never knew the "pure and undefiled" Revival that clothed the naked or fed the orphan. The Catholic religion saith, *add to* your faith, *virtue;* and to virtue, *knowledge;* and to knowledge, *temperance;* and to temperance, *patience;* and to patience, *godliness;* and to godliness, *brotherly kindness;* and to brotherly kindness, *charity.* This is the pyramid of virtues by which, if we successfully erect it, we "make our calling and election sure," and shall be able easily and certainly, to climb to heaven. The foundation is JESUS CHRIST: to faith is assigned the honorable task of finding the foundation, and laying on it the first stone cemented in the tear of repentance. Yet this is the bare beginning. "*Add* to your faith, virtue;" and so on up to "charity," the highest grace we can attain on earth, the beginning of all graces in heaven. Not only is such a superstructure a safe path to heaven, but it is a house of light and a beacon of love to a rational world. As Christianity is not a one-idea, but is, in this respect, a science in which no one idea stands alone, but each is a link in an endless chain, reaching from first truths up to boundless demonstrations: so practical religion is also a holy chain; link fastened to link, Christ to faith, faith to hope, hope to charity, charity to holiness,

holiness to heaven, and heaven to Christ again, in God. They who see nothing else but repentance and faith in the Bible, cut the celestial chain that reaches from this dark world to heaven. By this chain—of which Christ crucified is the earthly anchorage, and Christ glorified the heavenly, with the long series of virtues and graces glittering between—we are to be drawn to God. No single separate link will raise us to the heavens. Together the bright and polished parts must stand: or, let but one be missing, and the whole must fall. To the faith that exalts CHRIST, we subscribe with a thousand hearts: but the faith that exalts FAITH, and makes faith, or an inward experience, its "all in all," we cast to the moles and to the bats. When we see this vaunted "faith" powerless to heal throughout whole neighborhoods "bitter envying and strife," mutual "biting and backbiting," unwearied "tattlings" and "evil surmisings;" when we see the tongue "a fire, a world of iniquity, setting on fire the course of nature, and itself set on fire of hell," an "untamed serpent" creeping along its slimy path from house to house, a "deadly poison" pouring "blessing and cursing out of the same mouth;" when we see "the fatherless and widows in their affliction" neglected and unrelieved: we remember that it is written, "The devils believe"—and are devils still! When we see whole communities acting virtually on the advice of Luther, *Peccate fortiter; credite fortius*—"Sin hard; but believe the harder"—

> "Backing their pious sabbaths, so to speak,
> Against the wicked remnant of the week;"

when we see the thronging multitudes about us, however worldly or profane, professing a reliance on Christ, and, on the death-bed, working themselves up with the utmost ease to the established *minimum* of a sudden repentance and "casting of themselves on Christ;" when we see vast numbers of the ignorant, on the old and easy advice, *Crede quod habes, et habes*—"Believe that you have, and you have it"—putting their faith in an inward *feeling* rather than in the Lord of life: the Catholic religion lifts up her earnest voice, and cries, "Though I have all faith, so that I could remove mountains, and have not CHARITY, I am become as sounding brass, or a tinkling cymbal." "FAITH WITHOUT WORKS IS DEAD," it cries, a subtle and soul-murdering imposture! A man "may say he hath faith and hath not works:" the Catholic religion does not hesitate to raise the awful question of her fearless Apostle, "*Can faith save him?*"

My own conviction, after long and painful attention to the facts, is, that *the manner* of preaching the great doctrine of justification by faith, isolating it from the virtues, and making it a reflexive operation, terminating in a *feeling* rather than in Life from Christ, is, among sectarians especially, *the* soul-destroying heresy of the age. The world without know that they have already this *minimum* in some degree; and they see daily before their eyes the dying, without difficulty accepting the terms of sectarianism, and "casting themselves on Christ." I was once called, at the break of day, to see a youth whom I knew to be wild and profane, and perhaps intemperate. He had sent for me. I had seen him the evening before, in vigorous health. Already had disease half done its work. I saw his youthful form writhing in pain; but the miseries of his mind were greater. When I first came to him, between his paroxysms, he was earnestly exhorting several young men around him to "take warning from his fate." He was in an agony. It was despair! Now was the hour he should have rested from his pilgrimage; instead of which, his pilgrim's course was now to be begun. This was the hour when he should have laid the last stone with shoutings on the building; instead of which, he was to cast about for a foundation. Unfit for the awful blessedness of heaven, its transparent truth, its deep-toned worship, its generous love, its every word and work and look and thought and feeling, pure and unsullied and transparent as its crystal streams, a world unclouded by a passion, unpoisoned by a whisper, unsullied by a sin: and now the work of a life-time was to be begun and finished in a hurried and stormy hour! Earnestly as the ebbing moments would allow, I pointed him to "the Man" that was to be "the hiding-place from the tempest." Presently a reaction came, as striking as the collapse in his disease; and exhibiting all the phenomena of the revivalism I had seen in other days. He was calm; he believed; his sins were forgiven; his heart was glad. The bystanders were overjoyed; and I myself had had "hope in his death." Although I had seen stimulants and opiates largely administered before my eyes, it never occurred to me that they might have performed a part in producing the phenomena; until the attending physician told me, a few days afterwards, that the patient had died of *delirium tremens!* It then occurred to me, that I had often before remarked these sudden emotions of religious terror, penitence, and joy, to be more easily and more strikingly produced in persons addicted to intemperance, than in any other class of men. Let me not be understood as passing judgment upon this young man: it is not for me "to judge another man's servant." I have adduced the case because it has occurred within a few weeks, and is an illustration of my invariable experience of the perfect ease with which you may induce the dying to "cast the soul on Christ," and die, as the phrase is, "resigned!" A life of profanity, uncleanness, drunkenness, and debauchery, rewarded at its close with peace, joy, ecstasy! It is the great phenomenon of revivalism—*Crede quod habes, et habes!* But, in naked truth, it is a fearful thing, this mistaking the decay of expiring nature for the subjugation of the flesh; the ejaculations of pain for the language of prayer; the languor of disease for the peace of resignation; the agitations of guilt for the emotions of a true contrition; the throbbings of the undying conscience for the pulsations of a living heart; the triumphs of disease for the victories of grace; the repentance of a Judas for the tears of a Mary; the prayer of a Simon Magus for the *Nunc dimittis* of a Simeon: this is falling into the delusion so loudly condemned in others, of a sudden and hurried conversion; and, like the blinded papist, glossing the disorders of a whole life with the extreme unction of the dying hour; or, like the victims of the ancient Flood, clinging in the wild storm to the outside of the Ark, flying to the Sacraments and externals of the faith! O frightful task, to offer to God the miserable leavings of a misspent life; the gleanings of a vintage pressed into the cup of pleasure; a victim taken from the fold for heaven, when, no longer fit for the world's use, its limbs are palpitating in the jaws of death! In the Papist, who believes there is another period in which to carry forward the work begun anywhere this side the grave, all this is reasonable: but that we are thus to be ushered directly from the body into heaven—unprepared, uncongenial in habit, character, or temper for its unsullied purities—how can a true Protestant believe? And why are millions in our land procrastinating repentance to the dying hour, except that they are taught that a short prayer-meeting or a short half-hour is more than enough for all the *essential* acts of repentance and of faith? No, no! As at the charming of the lyre of Amphion the stones are said to have risen into their places in the walls of Thebes: so a true *faith*, chiming with the music of a good conscience, will gather all the other virtues to itself in the spiritual building. "The fruit of the Spirit is love, joy, peace, long-suffering, gentleness, goodness, faith, meekness, temperance." "Add to your faith virtue, knowledge, temperance, patience, godliness, brotherly kindness, charity." Faith is but a single grape upon the cluster. Indeed, it is not so much a fruit, as it is the active, circulating junction of the branch with the heavenly Vine, of which the evidence will be its grapes hanging in rich clusters over it; and who can doubt that a branch bringing forth such fruits, ripening and mellowing until fit for angel's food, shall be gathered into the heavenly Paradise? Faith is but a single star in a single constellation in the firmament of grace,

> "Each, all proclaiming as they shine,
> The hand that made us is divine."

Why will you darken the radiant firmament, destined to glow and burn and brighten when the powers of heaven shall be shaken: and leave in human sight but the lone, cold star of faith, which, like the stars above us, is to fall and die? No! We express our firm conviction once more, that the doctrine of justification by faith is understood by the people generally to mean, what none but the Antinomian would desire to teach: in a word, that, as it is too often preached, especially among sectarians, it is *ad clerum*, or, in the theological sense, *true;* but *ad populum*, or in the popular apprehension, *false.* Here is one great secret, we fear, of our worldliness, our avarice, our starving missionaries, our stinted charities, our unprovided poor, our miserable broils, our gossiping, our vindictive, unforgiving tempers. They are all covered by the *imputed* but not corrected by the *indwelling* righteousness of Christ; all smoothed over and "*justified by faith:*"—a dunghill wrapped in snow, and presented as a pure offering to God!

But tell us not that we undervalue faith. We magnify it. We restore it to its ancient honors. We replace it in its ancient crown, among the lost jewels of meekness, and brotherly kindness, and truthfulness, and sincerity, and gentleness, and charity, and mutual forgiveness, and love. If *Churchmen* undervalue faith in the Redeemer's blood, explain to me, I pray you, why we have so much at heart the Altar, the breaking of bread, and the red cup of the awful Eucharist? Why is it that we lift aloft on steeple high, and would keep continually before men's eyes, *the Cross*, the symbol of the world's redemption? It is because we know we cannot obtain that blessing until we be covered with the fleece of the slain Lamb. We fill the windows of our sanctuaries with the thorns, the scourge, the cross, the hammer, the nails, the spear, the lamb: because it is through these that the light of Heaven dawns on us. Amidst the wild skepticism which you create, and with which you must for ever struggle, it may be well for *you* to dwell day and night on "the first principles of the doctrine of Christ;" but with *us*, they are the alphabet of our religion, no longer open to discussion. We have learned and believed them long ago, and raise everywhere *the Altar and the Cross* as symbols of a hope already attained. Churchmen undervaluing the "redemption by His Blood?" God forbid! I will take you to the bedside of a Churchman, who, after a brief life of sorrow, perished not long ago at sea. "Do you place," said a Presbyterian minister to him, as he lay dying, "Do you place your sole reliance on the merits and righteousness of Jesus Christ for your salvation?" The youth, fixing his eyes on those of the inquirer as if grieved at the question, said, "*Of course* I do!" The Presbyterian, to his credit be it said, has lately thought it worth while to relate the facts of the occasion in a Presbyterian journal, (the Lord reward him!) for the avowed purpose of doing justice before men to the memory of ARTHUR CAREY, whom he learned to love. Take now another—the hated and murdered *Laud.* "Good people," said the hoary-headed Archbishop, as he stood upon the scaffold high, "this is an uncomfortable time to preach, yet I shall begin with a text of Scripture: '*Let us run with patience,*' &c.—I have been long in my race, and how I have looked to JESUS, the Author and Finisher of my faith, He knoweth. I am now come to the end, and here

I find the cross and a death of shame; but the shame I must despise, or I shall not come to God. My feet, as you see, are on the brink of the Red Sea, an argument I hope that God is bringing me into the land of promise. I shall most willingly drink of this cup of the passover with its bitter herbs, as deep as He pleases, and enter into this sea, yea, and pass through it, in the way that He shall lead me." Then, having concluded his discourse, he knelt down on the scaffold and said, "O Eternal God and Merciful Father! look down upon me in the riches and fulness of thy mercies, but not till Thou hast nailed my sins to the cross of Christ, not till Thou hast bathed me in the blood of Christ, not till I have hid myself in the wounds of Christ."

We do not, for all this, boast ourselves as "evangelical" above all others, or as having made some great discovery in religion. To the Catholic heart these are "the first principles" which St. Paul exhorts us to learn, and then "leave, and go on unto perfection,"—the perfecting of *character* in concert with the harmonies of the heavenly world. That a man is "justified by faith," is a most true and comfortable doctrine. But to fritter away this vast circle of truth into a mere belief in Christ as a Redeemer; and this again into a trust in His atonement; and this atonement again into a satisfaction to divine justice; and this satisfaction, once more, into mere *suffering;* and this faith itself concentrated into a single act of "casting the soul" upon this suffering for hope; and Christ entirely unknown as the Second Adam, communicating from His body into ours a quickening and transforming life, purifying our flesh by the same agencies or operations that purified His: this is a mode of teaching which we must regard as unsafe and soul-ruinous in the highest degree.

Calvinism, in my observation of its influences, generates moreover an exaggerated and morbid conception of every thing in true Christian experience. I need not go over the ground—dreams, voices, impressions that one is forgiven; lights, sensations, passionate and self-consuming bursts of feeling; opening by accident to certain passages of Scripture; a constant effort at the marvellous, the counterpart of the Papists' hankering after mongrel miracles; a lifetime of laborious, parental, and pastoral teaching, ungratefully cast aside as having accomplished nothing, until by some accidental casting of the eye upon a passage of the Bible, or by some sermon of some passer-by, or some picked-up, half-torn leaf of a common tract, the mighty office of "regeneration" is performed; men willing to be damned, if it be for God's glory, before they can be saved; the prayers and charities of baptized but "unregenerated" men, an abomination to God: these and a thousand like things continually resulting from sectarian teaching, and contrasting amazingly with the calm and solemn Faith and Hope of the ancient and true Religion.

The sectarian pulpit partakes strangely of these exaggerations. What impressions, for example, are generally received from sectarian teaching, concerning the dying hour? I do not hesitate to say, One utterly at variance with the facts. The Christian—calm, collected, happy, triumphant when he comes to die: the sinner—anxious, agitated, terrified, and in despair! It is *not true:* else the Book is not true, in which it is written of the wicked, "There are no bands in their death; they are not in trouble as other men." A very extensive observation convinces me that good men are often more anxious than the wicked, when sick unto death; and that the wicked who have never reflected on the awful nature of a true preparation for heaven, who have never tasted the bitterness of sin, whose "conscience is seared as with a hot iron," are the first and easiest to receive consolation at death, and suffer a far less, and a far less lasting concern for the result. I have often made inquiries, on this subject, among medical men in the habit of observing such phenomena: and their observations have invariably corroborated my own. Nay, I have been admitted by them into the secret, in part, of the phenomenon which has too much surprised us—of that deplorable skepticism into which so many of the medical profession, in this and the last age, have fallen. The Calvinistic *pulpit* has made a *false issue* with the *profession.* Gentlemen see that these death-bed stories are *in general* not true; and that the "bad" man meets his fate often with the apathy and calmness of the "good:" or, if alarmed at all, can be as easily and as soon reduced to the same condition of "resignation" or "peace," by physical means and causes, in which, *as medical men,* they cannot be deceived. And as religion is held to be only a bright transition from cloud to sunshine in *feeling:* they compare the phenomena of the death-bed with those of a revival or a camp-meeting; and reduce the mighty paroxysm which "*preaching*" seeks to produce, to the same precise category with the effects of disease, and of a certain condition of the nervous nature. As to the rest, they daily see thousands dying without concern or fear, who have neglected religion all through life: and, seeing the pulpit contradicted continually by facts, they become skeptics themselves, and die in the apathy in which they have lived. One of the most saintly, heavenly men I ever knew—a Presbyterian missionary falling, in his youth, in the service of God—said, when he came to die: "Brother, it is an awful thing to die; unspeakably awful to appear before God! The best preparation falls unutterably short!" And David could not understand the mystery of the happiness of the wicked, until he went into the Sanctuary. And St. Paul tells us of good men "who through fear of death were all their lifetime subject to bondage." But if religion is reduced to a desultory act of casting one's self on Christ, and a consequent feeling of composure or peace, we must expect that misbelief will continue to blind, and procrastination to destroy the multitude. No!

We must cease this lullaby with which we have put the world to sleep! We must let men know that preparation for *heaven* is a task for which the longest life is short! And as they understand that gold does not drop on them from the clouds; that crowns do not grow for them upon the trees; that there is no such thing as acquisition without toil: so we must *tell them what that awful preparation is*, that is to fit men, in *body* and *soul*, for HEAVEN.

I will speak now of but one thing more—the austerity of the Calvinistic system. Calvinism, like Popery, has its terms of accommodation for the multitude who, in less than "two moments," can be prepared for death: while, on the other hand, it has its pains and rigors for others, disposed to be austere. In this aspect of it, Calvinism wants the meekness, the gentleness, the affectionateness of the Master. Oh, I have felt its cold repulses, and its distracting terrors, and its terrible tormentings, till endurance has been well nigh exhausted. I have felt the wheel, the rack, the torture! When I was a little child, it spoke to me and said: "Perhaps you are not one of the elect! Perhaps Christ did not die for *you!* The influences you feel are perhaps the 'common,' not the '*regenerating*' influences of the Spirit! Your prayers being done in impenitence, are an 'abomination to the Lord!' You have no power! If you have power, you have not the will! You must 'feel' thus and thus, or you cannot be saved! You can do nothing to save yourself!"*

Oh, I have felt my bones cry out under the torture! While yet a boy, I met with other boys in "prayer-meetings," to reach the solution of our terrors. Those boys, so far as I can

* A state of feeling reminding one of the pithy old distich:—

"You can, and you can't!
You will, and you won't!
You shall, and you shan't!
You'll be *lost* if you do! You'll be *lost* if you don't!"

trace their histories, lived all, except one, to despise the cheat, and to doubt the reality of all religion: one has lived, not to despise, but to mourn; and to find, in the glories of the ancient faith, the magnificent image and superscription of its Author. In a small company of seven, at sea, not long ago, the subject of sectarian revivals being introduced, I found that four of that little number had been subjected in boyhood to the fearful process: and three or four were now, on the subject of religion, like our bark, entirely at sea. I meet the like phenomena frequently. Is *this* the "regeneration" that we hear of? And I have now in my memory, as I have daily in my prayers, a dear one in this mortal life—*how* dear I cannot tell—dear *as a brother*. In boyhood and youth he was tossed up and down on the waves of revivalism: he is now laboring to beat back the billows of universal skepticism! Although he has glimpses, recently, of the Catholic religion flashing gorgeously upon his understanding: yet *the habit* of skepticism, generated by his old experiences, ever and anon suggests the thought that perhaps, after all, Christianity may have been some solitary effort of the natural mind, never made before, and not again to be repeated. Then comes the conviction, that it ought to be true; it is too good to be false! He trains his little ones in the ancient faith: not many besides himself have suspected the terrors of his troubled mind. He is himself devout—so devout that in the darkest hour, when he can say no more, he prays; "O God, if thou art God, scatter the darkness, and let there be light within me!" Even beyond this point the harmonies of the ancient faith are the daily admiration of his soul: but Calvinism, with its iron rod, has dashed the harmonies of his own pure mind—the purest I have ever known on earth. Calvinism and revivalism he encountered in early youth: and horrid Atheism brooded darkly over his mind for years, until the genial influence of a better faith began to dawn into it again;

which I feel assured will, by God's mercy, shine in him more and more unto the perfect day. My personal acquaintance embraces numbers of individuals led back, by a like experience, to the ancient and happy fold: while the pall of skepticism yet hangs over communities in our own land, and over empires abroad, where Calvinism has run its course; as we have already shown. O God, beat back the waves of such a system from thine ancient Church! O Spirit of God, lift up against the flood, when it cometh in, Thy glorious Standard!

But again, like Popery, this system has its compromises. It offers an easy escape from the true and useful austerities of the Christian life. Instead of living severely, it teaches only to believe severely; instead of writing bitter things against ourselves, to believe hard things concerning God; instead of austerity of self-discipline, the austerity of doctrine; instead harshness against failings of the tongue, the temper, and the flesh, it is too often satisfied with harshness of judgment on others. Instead of ascribing the straitness of the gate, and the way of life to its proper cause, in our lusts and passions: it would often make it the result of the arbitrary purposes of God. Instead of teaching that "few find it," because few seek it as they should: it teaches that few find it, because God hides it, save from His elect! Thus, through the whole circle of truth, it is, with its multiform anathemas, a vast gigantic system frowning and scowling sullenly upon the sons of men. When will the cloud pass over which has kept the earth wet with men's tears? When will the Catholic religion belt its dark bosom with the ancient mercies of God?

We have yet another illustration, in the memoirs of Franklin, as written by himself; where we may see a gigantic mind wrestling awhile between Calvinism and infidelity, and seeking in the latter a refuge from the harshness of the former! He tells us of the severity of the dogmatic training to which he was subjected when a boy, and which prepared him to resolve, with a young companion, to wear a long beard, subsist on a vegetable diet, and set up a new religion. Once, in his riper years, he listened with hope to a popular divine announcing for his text: "Whatsoever things are *true*, whatsoever things are *honest*, whatsoever things are *just*, whatsoever things are *pure*, whatsoever things are *lovely*, whatsoever things are *of good report*, if there be any *virtue*, if there be any *praise*, think on these things." But the expectations of the philosopher were woefully blighted, when this magnificent passage was made to cover, *seriatim*, the coldest observances of the Calvinistic creed. The result is known. Franklin was disgusted. The philosopher became *an infidel;* and ascribes his infidelity to paternal training, and the popular ministerial preaching.* Over such a calamity, although but the type of millions, the mountains and hills might take up their lamentations. Yet men persist in the barren dogma—a dogma worn out in the fields where once it flourished, and now sought to be introduced into the virgin soil of the Church!

Calvin himself, it is said,† preached nineteen hundred sermons, of which the texts are all recorded, and (with one doubtful exception) not one of them is taken from the Gospels. Luther went so far as to declare that "the *Gospel* is not in the Gospels!" But the ancient Church has had from the beginning, has now, and ever shall have, her "Gospel for the day."

* As to the sermon alluded to, he says: "These might be all good things; but as they were not the kind of good things I expected from that text, I despaired of ever meeting with them from any other, was disgusted, and attended his preaching no more."

† Dr. John Augustine Smith, of the medical faculty in New York, has stated the fact; and I am not aware that it has been, or can be, contradicted.

CHAPTER XXV.

RAGS OF POPERY.

A Presbyterian wag, on seeing, in an unfinished church, that some idler had written over the Altar, "I publish the banns of marriage between the Protestant Episcopal Church, and the Church of Rome:" took up the chalk and wrote beneath, "I forbid the banns, as the parties are too near of kin." We enjoy this. We laugh. It is wit, if it be not argument. It has the merit of good humor, if it have not the force of good logic. But when methods more deliberate are industriously resorted to, to bring down upon the Church a storm of popular odium by the hue-and-cry of Popery—a cry that the Independents employ against the Presbyterians on account of "some mysterious virtue" going out from "the hands of the Presbytery;" and the Baptists in their turn against the Independents, for holding the root of all abominations in infant baptism; and the Quakers in their turn against all others, for still adhering to the externals of a ministry and sacraments at all—when a wild and blind cry like this is fondly resorted to, to eke out the deficiencies of argument: if it were not for the interests jeoparded, we could hardly regret the opportunity, thus afforded, of seeing that Sectarians have in fact no easier way of coping with the ancient Church, or silencing her claims, than by invoking the scorn and hooting of her foes.

I have felt the influence of this cry. I abhorred Popery;

perhaps dreaded, more than I abhorred it. I had been taught, from a child, to "hate it with a perfect hatred." I spent a thousand hours in boyhood with an old copy of the "Book of Martyrs," copiously adorned with pictures intended to produce, in an opposite direction, the effect of pictures in the worship of the Papists: the former being designed to stir men's passions, the latter their devotions. While, with my little sisters and their playmates, we sat around the great volume, we kissed the wounds of the martyrs, and half worshipped their images; we got us deadly instruments—pins, needles, knives, scissors, and without compunction put out the eyes of magistrates, and tore off the limbs and ears of Kings, Queens, Bishops, Cardinals, and Popes: while, at the top of each engraving, the picture of the Prince of Darkness with axes, torches, chains, and serpents issuing from his brain, suffered indignities and mutilations showing, quite sufficiently, that we were not only disposed, unlike Saint Michael, to "bring a railing accusation," but would certainly have had the Evil One "tormented before his time." In fact, we were genuine little Protestants, that would have seen the Pope and all his followers at the bottom of the sea. And I was myself more than a full-grown Protestant, before I knew at all where Popery had struck at the foundations of the ancient faith, or at the unity of the ancient Church: suspecting as little that it was done by additions to the primitive Creed, and by riding over the conservative Episcopacy, as that my own Church had done the same.

What is Popery? Is it wafers? candles? crosses? Luther used wafers, candles, altars, crosses, crucifixes; and the Lutherans do still: was Luther a friend of Popery? Yet there are men who would play into the hands of Rome, by persuading the uninformed that the Reformation was a miserable squabble about crosses, surplices, candlesticks, and snuffers! No, Sirs! It was for no children's quarrel that Luther stood before the Diet at Worms, and Cranmer gave his body to be burned. It was for doing precisely what you have all since done yourselves—for tampering with the ancient creed, for riding over the ancient order of the Church. With us, this is Popery. We know what it is. You know not what it is.

In England you once, by act of Parliament, forbade prayers over the dead; as they did also in Scotland and Geneva: and, in New England,* it is but fifty years since the first prayer at a funeral was heard. This rag of Popery you have now put on.

Once you forbade chanting and choirs in your worship, both in Great Britain and America: but now one of your own ministers in Leeds has pointed the Psalms for chanting; a chant from our own Daily Service with the *Gloria Patri* was recently sung to celebrate the landing of the Pilgrims; and you have your choirs, in the classic phrase of a Puritan of better days, "bellowing the tenor like oxen, barking a counterpart like a kennel of dogs, roaring a treble like a sort of bulls, and grunting a bass like a number of hogs."

Fifty years ago, or within half that time, you had not in all the land a single organ to distract your worship; while in England "the devil's bagpipe," as you called it, was formerly splintered and strewn upon the streets: but now its Babylonish tones fall pleasantly on your ears "at meeting," and you can endure quite well the bellowing of "the ten-horned Beast."

Formerly, both in Old and New England, you held the gown and bands to be literally rags of "the harlot," and gown and surplice you put upon dumb beasts in England and stood

* On the occasion of the death of a Divine of the (Puritan) Establishment in Massachusetts, in 1685, although prayers at the funeral were by law prohibited, we find the following parliamentary record: "Voted, that some persons be appointed to look to the burning of the wine, and heating of the cider, against the time appointed for the funeral!" Expense £18. Bought 32 gallons of wine, cider in proportion, and 104 pounds of sugar! A regular Popish Irish wake.

them at our altars: but now the model-Presbytery of New Brunswick have formally recommended the gown, (a recommendation, however, that created a little breeze, and was reconsidered;) and the Dissenters in England have extensively introduced the gown, and some of them the white surplice; although in general they adhere to black, the distinctive dress of the Jesuits.

Once you denominated the Liturgy, the Church's "Lethargy;" and the Prayer Book, an "ill-mumbled mass-book," "belching the sour crudities of Popery" into your face; you made bonfires of it in the streets, and forbade its use in England; while the "possessed" young woman in the Rev. Cotton Mather's house, who was unable to read a syllable of the Bible, or a Puritan book, could read fluently, he tells us, the Episcopal Prayer Book, or any *other* Popish work whatever; but now the more enlightened Dissenters in England often use it in their worship; and your own Doctors and Reviewers were passing the highest encomiums npon it, until you discovered that your laity were taking you at your word; while even now your Barneses and Smiths and Winchesters and Springs and very best Divines, are engaged in the Popish work of writing and dictating prayers for others.*

Once the symbol of redemption, on brow or church, challenged the hootings of your armies in the field, and of your

* It may be remembered that Drs. Anderson and Hawes, no mean names among New England Congregationalists, took open ground, in 1844, that Bishop Southgate was guilty of wilful misrepresentation in asserting that the Congregational missionaries, in the East, had worn Episcopal robes and used the Prayer Book; and in short had deceived the simple-minded Christians of the East, who believed them to be members of the English Church. The Bishop reasserts it. The Missionaries are written to. Mark their answer to their "Board" in Boston! "By being ready, in accommodation to *the great weakness of men*, to use on special occasions our English gown,. . . . . to use occasionally an Episcopal Liturgy: we have shown that *we are immeasurably exalted* above all the littleness of mere form and ceremony, and of that which is only external, and have exhibited a spirit of *tolerance* which was not previously supposed here to have *any existence on earth!*" Suppose the Jesuits had done this, eh?

flocks at home; nay, your Divines and Diviners certified you that it was "*the mark of the Beast:*" but we see it now on Baptist and Unitarian temples, and glittering upon the bosoms of your children, and even speaking peace upon the sepulchral stone over your dead.

To get away as far from Popery and heathenism as possible, many of your ministers, in other days, refused to baptize by any name not found in Scripture, or not made otherwise appropriate by some act of Providence, or some pious personal experience; so that the damsels and youth of New England are afflicted to this hour with such names as Experience, Joy, Charity, Deliverance, Discipline, Piety, Mercy, Faith, Patience, Preservation, Devotion, Thankful, as also by all the nomenclature of the old Testament from Adam to Malachi; while in England, according to Southey, the sons and daughters of the elect were called Earth, Dust, Ashes, Kill-sin, Joy-again, More-fruit, More-trial, From-above, Praise-God, Fight-the-good-fight-of-faith, &c., and one poor fellow, it is said, had the ill luck to be called, Through-much-tribulation-we-must-enter-into-the-kingdom-of-heaven. Now, however, I believe the Puritans have overcome the scruple; and a deteriorated conscience gives way to a cultivated taste.

Once you were known as haters of Episcopacy by your dress, and gait, and rounded hair, and upturned eyes, and new-invented dialect, and "*nasal twang*"—with which New England is still afflicted as the "mark" of the Puritanism that once domineered over the land: but now, though in some instances the children of the parents that ate the sour grapes find their teeth still set on edge, and they cannot get rid of the "mark," yet I believe that all New England would be glad to cast off these tokens, which their forefathers adopted to prevent the probability of the Evil One's mistaking them for Papists.

By solemn act of Parliament you once commanded all

paintings and pictures in the public collections, that contained representations of our Saviour or the Virgin, to be burned: but now we may see pictures of our Lord, and of his Saints, and of her whom "all nations shall call blessed," hanging in your galleries, and adorning your domiciles; perhaps, with the Missionaries at Constantinople, to show that you have suddenly become "*immeasurably exalted above mere externals!*"

Once you detested "Sisters of Mercy and Charity" as daughters of "the mother of abominations:" but recently your more evangelical brethren in France and Germany have instituted like orders (in some cases under the scriptural name of Deaconesses) in hospitals and parishes; and are effectively proving (WHAT IT WERE DEVOUTLY TO BE DESIRED THAT WE ALL MIGHT LEARN) that our only plan at last must be, to take the good and true in Popery, to conquer the evil and the false.

In those days you would not endure Daily Prayer and Weekly Sacraments, and you still object to them if restored among *us:* but vast numbers of your own selves have risen up, under the names of Sandamanians, Christians, Disciples, Irvingites, &c., to the ancient and scriptural privilege of continual communion; while we have seen among you often the experiment of a daily "prayer meeting" which you have, however, as often been compelled to abandon, not a man among you being able to endure for three hundred and sixty-five successive days the infliction of extemporaneous prayers.

Once by penal statutes, out of sheer abhorrence of Popery, you forbade any man or woman to be married by a minister, even of your own sect; running as usual from the Popish to the Protestant extreme, making entirely secular what Papists had believed to be entirely sacramental: but now we do not know the Divine in all New England, in whose pocket a wedding fee would not repose as comfortably as on the conscience of an Episcopalian—one rag more of Popery. If we go on thus, we shall soon have you covered from head to foot!

Once it was your loathing to see the lofty tower and pointed spire, the open roof and "dim religious light," the clustered column and symbolic tomb, as being so many expressions of Popery; with axes and hammers you broke down the carved work of the sanctuary; and it was one of your charges on the trial of the martyred Laud, that he had caused some painted windows at Lambeth to be mended: but now a man is famous among you according as he hath lifted up axes upon the thick trees, and wood, and stone, and all manner of material, to adorn with cunning device the place of your worship, according to the pattern of the "Dark ages," so that they require but little emendation to make them once more "Christianity petrified."*

I might trace this change that has come over you, into details innumerable. If you will have it that the leprosy of Popery is in our skirts, we cite the proverb, Physician, heal thyself! Away with these organs and bells, these steeples and towers, these carved stones and Gothic temples, these chants and choirs, these gorgeous sepulchres, these prayers over the dead, these commendations of liturgies, and these books of printed prayers, (as if the Spirit could be bound,) these pictures of the Lord and of His saints, and these crosses, and the "*Ave sanctissima*" now sung by your children to the piano and the harp! Depend upon it, ye are

* We confess ourselves at a loss to explain these strides of Presbyterianism toward the solemn and grand in architecture. We avow our motives: 1st, to make habitations worthy of the Being dwelling in them by His Presence; and 2dly, to exhibit symbolically to all coming ages the mysteries of our faith and hope. We *should like to know* the motive of Sectarians—who profess that God is better pleased with *simplicity*, and who have no mysteries to perpetuate—in resorting again to spires, towers, naves, &c.

fallen, ye are fallen from the simplicity of your forefathers; and if that be Popery which you once solemnly affirmed to be Popery, and with which you inflamed a nation to slay its Archbishop and its King: then your crusade against it is to be fought over again, and without a man left among you to fight it! Like the sea, which comes back to swallow again the trash that it threw up and left in an hour of anger on the beach, you are yourselves returning to the "vile things" which you once spewed out of your mouth, from a nauseated and excited stomach. There is not a man among you that would now wish to shed the blood of either Laud or Charles; and but few among you who would have deserted England's Church, if *all* the results of the experiment had been foreseen. Why, even the Dutch have lately erected a church in New York in the form of the cross; and the Board of Publication of the Presbyterian General Assembly has ornamented the most beautiful edition of Bunyan's Pilgrim's Progress I have yet seen, with a magnificent frontispiece emblazoned with a gorgeous cross! For nine years, as a Presbyterian minister, I wore on my breast a cross presented by a friend in a Revival, and was never taken to task for so doing until I became an Episcopalian; since when, first a carman whom I hired on the street, and then an organ-builder the first and last time I ever saw him, and after them, some half-dozen women, all "evangelical" Episcopalians, undertook to deprive me of my "liberty." *

* This rude declamation of the organ-man came with a very ill grace from him, to be sure, and so I told him. "What," said I, "do you pretend to talk thus to me, when this desk of yours has on it no less than four Popish periodicals, (with crosses in them, too,) to corrupt your visitors who may be tempted to read them, as I have been while waiting your return to your office?" "Oh," said the organ-man, "I am obliged to take them in the way of my business, as it brings me customers and makes the pot *bile*." "So then it is for *money*," said I; "for money, that you make these noble instruments to chant the lauds of Mary and the saints; but let me tell you, that though I wear the cross, and mean to wear it while I live, I would not for a universe of gold, encourage the circulation of those journals."

But you allege that there have been apostasies from the Church to Popery? I grant it. I lament it. But I can account for it. As far as my information now extends, the facts will show that, for the most part, the apostates to Rome have previously belonged, either within or without the Church, TO THE PURITANS; and have been, as Dr. Forbes (who was once one of them) expressed it with regard to himself, a "red-hot evangelical." Puritanism, within or without the Church, presents no fixed principle to the human mind, which is abandoned to the delirium of its own "private judgment," and by natural reaction, if not by the natural course of its own free-thinking, vaults from opinion to opinion, until it is lodged at last in the meshes of the Roman fisherman. Popery did not *draw* these men, but Puritanism *drove* them. They knew what had been everywhere the career and the goal of the Genevan sects; they had been in the secrets of the so-called "evangelicals:" they became dismayed at the thought that the Church was to run the course of the sects around her: and, in an hour of half-maddened grief, they rushed back from the precipice over which the sects had slidden, to the embrace of Rome. It was Puritanism *in* the Church, combining with Puritanism, Popery, and Atheism without, that in 1833 abolished ten Bishoprics in Ireland at a blow; and, instead of "Christian" education, substituted the present "National" system in Ireland, by which the Word of God has been taken from nearly half a million of children, and the children of the Church (as a bait to the Papists) have been allowed thereafter only such "Scripture Extracts" as the Papists shall approve. Gradually Maynooth, the hotbed of Popery, was endowed; Romish Prelates were allowed precedence on public occasions,

So leaving him to judge which of us was the Papist, I bade him good morning, and have never seen him since.

I despised such cant as a Presbyterian; I am quite sure Episcopalians cannot teach me to admire it.

of those of the Church; Romish Churches, Schools, Colleges, and Seminaries, in Canada and other colonies, were endowed with lands reserved for the Church: and all this, you will say perhaps, under a High Church Premier and Government in England? Not at all, dear reader. The first blow was struck in 1832, and the contest went on, under Lord Melbourne—not a High Churchman, but the "Liberal" Melbourne—who played a desperate game into the hands of the Jesuits, and had the so-called Evangelicals for his most potent allies; and who is now, by many, supposed to have sold his conscience to the Jesuits while he was Premier of England, and to have died a Papist, and a Jesuit of the short robe! The "High-Church party" remonstrated from the very first. But the "Evangelicals" and Puritans, within and without the Church, held the balance of power: and Popery understood how to make capital of the Latitudinarians. So I have reminded the reader before, that there was not a Romish Bishop or Priest, or a Romish separatist in England, *until the very year* the Puritans, calling themselves in that day "Gospellers," as they now do "Evangelicals," went out of the Church, and Rome entered through the breach. Please *remember* this!

And what do we now see? We see "evangelical" men, so-called, appealing from their Bishop to a secular court of Presbyterians and others, to settle great and grave questions of discipline and heresy; leaning on the secular arm, and teaching the nation to look to the Queen as "the supreme Head of the Church." We see another Melbourne in Lord J. Russell, seeking to recognize the Pope as a Sovereign, and to open direct diplomatic intercourse with Rome; and, if we are to believe the intruding Bishops in England, intimating to the Pope that such a measure would not be resisted: and all this while he was forbidding the Church to hold even a Convocation of her clergy, promoting men of "liberal" sentiments to all Episcopal vacancies, and himself procuring the baptism of his own child from a Presbyterian minister; and, when he sees all England dismayed at the results of the Melbourne-Russell policy, and threatening to lay him in an ignominious grave, *joining the Evangelicals* again in their cry against Church principles! If the Jesuits have not made good use of the Puritans within as well as without the Church, then such a man as Loyola has never lived.

What do we see! *The same combination* in the British colonies at the north, in the British possessions at the south, and IN THE UNITED STATES—we see everywhere *the same combination* between the "evangelicals," so called, and the dissenter, the profane, the lawless, and the infidel—in vestries, in conventions, in parishes, in newspapers, in books, by raising tumults, by threatening the clergy, by direct persecutions and broils and mobs, *per fas et nefas*—resisting all return to the principles of the Reformation, all return to the scriptural precedents of Prayers and Eucharists and Alms, and even avowing the determination, when they shall get the power, to alter and "reform" the Prayer Book of its "remnants of Popery!"

My Brethren of the "evangelical school" within the Church, listen to me while I raise in your ears the cry of warning! Abstain from your present work. Return to the principles you once embraced, and to which the party you despise are *the true successors.* Return to alms-deeds, and charities, and labors, and fastings, and eucharists, and prayers, and meekness, and gentleness, and love! Return to the principles that made *you* the friends of the *poor*, and the *poor* the friends of the *Church;* and fly from the teaching into which you have degenerated, and which has gathered around you the wealthy and the proud and the powerful, and has made the world without, regard you as essentially *with them* in their purpose to obliterate altar, priest, sacrifice, self-discipline, from the earth, together with the last vestige (unless it be looked for in Rome) of the cross and the keys. Once the wealthy and the worldling hated you; now you agree. Brethren, stop! My feet have trodden on the frightful precipice. My eyes have seen the dark and dismal gulf. My ears have heard the moans of the millions that have fallen over. And I tremble to see *you* joining hands upon the precipice with parties just hanging over, and they with others who are in the act of falling, and they with *the fallen!* What are you to gain? If you *fail* of your object, your labor is lost; and with it your time and opportunities. If you succeed, if the Church shall be Puritanized, if you even blot out Baptismal grace and the Eucharistic Presence from our Prayer Book: your league with the sects is complete, the link with antiquity is lost; and, instead of here and there one, you will see thousands, tens of thousands, millions flying in dismay to Rome, and yourselves or your successors falling off to Socinianism; and the meaning, we fear, of that awfully mysterious Scripture will be cleared up by a fulfilment which your own agency shall give it: "HIS DEADLY WOUND WAS HEALED. *And all the world again wondered after the Beast!*"

There is one Presbyterian Church already, why do you want another? Nay, there are several hundred; why another? Wait and see! See first to what goal Presbyterianism is striding! Why, Brethren, since these pages were begun, all the "evangelical" associations of Connecticut have proven themselves powerless to censure the wretched doctrines of their brother Bushnell, who assails their faith in the Holy Trinity as hitherto held, and their various views of the atonement, concerning which he tells them, that they all teach at last that "God must have his satisfaction somehow," and again "must somehow get his *quantum* of suffering out of His Son!" Brethren, let go their hands! If you will hold on to theirs, you must let go ours. Let our Church be again what she was under Elizabeth—the noble Queen who (unlike Victoria) refused to be called "the supreme Head of the Church"—when our doctrines and our ritual had fair play: and there can be again, as there was then, no danger! It was the exiles under Mary, returning from the Continent, that first rent the Church with the Genevan doctrines. While the Church was one, she conquered the strongholds of Popery, and she can do it again. She has kept off the malaria of infidelity from England, and she can do it here! She stands with open arms to receive the thousands and ten thousands that, except for her, would have no other home to flee unto from the apostate sects, but to the bosom of Rome! *Puritanize the Church, and Rome's work is done!*

CHAPTER XXVI.

THE TWIN SISTERS.

THE political world presents at this moment a painful illustration of the maxim, that "Extremes meet." The feeling at the North against involuntary servitude, carrying men's minds in one direction; and the settled conviction at the South, that the circumstances of the case make such servitude both lawful and humane, operating in another: have produced, under our eyes, the one result of trampling under foot the wholesome compromises of the Union. In like manner Popery, by pressing its pretensions in one way, and Presbytery, by doing the same in the opposite direction, agree only in the common result of disregarding the ancient compact under which the Church was One, at the beginning: while the Episcopal Church, adhering still to the sacred terms of that original Bond, holds both the extremes in check, and invites all, who profess and call themselves Christians, back to the basis of the Ancient Union, for which the noble army of Martyrs fell gloriously in the field. If the page were sufficiently wide I should exhibit in parallel columns the two extremes, and between them the Church of our love crucified, as between the two—bearing alike the taunts of both, and yet ever holding forth the Lord, the Faith, the Baptism of Antiquity.

Popery affirms that the Church of Rome, or, as some say, the Pope

Presbytery (or old Calvinism) teaches that every man of the elect

himself, (which, now that Mary is deified, will probably be the next article foisted into their creed,) is infallible in doctrine, although either he or his may fall into sin and perish.

is individually infallible in things essential to salvation, and can never deny his Lord; and out-popes the Pope in insisting that no man, once a Christian, can be ever left to depart this life in any grievous sin.

The true Catholic believes that an individual, or even a particular Church, may fall for ever away: and that it is only the Church in its totality that cannot fall from the faith, or yield to the gates of hell.

Popery refuses to be governed by antiquity; alleging that the Pope and his underlings are capable of defining and discovering truths that the times were not ripe for in the days of St. Paul.

Presbytery refuses to be governed by antiquity; alleging that every man is capable of interpreting for himself: and whole sects of Presbyterians are, even now, discovering new doctrines for which they imagine the less enlightened ages were not prepared.

While these Twin Sisters, Trent and Geneva—born, as we said before, in the throes of the fifteenth century—refuse to have their legitimacy tested by calling into court the ancient Mother: the true Catholic flies to her arms, and appeals confidently to her testimony, that the Church,—as he holds it in the Creed, and the Episcopacy,—is the Church that was born in the throes of Calvary.

Popery, without remorse, adds to the ancient Creed her incongruous dogmas concerning relics, and dead men's bones, and purgatorial fires, and—in short, the decrees of the Tridentine Synod.

Presbytery has also, without compunction, added to the ancient Creed, or substituted for it, the dogmas of predestination, limited redemption, and—in short, the resolutions of the Synod of Westminster.

Episcopacy maintains the ancient Creed *intact*, as the ancient compact and sacred bond of union: and would no more presume to add to that sacred instrument, or to take from it, than she would alter or mutilate the Scriptures. You may see her agitated to her centre, but in her rashest hours she has never tampered with the Creed.

The Papists, with unhallowed hand, have touched the ark of the Testament: and, as late as the fifteenth century, have added to the Holy Scripture the Apocrypha as of equal inspiration and authority.

Sectarians, from Luther to the "evangelical" Neander, have cast out one and another and another of the Books of Scripture, until all in their turn have been *rejected:* while some have *added* the words of Swedenborg, and others the Book of Mormon, and others the Revelations of Davis, and others the ethereal ravings of Madame Hauffe, the seeress of Wittemberg, whose "spirit-nerve" and "illuminated eye," and "epigastric ghost-seeing" and "language of spirits," are esteemed by many of the *savans* of that place, as more entitled to philosophical belief than the Bible, which Luther has been, poetically enough, represented as exhuming from its monastic sepulchre, in that very city.

Only the Episcopal Church, with her Northern and Oriental sisters, has kept, and will ever keep, the ancient Word of God intact.

Popery fetters "private judgment" by binding it down to insufferable trifles in the dogmas of Trent, each one of which must be received on pain of damnation.

Presbytery leaves also little room for the free exercise of "private judgment," by the multitudinous dogmas required of her ministers to be subscribed, as essential portions of a consistent system.

Episcopacy, still content with the articles of the most brief and ancient Creed, leaves mankind free to differ on other questions, for the sake of promoting the chances of agreement and of peace in those matters which are alone *essential.*

Popery is still employed in tinkering at the faith, and has lately added, or is about to add, the dogma of the Immaculate Conception of the Blessed Virgin, with which it appears all parts of the Romish Church have been simultaneously *inspired.*

Sectarianism likewise is yet occupied with mending her creeds; and new and startling dogmas, often based also on alleged inspiration, are so often propounded, that both the novelty and the enormity have ceased to create surprise.

The Episcopal Church has no such work to do, and never had: but has received her faith, as she has received her Bible and her Priesthood, complete from a pure and inspired antiquity.

Popery rides over the Bishops, as being in the way of the supremacy of the Pope.

Sectarianism rides over the Bishops, as being in the way of the supremacy of the pastor.

The follower of the ancient Church insists that the pastors should bear themselves meekly, and set their flocks a heavenly example by showing docility and obedience to *their* pastors. It is a discipline for the clergy, but it fits for the kingdom of heaven.

Popery destroys the nature of a sacrament, (which, to be a sacrament, must have both an outward and an inward part,) by denying that, after consecration, the *outward* elements of the bread and wine remain.

Presbytery destroys the nature of a sacrament, by denying that, after consecration, the outward elements have an *inward* part, or convey to the soul the Body and Blood of the Lord.

True Catholicity adheres to the ancient definition of a sacrament, and retains both the outward or visible, and the inward or invisible: alleging that the bread and wine are still bread and wine, but that the Body and Blood of the Lord are conveyed through them, to our condemnation or glory.

In a way we have explained before, Popery avowedly gives a

Presbytery gives to the cheated infant a *blank baptism,* signifying *blank communion*, an unconsecrated wafer, without the inward part or thing signified.

apparently as much as in an adult, but conveying nothing but cold and soulless water to the forehead, without the inward part or thing signified.

The ancient Catholic holds that Baptism with water only, is not Baptism ; and that when we baptize with water, if there be no resistance, (and in infants there can be none,) God, according to the promises of His word, does baptize with the Holy Ghost: and that a blank or white baptism is as solemn trifling as a "white communion."

Popery denies the intermediate state betwixt death and the judgment: and was the first to allege that those dying in mortal sin go instantly to *Gehenna* after death; and the good instantly, or very shortly after death, to heaven.

Presbytery, with the exception of a few Divines, denies the doctrine of the intermediate state: alleging, with Popery, that the good and the bad go immediately to heaven or *Gehenna*.

Episcopacy maintains the ancient faith, that there is a place of repose for the good,* and of awful forebodings to the

* The rich man was not *in hell proper*, but in "Hades;" Lazarus not in heaven, but in "Abraham's bosom;" the penitent thief not in heaven proper, but in "Paradise," for our Blessed Lord had "not yet ascended" into heaven: even David was yet in that intermediate world, when St. Peter preached on the day of Pentecost. *Read attentively* St. Peter's sermon; "Death and hell"—not Gehenna, but *Hades*—"were cast into the lake of fire." So throughout. It were strange indeed to be rewarded or punished first, and judged afterwards! No! Let wheat and tares ripen fully until the harvest, which is "the end of the world." I was never more fairly disconcerted and *non-plussed* in my life, than I was the very year that I left Princeton, by a half-intoxicated man at a country inn. "Mister!" said the man, "they say you are a parson; now there is one thing I should like very much to know, and I suppose you are the man can tell me!" "Yes, sir," said I, "with much pleasure, if I can." "Well," said my new acquaintance, "can you tell me where the wicked go when they die?" I answered, according to the best of my knowledge at the time, "To Hell." "Well," said he, "isn't it said that they shall 'by no means come out thence until they have paid the uttermost farthing?'" "Yes." "Well, do they come out on the day of judgment? And if they do, isn't it very strange that the wicked should be sent to hell first, and judged afterwards?" What I could have answered, I do not know; as what I did answer I do not remember. The eyes of several bystanders were by this time drawn to

wicked, until the judgment; and that even the devils are not to be "tormented before the time."

Popery well nigh abolishes, among her followers, the fear of hell, by the doctrine of purgatory.

Puritanism has fifteen hundred ministers in this land alone, that hold the doctrine of a purgatorial process, and no hell hereafter.

The Catholic religion, before Popery was, and in the East where Popery has never been, denies a purgatorial fire, as a most dangerous innovation on the ancient faith, and a great wrong to the Divine government; since it represents the punishments of the world to come as vindicive exactions extending even to the good.

Popery exaggerates *faith* to an extent that is fearfully abused among its followers, who are taught that all die safe, who die *believing* what the Church believes.

Calvinism exaggerates *faith* to a degree which by easy abuse lulls its followers into complete security, for when they come to die, whatever has been the life, they *believe* and trust only in Christ.

The Catholic religion, while it makes faith the foundation, requires the superstructure of *character*, as obviously requisite for mingling with the pure and unsullied spirits of "just men made perfect."

I could greatly extend this list of coincidences between Romanism and Presbyterianism, but time would fail me. And as they coincide in dogma at so many points, (including the famous doctrine of *election* first invented by Augustine,) so do the two systems meet in their practical workings, as we shall now discover.

us; and I felt myself in such close quarters, that I wished my new acquaintance of the Socratic school had joined the tee-totallers before I met with him, or had found such cause to ask, in the words of Scripture, "Who hath babbling?" This incident turned my attention to the subject; and, long before I was an Episcopalian, I believed, with a few others of my brethren, in the Intermediate State. With eternity before us, there is no occasion for precipitancy; and the majesty of redemption, and the importance of the issue, justify deliberation and delay.

If Presbytery has dared to talk of "elect infants," she has borrowed this horrid dogma from the Papists, whose doctors have often held the damnation of (unbaptized) children.

If Presbyterianism has relied much on frames and feelings and transports in religion, as an evidence of saintship, she has borrowed a leaf from Popery, which deals often in this same enthusiasm, and has lately done so in the raptures and rhapsodies of the virgins of the Tyrol.

If Papists say, as did Bishop England to a friend of mine, that they would not desire more than two hours to prepare any man for death: so Presbytery, by reducing preparation to a minimum, declares that faith and repentance may take place in a moment of time; and I sat in the pulpit once, while a celebrated divine, in an elaborate treatise, sought to satisfy his hearers that it took no longer to prepare a man for heaven, than would be necessary for the two propositions to pass through his mind, "I have sinned," "Christ has died." He made it out less than a quarter of a minute. What mind can conceive the amazing mischief of such soul-deluding teaching? With Bishop England it is reasonable, for he allows a place within the limits of probation for carrying forward a work begun here; but the Calvinist translates to the unsullied light of heaven without *any* cultivation of character!

If Papists too often substitute severity of dogma for severity of morals: so Sectarism does away too often the rigor of a life-long charity, by the rigor of a sudden and harsh conversion; the severity of fastings and prayers, by the severity of doctrines; the discipline of brotherly kindness and forgiveness, by the discipline of censoriousness and denunciation; the severity of watching over self, by the severity of watching over others: until, in some quarters, it has almost become a proverb, that a man is made a worse neighbor and a worse man by his "getting religion."

If Popery allows the taking of oaths with "mental reservations," "Evangelicalism" permits the same: and hence the Presbyterian Church has been overrun by a ministry subscribing the "Confession of faith," and then trampling it under foot and rending the communion; and the Church of England has been cursed with the principles of the Tract No. XC., written by a man who had learned this lesson from the so-called "evangelicals." Yet he did no more as a Papist, than he had done before as a Puritan. Only as a High Churchman—high above all "mental reservations" of Puritan or Papist—could *I* have subscribed the Prayer Book, or have ever allowed myself to say, "We yield Thee HEARTY THANKS *most merciful Father*, that it hath pleased *Thee* to *regenerate* this infant *with thy Holy Spirit*"—a doctrine on which hangs all the after-teachings of the Church.

If Popery has created schism in England to establish her supremacy: she waited until the Presbyterians had first separated from the Church, and set up altar against altar.

If Popery has openly avowed that heretical princes must be set aside: Puritanism has avowed and carried out the atrocious doctrine in the murder of King Charles, who offered them a law of universal toleration—which was *not the thing they wanted.*

Popery excludes a large portion of the word of God from the sanctuary: Presbyterianism does the same, allowing almost universally but a chapter or two in a week, and in many European Presbyteries not even that.

If Popery, reducing things to an accommodating *minimum*, has yielded to the fashionable phrase of going "to hear" *Mass:* so Presbytery has reduced the magnificence of worship to the lowest quantity of going "to hear" *preaching.*

If Papists worship God by proxy of priests and choirs, as in many places they now do: Sectarians, excepting a few lines of rhyme said over by the people, commit their worship to their preacher.

If Papists substitute certain outward abstinences for purity and piety: Sectarianism too, is often eminently satisfied with abstinences from what it calls the world—balls and dances, drinks and parties of amusement.

If Popery has bound grievous burdens, and broken the unity of the Church by unheard-of terms of communion: Puritanism has been guilty too, in several thousand congregations, of compelling all who would receive communion to confess that they belong to a "Temperance" society, an Anti-slavery society, &c.

If Papists have laid their hand upon the CUP and withdrawn it from the Laity, to make the doctrine of transubstantiation consistent with itself: we are told that the Sectarians have, in the State of New York alone, eight hundred congregations where the CUP that Christ commanded is forbidden, and boiled raisin-water or other wretched drink is substituted! As far as Sectarianism can do it, it is ripening the whole land for Popery.

If Papists have a strange fancy for relics and dead men's bones: there may be seen, projecting from the tower of "The Church of the Pilgrims" in Brooklyn, a mammoth fragment of the Plymouth Rock, (they would have shuddered at a fragment from the rock of Calvary;) and my own eyes have seen the chair in which "the Dairyman's Daughter" sickened and died, transported across the Atlantic, and held up as high as arms could reach in the Broadway Tabernacle, for the weeping gaze of "all the evangelical denominations." Nay, I myself made a pilgrimage to her tomb in the charming Isle of Wight, with a "guide-book" in my hand, saw a volume of names, (including, I observed, that of one of our own Bishops, who is zealous against altar-tombs,) and after inserting my own, plucked a sprig of the box tree, which her sainted hands had planted, and which I held for a time in as great veneration as the Papists in Rome are said to hold the tail of Balaam's ass.*

If Popery has dealt much among the superstitious in dreams, voices, visions, smells, &c.: who does not know that among the ignorant, modern Revivalism has made large capital of these same impostures, as evidences of the Spirit's descent into their hearts? An extensive "awakening" was a few years since carried on among the negroes of Jamaica, in which they were required to dream three times on subjects assigned them, before they could be admitted to communion; and the revival (as all "revivals" depend more on the *music* than the preaching) was greatly promoted by a solemn tune to "the house that Jack built."† Stop the *music*, and you kill any such "excitement" in a week!

If Popery has the faculty of adaptation so that its system sits easily upon her members, from the wild enthusiast to the most vicious and profane: so Sectarianism, in its multiplicity of forms and opinions, even to the denial of future punishment, has adapted itself completely to all sorts and conditions and opinions of men, from the fanatical revivalist and revelationist, to the cold Socinian and the German Pantheist.

This parallel of abuses and corruptions, we might pursue almost without limit.‡ But, to sum up all, both systems—

* "The keeper of the Wartburg" [Castle,] says M. D'Aubigné, "regularly points out to travellers the mark made [on the wall] by Luther's inkstand," which he threw at the "gigantic form of the devil, grinning triumphantly, and grinding his teeth at Luther, (who was engaged in translating the Bible,) tormenting and vexing him, and moving round and round him, like a lion ready to leap upon his prey." Very odd, certainly. We are told, on the authority of Luther himself,—a man of strong nerve,—that he very often saw and conversed with the devil!

† This account, by a Sectarian Missionary in that Island, I can well believe, after scenes and songs that I have seen and heard at the South, and in camp meetings, in our own country. Who has not noticed the similarity between Revival Hymns and the songs of the popular "Negro Minstrels?"

‡ And we might also say to a ridiculous extent. Let one example suffice for each. The Puritans tore down from the altar *the commandments of God;* and posted

having broken away from the ancient uniformity of Creed, the ancient discipline of the Bishops, and the ancient terms of Communion, and refusing to abide by the verdict of antiquity—have substituted strange doctrines, a new discipline, and unheard-of terms of communion. Both too have exaggerated truths into miserable fables. Popery exaggerates the intermediate state into a gross purgatorial fire; the Real Presence in spirit and power in the Eucharist, into a carnal and local presence; respect for the ashes of the dead who sleep in Jesus, into a veneration for their bones; the indefectibility of the whole Church into the infallibility of the Roman; the Divinity of Christ, into a naked and absolute Divinity not now to be approached but by the mediation of Mary; the humanity of Christ, into a subjection to Mary whose maternal behests he must obey; the purity of Mary into her "immaculate conception," &c., &c.: while Puritanism pushes the Divinity of our Lord to the practical exclusion of his Humanity as a man like ourselves, whose life of prayers and fasts and sacraments and sufferings and charities we are bound *to make our own;* or else it presses His humanity to the denial of His Divinity; it magnifies an overruling, into a predestinating Providence; the election to privileges, into an irreversible election to salvation; a watchful care of the people of God, into their *nolens-volens* "perseverance;" the atonement itself, into a harsh, stern commercial transaction between what they style "parties in the Godhead;" the gentle influences of the Spirit, into a sudden and irresistible *ictus* from above; the divine method of patient-

in their stead, in the Churches of England, the celebrated "*Covenant*:" while a Popish saint, regularly canonized, travestied the Book of Psalms, and applied their majestic worship to the Virgin. The Papists too, have adapted our gorgeous *Te Deum* to the Virgin: as the Puritans did our *Litany* and *Benedicite* to their wars against their Church and King. The Papists have a set day at Rome, in which they gather and kneel around the Pope—their Grand Lama—on his throne, and kiss his toe: not long ago, the "Presbyterian" was compelled to take to task a congregation for "singing to the praise and glory of" *their Minister* just returned from Europe, a *hymn* of fulsome flattery to himself and his *wife* and *children!*

ly wearing out evils and abuses, into violent, spasmodic indiscriminate eradication; the utility of preaching, to the almost exclusion of worship; and sins God can easily forgive, into the "unpardonable sin against the Holy Ghost." I have seen a whole school of boys tortured on this last-named engine of revivalism, without a man to let us know that such a sin was, in us, well nigh impossible!

Thus do extremes meet. Thus are Popery and Puritanism mysteriously united, by some tie through which they seem to act and think and feel together: not unlike the Siamese twins, that seem sometimes to be one, and sometimes two. How often have we seen Popery and Sectarism combining —together with Infidels, Agrarians, and selfish Politicians, and profligate and debauched men, against the Church: both in England and America—Popery as bitter as Puritanism, and Puritanism as violent as Popery. O Popery! Popery! It is of *thy* doing that the bewildered world is doomed to tread this maze of dogmas, before arriving at the ancient fixed goal of truth! If *thou* hadst preserved the Creed *intact*, as the Churches of the East have done; if thou hadst even been content with thy ancient honors as Umpire in matters of local disagreement; if thou hadst left the Scriptures untainted by the Apocrypha; if thou hadst pinioned thy hand in the fearful hour that it was extended to rob the laity of the Cup; if thou hadst bridled thy tongue when thou framedst it to pronounce anathemas against the word of God in the hands of the people; if thou hadst stood fast by the ancient terms of communion in the early centuries; if thou hadst been as silent as the ancient fathers are, about the worship of Mary, and the angels, and the saints, and pictures, and images, and dead men's bones, and about purgatorial fires to *satisfy* justice, and about works of supererogation; if thou hadst left voluntary celibacy with the honors assigned it in Scripture and antiquity, and the celibacy of the clergy to the honorable choice of pure and self-denying and heavenly-minded men, as it was left in the days of Jesus and of Paul; if thou hadst been content that "all generations" should call Mary "Blessed;" if thou hadst taught the ancient doctrine of the glorious Presence; if thou hadst been satisfied that the whole Church should enjoy conjointly—but separately should forfeit—the promise of safe-keeping from the gates of hell; if thou hadst not interpolated the fathers; in a word, if thou hadst ADHERED TO ANTIQUITY: the world would have been spared these endless distractions, doubts, and protests. You have so mixed up the worship of Mary and the saints, with the worship of Jesus: that Sectarians by millions, without discriminating, have set the whole system down as an imposture, and denied the Lord who bought them with His blood! You have so confused modern inventions and traditions with those of high antiquity and apostolic dignity, that unless men can see a dogma categorically set forth in Scripture, they reject it, and fill the world with the denial of infant baptism, and of other blessed and refreshing truths. Thou hast so perverted, too, the Episcopacy into the Papacy, that men in disgust reject the one as the germ of the other. Thou has so mixed up "works of supererogation" and the merits of your "saints" and societies and your "Banks of Piety," with the merits of our Only Redeemer: that the whole doctrine of justification by merits other than our own, is ruthlessly despised. And, in fine, thou hast so set thine own self-will and "private judgment" against all the doctrines, teachings, and usages of the Ancient Church, that every Sectarist, in breaking away from unity and from authority, pleads the example of the Pope! Rome! Rome! Twin-sister to Geneva! Is all the fanaticism, false doctrine, heresy and schism, bewildering and blighting the minds of men this hour, to be found in *thy* skirts? And thou Geneva—exalted to heaven, but thrust down to hell, for the denial of thy Lord—as thou art the child of Rome, art thou not the

Mother in thy turn, of this miserable brood of schisms, and strifes, and heresies, and horrid and blasphemous opinions, that darken and curse the sectarian world? "Come out of her, my people, that ye be not partakers of her plagues!" Drink not the cup that Rome and Geneva drink, lest ye be baptized with their baptism: but go to the pure fountains of Antiquity, the cool, clear, refreshing sources of an Ancient and Catholic religion.

CHAPTER XXVII.

VARIOUS OBJECTIONS ANSWERED.

It is singular how the whole outside world is fretted and worried with the family affairs of the Episcopal Church. The General Assembly of the Presbyterians may dispute, divide, go into the secular courts, fly into a hundred sects and schisms, and the Episcopalian not even know it. Baptists may hatch their brood of fifteen different communions: and the Episcopalian will still be calm and serene as a sunny day in June. All Germany may become infidel, or Scotland Arminian, or Ireland Arian, or Geneva Socinian, so far as regards the Presbyterian population: and the Episcopalian will scarcely chronicle the fact. Fifty thousand sectaries may follow Joe Smith into the wilderness, or thousands of Presbyterian Protestants in Europe, terrified at the results of their experiment, may revert to Popery: and Episcopalians not notice it. But let there be an apostate to Popery from the ancient Church of God, east or west, north or south, in England or America: and all the sects are at once thrown into dismay, and the curtains of the land do tremble. Newspapers, magazines, mobs, platforms, parliaments, echo the wild dismay. Is not this the leaven heaving the bosoms of the nations? Is not this the Bride, startling the earth by the slightest imputation on her fair fame? Is not this the Church of God—the city that cannot be hid?

As an individual, unable to grapple with the defences of a Divine Episcopacy, I was glad to be diverted with the blemishes and weaknesses of its human administration. *Any thing*—to get rid of the interminable shower of arguments falling heavy and thick, like iron hail, around me.

Thus, for example, I would fly across the waters, and renew the political alliance of my forefathers with the Papists, and join in the outcry against the alleged exactions and oppressions of the Episcopal Church. Nor did I care to be informed that the present Episcopal Church in Ireland is the true and lineal Church of St. Patrick, whose successors in the Episcopal line became, in the sixteenth century, the reformers of the Church, without exceptions sufficient to keep up the Popish schism: so that that schism was reproduced entirely by the influence of Spanish and Italian gold, and the fresh importation of Italian and Spanish Bishops. Nor did I care to be informed that the average income of the Irish clergy was but $1,000 a year: while the result of their labors, since the beginning of the present century, has shown an increase of clergymen from 1,000 to 2,000, of whom eight hundred are laborious curates; a still larger increase of churches, from 639 to 1,375, besides 200 licensed chapels; and the restoration from Popery of "a great company of the priests" to the ancient church, so that the establishment of an asylum for their reception has been found necessary; and all this in the face of a hostile government, the abolition of ten bishoprics, and the confiscation to the State, for secular uses, of 1,480 glebes, and of an annual income of $1,500,000, once devoted in good faith by men, in their last will and testament, to pious uses.

Again, my sympathies were lavished on the poor, down-trodden, tithe-paying English—unconscious, as I supposed, of their burdens and their wrongs. Nor did I care to understand, that, if these tithes were abolished to-morrow, the greedy landlord would receive exactly one-tenth more of income, as his estates would be rented for the difference: while the peasant would be robbed of his time-honored church, and his child of its parochial school. I did not understand, that pious proprietors of estates had, in days gone by, erected these churches for their villagers and farmers; and, instead of enriching the church with lands, had entailed on their children the parochial tithes, for religious and charitable uses among the poor. I did not care to understand, how deeply seated must be the religious principle in the breast of a nation accustomed to understand their rights and to redress their wrongs, and to require a *quid pro quo* in all their compromises; yet willing, against the combined opposition of Papists, Dissenters, and Infidels, to surrender, with Abraham, a tenth of all to the great Melchizedek. I did not care to know, that the large incomes of some of the Bishops and clergy were the result of a providential purpose, developing the wealth of a highly-favored nation, on a small island of the sea, and enhancing the value of the property which was little worth when first donated by a pious ancestry to a poor and suffering Church. Nor did I care to know that, after all, there were *twelve thousand* clergymen in England, each living on *less than fourteen hundred dollars;* that out of thirteen thousand working clergy more than *ten thousand* subsist on a salary of £114, or *five hundred dollars* a year! Mr. Baptist Noel, who furnishes an unexceptionable testimony to most of these facts, tells us that 5,230 hard-working curates receive but the average income of $370, while 4,882 incumbents receive themselves but $700 a year. There is but one living in England, which, by the accidental rise of property, is worth $30,000; and but one other that is worth $20,000; three others of the value of $14,000; thirteen of $9,000; thirty-two of $7,000; and only 1,425 of the value of $2,300 and upwards. Nor did I know any thing of the interior or domestic policy of the Church of England, under which the clergy are expected to head all subscriptions for charitable purposes and public improvements, to an extent unknown, undreamed of, this side of the waters: besides employing their curates at their own expense. Lately a venerable Bishop has gone to his rest, of whom it was ascertained, at his demise, that more than a million of dollars from his income and private fortune had been expended on public and charitable uses. A noble Bishop, of the order and spirit of St. Thomas in the distant East, has lately given out of his private fortune $100,000 towards the erection of a Cathedral in a heathen land. A Bishop, worthy of the name of Coleridge, and lately gone to rest, surrendered, years ago, one-half of the Episcopal endowment, to erect a new Diocese. An unendowed Bishop in the Church of Scotland has lately, from his private fortune, endowed another Diocese in the North. The erection and endowment of churches, schools, and charities, by Rectors in England, at an expense of five, ten, twenty, fifty thousand dollars, is an every-day occurrence; while these donations have sometimes reached, and are reaching at this moment, in some instances, the enormous sums of hundreds of thousands! We have nothing like it on this side of the Atlantic. These large livings are sometimes given back, with as much again, to the Church and to the poor. Their system of curacies absorbs another vast portion of these revenues; so that, in the majority of cases, the clergy are supported in a great measure by their private fortunes, or their personal exertions. One of the most devoted and most hated Bishops in England, and one continually cried down as a wealthy and pampered Lord, said solemnly to an American Bishop long ago, that so great were the demands upon his income for charitable and public purposes, he should not leave his family, from the income of his Episcopate, a single farthing at his death. The British people are not an ignorant or superstitious people, wont to submit quietly to grievances and wrongs. They are acquainted with these facts; and every hour a wealthy and noble laity, with a virtue and piety unknown in any land before, are pouring their unbounded voluntary offerings, besides their cheerful and accustomed tithes, into the lap of such a Church; while every hour gives fresh demonstration to the saying of Lacon, that "in no country do the clergy have so much power, and in no country do they abuse it so little, as in England." With all its real wealth and alleged luxury, and with all the tempting and corrupting influences of state-patronage and state misrule, it is the only state-religion or state-church since the Reformation that has preserved the succession of an uncorrupted doctrine; and ever and anon has shown its inherent vitality by a re-awakening, and made its power felt, as well abroad as at home.

Yes, for every Presbyterian preacher in America living on a minimum salary, I will undertake to produce three of the Church of England living, in a more expensive country, on a smaller income. Will you accept the challenge? When will you produce 10,000 hard-working ministers, as the Church of England can, subsisting each on less than $500? When shall we see, in this land of cheaper bread and of alleged cheaper religion, 5,300 pastors subsisting on $370? No, no! The hardship is not in England, nor yet in Ireland, where the landed property is Episcopal, and its proprietors consent gladly to this reduction from their profits. The hardship is in Scotland, where a Presbyterian kirk is supported by tithes from property of which, as the Edinburgh Review admits, three-fourths belong to Episcopalians. No, no! The people most taxed for the support of religion are not the people of England, but the people of the quiet villages of our own beloved land: where, instead of one venerable village spire, five or six churches, for as many different sects, must be erected; and as many bells—if each "denomination" be not too poor and mean to have one—ring their discordant jar upon the air; and, instead of one spiritual parent to the united family, there are five or six preachers of different "persuasions" to be supported—that is to say, nineteen thousand in all, throughout the country—and all without the schools and charities which ennoble the villages of England. Even in England, the individual tax on the dissenter to support his preacher, is allowed, by Mr. Noel, to be greater than on the member of the Church of England for the support of the recognized religion of the land. And as to declension in doctrinal purity, neither Rome, nor Germany, nor Switzerland, has been able to bear the corrupting influence of an Establishment: the Church of England alone has had the vital force to beat back neology and its corruptions; and this inherent life within the Church has had its share in convincing me that it is the Church of Christ.

As a modest Presbyterian, I did not suppose the fact could be disputed, that Missionary zeal and Missionary societies were exclusively the offspring of an anti-prelatical religion. I did not know, or care to know, that while the oldest of our sectarian Societies for Missions, Tracts, and Bibles was scarcely half a century old, the venerable Society for the Propagation of the Gospel was founded in England in A. D. 1700; and that the Christian Knowledge Society, for the diffusion of tracts and books and Bibles, entered on its glorious course in 1698; and that the Church of England was vigorously planning for the world's conversion, even while the towers of her cathedrals lay prostrate before the batteries of a Puritan artillery, and her altars were yet smoking from the fires of the fanatical incendiary. What Presbyterian knows that the former of these societies is in the annual receipt of $400,000, and the latter of more than $500,000, while the Church Missionary Society of London receives half a million more, and innumerable charities, amounting to a great many annual millions are incessantly pouring in from a people, whose ideas of obligation to Almighty God are not satisfied with even a Nation's tithes. See $600,000 raised within a little while to increase the number of free churches in London; see three hundred new churches spring up in the lifetime of a single Bishop in the Diocese of Chester; see sixty new churches, nearer by, grow up in a single year in the desert-diocese of Toronto. And what this Church is doing at these points, she is doing everywhere. And pray what was Presbyterian Scotland doing all this while for the world's regeneration? or Presbyterian Holland? or Puritan England under Cromwell? or Presbyterian Geneva? or Presbyterian Germany, or Denmark, or Prussia? *Nothing.* While the Episcopal Church numbers but one-fifth of Protestant Christendom: her voluntary annual charities, as figures show, are five times larger than those of the whole Protestant world besides. The public charities of London alone, amount to a greater annual sum than those of all the rest of Protestant Europe! And while the Protestant world slumbered, and even lost the faith, at home: the Church of England was reaping the ripe field, and would never have put her sickle in the belt, only that the Spanish Armada, or the Gunpowder plot, or the arming of the Puritans for civil war, obliged her to draw, in its stead, the sword which she was never first to draw against Puritan or Papist. And while the colonies of England are circling the earth with light, and raising up Christian empires in Asia, or Australia, or wherever the pillar of cloud directs her hosts: what—what have Geneva, and Germany, and Prussia, and Denmark, and Holland, and Scotland, done towards the illumination of this globe? While they have lost the faith at home, I am personally told by the Moravian missionaries at Surinam, that not an individual in that colony, of the Dutch, is a married man; and it is perfectly well known that in the important colonies of Holland in the East, the conversion of her Christians to Mohammedanism, is altogether a more frequent occurrence than that of a Mohammedan to Christianity! In one of the Dutch colonies of Southern Asia, drummers have recently been sent forth, by order of government, throughout the country, to beat the people to baptism, at so much a head. And if the ringing of bells, by Tetzel and his companions on the streets, selling releases from purgatory at so much a month, was enough to rouse Luther to his task: so is this beating of drums in Presbyterian colonies, and beating of pulpit-cushions everywhere resorted to now, to convince men of even the propriety of baptism, enough to wake the earnest mind of universal Protestantism to a repudiation of principles that lead to such results.

I grant that the outburst of Puritanism in England was succeeded by a deep and deadening torpor. I grant that the short reign of evangelicalism in England, except as it was a step toward the earth-comprehending views of the Catholic faith, did little toward the extension of the Church. Yet it was well. It was the spasmodic respiration that, after the apparent suspension of vitality, precedes the healthy and deep-drawn breathing of a natural life. Evangelicalism was too nearly allied to Puritanism to rebuild the altars that the latter had cast down, to restore the daily sacrifice which the latter had supplanted, or to abhor the schism which the latter had perpetrated. At length, an event occurred that waked the lethargic lion from his slumbers. The Puritan and Papist, returning to a combination formed repeatedly under Elizabeth and Charles and Anne, swept from the Irish Church ten bishoprics at once. Good men grew pale. The alarm reached the Universities. Oxford stood in the breach, and asserted once more the prerogative and destiny of the true Catholic Church. And since that perfidious deed of 1833—which the Papists could never have perpetrated but for the aid of the Puritans, nor the Puritans but for the help of the

Papists—what have we seen? Two thousand new churches erected in England alone; the churches throughout the kingdom universally restored at an expense never to be estimated; an increase of clergy exceeding the increase of churches; the number of *congregations* added to the Church exceeding the number of *individuals* drawn off to Geneva or Rome; more than a million of money raised by voluntary subscription for the scriptural education of children; a whole system for the training of school-teachers established; the reorganization of almost every diocese, on the principle of its spiritual unity; the founding and endowing of twenty-five new dioceses, with their Bishops, in the distant colonies, with the prospect of a still greater increase; the number of missionaries and catechists nearly doubled; a missionary College founded and endowed on the site of the old St. Augustine's in Canterbury, by the charities of heavenly-minded laymen, for training missionaries in all the languages of the earth; the erection of Colleges and Cathedrals on lasting foundations in many of the colonies; 500 villages, in India alone, brought into the Church; a diocese permanently endowed in China, in Jerusalem, in the Holy City, and nine others in heathen lands; sixty new churches erected in Toronto alone, in a single year, with one hundred and fifty clergy in that single diocese; more than a hundred clergy with their churches and their Bishop in Jamaica, where Puritanism and Evangelicalism had been able to produce, as their combined result, but twenty churches that, altogether, might seat two thousand in a population of near half a million; a large number of Irish priests restored to the ancient Church; and the total number of dissenters in Great Britain materially lessened: and all this the result of some seventeen years' experiment of the Catholic principle, and in the face of the oppressions of a time-serving government, and the persecutions of a mixed multitude of Papists and ultra-Protestants. No wonder there has been a hue and cry. When the Ark moves, the mountains skip like rams, and the little hills like lambs. And the late appeal of the "Evangelical" party to the secular authorities, to determine a question of heresy; and the appeal of that party, and all its Erastian brood within and without the Church, to the secular arm, to repel a "papal aggression"—contrasting so painfully with that quiet confidence in the goodness of their cause, which has lately enabled the Patriarchs of the Eastern Churches to beat back effectually the encroachments of the Pope, by appealing calmly and without invective to the Fathers and Councils of antiquity—will have but the ultimate effect to rouse the remaining energies of a principle in the Church of England, which needs only to be roused, to conquer.

I confess, however, that I was drawn toward the Church, not so much by these outward phases, which I had little noticed, as by observing the influences, on individual character, of that hidden and inner life of which these are but the outward signs. "Whatsoever things are true, whatsoever things are honest, whatsoever things are just, whatsoever things are pure, whatsoever things are lovely, if there be any virtue, if there be any praise," I had seen the happiest combination of them all in individuals moulded under the lofty and ennobling influences of the Church of England. I became intimate with numbers of persons whose simplicity, and fervor, and single-mindedness, and innocence of speech, and purity of life, and daily benefactions, graced with all the charms of a cultivated intellect and expanded heart, introduced me, for the first time, to a religion which certainly I had not supposed to exist upon the earth. I saw a piety without cant, that I had never seen before; a zeal without noise, a charity without show, a fixedness in doctrine, a heavenly-minded quietness of character, an ease and natural free-breathing of religion, a warmth of hospitality, a rootedness of friendship, a daily entering into the details of neighborhood sufferings and sorrows ; in short, a doing and a way of doing every thing, which I had never seen before, combining, as I had never seen before, the features of the beautiful ideal, in a character moulded by the precepts and penetrated by the Spirit of the Blessed Master: so that I could not but feel that this was the finger, and this the Church, of God. I had opportunities also of seeing a number of those earnest and heavenly-minded Curates in the village and country parishes of England, who are spending and being spent in daily and unwearied alms-deeds, to an extent and an amount that I had never dreamed of as existing on this earth; and, after what I had seen of my own dwindled, dwarfish, sluggish, and degenerated faith, and its terrible results in Switzerland and Germany and Europe generally, these things led me to marvel the more, that a Religion which I had despised could, even though established and fettered by the law, form hearts so true and lives so pure, neighborhoods so happy and a nation so good and great.

Besides these things, I marvelled much at the weakness of the Brethren in the Episcopal Church in observing fasts and festivals. Why keep Christmas-day, it is said, when there is no command to keep it, and no certainty that our Lord was born upon that day? Sirs, ye do err, not knowing the affections nor intentions of the Church. The Church does not keep the *day:* but as the faithful and true Witness, she keeps the *doctrine* of the mighty Incarnation, by which the Lord from heaven is made the second Adam, or the second representative and life-imparting Man. Ye, who have not kept the *day*, have lost the *doctrine* of the Word made flesh, and the Word-flesh made a quickening Spirit. To *you*, a full-grown Sacrifice, to suffer and make over the merit of those sufferings to man, is the sublimest, as it is the only essential conception of the purposes of the Incarnation; and a body dropped for our Saviour from the clouds, or moulded from the clay, would have answered the purposes of this theological abstraction. To *us* who have other views, who see other purposes, to be accomplished by the assumption of our Nature: it was necessary that our Lord should pass through all the stages of a human life. Wait for a command to keep the bright day of rejoicing? Oh, no! A Catholic heart would require a "Thou shalt *not*," to restrain it from this tribute. Away with the quibbling of an unbelieving age, "Ye do not know the day!" Again we tell you, that it is not the day, but the doctrine, that we keep. Besides, the settling down of universal Christendom upon this as the right day, is as much a presumptive proof that it is the proper anniversary: as that all Christendom agreeing, after fierce controversies for three hundred years, upon the present books of Scripture, is demonstration of the care and caution exercised in arriving at the truth. And there are reasons, based on the chain of incidents recorded by the Evangelists, in connection with the established data of the twenty-four courses of the priests, which, as men profoundly learned in chronology assure us, lead to the very date that we actually observe. But what if they did not? Are the devotions and rejoicings of a nation any the less loyal, when a sovereign, because his court may be in mourning, has postponed for a month the festivities of his birthday? Is our patriotism or enthusiasm the less earnest or less lawful, because, when the "glorious Fourth" falls on a Sunday, we defer the celebration of it to the following day? Is the Sabbath any the less acceptably kept, because it begins and ends differently in different longitudes? Or have the Puritans been less sincere or dutiful to their ancestors, because, by an error in translating from the Old Style to the New, they have rent the air with their hosannas on the 22d of December: whereas the true "forefathers' day" on which they actually touched Plymouth rock,—was the

21st?* Away with such cold, *calculating* quibbles about the exact day or hour! It is but a cavil. You know the day and hour, on a Wednesday, when the Lord of glory was betrayed into the hands of sinners: yet you do not keep it. You know the exact day and hour of his grief and passion, on an awful Friday: yet you do not keep it. You know the day and hour when He rose from the dead, and all the members of his body became partakers of His resurrection: yet you do not keep it. You know the day that he ascended into heaven, to appear in the presence of God for us: and yet you do not keep it. You know the day and hour when the Holy Ghost came down to dwell in our mortal bodies, and impart the life of Jesus to a universal Church: yet you do not keep it. Will you keep nothing that is not commanded in the Bible? Nay! You baptize infants, you give females the communion, you pass the Sabbath over to a different day, you build temples, you form voluntary Societies and keep their anniversaries, and do numerous other things nowhere commanded: while things that are commanded—the washing each other's feet, the anointing of your sick with oil by the Elders, the kiss of peace, the love-feast, and many other such things—you repudiate. Our Lord himself kept forms and feasts which Moses had not commanded, but which commended illustrious deliverances by the hand of God, to the devout remembrance of a pious nation. Waiting for a commandment? No! I remember how vainly, when I was a Presbyterian preacher, I looked for a command to observe Family Prayer; and, when I could not find the commandment, I looked as unsuccessfully for an example of this practice. I could find commands and examples enough for daily morning and evening prayer; but it was in the Temple, which comported rather with Episcopacy than with Puritan-

* So the "Family Christian Almanac" of the American Tract Society, bearing the testimony of "all the Evangelical" denominations, tells us.

ism: yet for Family Prayer I could find neither example nor precept. The truth is, the Gospel is a "*law of liberty:*" law, as it settles the principle; liberty, as it respects the time and mode. The temple is the place for prayer. If I cannot reach it, with Peter and John: let me, with Daniel in Babylon, Cornelius in Cæsarea, or Peter on the house-top in Joppa, join the adoring throng where I can; and, if I can, at "the hour of prayer," be it the third, or the sixth, or the ninth. This modern Family Prayer, which has how dwindled into nothing, has become a sad substitute for God's ancient way. The "*law*" is *prayer;* I have a liberty as to time and place and circumstance. The *law* is *fasting;* the Church herself has a "liberty" only as regards the time. Moses and Elijah, without commandment, fasted forty days. The Jewish Church had its fast likewise of forty days. The cold sectarian world asks,

"Wrapped up in majesty divine,
Doth God regard on what we dine?"

The warm-hearted Christian, keeping a fast kept by the ancient Jews before the passover, and kept by Christ, and kept by Irenæus and his companions who were born in the days of the Apostles, takes down his harp and sings:

"Welcome, dear feast of Lent! who loves not thee,
He loves not temperance, nor authority,
But is composed of passion.
The Scriptures bid us *fast;* the Church says *now,*
Give to thy mother what thou wouldst allow
To every corporation.
It's true we cannot reach Christ's fortieth day;
Yet to go part of that religious way,
Is better than to rest.
We cannot reach our Saviour's purity;
Yet we are bid *be holy even as He,*
In both let's do our best.

Who goeth in the way which Christ has gone,
Is much more sure to meet with him, than one
That travelleth by-ways;
Perhaps my G[illegible] though He be far before,
May turn, and take me by the hand, and more,
May strengthen my decays."

But the flesh pleads that Christ was miraculously supported in His fast. This is not so certain. Yet, if this is to be the cavilling of those who ought to be believers, let us carry the cavil farther, and say we will not visit the sick because we cannot heal them by a touch; we will not pay our debt to the house of mourning, because we cannot call back the dead of Nain and of Bethany to life; we will not feed the hungry, because we cannot multiply our loaves and fishes to suffice the whole multitude; we will in fact do nothing, because we can do nothing as He did. Sectarians tell us that they have tried fasting, and it has done them no good. I have seen unhappy men who have told me that they had tried praying, and that it had done them no good. No wonder. *Such* praying, *such* fasting, by fits and starts, can never do one good. Prayer once a month, or once a year, can effect nothing. Think you the Lord intended this, when he declared, "This kind goeth not forth but by prayer and fasting?" Think you St. Paul meant only this, when he said to wives and husbands, "Defraud ye not one the other, except it be with consent for a time, that ye may give yourselves to fasting and prayer?" As these are texts (and there are many others) which the Ancient Religion alone can understand or explain, since they are *allusions to customs already established* before the New Testament was written: so they compel me to condemn the schisms of Presbytery for their recent repudiation of all true and proper fasting, as I would a system that should repudiate alms-giving and prayer. None but the Catholic religion, it would appear, can perpetuate those awful impressions of our duties and our dangers, those mighty conceptions of the Incarnation the Cross, and the Resurrection, which shall *compel* the heart, conscious of the magnitude of the occasion, to fastings and commemorations. What would Jesus have thought of St. Peter and St. James and of him who leaned upon His breast that night: if on the second, or the third, or the thirtieth anniversary of that tremendous moment, no prayers, no preachings, no sacraments, no communings with each other, should commemorate the mighty mystery of that day and hour? Who can imagine that St. John would not say to Polycarp: "This, Brother, is the day on which the Lord of glory hanged upon the cross?" Who can imagine that Smyrna, and Antioch, and Jerusalem, and Rome, were not made glad when Peter and Paul and John and Ignatius and Polycarp let fall in their discourses the hint, that "To-day He became the first-fruits of them that slept?" Who can suppose that, to such a mind as St. Paul's, or to such a heart as St. John's, the illustrious day and hour had been suffered to pass over without notice? Nay, St. Paul "must by all means keep this feast that cometh, in Jerusalem;"* and "hasted, if it were possible for him, to be at Jerusalem the day of Pentecost;"† and when there, with St. James and the great multitude, would there be nothing said of the descending, on that day, of the adorable Comforter, in visible and glorious majesty, to take the place of Christ in His Body which is His Church? Even Neander allows the force of these considerations.

But Dr. Miller tells his classes that Easter is a word derived from the name of the Saxon goddess Eostra. Well; altar, temple, divinity, piety, religion, are the *altare*, *templum*, *divinitas*, *pietas*, *religio*, of the ancient Pagans. But Dr. Miller and Buck's Theological Dictionary do err. Easter is from the ancient word East, or Est, or Ost, the same in

* Acts, xviii. 21. † Acts. xx. 16.

Saxon, French, and German, signifying the *Rising*—the day of the Lord's rising from the dead. But Dr. Miller tells us that "there was a great controversy in the second century about Easter," proving conclusively that it was not of Apostolic origin. Indeed! "So there was a great controversy," may the Baptists say, "in the third century about Infant Baptism, demonstrating that *it* was not of Apostolic origin." But let us sift this thing a little. Two hundred and sixty-six bishops met in Egypt to settle the question, not whether infants were to be baptized, but whether they were to be baptized on the eighth day: and the greatest proof of infant baptism, like that of Episcopacy, is that no Council ever established it, or even debated the question. So it was with Easter, or rather the time and duration of the preceding fast: it was a question of time; and, moreover, like baptism on the eighth day, a question between Christianity in the East, where the Jews controlled the details of discipline under the lenient permission of the Apostles, in innocent accommodation to their ancient predilections; and the freer Christianity of the West, which desired to combine the Easter with the Sunday. So it was with the question of Circumcision, and the seventh-day Sabbath, and various other matters. In this, as in many Jewish rites and prejudices, the Apostles had always allowed a latitude and liberty. The travelling of a Bishop and convert of St. John from the distant East, to produce uniformity between the Jewish Churches (so to call them) and the free Gentile Churches in the West, on the mere question of date and duration: is of all proofs the best, that the Lenten fast and the feast of Easter were observed from the times of the Apostles. But why reason longer? To the cold, ultra-Protestant, more would not suffice: to the warm and bursting heart, who lives in antiquity with the Manger, and the Cross, and the Sepulchre, less is enough.

Thus I was compelled to listen, to the last, to all the miserable quibblings which, in the aggregate, might perhaps reconcile me still to my separated sojourn, out of God's ancient Church. But now that I have been adopted into the glorious Household tracing its genealogies to the ancient ones, and living familiarly amidst the sweet anniversaries kept in the Family from the beginning: how beautiful and bright dawn the days as they come round. On Christmas we go with our children, and show them the little hands and feet of the mysterious Babe; and tell them the story of the manger, of Herod and the Innocents, and the cruel flight into Egypt: and make on them impressions they can never lose. We show them His star in the East, and keep alive His manifestation to the Gentiles. We bring the fir, and the pine, and the box together to beautify the sanctuary, and make the place of His feet glorious, *now*, when the Lord whom we seek hath come to His Temple, and as our Simeons explain it, the glory of the latter Church is greater than the glory of the former. We fast—we must fast, we cannot abstain from fasting, for that were a more painful abstinence—as the awful mystery of His Passion is approaching. We keep, throughout the year, the Wednesday and the Friday Litanies, as if to robe in penitence the days of the Betrayal and the Crucifixion. We keep the forty days of Lent, to consider well the sins that procured this terrific Mystery, and to wash with our tears the feet that our sins had first bathed with blood. No sudden burst of penitence will satisfy the Catholic Religion: and once a year she calls her children to withdraw from the vanities of life, and spend a protracted period in sorrow and in prayer. We follow Him to the grave, and watch the Holy Sepulchre. We wait for His return from the place of the departed, whither His soul descended, while separated from the Body. On Easter morning, we pass the exultation round the globe, wherever there are voices to repeat "The Lord is risen!" The forty days of joy go over, and we follow our second Adam into the heavens. And on the tenth day afterward, we keep the joyful Pentecost. Then comes the feast of Trinity, the two Persons of the Godhead having visibly descended. And from that day onward the Church draws our attention to the precepts and practices, as she had done during the previous division of the year to the great facts and doctrines, of our Faith. All this is solid gold. We cannot part with it for tinsel.

As the relative positions, and distances, and mutual relations and bearings of the heavenly bodies, present but one strange chaos to the vulgar eye: so, but a few years since, on opening a Prayer-Book, these objects stamped upon its pages were to me but a congeries of unmeaning, arbitrary ordinances. Now I see in them a heavenly science. For as the earth and sun and heavenly bodies return this year to the same relative position that they occupied a year ago, and begin the same course that they then began: so the Church wanders in search of nothing new, but is for ever laboring to keep herself and her children in the old beaten path, swerving never from her orbit. As we see, in our day, the same stars of heaven that Ignatius and Irenæus saw: so we hold the same truths that Ignatius and Irenæus held. The Incarnation, the Advent, the Redemption, the Resurrection, the Ascension, the manifold operation of the Pentecostal Spirit; these are her teachings, these the stars that glow and brighten in her sky: while the still lesser lights of truth and grace twinkle and glitter as gems between. They always were her teachings, her lights that gave shine unto the world. And for fear that one of them should be eclipsed, she has ordained that every truth and precept of religion shall have, in turn, its blessed anniversary. Thus, as the sun comes and goes from tropic to tropic, or as the earth revolves from solstice to solstice: so the unvarying round of truth returns again and again, continually from Advent to Advent, in an eternal circle; while the old Church, like the old Earth, in all Her revolutions, and in calm or storm, points always to Her one, everlasting, Bright and Morning Star. When they cry, "Lo, here is Christ; or, Lo, He is there:" her voice is, "Go not after them." And they who quarrel with her exact immutability, or weary of her annual round, may as well quarrel with the fixed and unalterable laws of the universe, and with the established routine that they, with majestic regularity, for ever reproduce.

CHAPTER XXVIII.

RETROSPECT.

But for this *via media*—this *via vera*, too—I must have followed my own private reasonings into all the vagaries of German rationalism; or have been led, by the yearnings of a better disposition, into the mazes of Popish superstition. As it has been therefore, to me, a matter of life and death, perhaps I may be forgiven if I have sometimes given utterance to the exuberance of my joy:

> "As the wave, while it welcomes the moment of rest,
> Still heaves, as remembering ills that are o'er."

I. Who shall blame me for renouncing a religion that taught me, before I could read, that "God, from all eternity, for his own glory, hath fore-ordained *whatsoever comes to pass?*"

II. Who shall blame me for renouncing a religion that, before it would allow me to teach or preach, obliged me to confess that, "by the decree of God, some men and angels are predestinated unto everlasting life, and others *fore-ordained to everlasting death;*" and that "these men and angels, thus predestinated and fore-ordained, are particularly and unchangeably designed, and their number is so certain and definite, that it cannot be either increased or diminished?"

III. Who shall blame me for renouncing a religion that

required of me, as its minister, to believe, that "neither are any other *redeemed by Christ*, but the elect only?"

IV. Who shall blame me for renouncing a religion which taught me that, for Adam's sin alone, his whole posterity are "by nature children of wrath, bondslaves of Satan, and justly liable to all punishment in this world and that which is to come, everlasting separation from the comfortable presence of God, and most grievous torments in soul and body, without intermission, *in hell fire for ever?*" Lo. Cat. Qu. 29.

V. Who shall blame me for renouncing a religion which taught me, that "*elect infants*, dying in infancy, are regenerated and saved, and so also all other elect persons [i. e., idiots, &c.] who are incapable of being outwardly called?"

VI. Who shall blame me for renouncing a religion, which, while it declared that "neither are any other redeemed by Christ but the elect only," still allowed me, and expected me, to "preach the Gospel [i. e., glad tidings] to every creature;" —an insincerity a Jesuit should blush for, which many Calvinistic preachers will not submit to, and which, I well remember, was to my fellow-students a *crux sinceritatis* of the most distressing nature?

VII. Who shall blame me for renouncing a religion which, while it held that only the elect can have the "effectual calling" of God's Spirit, "enabling them to repent:" yet required me to summon all others to repentance, on pain of an aggravated damnation for not repenting?

VIII. Who shall blame me for renouncing a religion, which, by these startling imputations on our Maker, obliges its ministers to disbelieve what they subscribe, or to keep back what they believe, or boldly to allow the imputations, and thus become at once the accusers and defenders of their Maker, employing their discourses constantly in painful, intellectual, hair-splitting explanations, quite to the satisfaction of the people, but—as we have often confessed in our little coteries—never to our own?

IX. I have done also with those off-hand prayers, in which dissent is happy; and with those rhymes which, with the "long" prayer, are all that it possesses to impart a conception of the dignity and sublimity of Christian worship. It has expelled the Psalms, as inspired and sung by David, chanted by the prophets, echoed through the temple and the synagogues, adopted by Christ and his Apostles, and sung in all churches in all lands for fifteen centuries: and instead of them has substituted its jingling verses, made often ridiculous enough by the solemn pauses and repetitions demanded by the musical taste of sectarian composers.*

X. I could not approve the religion that forbids the laity joining in the worship of God, and has even silenced the "Amen" of the *profanum vulgus.* As we said before, Give back, thou man of Rome, the cup to a thirsting flock: give back, thou man of Geneva, the liturgy to a congregation of dumb worshippers!

XI. Thank God, I have now A LITURGY, venerable for its years, glorious for its associations, heavenly in its strain, divine in its composition, nine-tenths whereof are from the word of God, and able to set us amidst the choirs and voices of angels and archangels, and all the company of heaven; "a truly lordly dish; a fatness that never corrupts; the more we taste, the more we hunger, with desires that are ever fed and never cloyed."

XII. The reasons I have given for returning to the use of liturgies are too many to be repeated here, and I shall only add to them the precious balm which they shed around the

* Good Bishop Seabury replied to a music-teacher, who had given a public rehearsal, and who sought the commendation of the bishop, That his sympathies were so engaged with poor Aaron, while they "ran down his beard" five or six times over, that he really could think of nothing else.

47

sick-room. Since these chapters were begun, my venerable father (may he rest in peace!) has gone, as I believe, to receive in Paradise the foretastes of a bright reward. Long he lay ill. But in all that time, no mortal, save a Methodist minister passing by, knelt beside his dying bed. His daughters—daughters now also of the Church—were with him, rendering all human sympathy and succor; but disallowed by sectarian habit from even proposing the solace of written words, to a dying parent. Thus ten thousand sicken, and the silence of the sick-room is not broken by the voice of prayer. And thus by sea and land ten thousand die, and are sent like dogs to the grave, without the embalming of a Christian hand; while thousands are daily saved from these worse than heathenish alternatives, by one little "Book of Common Prayer."

XIII. In returning to liturgical worship, I have returned to a principle once buffeted and crucified by Dissenters, but now regarded by some of them with very great respect. Calvin, Luther, Knox, Baxter, Wesley, all prepared liturgies for their followers; Doctors Winchester and Smyth, both classmates of mine at Princeton, have both put forth books of prayers; the Seamen's Society has set forth forms; and even Doctor Spring has given us a volume of devotions. What a change has come over us! How fast the deadly wound of the Beast is healing! Are we not all moving on towards Popery together? From circumstances within my knowledge, I am quite sure that the more enlightened and grave of the Presbyterian ministry would delight to see a liturgy adopted at once, but that it would look like backing out from an advanced position. *But liturgy they can never have.* A jewel once lost among them, they can never recover. But though sectarians pretend that the night hangs dark over the Church, yet hear how, even in this our darkest hour, the voices of the night fall upon the ear of a favorite son of dissent:—The Rev. H. W. Beecher, of Brooklyn, writes thus from Scotland:

"The services began. You know my mother was, until her marriage, in the communion of the Episcopal Church; this thought hardly left me, while I sat, grateful for the privilege of worshipping God through a service that had expressed so often her devotions. [Aye, this is a sweet and holy tie among us, whether separated by sea, or land, or death.] I cannot tell you how much I was affected. *I had never had such a trance of worship, and I shall never have such another view until I gain the gate.*

"I am so ignorant of the Church Service, that I cannot tell the various parts by their right names—but the portions which most affected me, were the prayers and responses which the choir sang. I had never heard any part of a supplication—a direct prayer—sung by a choir; and it seemed as though I heard, not with my ear, but with my soul. I was dissolved—*my whole being seemed to me like an incense wafted gratefully towards God.* The Divine presence rose before me in wondrous majesty, but of ineffable gentleness and goodness; and I could not stay away from more familiar approach, but seemed irresistibly, yet gently, drawn toward God. My soul, then thou didst magnify the Lord, and rejoice in the God of thy salvation! And then came to my mind the many exultations of the Psalms of David, and never before were the expressions and figures so noble and so *necessary to express what I felt.* I had risen, it seemed to me, so high, that I was where David was when his soul conceived the things which he wrote. Throughout the service, and it was an hour and a quarter long, whenever an "Amen" occurred, it was given by the choir, accompanied by the organ and the congregation. Oh, that swell and solemn cadence yet rings in my ear. Not once, not a single time did it occur in that service, from beginning to end, without bringing tears from my eyes. I stood like a shrub in a spring morning—every leaf covered with dew, and every breeze shook down some drops. *I trembled so much at times, that I was obliged to sit down.* Oh, when in the prayers breathed forth in strains of sweet, simple, solemn music, *the love of Christ* was recognized, how I longed then to give utterance to what that love seemed to me. There was a moment in which *the heavens seemed opened to me,* and I saw the glory of God! All the earth seemed to me a storehouse of images, made to *set forth the Redeemer, and I could scarcely keep still from crying out.* I never knew, I never dreamed before, of what heart there was in the word *Amen.* Every time it swelled forth and died away solemnly, not my lips, not my mind, but my whole being said—Saviour, so let it be.

"The sermon was preparatory to the communion, which I then first learned was to be celebrated. It was plain and good; and although the rector had done many things in a way that led me to suppose that he sympathized with over much ceremony, yet in his sermon he seemed evangelical, and gave a right view of the Lord's Supper. For the first time in my life, I went forward to commune in an Episcopal Church."

XIV. I was constrained to leave my much-loved church, because I believed it to be without sacraments. Long ago have both the golden ear-rings dropped from its ears. Once it held that a sacrament must consist of two parts, "the outward and the inward." But now ye deny the inward and invisible part, and hold only the outward form. Ye talk of a sacrament as if it were only intended to keep us from forgetting that Christ died. To us, in this poor sense, all nature is sacramental, being consecrated by the word of God. Our morning ablution reminds us often and often of our birth from above, aye, and conveys grace by the dear remembrance; and bread and wine, upon our tables, bring to us often the recollection of a Saviour slain. Are these, therefore, sacraments? Yes, in your very highest sense. Why, sirs, all things should be sacramental, in this degree, to a devout mind; for scripture hath made them so. Sun, moon, and stars; earth, wind, and water; rains and dews; the cloud and bow; mountain, vale, and garden; fountain, brook, and river; darkness and light; lightning and fire; trees, grass, and seeds; the plough and the sickle; the tares and the wheat; planting, watering, reaping; the harvest, the barn; the shepherd, the fold, the lamb; the wolf, the leopard, the ox, the fatling, and the lion; even the little sparrow; even the disgusting serpent; dust and ashes; wood, hay, and stubble; gold and silver; crystal and glass; pearls and jewels; kings and kingdoms; thrones and crowns; the ship, the fisherman, the net, the anchor, the rock; our suppers and feasts; the bridegroom and his friend; the bride and her virgins; the marriage, the birth, the little child, the son, the brother, the father, the family, the prodigal; our very food and drink; our sleeping and waking; even our walking, running, stumbling, rising; the very roads we travel, the gates and doors we enter; in short, every thing in nature, and in life and its occupations, the word of God has consecrated, to the devout mind, as remembrancers of the truth and vehicles of grace in Jesus Christ. They even make Christ present to our faith. Are they therefore sacraments? I trow not. You must raise your vision higher.

XV. They have no Baptism. The sprinkling with water among them is *without* the *Spirit;* but Baptism is the Baptism "of water *and* the Spirit"—not a dead sprinkling under the law, but a living, life-conveying reality; something of dignity and excellence enough to be the parting gift of an ascending Saviour to the "nations." Away with your Jewish washings! We are not under the law, but under grace. The shadows are gone. The substance is come.

XVI. And yet the brethren I have left cannot escape the charge, that they have two baptisms: a baptism signifying positive regeneration in the adult, and a baptism signifying —no mortal can tell what—in the infant. Yet there is "one baptism," as there is "one God, one Lord, one faith, one hope;" "for by one Spirit are we all baptized into one Body;" and, could there be a difference, more certainly would that difference be in favor of the little child, "for of such is the kingdom of heaven." Dr. Alexander confesses, and so perhaps do all his brethren, that regeneration takes place *sometimes* in infant baptism, and that there is "such a thing as *baptismal regeneration.*" This seems to shut the question in a nutshell. If it take place only *sometimes*, there is an *election.* Take away this election, or selection, and let all be equal in the sacrament, and all must be regenerated. But that dark system comes to my children, before they have done good or evil, and says to one,—"Sweet child, weep not; thou hast been chosen to an eternal life, and over thee I set a loving angel who shall cover thee with his wings;" and to the other, —"Thee, doomed child, I leave [theologically, "præterition"] to the vexings of a tempting demon, who shall cast his toils about thee, and bind and blind and drag thee to his burning cell, for thou wast not in the slain Man's thoughts when he hanged upon the tree." Take this dogma away; say that God is no respecter of persons; remember that there is less in an infant's heart to resist the entrance of the Spirit, than in the most approved of your adults: then, if *one* infant, since the world began, has ever been the subject (as Presbyterians allow) of "baptismal regeneration," it follows, as a consequence, that *all* who have been thus baptized must have been also thus regenerated. The same water; the same infancy; the same form; the same words; the same thing. "I baptize *thee*"—and "*thee*"—and "*thee*." So it is written —"ONE BAPTISM."

XVII. I left my religion, because I could not remember that it had ever admonished me of any duty, grace, or privilege, accruing from my baptism. Nay, I do not know, except by inference from the ecclesiastical faith of my parents, that I was ever baptized at all. Who ever heard a Presbyterian sermon, to children or youth, regarding any duty, grace, or privilege, growing out of Baptism? The popular interpretation of Baptism, next to giving the child a name, is, that it is to bind *the parents* to certain promises and duties. Then a rite should be performed *on the parents*. But Baptism addresses not a word to the parents, performs no rite upon them. "I baptize *thee*"—all that is said or done is said and done to *the child*. Another cause of this neglect is the excuse of many, that the child was not a consulted or consenting party to its baptism, and therefore is not bound. Sirs, you strike deep! You strike high! Neither was it a consulted or consenting party in being born; the family obligation ceases! Neither was it consulted in being created; you undermine the throne of God! So sure as its being born binds it to *you*, and places it under your authority and love: so sure its being born again of water and the Spirit binds it to its God, and lays it under His wings.

XVIII. I abjured my religion, because it kept from the people all the clear passages that speak of Baptism:—"One body, one Spirit, one Lord, one faith, *one Baptism*"—"the washing of *regeneration*"—"except a man be *born of water and* of the Spirit"—"the Baptism of repentance for *the remission of sins*"—"Repent and be Baptized, every one of you in the name of Jesus Christ for *the remission of sins*, and ye shall receive the gift of the Holy Ghost"—"arise, and be Baptized, and *wash away thy sins*"—"buried with Christ *by Baptism* into death"—"by one Spirit are we all *Baptized* into one Body"—"that He might sanctify and cleanse it [the Church] *with the washing of water* by the word"—"the like figure whereunto [antitype] even Baptism doth also now *save us*"—"Jesus also [second Adam or Representative] being Baptized, the heaven was opened, and *the Holy Ghost descended* in a bodily shape, like a dove upon Him." Who ever heard a sermon from a Presbyterian pulpit on any of these texts? I never did. Dissent ignores them. The Church alone is their interpreter. The Church alone is their proprietor.

XIX. I have cast off a religion that, because the parents are not actual communicants, refuses baptism to the child, and leaves it to the serpent's coils. The old days have returned, when "the fathers eat sour grapes, and the children's teeth are set on edge."

XX. I have given up a religion that has given birth to the wide-spread sect denying baptism to all infants alike. Ye say, Infants cannot repent, and it is written, "Repent and be baptized." Jesus could not repent, yet it became him to "fulfil all righteousness." Ye say, Infants cannot believe, and it is written, "He that believeth and is baptized shall be saved." Then (as some of you have held) infants cannot be saved, for it is added, "He that believeth not shall be damned." Away with your freezing faith! A thousand times away with it! I would not believe a religion that, when I fly to the ark, forbids me to take my child in my arms. Would this make Baptism St. Peter's antitype of the Ark? I could not believe a religion that should involve the infant universe in the overthrow of the first Adam, and pour the stream of death into its being, and not allow one single drop from hands or feet or side of the second Adam to be conveyed into its veins; that should involve it in all the sorrows that overtake humanity, and give it no share in human redemption. Is the first Adam stronger than the second? Has judgment triumphed against mercy? Nay, He who spared Nineveh for its idol-dedicated infants, has, in an empire of grace, provided for the babe. If the covenant of the Gospel include it not, it is the first covenant with men that has shut infants out. With Adam and with his seed was the covenant made; with Noah and his seed; with Abraham and his seed. Has the Gospel abridged the love of God? I trow not. Ye say, Away with the children! But there standeth One among you who is "much displeased," and says, "Suffer the little children to come unto me, and forbid them not, for of such is the kingdom of God [the Church]." See His outspread arms; see Him fold them to His bosom; watch His symbolic act in laying on His hands; hear His sweet voice bless them and give them to their mothers again!

XXI. I felt it my duty to leave my denomination, because I saw that it was itself fast becoming Baptist. I have already adduced figures; here are more. The Presbytery of New Brunswick—the nursery from the beginning, and the present model, of Presbytery—in 1830, reported 40 ministers, 2300 communicants, and 220 baptisms; or, one to every ten communicants. In 1847, it reported 53 ministers, 4322 communicants, and 174 baptisms; or, one to twenty-four. The Synod of New Jersey, the stronghold of Presbytery, in 1830, reported 104 ministers, 831 baptisms; in 1847, 140 ministers, 778 baptisms. In contrast with this, the Church, claiming to be "the mother of us all," had but 15 ministers and 900 communicants, yet baptisms 450, or one to every two communicants; in 1847, 60 clergy, 2270 communicants, and 1170 baptisms, or one to less than two. Such is a true mother's love.

XXII. My religion I threw away, because it threw away the golden tie of CONFIRMATION, that had ever bound our youthful Isaacs to the altar. Yet when the Apostles heard that Philip the Deacon had baptized a great multitude in Samaria, they sent to them Peter and John, "who laid their hands on them, and they received the Holy Ghost," "both men and *women*." And when St. Paul goes to "the *foundation*," and recites the "*first principles* of the *doctrine* of Christ," he says, "the foundation of repentance—of faith toward God—of baptisms—of *laying on of hands*—of the resurrection—and of eternal judgment." This rite was retained by Luther, desired by Calvin, approved by Beza, coveted by Owen, commanded by Adam Clarke, sometimes practised by the older Puritans and Baptists, and to this day approved by prominent divines who bewail its loss—but still it is among the things that schism cannot keep. It tells its followers now, as they grow up, that they are "strangers to the covenants of promise, and aliens from the commonwealth of Israel," "children of the devil," and that their very baptism is designed to teach the fact—and turns the lambs from the Shepherd's full hand, to feed on the world's harsh husks. They are addressed in the same tone as if they had been crowned in infancy with the turban of Mohammed, or devoted in the Ganges to the pollutions of Brahma.

XXIII. By the change that I have made, I have now an ALTAR. Saint Paul says, "We have an Altar;" and that we may not mistake, he adds, "whereof they have no right *to eat* which serve the tabernacle." Oh, it is sweet to see the Altar holding the chief place of honor in our sanctuaries—emblem of sacrifice, type of "things in the heavens"—sweet, holy, joyful place of intercession and prayer!

XXIV. And I can now worship God with SACRIFICE. We have the Bread and Wine of the great Melchisedek pleading on our altar for the sins of the people. As the Jew laid on his altar the lamb bleeding and pleading, "O Lamb of a future age, have mercy upon us!" as the heathen had in all lands the smoking sacrifice crying, "O Seed of the Woman, who art to bruise the serpent's head, have mercy upon us!" so do we offer everywhere the Bread and Wine, a more excellent offering, silently and sinlessly interceding, "O Lamb of God, who takest away the sins of the world, by thine agony and crown of thorns, thy cross and passion, have mercy upon us!" And thus, while Jesus presents his pleading wounds in heaven, His members on earth present them, in glorious symbols that have been from the beginning of the world. As in Baptism our Lord retained the use of water, which at the time bore a part in the sacrament of circumcision: so He laid aside only the bloody part of the sacrifice of the Altar, retaining the "meat-offering of flour and the drink-offering of wine," which had from the first accompanied the lamb slain in the Temple each morning and evening—Himself to provide hereafter the Lamb, and to be verily and indeed present at His Altar. In both these changes of the form, He hath magnified the sacraments and made them glorious—surely He hath not made them less. It is the only pure offering on earth; and so it is written, "In every place incense and a pure offering shall be offered in my name." O how it quickens faith! O how it kindles prayer! O how it strengthens hope! How we hear the voice of the Intercessor and the choirs of the angels! How "earthly things are joined with heavenly, and things visible and invisible made one!"

XXV. And as Christ was given to be "once our ransom, but daily our food," the commemorative rite among my former brethren seemed to be quite unworthy to be called the SUPPER OF THE LORD. If I partake of nothing but bread and wine, it is to my soul no feast. But now as I come to that holy table, it is not to eat bread and drink wine only, but it is to "eat the Flesh and drink the Blood of the Son of Man,"—each in the only manner in which each can be eaten—the one with the lips of Sense, the other with the lips of Faith. It is now a Supper, a Feast, a glorious Eucharist. Schism has lost it. Its ministers do only what men, women and children may at any time anywhere do—break bread and drink wine in affectionate remembrance of their Lord. There is perhaps no harm in it, more than in the annual bathing of the Pilgrims in Jordan, in commemoration of the Baptism of our Lord and Saviour therein. O it is delightful to have done with types, and to live amidst realities—the Baptism of the Spirit, and the Sacrifice and Supper of the Lord!

XXVI. My religion was here again at a loss to explain for me the Scriptures. I shall cite from one place only. The Corinthian Christians *must* have known that the bread and wine were in remembrance of the death of Christ: and yet, for their irreverent reception of the sacrament, they were smitten with disease and visited with death. Why *so terrible* a breaking forth of the Lord's anger for the careless performance of a "commemorative rite?" Schism cannot answer. The Church answers with Paul, for "not discerning"—mark this word—"not discerning the *Lord's Body.*" The majesty and glory of the august sacrament, they had fallen from, into lower views. He asks, as of a fact strangely forgotten:—"The Bread which we break, is it not the communion [κοινωνία—partaking, imparting] of the Body of Christ? The cup which we bless, is it not the communion of the Blood of Christ? Wherefore"—notice the inference —"whosoever shall eat this bread, and drink this cup of the Lord unworthily, shall be guilty of the Body and Blood of the Lord." And besides this fearful reasoning, an impressive miracle—judgment and *death*—are sent among them to arrest, at the beginning, and once for all, in the eyes of the whole Church, these low views of the stupendous mystery: just as the same messenger was sent to stamp the first schism with the divine reprobation, in the frightful death of Korah and his company.

XXVII. And I can now understand, not only Jesus and Paul, but the good Cyprian when he says, "We offer our daily sacrifice because of our daily sins," and the mighty Augustines and Chrysostoms, and the glorious Basils and Gregories, when they speak on this theme; back to the martyred Ignatius, the disciple of St. John, who says, almost in the very words of St. Paul:—"There is but one Altar."

XXVIII. I gave up my religion because, with its meagre resources of extemporaneous devotion, it can never return to the daily prayer and sacrifice, which were practised throughout the world in the beginning, and were never intermitted until Puritanism reared its head in the Church.

XXIX. I grew dissatisfied to see the withdrawal of the Cup from the laity, and strange mixtures used instead of Wine; striking, effectually with many minds, at the foresight, the prudence, the Divinity of our Lord, for instituting the sacrament in Wine.

XXX. My religion continued to grow distasteful, as it denied such poor sacraments as it had, to the sick and the dying —an abuse never perpetrated in the most cruel days of Rome.

XXXI. Nor could I endure those arbitrary tests, with which thousands of congregations had fenced the communion-table, varying capriciously and constantly, destroying charity, and making the feast not one in which "His banner over us is love," but one at which each guest sits down with a hair-hung sword above his head.

XXXII. While this religion professes to abhor popish absolution, its mode of separating "converts" from "inquirers," and of pronouncing formally, after deliberate examination by the brethren or the elders, upon their spiritual state, imparts an absolution far more soothing and soul-destroying than that of Rome, which reaches only to the next sin; for the elders in effect say, "We believe you to be now converted, and that, however you may fall, you can never fall from grace." It has a paralyzing, deadening effect. The ministers perceive it, and lament it.

XXXIII. I have done with this religion, because it varies continually the terms of its salvation. Formerly the "law-work" and "grace-work" with the soul, required months and years; but latterly a regeneration, and repentance, and faith, can all be crowded into the compass of a single night or hour! and the stupendous preparations for eternity are made!

XXXIV. I have repudiated my religion, because, in its latest evangelical form, it reduces the mighty circle of religious Faith to a faith in the person only of Christ; and this again to faith in His redemption only; and this redemption again to His mere sufferings; and this faith again to a single act which casts the soul on Christ once for all, and for ever.

XXXV. I have repudiated my old faith, because, in no small degree, it reduces the great conflict of life, and the life-long sorrows of repentance, to the "strivings" of an hour or a night in a camp-meeting or a revival; and so defines the mighty office of repentance, as to overlook the essential element of reparation to the injured, and restoration to the robbed and wronged.

XXXVI. This faith moreover has latterly reduced practical conversion to phenomena which nervous sympathy, sickness, opiates, deliriums, not unfrequently produce; which can be produced in most instances with ease upon the deathbed; and which have thus become a chief stumbling-stone in the way of men's salvation. The great object of life and of life-long agony seems forgotten, the formation of character —CHARACTER fitted for the seats and the circles of HEAVEN!—Heaven! an atmosphere pure enough for God and the Lamb to breathe! How vast must be the discipline that shall fit a soul for heaven! The slightest whisper of your busy-body or your "converted" slanderer, would silence every harp and break every heart in heaven!

XXXVII. This was another cause of my dissatisfaction; that, to a sad extent, the cultivation of the social virtues was overlooked, as though conversion were a discharge in full of all other obligations. So bare is this fact to men's eyes, that they express it in proverbs. Who has not noticed with what melancholy uniformity disputations, strifes, jealousies, gossipings, and broad censoriousness, follow a revival? "No roads so rough as those newly mended; no sinners so intolerable," says the world, "as those just turned saints." "Saints in the parlor," says the world, "and furies in the kitchen." "*Moral*" teaching is avowedly discarded; and the tongue, the temper, and the passions, are left to their own way and sway. Who can wonder at the result? Milton thought, "there had never been a more ignominious and mortal wound, to faith, to piety, to reformation, nor more cause of blasphemy given to the enemy, since the first preaching of Reformation." Another thought, that "Instead of a Reformation they had a Deformation of religion." And so it went on to the days of Edwards, who confessed, after a long and world-renowned revival, that, "If envy, strife, variance, emulations, wrath, worldliness, selfishness, be badges of the Christian, we have Christians among us in abundance." It has been always so. So is it still.

XXXVIII. I have discarded a religion that produces constantly distempered frenzies, and has settled thousands of its followers into irretrievable melancholy, and has prompted to many a mournful suicide.

XXXIX. I have repudiated the whole Puritan system, because it compelled me to judge my brother. And unless a brother could say *my* shibboleth, and talk *my* talk, I branded and disowned him. Each member of the family allowed to choose who shall be his brothers and sisters, where is charity? Charity, like faith and hope, begins where doubt begins. But this snarling system, in the Church and out of it, when doubt begins, sets up its cry. This concision and excision I have done with. The wheat and the tares, the good fishes and the bad, I can now leave together, for a merciful God to send His rain upon them both. There are "branches *in Christ*" that "bear no fruit." It is the Husbandman's place, not mine—and His not yet—to cast them into the fire.

XL. The most painful part, in my experience of Dissent, was the lone conspicuity it gave me as a preacher. In Scripture I read that when men "went up to the temple," it was "to pray;" and when "the disciples came together," though St. Paul was to be there, it was "to break bread," "to pray," "to eat the Lord's Supper." *I* went to the temple to preach, as others came to hear. I saw beneath its roof no sign of the Son of man—no altar, no place of prayer, no emblem of alms and offerings, no memento of redemption, no glowing litanies for a blazing shield between the people and the preacher. He was the all in all. I was to be the grand Llama of the day. I went into the pulpit, feeling that I could creep into the earth: I came out of it, feeling that I could there find room among the ants.

XLI. And with what kind of preaching has sectarism flooded the land! I have heard schismatics reason, that the ignorance of their ministry was the proof of their inspiration. Did you ever hear them preach, by their tribes and by their companies? Did you ever hear a Mormon sermon? Did you ever sit before one of the two thousand elegantly decorated pulpits, where you might hear the redemption of the world by God our Saviour denied? Did you ever sit before one of the fifteen hundred preachers among us, who deny the sin and the punishment from which that Saviour came to redeem us? Have you ever heard—but the time would fail me. Glorious pulpit! Manufacturer of religions made palatable to the tastes of all! Presbytery! thou in thy genealogies art the true and lineal parent of all these, of more, and of more to come!

XLII. I have repudiated my old religion, because it is solely and wholly responsible for all the humiliation and dishonour done to pulpit as well as altar, in the fanaticism that disgraces and degrades thousands of neighbourhoods throughout the country. Only those familiar with the facts could know their nature and extent; others would not believe:—gestures, rollings, tossings, tumblings, shoutings, faintings, screamings, in confusion inextricable. Doctor Potts tells us, that the call to the ministry consists in an inward moving of the Spirit, the sanction of the congregation, and the Lord's seal in the conversion of souls—a triple test in which the wandering Mormon and Deistic Campbellite claim to excel you all—a test all fanatics who count their followers submit to; but one in which the preaching of the Lord of Glory would seem to suffer by the contrast. Yet it is written, as did Aaron, "So also Christ glorified not himself to be made an high priest; but He that said unto him, 'Thou art my Son.'" Thirty long years His soul, with all the burnings of eternity upon it, waited until the anointing of John, and the Voice from Heaven, called Him to His task.

XLIII. My religion, consequently, could never have assured me that I had received any sacrament, or had heard the Gospel from any true minister. As the Romanist holds that the validity of a sacrament depends upon the intention of the priest: so schism maintains that it has been administered by no true minister, unless he be truly a converted man, called by the Spirit of God. Doctor Potts says, a minister is no minister, unless he have "the spiritual succession." How, in this world, then, am I to know whether I have ever been baptized, have ever received the communion, have ever heard the Gospel from a lawful minister? The Baptists complicate the difficulty, by making baptism dependent on the regeneration or *animus* of the subject. Who, then, is baptized? Who is a brother? On every hand suspicion, in pulpit and in pew, must reign in the home of charity.

XLIV. My old religion teaches that three or four good laymen may come and lay their hands upon my pious boot-black, and make him as true a minister of Jesus Christ as myself; equal in dignity, and right, and power. How was it possible that a religion like this could have ever given me, in its highest reaches, that exalted and inspiring apprehension of the tremendous calling which now I feel, as one clothed with the authority of the universal Church, to proclaim her universal faith, without a "perhaps" or an "if," or doubt or contradiction; and "as the minister of Christ and steward of His mysteries," to imitate His mighty act in heaven, and, in a figure appointed by Himself, to offer up the one, pure, only, everlasting sacrifice for sin, pleading sinlessly and gloriously upon our thousand altars?

XLV. And I regard it as no small thing to have recovered the ancient Episcopacy—the chaff that protects the seed, the shell that protects the kernel, the casket that keeps the crown-jewels of our Lord—true by the external demonstrations of history, analogy, universality; true by its unity, its never altered faith, its perpetuity, and its power of self-recovery; proven, as no other fact but those in Christianity are proven; so demonstrated that, even without the Church, ripe scholars have given it their assent, and a yearning, almost national, has been sometimes felt in parts of Europe for its recovery.

XLVI. I find it delightful, too, to be *satisfied* regarding one's ordination, especially as introducing to a priesthood and service, of which schism has lost the memory. Doctor Adam Clarke, the Methodist commentator, shortly before his death, said, "I preach, and have long preached, without any kind of Episcopal ordination. I would greatly have preferred the hands of a Bishop; even now, at this age of comparative decrepitude, *I would rejoice to have that ordination.*" The man is living in Maryland, who remembers the wide excitement among the Methodists, occasioned by the first baptism of an infant by one of their preachers. No man in England was more indignant than Mr. Wesley, at hearing that some of his preachers had undertaken to baptize; he likened them, in an earnest, public discourse, *to Korah and his company.* About this time, he made application to a Bishop of Crete, who was then in England, to ordain his "preachers," and, it is also said, to consecrate himself a Bishop. But the scruples of the good Bishop concerning the ancient canons, prevented him. Twenty years afterward, when in his dotage, he laid his hands on Doctor Coke, and made him Bishop of the Methodists in America. Wesley's own brother, on this occasion, wrote a brief satire on the affair, whereof a portion runneth thus:

"So easily are Bishops made,
By man's or woman's whim;
Wesley his hands on Coke hath laid,
But who laid hands on *him?*"

But Doctor Coke was *not satisfied.* He *wanted* a line from Christ, not from himself. It was the old *hiatus valde deflendus.* Accordingly he proposed to Bishops Seabury and White the consecration of himself and Mr. Asbury as Bishops of the Protestant Episcopal Church; and, on certain conditions, the re-ordination of their "preachers." Failing in this, he returned to England; and in 1813, when he had now been "Bishop" twenty-nine years, he wrote an humble letter to the late Hon. William Wilberforce, offering to "*return most fully and faithfully to the bosom of the Church,*" if he might himself be consecrated Bishop of India! These may be taken as conspicuous examples of that *dissatisfaction* with their ordination, which pervades extensively the ministers of schism, and which is turning the thoughts of not a few toward the Church. I have said "three hundred" within a few years; but I have received, in several letters, the advice to make my signature "One of *Five* Hundred." Many old-fashioned Presbyterians look at their ordination as far corrupted by the Congregational influx. How agreeable, therefore, to have done with all this misgiving, and to be *satisfied* with one's ordination! I am satisfied with mine. It is Congregational; for it was done in the presence and with the approbation of "the Brethren." It is Presbyterian; for Presbyters, together with the Bishop, laid hands upon me. It is Episcopal; for it was done by the Bishop himself. It is Papal, if you please; for, under Elizabeth, the Pope acknowledged our Orders, and offered to receive us as we were, if we would allow his jurisdiction.

* * * * * * *

But enough, and more than enough! My heart is sick, my hand is weary with the lengthening catalogue. The conflict is over: it is useless further to recall the particulars of the strife. Let us hasten to the end.

CHAPTER XXIX.

THE CHURCH FOUND.

The rest of the story may be soon told. A voyage I would not make again for a universe of gold was now at an end. I would not be again among those rocks, again upon those shoals which reason is allowed to fathom, again in those currents that glide rapidly but imperceptibly along, again perilled in those collisions with barks as well-constructed and well-manned as mine, again lost in the ice of chilling speculation, again circling in the verge of the German maelstrom, again steering by the lights of wandering stars, again trusting to the reckonings of my private judgment for my place and bearings, again in the vessel which had been split in a hundred storms, and had lent its fragments to be reconstructed into things more frail and perishable still—again in such a bark, on such a sea, at such a time, for all the wealth omnipotence could create. On this sea I was born; but the voyage was now over. Land spread out its wide, bright coasts before me. Land! Land! Columbus and his men knew nothing of the joy! And I had now but to leap from a sea of uncertainty, and division, and chaos, and change, upon the *terra firma* of unities and harmonies, of certainties and perpetuities.

But duties involving principles and results of any magnitude, are nearly always, in Christian experience, embarrassed with influences seemingly intended to delay or defeat their accomplishment; although, in fact, only permitted to confirm the genuineness of a true and earnest conviction. So it was in the present instance. Considerations innumerable now sought a final hearing, to hold me back from acting under the light which God had been pleased to throw into my path. It was a conflict I cannot describe. I only know it was terrific. I can hardly imagine that it would have cost him, who boasted that he would, alone, overthrow the religion that it required twelve men to establish; or him, who labored to impose upon the world the sophism that no amount of testimony could establish the truth of a miracle; a greater sacrifice of intellectual pride, to have made, with the Ephesians, a bonfire of his books, and to have done homage to the majesty of revelation: than it cost me to publish my adhesion to the faith which I had pitied as superannuated, by virtue of the very antiquity of which it boasted; and which I had despised for its unaccommodating temper, by virtue of the petrified, unbending form in which it gloried as the perpetual representative of "the *everlasting* gospel." Fast as my hours went by, reasons on reasons crowded to my thoughts, why it would be better to abandon, or at least delay, the final step. The fountains of the deep within me were broken up, and the billows went over my soul. But He, whose goodness is equal to His power, comforted my heart, as He covered my head, in the day of battle.

Something called "flesh and blood" said in my ear, "The mother that bare thee fell asleep, after a blameless life, in the assurance of a blessed resurrection: and thou wouldst cast dishonor on her dust, and suspicion on her faith!" Not so, I said; I have not seen so great faith, no, not in Israel. But if Catholicity be true, the dead know it; and my departed ones behold it in the order of the heavenly hierarchies, and the unities and harmonies of the material and moral universe; and it is joining myself again to their company, to embrace the convictions that they have reached, and the hierarchy on the earth ordained first in the Mosaic tabernacle "*after the pattern of the heavenly.*"

"Go," said this voice again, "go first, and bury thy father, and do not, by abandoning his faith, bring down his grey hairs with sorrow to the grave." I do not abandon his faith, I said, but the securities on which it rests I abandon; for, although my father has stood so far from the precipice as hardly to discern it, yet a thousand thousand of his brethren have ventured to the verge and fallen. No, I abandon not the faith of my fathers; but the schism that has been almost everywhere fatal to that faith, I abandon and abhor. I do not abandon that faith; but where that faith has turned to reason, and is no more faith, I give it to the winds. I do not abandon that faith; but the vacancies around it and the sands beneath it, I replace and fill with the foundations and proportions of antiquity. "You are about," said a private letter from an eminent divine well known to the Episcopal church, "You are about to unchurch and give over to a sort of surreptitious, left-handed mercy of God, your father, your former brethren, and the largest portion of Protestant Christendom." *The very day* this letter was received, my venerable father, three hundred miles away, wrote in a letter intended for my eye, "With regard to ———'s removal to another branch of Christ's Church, it has no objection from me, but on the contrary my cordial acquiescence; as I trust and believe he is acting in the matter according to his best judgment, and the dictates of his conscience; and I sincerely pray that he may be eminently useful in the new ecclesiastical connection."

"But why," said a strong man armed who came to me, "why do you leave a body which even scribes and priests of Episcopacy acknowledge, with a slight qualification, to be a true branch of Christ's Church?" I answered, "If Esau despise his birthright, then shall I be the Jacob to inherit his blessing; and if the children loathe their bread, then shall I be the dog to eat the crumbs from their table."

Besides the great and real conflict that was passing within me, one, who loved me once, suggested that it could not surely be the gewgaws of a ritual worship that had drawn me over. Even the letter from the divine who expressed his solicitude for my father's fate, acknowledged— "If your change were a mere matter of taste, a mere preference for forms and robes, &c., &c., while I might lament over the weakness which such a change would betray, I would be far from charging it with the arrogance and heresy of the fashionable high-church, papistical Oxfordisms of the day."

Another, who was my fellow and my friend, was afraid that some in the church would suspect me of having left my "evangelicalism" behind me, and others of having brought my puritanism with me, and that, between the fires, I should be subjected to a roasting. And to another who hoped, with a patronizing air, that I would not be a high-churchman, I said, If I be a churchman at all, I must cease to be a Puritan; I have been a high-church Presbyterian; I shall probably be a high-church Episcopalian; else why should I not continue as I am? Whatever system I embrace, I must hold it in its highest conservatism, as the truth and institution of Christ. To instance a single fact:—as a Presbyterian, I had many a time said, that I could never have been satisfied with Congregational ordination, nor did I ever allow a minister so ordained to aid me in the ministration of the sacraments, nor did I ever receive communion from a person so ordained; and it was the Congregational admixture, and consequent corruption of a Presbyterian ordination (delivered, as I had held, by succession from the apostles) that first shook my confidence in Presbyterian orders in general, long before I doubted the validity of my own; for my own I could trace through a Presbyterial succession.

And, yet once more, it was suggested by a friend, that I could not expect to reach, in the Episcopal Church, the position I had earned in the Presbyterian. I already occupied a post sufficiently lucrative. A new pastoral situation was offered me, with emoluments not exceeded by any in the Presbyterian church. And yet another office, of Missionary supervision over the southern portion of the church, was within my reach; and yet another, that would have given me easy duty, and opportunity of travel in every corner of Europe and the East, besides the probable acquisition of a post of repose and dignity in a literary institution. Some one of these proposals I should certainly have accepted, but for a sense of honor that would not suffer me to do so, until my mind should be settled on the questions that disturbed it. It was the same feeling that prevented my acceptance of a considerable sum of money, most kindly presented me during my above-mentioned illness, by my former companion and brethren. Things such as these I should long ago have forgotten, except that I know there are minds weak enough and censorious enough (for the two infirmities go commonly together) to suppose that loaves and fishes can influence the faith of a truth-loving mind. As a Presbyterian, I was never in the receipt of less than two thousand a year; as a Churchman, I have been sometimes content with four hundred, and have never sought or desired emolument or power.

Meanwhile the truth was mighty. *Magna est veritas* had been, before, a rhetorical or philosophical flourish: but now I felt its power. Intellectual pride; hereditary prejudices; local and personal influences without number; friends, foes, earth, time, fame, family, all were compelled to do it homage. I could no more arrest the progress of conviction, than I could stay the marches of the sun in heaven. Having rid myself of all other relations and ties in the Presbyterian communion, that I might glide out of it as inoffensively as possible, I resigned, last of all, my pastoral charge. The next day I was taken violently ill, and, through a dreary winter, lay, in the estimation of my friends, at the gates of death. And, with the opportunity thus given me to review the motives and disposition with which I had prosecuted my inquiries, I desired to live, mainly that I might recant before the world the schism of which I had been guilty in rending the body of Christ.

My prayer was heard. As soon as my yet feeble health would allow, I penned a letter to the moderator of my Presbytery, beginning thus:

"Rev. and Dear Sir,

"It is my desire, if it shall please God to count me worthy, to resume the duties of the ministry, in connection with the 'Protestant Episcopal Church.' The right of that church to embrace in her immediate communion all christians of Anglican descent at least, has been for many years the subject of my most earnest consideration; and, in conceding her pretensions on this point as supported by Scripture and by Ancient Authors, I have not yielded to my convictions until they were mature, and could no longer with a safe conscience be set aside. I have rather labored to rid myself of them, by allowing undue influence to former prejudices, as well as by the more lawful expedient of consulting largely the soundest and most esteemed authorities upon the other side. But, after having over and over sifted my convictions, and the motives with which I had either cherished or repressed them, in the light of another world, as I lay for many months at the door of death, I cannot now approve the timidity which held me back; and have resolved to lay the sacrifice of whatever it may cost me, (and only He who made the heart can know what it has already cost me,) at the feet of Him whose great sacrifice alone can make any of our offerings accepted. It would be a departure from the respect which I owe to the body over which you preside—in which there are fathers as much beyond me in years, as they are beyond me in the attainments of piety—to state the reasonings that have led me to these conclusions; but I may be allowed to add, that I have studiously chosen, as the most suitable moment for making the change, one that should hazard no interest of Presbyterianism, however small, confided to my hands, in the pastoral relation, or in any other official tie whatever. . . . .

"With great respect for the body over which you have the honor to preside, and with assurances of personal esteem and affection for every member of it individually, I remain, Rev. and Dear Sir,

"Yours, in the grace of the Lord Jesus,

"—— —— ——."

On the receipt of the foregoing, the Presbytery appointed a committee of its most distinguished members to confer with me upon the subject. The matter was conducted with a courtesy and kindness as honorable to themselves as they were grateful to my own feelings. The interview soon satisfied them that my convictions were not likely to be shaken, and, I must also believe, that my intentions were pure. On their report to the Presbytery, the following minute was adopted, and transmitted to me with a kind letter from my old friend the clerk: "Whereas, it is satisfactorily ascertained that the Rev. —— has made application for ordination to the Bishop of the Protestant Episcopal Church in the Diocese of ——, and has thereby implicitly, as otherwise explicitly, renounced his ordination as a Presbyterian minister, and withdrawn from the jurisdiction of this Presbytery; therefore

"Resolved, That the name of Mr. —— be stricken from the roll of this Presbytery.

"Resolved, That a copy of this minute be transmitted to Mr. ——."

In this quiet result I was more fortunate than the Rev. Messrs. Leach and Richie, who were deposed, by the Presbytery of Toronto, for returning to the Church of England in 1843; as, in having with impunity had my children baptized some time before in the same church, for motives stated in the beginning of this narrative, I was more fortunate than a clergyman in the Scottish kirk, who about the same time was degraded from his office for the same offence.

Thus terminated, as pleasantly as the case would allow, with a due regard to christian courtesy, an intercourse which had always been agreeable and friendly, and which could have been brought to a close by nothing under the wide heaven but that voice in the breast, which never commands except to be obeyed. My venerable father, knowing that a long illness had exhausted my resources, gave me immediately an earnest invitation to come with my children, and make my home with him, until I should take Holy Orders, and obtain the means of living in the Church which I was entering. And in this, once more, I was more fortunate than the sons of a distinguished Presbyterian divine, who were parishioners of mine, and dwelt with me in the same house, whose father refused to support them (although yet but boys) so long as they should persist in their purpose to return to the Ancient Church and take Orders at her Altar.

I was kindly received by the Bishop and clergy in my new relations, and after the customary probation, one who had pretended to be a successor of Peter and Paul, and to be the Bishop of —— street church, (phraseology unknown to antiquity,) was admitted, in company with two other Presbyterian ministers, into the humble order of Saint Stephen.

Never, for the briefest instant that time could mark, have I desired to return, or regretted the step I have taken. "My heart is fixed: O God, my heart is fixed." I breathe the free, bright, sparkling atmosphere of the purest antiquity. I live again in the times of Irenæus, Ignatius, and Saint Paul. I am held by a line of a thousand links going back to the Cross. I am a member of the Body in which the Faith has lived from the beginning until now; and, with no measured satisfaction, I can join the cry of ten thousand times ten thousand, and thousands of thousands, in which the voices of Three Hundred can be scarcely heard, "We have found it! we have found it!" and while we live, the joyful Eureka and the adoring Alleluia shall go up together!

ONE OF THREE HUNDRED.

THE END.

www.ingramcontent.com/pod-product-compliance
Lightning Source LLC
LaVergne TN
LVHW021223110826
845150LV00002B/230